Ethics: The Fundamen. W9-CTW-234

Fundamentals of Philosophy

Series Editor: A. P. Martinich, University of Texas at Austin

Each volume in the *Fundamentals of Philosophy* series covers a key area of study in philosophy. Written with verve and clarity by leading philosophers, these authoritative volumes look to reveal the fundamental issues and core problems that drive interest in the field.

Ethics: The Fundamentals

Julia Driver

Blackwell
Publishing

BLACKWELL PUBLISHING
350 Main Street, Malden, MA 02148–5020, USA
9600 Garsington Road, Oxford OX4 2DQ, UK
550 Swanston Street, Carlton, Victoria 3053, Australia

First published 2006 by Blackwell Publishing Ltd

1   2007

Library of Congress Cataloging-in-Publication Data

Driver, Julia, 1961–:
    Ethics: the fundamentals / julia Driver.
       p. cm. (Fundamentals of philosophy series)
Includes bibilographical references and index.
    ISBN-13: 978-14051-1155-3 (hardcover : alk. paper)
    ISBN-10: 1-4051-1155-0 (hardcover : alk. paper)
    ISBN-13: 978-1-4051-1154-6 (pbk.: alk. paper)
    ISBN-10: 1-4051-1154-2 (pbk.: alk. paper) 1. Ethics. I. Title. II. series: Fundamentals of philosophy.

BJ71 D75 2006
170 dc22   2006012513

A catalogue record for this title is available from the British Library.

Set in 10.5/13pt Photina
by SPI Publisher Services, Pondicherry, India
Printed and bound in Singapore
by Markono Print Media Pte Ltd

For further information on
Blackwell Publishing, visit our website:
www.blackwellpublishing.com

Contents

Acknowledgments

I would like to thank a number of people for helping me along with this project. Al Martinich approached me a few years ago, to ask if I'd be interested in writing a book for this series. Since I do a good deal of teaching ethics here at Dartmouth, I had some very definite ideas about how an introductory text should go. I also wanted to write one that was accessible and fairly fun to read. So I agreed to the project and am very happy that I did so.

I would also like to think Walter Sinnott-Armstrong, who read drafts of Chapters 1 and 11 and offered valuable comments, as well as Roy Sorensen and Timothy Rosenkoetter, who also read portions of the manuscript and offered comments and ideas on how to improve it. I would also like to thank my Presidential Scholar at Dartmouth, Christopher Schooley, who offered insight from the undergraduate's point of view.

There were also several referees from Blackwell who wrote up extensive comments and I would like to thank them for their efforts. I found their advice valuable.

Portions of the material in the book have appeared previously in my article "Normative Ethics," for the *Oxford Handbook of Contemporary Philosophy*, edited by Frank Jackson and Michael Smith (New York: Oxford University Press, 2005); © 2005 by Oxford University Press; reproduced by permission of the publishers. Some parts of Chapter 9 first appeared in James Dreier's *Contemporary Debates in Moral Theory* (Malden, MA: Blackwell, 2005); © 2005 by Blackwell Publishing Ltd; reproduced by permission of the author and the publishers.

Julia Driver

Introduction

[T]he justification of an ethical principle cannot be in terms of any partial or sectional group . . . Ethics requires us to go beyond "I" and "you" to the universal law, the universalizable judgment, the standpoint of the impartial spectator or ideal observer, or whatever we choose to call it.

Peter Singer, *Practical Ethics*[1]

Every human being thinks about how to live a good life – how to make the right sorts of decisions, and what sorts of conditions contribute to a morally good life. This naturally leads to thoughts about the following questions: What should we do in order to be good? What considerations make our actions right or wrong? How should we go about deciding how to act in a morally appropriate manner? This book explores various responses to these questions by looking at a wide range of different moral theories.

We should first distinguish moral "oughts" from other types of "oughts." Some different normative concepts are associated with prudence, some with rationality, and some with aesthetic norms. Moral norms primarily concern our interactions with others in ways that have significance to their well-being. Thus, while it is true that we *ought* to eat at least five servings of fruits and vegetables a day, this ought is not a moral one. If we fail to do this, we have harmed only ourselves – so it is a failure of prudence, not of morality. Also, one *ought* not to hang a psychedelic black velvet painting over one's colonial fireplace. However, doing so is not a moral failure. If anything, it is an aesthetic failure. But if we do something that could harm or benefit someone else, then arguably this is a *moral* matter. Someone who wrongfully harms another does something that he or she ought not

---

[1] Peter Singer, *Practical Ethics* (Cambridge, UK: Cambridge University Press, 1979), p. 11.

do in the moral sense of "ought." It is this sense that is the subject of normative ethics, and it is an understanding of this sense of "ought" that is at the heart of normative ethical theories.

Normative ethics is the area of philosophy that, broadly speaking, is concerned with standards for right conduct and moral evaluation. Generally, such a theory will give an account of right action and try to give some idea of what makes it right. Some writers, however, tend to focus more on character evaluation; that is, on criteria for evaluating a person's character. In fact, in recent years there has been a move away from simply focusing on right conduct in articulating a moral theory and toward placing more emphasis on character evaluation – that is, moving away from focus on right action and toward the issue of what is involved in being a good or *virtuous* person. Still, whatever the focus, moral theories are primarily concerned with (1) providing moral guidance and (2) the moral evaluation of human conduct. Central concepts such as "right," "wrong," "good," "bad," "permissible," and "impermissible" need to be articulated to accomplish these tasks. Different moral theories spell out application of these concepts differently, and one task of this book will be to discuss the various approaches that have been taken to, for example, providing an account of "right action" and "good character."

An example of a moral problem might help us to understand the tasks of moral theory. Consider the case of Mary, who must decide whether or not to authorize additional medical treatment for her mother. Her mother is in intense pain from her illness, but because she is also suffering from dementia she cannot authorize cessation of treatment herself. Only Mary now has that authority. An ethical theory would first of all try to provide some guidance for Mary – for example, it might offer a principle such as "One ought to try to minimize needless suffering," in which case there is a reason for Mary to authorize that her mother's treatment cease, since her mother's suffering is so intense and since her mother also has no prospect of recovery. Or a theory might present the principle that "One ought to do whatever one can to keep a human alive at all costs," in which case Mary would have a moral reason for continuing the treatment even though this will mean continued suffering for her mother. The point of this example is not to argue which putative moral principle is right, but to give some idea of how such principles can help *guide* action. Depending on which reason Mary has justification to believe is the best in this particular case, she will be guided by that reason to do what she believes to be best for her mother.

An ethical theory may also provide criteria for *evaluating* an action. For example, whatever principle Mary uses to make her decision, a theory that held that she should be acting so as to minimize needless suffering would argue that she should be criticized if she knowingly failed to do so, and instead allowed her mother to continue living in intense pain, with no prospect of recovery. Therefore, not only does an ethical theory guide our actions, but it also provides the criteria used to evaluate actions. In short, normative ethical theories give us some idea of how we ought to act, and what reasons are relevant in justifying praise and blame of action.

Some of the theorists discussed in this text sought to apply their theories to problems that people faced at the time. One very famous example of this is the philosopher John Stuart Mill (1806–73), who used his theory of *utilitarianism* to criticize laws that he felt were pointless and even harmful to society. Utilitarianism holds that an action, or a law, is right only if it produces the best outcome – only if it brings about the "greatest good for the greatest number." But some laws seemed to only cause misery, or bought happiness for some by degrading others. Mill would go on to be a champion of women's suffrage and a vigorous defender of free speech. He would argue that numerous social benefits would be realized by granting women a say in government. If the state tolerates diverse points of view within its borders, then the ensuing debate improves intellectual development and offers a force to counteract complacency and reactionary tendencies. Mill's books *Utilitarianism* and *On Liberty* eloquently argued for these changes.

Similarly, when we look at some modern moral theorists, we see people who believe that ethical theory can be used to provide arguments that will morally improve society. Feminist writers have long argued, for example, that female perspectives on how to approach moral problems have been ignored or set aside as inferior. Some writers, such as Carol Gilligan and Virginia Held, have argued that this attitude toward women's experiences has led to the systematic overlooking of alternative approaches to moral issues, approaches that treat our relationships with others as central to morality, as opposed to an impartial standard of justice. In Chapter 9 of this book, we will examine these approaches in more detail.

But aside from the practical significance of ethical theories, they are also intrinsically interesting. It is one thing to know that, let's say, killing is wrong; it is another to hear what other people have to say about what precisely *makes* it wrong. Theory enables us to delve beyond our surface intuitions about what is right and wrong to get at the underlying explanation for that judgment – a very important judgment, since it enables us to provide justifications for our actions and evaluations. We frequently want and need to provide justifications for at least some of our actions. For example, whatever Mary decides to do for her mother, she will want to do it on the basis of good reasons, reasons that she endorses. This means that she has a justification for her decision and subsequent action, and it also provides her with the tools to justify that decision to others. An understanding of underlying moral justification, which normative ethics supplies, helps us in our justificatory and critical practices. For example, a Kantian ethicist agrees with the classical utilitarian that killing an innocent person is wrong. He or she disagrees with the utilitarian about what makes it wrong – for the Kantian, it is a failure to adhere to a universal norm and a failure to treat the person who is being killed with respect; for the utilitarian, the person who is killed is being deprived of his or her future pleasant experiences.

Because the role of normative ethical theory is to better understand moral justification, one important point to stress is that normative ethics is about giving an account of what we *ought* to do, or what we *ought* to be like. This is distinct from giving an account or a theory of how people do in fact act, and how they do in fact go about praising and blaming. That is the subject of *descriptive*, not *normative*, ethics. Descriptive ethics is not evaluative – for example, an anthropologist studying the ethical beliefs prevalent in a given culture will describe those beliefs and practices, but will not evaluate them and will not (generally) endorse or criticize them. But normative ethics is a different enterprise entirely. Normative ethics is about how we ought to act. If someone makes a claim of the form "x ought to do y," this claim cannot be shown to be true or false by simply pointing out what x actually does. That's because x may in fact do what is wrong. There is a difference between how we *ought* to act and how we *do* act, though in practice we hope that those coincide.

Normative ethics is also distinct from the law. Just because a procedure or outcome is legal does not make it morally good. Sadly, history is filled with examples of laws that were (and are) immoral. Laws permitting slavery, laws forbidding women the vote, legal permissions for child labor, and laws that allowed for bloody expansionist warfare all qualify as immoral since – for one thing – they were laws that allowed some to profit unfairly at the expense of others, or they denied an equal voice to all persons. Again, ethics and the law are distinct, though we hope that true ethical norms will inform the content and enforcement of the law.

Normative ethics is also distinct from what philosophers call "meta-ethics," though the two are closely related. Meta-ethical issues are issues *about* ethics – for example, the status of moral claims, their truth-value, whether or not there are such things as moral properties, and so forth. We will discuss a few meta-ethical issues that have to do with challenges to ethical theory – one is the issue, for example, of moral relativism, which will be covered in Chapter 1. Moral relativism is the view that there are no universal moral standards, no standards of "right" and "wrong" that apply across all times and cultures. Instead, moral relativists think that the truth-value of the claim

(1)   Torturing innocent persons is wrong.

is *relative*. Usually, they understand the truth or falsity of a normative claim, such as (1), to be relative to what people happen to believe in a given culture. Thus, there may be some cultures in which (1) is true and others in which it is false, depending on what people happen to believe about the permissibility of torture. Some argue that if moral relativism is true, then there is a problem for normative ethics because no universal justifications can be provided. I will be arguing that we have good reason to doubt the truth of moral relativism, but even if it were true, this needn't undercut the authority of morality. There are degrees of universality, and even if it is only true that the norms are universal within a culture, we can have some basis for principled moral appraisal. However, the focus of the book will be on normative ethical theory.

One central problem in ethics has to do with accounting for the *source of normativity*. Normative claims are evaluative. In ethics, the kind of evaluations that occur are those that have to do with moral value and disvalue, moral rightness and wrongness. Further, these claims in ethics are thought to have a peculiar authority over us. If an action is judged to be wrong, it is not to be done – it is impermissible. A person performing this action would be subject to blame and possibly even more severe punishment. What gives these claims such authority over our actions? Very roughly, normative theories can be divided into two categories on the basis of how they answer this question. The first group comprises those theories that identify this source as being external to humans. Some believe, for example, that it is God's authority that underlies the authority of morals. The second group comprises those theories that identify this source as being dependent in some way on human nature, or facts about human beings. For example, some ethical egoists believe that human beings are essentially self-interested creatures and so morality must tie into promotion of self-interest. Thus, they appeal to a particular account of human nature – what human beings are like – to provide the basis for their theory. We will compare these two approaches in Chapter 2. The issue of where morality gets its content and authority is meta-ethical, but views about this issue, I believe, have helped to inform how people have developed different theories in the past – it helps sometimes to understand the motivation behind acceptance or rejection of some theoretical approaches to ethical evaluation.

Moral Evaluation of Actions: Terminology

It might first be helpful to spell out some of the terminology that we will be using. It is fairly clear that the concepts of "right" and "wrong" are important to our thinking about moral issues. Loosely, the right action is the one that we ought to do and the wrong action is the one that we ought to avoid; however, this will be spelled out differently with different theories. Other important concepts include the following:

- *Obligatory actions.* These are the actions that we ought, morally, to do; they are morally required and not morally optional. Failure to perform an obligatory act is wrong, or forbidden. "Obligations" are generally understood to be *prima facie* and not absolute. We have a moral obligation to tell the truth, for example, unless there is some countervailing consideration – such as the fact that under the circumstances telling the truth would lead to the death of an innocent person. Thus, telling the truth is obligatory, and we have an obligation to tell the truth, although the obligation is *prima facie* and can be overridden by other moral considerations.

- *Right actions.* A restrictive sense of "right" would be synonymous with "obligatory"; however, some would argue for a less restrictive sense of "right" that would include obligatory, supererogatory, and even morally neutral actions. In this sense, "right" would just mean "not wrong." However, people who would argue for this broader understanding of "right" would probably not include the suberogatory and, indeed, might argue that no such category exists – that all putative examples involve forbidden acts.

- *Forbidden actions.* These are wrong; these are actions that one is morally required not to do – they are morally impermissible. All other things being equal, failure to keep our promises, for example, is forbidden since when we make a promise we are taking on an obligation to keep the promise (barring unusual circumstances).

- *Supererogatory actions.* These are actions that are good, but not obligatory. For example, if someone rushes into a burning building to save someone else's life, this is supererogatory. It is admirable, but not obligatory, since that person would not be blamed for failing to risk his or her own life even to save another. There are very many examples of supererogatory acts. These acts involve rendering aid to others when they are not, strictly speaking, entitled to that aid.

- *Suberogatory actions.* These are actions that are bad, but not forbidden. This category is more controversial, since some writers would hold that actions that are bad are always forbidden. However, putative examples of the suberogatory would involve failures to help others when they are not entitled to the help. For example, if (assuming that you are a healthy adult) you refuse to give up your seat on the bus to an elderly person who sorely needs it, this could be regarded as suberogatory: if you are entitled to the seat given a "first come, first served" rule, then failure to give it up is not forbidden – it does not violate an obligation that you have. However, it does seem bad to fail to help the elderly person, who will then have a very unpleasant ride on the bus.

- *Permissible actions.* These are actions that are morally acceptable. This category includes the obligatory, the right, the supererogatory, and the suberogatory, as well as morally neutral actions. For example, under normal circumstances, eating an apple as opposed to an orange is morally neutral, and therefore permissible.

Value Terms

Value theory is an important part of ethics. For example, if part of our theory of right action is that it brings about a good – or at least better – state of affairs, then fleshing out the theory requires an account of what is good. The fundamental or basic good is often referred to as *intrinsic* good. Thus we can note a distinction between various types of value – intrinsic, extrinsic, and instrumental. We will discuss substantive accounts of value later in the book, when we discuss specific ethical theories.

- *Intrinsic value.* Something has intrinsic value if it has value in and of itself. For example, some philosophers think that pleasure has intrinsic value, since the goodness of pleasure does not seem to depend upon anything else – it requires no explanation.
- *Extrinsic value.* Something has extrinsic value if it has value that depends upon some factor that is external to it. For example, we might hold that a beautiful painting has value, but the value is extrinsic since it depends on the reactions of sentient beings.
- *Instrumental value.* Something has instrumental value if it has value through what it brings about, or through its consequences. For example, a hammer has instrumental value due to its being used to create things.

"Testing" a Moral Theory: How Do We Evaluate the Theories Themselves?

One of the most basic criteria of goodness for a theory is consistency. If a theory is inconsistent, then it must be revised or rejected. This is true of any theory, not simply ethical theories.

In looking for other criteria for evaluation, it may be useful to make a comparison with other sorts of theories – scientific theories, for example. Another very basic question is how well the theory explains the phenomena in question, or, in the case of ethics, how well it identifies reasons that are justifying. A person concerned with providing justification doesn't want to merely explain why he or she performed a particular action. He or she also wants to try to give reasons that are taken to be good reasons for the action. All actions have some explanation or other, but not all can be morally justified. Mary's testy remarks on Saturday morning may be explained by the fact that she stayed out too late on Friday night and is tired. But these facts don't morally justify the testiness. When she writes a check for Oxfam later in the day, that may be explained in part by her feeling sorry for the starving children. The action is morally justified because it is one that is motivated out of a desire to alleviate human suffering. What are the features that the ethical theory identifies as morally relevant, and can they be generalized to other cases? For example, one theory we will look at in this book is utilitarianism, which holds that right actions maximize the good. The classical utilitarians identified the good as pleasure, so on this premise the action that brings about the most pleasure is the right action. This theory can explain why a wrong action is wrong and justify the judgment that it is wrong – because it causes pain as opposed to pleasure, for example, and in a way that is generalizable. For example, one implication of the theory is that if animals feel pleasure and pain, then we can behave rightly and wrongly toward animals.

The analogy with scientific theories suggests another mode of evaluation. Most of us are familiar, at least roughly, with how scientific theories get tested – a scientist comes up with something as an explanation for an observable phenomenon, for example, and then makes predictions that are either true or false. Crudely, if the prediction is true, the theory is at least slightly confirmed; if false, it is at least slightly disconfirmed. Testing a moral theory can work like this as well. For example, in this book when we discuss a specific theory, after considering some of its advantages we may take a critical look at both its structure and its implications. If those implications conflict with our strongly held and reflective moral convictions, then this is viewed as presenting a problem for the theory – the theory then needs to be either revised or rejected in the light of this problem.

When it comes to ethical theories, we also frequently look for novel guidance. Ethical theories are supposed to provide us with decision procedures and/or criteria for evaluation of actions and character. They are, in that way, practically oriented. If a theory does not give us answers that go beyond our intuitions, then the theory is not doing any independent work for us, and this would be a drawback. For example, a scientific theory that is powerful will make novel predictions, and lead to further fruitful areas of inquiry, and even suggest surprising and interesting connections between disciplines that had previously been regarded as unrelated, or irrelevant to each other. Ideally, we'd like to see the same thing in an ethical theory.

We also seem to regard simple theories as superior to complicated ones. This criterion is controversial – critics will wonder about it since, off hand, there seems to be no connection between simplicity and truth. But, *all other things being equal*, the simple, elegant theory is preferred. This may have something to do with pragmatic considerations – for example, simple theories are easier to use and we are less likely to make a mistake implementing a simple theory as opposed to a highly complex one.

Before moving on to a discussion of the substantive moral theories, we should first take a look at a popular, though misguided, challenge to normative ethical theory – in Chapter 1, we will consider the issue of moral relativism.

Chapter 1

The Challenge to Moral Universalism[1]

What, to the American slave, is your 4th of July? I answer, a day that reveals to him, more than all other days in the year, the gross injustice and cruelty to which he is the constant victim. To him, your celebration is a sham...There is not a nation on the earth guilty of practices more shocking and bloody than are the people of the United States, at this very hour.

Frederick Douglass, July 5, 1852

We are all familiar with the practice of moral appraisal. Whenever we assess an action or policy as right or wrong, or a person as good or bad, we are evaluating. There are whole ranges of behaviors that people tend to view as wrong – killing innocent persons, theft, lying, or cheating, for example. Others we typically evaluate as right or good – charity, promise keeping, and respect for others, for example. It would be very difficult to imagine living as we do without this practice of evaluation and moral appraisal. We need to evaluate potential courses of action in order to decide what to do. We need to evaluate in order to convey our moral concern to others. Positive social change also requires evaluation. For example, when Frederick Douglass, the great American orator and reformer, condemned the institution of slavery, he was evaluating the institution, judging it to be wrong and a social evil.

Yet, in spite of its seeming significance, there are some people who are very skeptical about morality – about whether there is such a thing

---

[1] In reality, this chapter focuses on a particular type of argument for moral relativism – one based on a consideration of cultural differences.

as a truly universal moral system, and whether any moral claims are true or "just a matter of opinion." Some argue that what is morally good is a matter of taste, or a matter of convention, so moral judgments are like aesthetic ones, where just about anything goes. We can trace such a view back to the historian Herodotus, who noted that there was enormous cultural diversity on moral issues – in some countries, cannibalism is permissible and in others it is immoral; in some nations it is acceptable to eat beef, while in others, it is not. Who is to say what is "really" right or wrong? There is no universal fact of the matter about "rightness" and "wrongness," and so forth.

On this view of moral evaluation, normative claims will be radically different from descriptive claims. For example, if someone were to make the descriptive claim

(1)   Wombats are mammals.

she would be stating something that has a truth-value that does not vary across individual beliefs, or across cultures. If (1) is true, it is true not in virtue of what someone happens to believe. The truth-value of (1) is not a relative matter. How do we find out whether or not (1) is true or false? We look at the features of wombats relevant to their classification as mammals – Are they warm-blooded and furry, and do they give birth to live young? The answers to all of these questions are affirmative, so (1) is true. In determining the truth-value of (1), we don't look at what people happen to believe about wombats. After all, people can be mistaken.

Moral relativists hold that normative claims, such as moral ones, however, are quite different from descriptive claims such as (1) and do have truth-values that can vary. The most prevalent forms hold that the truth-values depend upon what people happen to believe to be right and wrong, or good and bad.

These sorts of views pose challenges to normative ethics in the sense that they challenge its status and authority. It's worth discussing the most significant challenge, that of cultural moral relativism, before turning to specific normative theories. First, though, we will look at a similar, though more restrictive, view – that of individual moral relativism.

One form of moral relativism is very restrictive, holding that the truth-value of moral claims can vary from individual to individual.

This view is sometimes referred to as *simple subjectivism*.[2] Consider the claim

(2)   Abortion is always wrong.

There are some people who believe that (2) is true and others who believe that (2) is false. If we think that the correct way to relativize moral truth is to the beliefs or attitudes of individuals, then we need to hold that (2) is true for those who believe it, but false for those who believe it false. Then (2) is both true and false – but false for one person, and true for another.

One way to spell out this theory more plausibly is to hold that claims such as (2) are just reports of approval or disapproval, so that when Mary utters (2) sincerely, that is just the same as saying something like

(3)   I (Mary) disapprove of abortion.

If Mary is being sincere, then (3) must be true. If (3) is the same as (2), then (2) must be true as well. But note that if Ralph says

(4)   Abortion is always permissible.

which is the same (on this theory) as

(5)   I (Ralph) do not disapprove of abortion.

then if Ralph sincerely utters (4), (4) must be true as well. Thus, (2) and (4) are both true, albeit relativized to different subjects. This has

---

[2] Subjectivism can be spelled out in a wide variety of ways – this is just one. For example, some subjectivists, discussed in a later chapter, hold that moral utterances have no truth-values at all, since they are just expressions of an individual's emotional response to an action. This version is sometimes called *meta-ethical subjectivism*. For more on this distinction, you can look at Russ Shafer-Landau's "Ethical Subjectivism," in *Reason and Responsibility: Readings in Some Basic Problems of Philosophy*, edited by Joel Feinberg and Russ Shafer-Landau (Belmont, CA: Wadsworth/Thomson Learning, 2002), pp. 604–16. But in this chapter we will discuss the variety that is more naturally contrasted with cultural moral relativism.

the very odd result that when Ralph and Mary argue about abortion, there is really nothing that they are disagreeing about. How can Mary disagree with Ralph, really, when all he is actually saying is that he does not disapprove of abortion? But this goes against our views about what takes place in moral argumentation – we do believe that something more substantive, more objective, is at stake.

Subjectivism seems to be an attractive view to some because it seems highly tolerant. What is "right" for me may not be "right" for you, since you have different beliefs. We sometimes hear people talking as though, for example, "Abortion is right for some, but for me would be murder," but – upon reflection – most people find the view that "right" is purely a matter of opinion to lack plausibility. It seems quite counter-intuitive, since it would result in the truth – albeit subjective truth – of claims such as "For me, mass killing is perfectly permissible," as long as the person making the utterance actually believed that mass killings were permissible. But a genocidal maniac cannot be acting rightly just because he happens to believe that he is acting rightly. There are lots of cases to which we could refer to show how unappealing such a criterion of rightness would be. There have been many people who have done terrible things and yet have felt very self-righteous about their actions. The Nazi commander Heinrich Himmler, for example, believed that morality demanded that he obey his leader for the sake of German society: of course, he was horribly wrong about this, and his individual beliefs in no way provide justification for what he did, and the horrors that he inflicted on others. So mere individual belief about what is right and what is wrong cannot morally justify someone's actions. In doing anything, whether it is right or wrong, a person is not acting rightly or wrongly just because she happens to believe that what she is doing is right or wrong. There must be something else that justifies her action (or not), some moral reasons for or against the action. So, most people who find moral relativism attractive do not find subjectivism attractive. Instead, the alternative formulation – which involves appealing to *cultural* relativism – seems to be favored: the rightness of an action is determined by what people in a given culture, by and large, believe.

Thus, many relativists will argue that instead of relativizing to individual beliefs we relativize to cultural beliefs, and it is those beliefs that determine the truth-value of the moral judgment or claim. So, when someone makes the claim that, for example, "Stealing is wrong," whether or not this is true depends on what people believe about stealing in the *culture* of the person who makes the claim.

The major consideration in favor of this theory is that it seems to reflect actual moral practice. That cultural differences in moral beliefs and attitudes exist is a certainty. Burial practices vary from culture to culture, female circumcision is practiced in some cultures and condemned in others, certain animals are approved eating in one culture, but not another – and the list could go on. These differences exist across time as well as geography. There is huge temporal variation in cultural beliefs about moral issues. For example, in the United States over 200 years ago, the vote for women was, by most, considered ridiculous. In fact, when Abigail Adams wrote her husband John (who would later become the second president of the USA) and broached the subject of extending further rights to women, this was his response:

> As to your extraordinary Code of Laws, I cannot but laugh. We have been told that our Struggle has loosened the bands of Government every where. That Children and Apprentices were disobedient – that schools and Colledges were grown turbulent – that Indians slighted their Guardians and Negroes grew insolent to their Masters. But your Letter was the first Intimation that another Tribe more numerous and powerful than all the rest were grown discontented . . . Depend upon it, We know better than to repeal our Masculine systems.[3]

He then goes on to argue – jokingly – that otherwise men would be entirely subject to the "Despotism of the Peticoat." Well, things have changed a bit since 1776. There is a difference between how people in the USA feel about equality and the scope of equality today, as opposed to 250 years ago.

What significance do these observations of cultural variation in moral belief have for moral theory? Some writers, particularly anthropologists such as Ruth Benedict, believe that this fact establishes the truth of moral relativism. This view is very attractive to many people because it is viewed as tolerant of moral diversity:

[3] Letter from John Adams to Abigail Adams, April 14, 1776 (electronic edition). *Adams Family Papers: An Electronic Archive*. Massachusetts Historical Society; www.masshist.org/digitaladams/

We do not any longer make the mistake of deriving the morality of our locality and decade directly from the inevitable constitution of human nature. We do not elevate it to the dignity of a first principle. We recognize that morality differs in every society, and is a convenient term for socially approved habits.[4]

Most cultures distinguish between morality and good manners, so this quote doesn't seem quite right to me. Everyone thinks of morality as something more than just socially approved habits. However, this quote from Benedict does, I think, capture the spirit of moral relativism, which is based on a recognition of cultural diversity – there is no "right" or "wrong" that transcends a given culture, no universal truth to morality.

It is important to note that relativism is a radically strong claim. It is not to be confused with the view that rightness is somehow context sensitive – which is a fairly uncontroversial view.[5] Instead, relativism maintains that there are no universal moral truths *at all*, where "universal" is understood as "across all cultures," precisely because moral quality is understood relative to beliefs of persons in a given society. A person who believed that the claim "It is wrong to cause unnecessary suffering" was universally true (and thus disagreed with relativism) would be free to concede that what counts as "unnecessary suffering" might vary from context to context, depending on the facts of the situation. So, for example, it might be wrong for Al to buy a carpet in a situation in which that carpet was made using child labor and unjust labor practices, but it would not be wrong for Stephanie to buy a carpet given that it was made without harming anyone. Thus, it is true to say that whether or not it is acceptable to buy a carpet depends upon the circumstances – but not in any way that undercuts moral universalism. This is because the rationale for whether or not it is acceptable does not itself vary from context to context. Again, the universalist can claim that the relevant basic moral truth is that it is wrong to cause unnecessary suffering – and this holds in both of the cases mentioned above. Relativism denies that claims such as this have any universal or objective standing. Instead – if we believe the cultural

---

[4] See Ruth Benedict, *Patterns of Culture* (Boston: Houghton Mifflin, 1934).

[5] Some – such as moral absolutists – would disagree with this. However, their view is not commonly accepted.

differences argument – we believe that the "truth" of a moral claim depends completely on the beliefs that are common to the culture in which the judgment is made. And, as we have noted, those beliefs and practices can vary dramatically across cultures.

The position that is generally contrasted with moral relativism is moral *universalism*. This is the view that at least some basic moral norms and values are universal. "Basic moral value" refers to a value that explains other norms. For example, in one society people may judge child labor to be immoral – thus they condemn this sort of behavior. This is turn is explained by appeal to a more basic norm or value, such as "Causing unnecessary pain is bad." The moral universalist believes that there are derivative norms that may differ across cultures, but at least some basic norms don't. One candidate for a universal norm would be something like "Causing unnecessary pain is bad." It may be that cultures differ in their derivative prescriptions – in one culture child labor is permissible, and in another it is not. But this would be explained by saying that either (i) one culture is just mistaken about the permissibility of child labor or (ii) the different cultures are faced with different circumstances; and in one culture child labor is unnecessary to family survival, whereas in another culture – one, for example, without public education and a social safety net – it is necessary for family survival.

The denial of universalism has been a popular view. Part of this appeal is due to the fact that some think that in order to be tolerant of others, we need to reject universalism with respect to truth in morality and instead ascribe to relativism. Moral relativism does not deny that moral claims are true or false – only that their truth-value is relative. Thus, though we may disagree with what people believe about torture in one culture, we can always adopt a tolerant attitude by holding, as relativism would seem to demand, that "Torture is not okay by me, but it is okay for them." And tolerance is a moral virtue. If there is no objective truth to appeal to, then criticisms of various cultural practices seem unjustified. What we call "morality" is just a construct of various societies and cultures, each with its own set of norms and not subject to criticism or praise from outsiders. Of course, we are free to ask whether or not tolerance is, universally, a virtue. If so, relativism is false. If not, then what about cultures that reject tolerance themselves?

Relativism also seems to offer a principled way of approaching moral disagreement, at least at the cultural level. If someone wants to know whether or not stealing is wrong, he just has to determine what the prevailing beliefs are in a given culture. However, this really just seems to favor a moral conformity. Moral progress is often achieved through the efforts of rebellious individuals with beliefs that do not conform to popular cultural beliefs. It seems odd to say that they were wrong and that everyone else was right, until others just happened to start sharing their beliefs.

But relativism also has some very serious disadvantages. Tolerance of the behavior of others only goes so far. As long as there is a view that rights – moral rights – are being violated, most people will not think tolerance in that context a virtue. This indicates that there is some universality to morality in that oppression is wrong, no matter what the prevalent cultural beliefs happen to be. Jeffrey Stout puts the problem for relativism (or, actually, anti-realism) this way:

> I deny the wrongness of torturing innocents is simply a belief we have that is justified by some expedient social convention. Knowingly and willingly torturing innocents is wrong, impermissible, and unjust. It always has been...
> That is the moral truth of the matter, whether we recognize it or not – a truth I deem more certain than any explanation I could give of it or any argument I could make on its behalf.[6]

Another example that illustrates this point is female circumcision. This is the practice, in some cultures, of excising a portion of the female genitalia. It is usually practiced on young girls. It is quite painful and can lead to numerous health problems for the girls, but it is practiced for cultural reasons and, some argue, as a way of depriving females of sexual enjoyment. Of course, in Western cultures such a practice is considered quite immoral, so here we have a case of cultural moral disagreement. Moral relativism would hold that in Western cultures "Female circumcision is wrong" is true, whereas in cultures where people don't happen to hold similar beliefs that claim would be false, and it may well be true instead that "Female circumcision is right."

But someone might argue that, of course, it is perfectly clear that there is no universality – after all, we have the empirical evidence of

---

[6] See Jeffrey Stout, *Ethics after Babel: The Language of Morals and their Discontents* (Boston: Beacon Press, 1988), p. 245.

moral disagreement – so doesn't this show that universality doesn't exist? No, it does not. And, as philosophers such as James Rachels have noted,[7] there are three reasons why:

1   Cultural differences are not evidence for the view that there is no universal truth to morality – there could be such nonrelative truth, but people are mistaken about it or unaware of it, just as it was true that "The earth orbits the sun" even 500 years ago when few people, if anyone, believed it. The premise that there is diversity of belief cannot support a conclusion that there is no universal truth to morality. Some people – or everybody, even – might be mistaken.

2   Further, when philosophers claim that morality is universal, they are making a normative or prescriptive claim to the effect that people ought to abide by these norms, rather than a descriptive claim that they do in fact abide by these norms. The claim that there are universal moral norms is the claim that there are norms that have authority over the actions of people universally; it does not mean that there are moral norms that have been accepted universally. Only the latter claim is impacted by the empirical evidence that different norms seem to be accepted by different cultures. The latter claim may be false given our empirical evidence – but the empirical evidence does not affect the truth or falsity of the first claim. As many other philosophers have noted, we can't derive something like "There is no universal moral truth" from a claim such as "Different cultures have different moral codes" – the second is simply a descriptive claim, whereas the first is interpreted as having normative significance. And what people ought to do and what they believe about what they ought to do are very different. People can be morally mistaken.

3   Even descriptively, it is not at all conclusive that values differ – it could simply be the circumstances that differ, or the nonmoral beliefs that affect moral practices that differ.

So, it does not follow from variation in practices that we have even descriptive variation in values. The same values may be accepted, but differing circumstances or beliefs result in different practices.

[7] In his chapter on cultural relativism in *The Elements of Moral Philosophy* (New York: McGraw-Hill, 1978), Rachels very clearly explores the same issues as are raised here. It does not follow from variation in moral practices that no objective standard of morality exists.

Further, we intuitively like to think that within cultures we can observe moral progress; that is, things seem to be getting better in some cultures at least. So, for example, some take the facts that slavery is illegal and that women now have the right to vote as a sign of moral progress in the USA. Recall Frederick Douglass and his condemnation of slavery. That slavery is a moral evil is a compelling reason to abolish it. The abolition of slavery throughout the USA – this change in the culture of the USA – denotes genuine moral progress and not simply a shift in what people happen to believe. Recall also the interchange between Abigail and John Adams. The view that John Adams espoused, which would likely have been typical within the culture at the time, is no longer viewed as legitimate – restricting rights on bases we now view to be arbitrary is unjust, and was unjust at the time. Thus, it does seem plausible to maintain that there has been moral progress in the USA since 1776, at least with respect to some issues. However, this would have to be rejected as illusory if moral relativism is true, since there would be no objective standard along which to measure progress. Instead, there would just be change, but we wouldn't be justified in claiming one sort of change to be better than another – or worse either, for that matter.

None of the above considerations provides a knockdown argument against relativism, since the relativist could simply bite the bullet and accept all of those unpalatable intuitions. The point of the above criticisms is to note that many people find themselves attracted to relativism because they mistakenly identify it with tolerance, or think that such relativism is necessary to adopt an attitude of tolerance toward differing social customs and conventions. But closer reflection reveals that, instead, the view has implications that are quite unattractive, and implications that most persons would be unwilling to accept. While tolerance is valuable, it only goes so far – it clearly can't cover morally outrageous behavior such as mass murder, baseless discrimination, or a host of other moral problems that we've seen in play throughout human history.

Of course, this is not to deny that tolerance is a good thing in the right circumstances. Tolerance is a good thing as long as we're not talking about practices with moral import. The feeling that relativism is supported by the value of tolerance can be explained away in the following way, by noting a distinction between morality and moralizing. Sometimes people illegitimately moralize nonmoral norms. They try to turn a nonmoral issue into a moral one by projecting emotional responses of various sorts. So, someone might view a deviation from norms of taste as a moral deviation ("How dare he wear a robe instead of trousers!"), or a deviation from norms of etiquette as a moral deviation ("How dare she use the entrée fork for her salad!"). This is a natural human tendency that needs to be guarded against. Some things – even things that people feel very strongly about, such as manners and fashion – are not moral. They may be aesthetic, in which case these norms lack the authority of moral norms. Constance may experience deep revulsion whenever she sees someone mixing chartreuse fabric with a plaid. She may form the judgment "One ought not to mix a chartreuse fabric with a plaid." But this use of "ought," though normative, is not moral. The person who is mixing clashing fabrics is not harming anyone. Of course, if Sandra wears chartreuse and plaid for the purpose of making Constance feel bad, that's a different issue. But what makes her action bad is the fact that she's trying to make Constance queasy, not that she's mixing fabrics in an aesthetically inappropriate way.

Whether or not someone wears a robe instead of trousers is not a moral issue. Yet, throughout history people have mistakenly turned such issues into moral issues – labeling, for example, non-Western clothing as "indecent," when it fact it was perfectly suited to non-Western climates. This sort of moralizing, I believe, is what makes many people attracted to relativism. However, universalism does not condone moralizing and is perfectly compatible with tolerance of cultural variation that does not violate universal moral norms. So, for example, it is compatible with condemning female circumcision, while being neutral on the issue of alternative forms of clothing and self-adornment.

In this chapter, we've discussed a major challenge to ethics. I hope to have shown that this challenge, while initially appealing, is untenable. Still, if there is a universally true content to morality, what is it? Various writers have offered accounts of morality by citing different fundamental norms and values. We will spend most of the remainder of the book critically examining these alternatives.

Further reading

Benedict, Ruth 1934: *Patterns of Culture*. Boston: Houghton Mifflin.
Rachels, James 1978: *The Elements of Moral Philosophy*. New York: McGraw-hill.

Chapter 2

God and Human Nature

One issue of enduring interest to philosophers working in normative ethical theory is the issue of the source of normativity. When someone makes a claim such as

(1)   Robert stole the television.

she is first of all describing something that Robert did, but she is also, generally, making a claim about the normative status of what he did. She is judging what he did, or evaluating it. Normally, stealing is wrong, so she may also be making the claim that

(2)   What Robert did was *wrong*.

But what makes what he did wrong? This is where theory comes in. Some ethical theorists believe that the source of normativity falls outside of – or, rather, transcends – human nature. Others believe that morality is a result of human nature – one of the outgrowths of our sociality, for example. Thus, the normative force of statements such as (2) depends upon features of our nature in some way. We begin this book by looking at two classic theories that embody this contrast – divine command theory and one form of ethical egoism.

Divine command theory holds that moral norms depend upon God's will, and in that way these norms find their authority outside human nature. Ethical egoism, on the other hand, is the view that moral norms serve the function of promoting the self-interest of individuals – thus, what we ought to do depends upon what promotes our own individual self-interest. Ethical egoism need not be based on any particular view of human nature, but it often is. In contrast to divine command theory, the version we will look at here is based on the view that human beings are fundamentally motivated by self-interest, or – to put this more strongly – that the only thing that motivates human beings is self-interest. This version of ethical egoism then depends upon a very simple view of human nature. Once problems with divine command theory became accepted, writers began to look at ways to ground ethics in human nature. This was a trend that continued up to Immanuel Kant (1724–1804) and beyond. Kant was not himself a divine command theorist; however, he accepted the intuition – which many people shared – that morality could not depend upon contingencies of human nature.

Divine Command Theory

> There are, however, certain exceptions to the law against killing, made by the authority of God himself. There are some whose killing God orders, either by law, or by an express command to a particular person at a particular time ... When Abraham was ready to kill his son, so far from being blamed for cruelty he was praised for his devotion ...
>
> St Augustine, *The City of God*, Book I, 21[1]

In the Bible, the prophet Abraham is commanded by God to kill his son Isaac. Abraham, though he loved his son, was willing to obey God and kill his son (Genesis 22: 1–2). But, at the last moment, as Abraham was just about to plunge his knife into Isaac, God intervened and told Abraham he need not make the sacrifice after all. Abraham's faith in God was tested successfully, and Isaac's life was spared.

Over the years, this story has been taken to represent a view of morality, Divine command theory, which is the view that what is right is completely a matter of God's will. Thus, in killing his own innocent son Abraham would have been doing nothing wrong, because that death was what God would have wanted – it was what God had actually commanded him to do. And that is just what it is for something to

---

[1] St Augustine, *The City of God*, translated by Henry Bettenson (New York: Penguin Books, 1984), p. 32.

be "right." The story of Abraham and Isaac is one of three stories used in the Judeo-Christian tradition to illustrate the dependence of morality on God's will. The others are, first, the command of God for the Israelites to plunder and loot the belongings of the Egyptians (Exodus 11: 2) and, second, God's command to Hosea to engage in sexual intercourse with an adulteress (Hosea 3: 1). These accounts in the Bible are sometimes referred to as "the immoralities of the patriarchs."[2] Because these cases involve God commanding persons do act in ways that seem inconsistent with the Ten Commandments – specifically, those against killing, stealing, and adultery – they are taken as posing a puzzle for divine command theory.

For many years, most people viewed ethics to be a matter of God's will. In fact, many people still hold this view. There is no doubt that morality and religion are closely connected in many people's minds. However, using God's will as the fundamental concept in the development of an ethical theory goes beyond recognizing a connection. The central idea behind the theory that treats God's will as fundamental to morality is that something is right if and only if it is God's will, or if and only if God commands it.

Thomas Aquinas (1224–74) argued that God was not in fact making an exception for Abraham contra the injunction against committing murder.[3] Rather, " ... when Abraham consented to slay his son [Genesis 12], he did not consent to murder, because his son was due to be slain by the command of God, Who is Lord of life and death: for He it is who inflicts the punishment of death on all men, both godly and ungodly, on account of the sin of our first parent, and if a man be the executor of that sentence by Divine authority, he will be no murderer any more than God would be."[4]

Divine command theory seems quite a natural theory to adopt, given that we believe that a divine, supernatural being created the universe in its entirety. If God created everything, then isn't it God who is responsible for morality's existence? Thus, when we make a claim

---

[2] See Philip Quinn's essay "The Primacy of God's Will in Christian Ethics," *Philosophical Perspectives*, 6, 1992, pp. 493–513.

[3] It should be noted that Thomas Aquinas was a natural law theorist.

[4] Thomas Aquinas, *Summa Theologiae*, translated by Anton C. Pegis, in *The Basic Writings of St. Thomas Aquinas*, vol. II (New York: Random House, 1945), pp. 843–4.

such as (2), the truth or falsity of that claim must depend upon God somehow – for example, it could be dependent on God's will, or what God wants to be the case.

But we need to take a closer look at this. What exactly does it mean to say that morality *depends upon* God's will? Perhaps we mean that God invented morality, just as Samuel Morse invented the telegraph. If Morse had not willed the telegraph, it would not have existed, and thus the telegraph depended upon Morse for its very existence. But the dependence specified in divine command theory must be much stronger than this. Once invented, the telegraph operates independently of Samuel Morse's will. What divine command theory holds is that God's will is necessary and sufficient in determining the content of morality – it actually defines it. Thus, for an act to be "right" it is both necessary and sufficient that the act be performed in compliance with God's will. God's will is necessary in that if the act is not in compliance with God's will regarding the right, it is not the right action. God's will is sufficient in that all that is required for an act to be "right" is that God wills it right.

If God had not retracted His command to kill and if Abraham had then followed God's command, would he have been acting rightly or wrongly? Again, on divine command theory, it would seem that Abraham would have had a moral obligation to kill his son, *just because* God commanded it.

But the ancient Greek philosopher Socrates (470–399 BC) raised a problem relevant to this theory, which is often termed "the Euthyphro problem" in honor of the dialogue in which it is discussed. Socrates was not, of course, responding directly to writers such as Augustine, since Plato's dialogues were written many years before the early Christian philosophers wrote their works. But the basic theory is not essentially a Christian one – very many religious perspectives could endorse a version of divine command theory and simply spell it out differently, according to the nature of the god set out in the religious tradition. It is simply the case that in Western philosophy this tends to be discussed primarily in the context of Christianity. When Socrates questions one of his fellow citizens about the nature of piety, he is raising the problem within his religious tradition. He asks Euthyphro to clarify what he means by "pious" – and at one point in the dialogue Euthyphro states that the pious is what the gods love. Socrates is still not clear, and asks "Is the pious loved by the gods because it is pious, or is it pious because it is loved by the gods?" (10a) Euthyphro, being led in the dialogue by Socrates, agrees to holding that the pious is not pious just because the gods love it. But then this means that there is some other reason or set of reasons that renders an action pious – so Socrates is not satisfied with Euthyphro's account. To get the full account, we need to know *why* the gods love certain acts as pious acts.

The same problem arises for divine command theory. If there are reasons why God deems an action to be "right" or "wrong," then it is really those reasons that provide the account of "right" and "wrong" – not God's will. It forces us to choose between two unpalatable options: either (i) what is right is completely determined by God's will, or what God wants, and is thus capricious in a way that seems incompatible with rightness; or (ii) God does not determine what is right, but is simply in the best position to discern or perceive what is right, since He is infallible.

With respect to the first interpretation, this seems capricious – What if God just decided that killing kittens for fun was right? Then, on this theory, it would be right – God's will is what would *make* it right. Recall Aquinas's rationale for why Abraham killing his son would have been morally good, given that God had not retracted His command: God is the source of life itself, and no person deserves life on account of original sin; thus if God wills that life to end, He is entirely justified and his servant justified in carrying out His will. Still, this may strike many as capricious, especially relying as it does on the morally dubious rationale of original sin. Why should a child be held responsible for the sins of his ancestors? This is not fair. Further, if we provide a rationale for God's willing a certain way, to avoid the charge of capriciousness, then we're actually giving other reasons why God made that particular decision. The idea is that God wouldn't will something as seemingly terrible as homicide without good reason – but then this brings us to the second interpretation suggested by the Euthyphro objection. If God's will is not what determines rightness but, instead, God is simply perfectly responsive to the right sorts of reasons that justify actions, then those reasons have their normative force independent of God's will. And, thus, a moral theory exists independent of God's will, and actions can be evaluated on the basis of the "right" or "wrong" reasons, which make no necessary reference to God's will.

Some writers who accept divine command theory would argue that this is not the right way to spell out the theory – morality does not depend upon God's *will*. They thus reject the "voluntarist" interpretation of divine command theory that makes morality dependent on the will of God. Rather, morality depends upon what God *believes* is right and wrong. This is often referred to as the "doxastic" interpretation of divine command theory. On this view God is, in effect, an ideal observer. He has all of the virtues that we associate with the ideal epistemic agent and moral judge. He is *impartial*, since He loves all persons equally; He is *rational* and thus makes no errors of reasoning; and He has *full information*, so He will not be making mistakes on the basis of partial information. If God, then, who is not swayed by bias or prejudice, who is completely fair, and who knows all of the relevant facts believes that x is wrong, then x is wrong. Thus a distinction can be drawn between the volitional and the doxastic versions of the theory. We could well believe that the volitional version has problems – spelled out in terms of what God wills or wants – but we could also believe that the doxastic version is true, and that what God believes really does determine the content of morality:[5] and not just the content of morality, but the content of mathematics and logic – the content of all the disciplines, even those characterized by necessary truths. Necessary truths are claims that are true in all possible worlds – any world that can be imagined. So, to use an example from René Descartes's *Meditations*, $2 + 3 = 5$ is a necessary truth; triangles have three sides; an object is identical to itself; and so on. We cannot conceive of a world in which $2 + 3$ does not equal 5. Yet, on the doxastic theory, if God believes that $2 + 3 = 19$, then it is true that $2 + 3 = 19$. Of course, this can be extended to moral claims, necessary or not. If God believes that torturing kittens for fun is permissible, then it is permissible.

My view is that this theory gets its initial plausibility for some people because there is a confusion between what counts as good evidence for something and what counts as a cause. Given that God is omniscient, given that He really does know *everything* there is to know, then if God believes that $2 + 3 = 19$ he must be right. Otherwise, he wouldn't be

---

[5] For more on the doxastic understanding of divine command theory, see Michael Loux, "Toward an Aristotelian Theory of Abstract Objects," in *Midwest Studies in Philosophy*, vol. 11, edited by Peter A. French, Theodore E. Uehling, Jr., and Howard K. Wettstein (Minneapolis: University of Minnesota Press, 1986), pp. 495–512. Philip Quinn (see note 2) believes that the doxastic and volitional version are equivalent, at least extensionally.

omniscient. So, what God believes, given that He is omniscient, is extremely good evidence of what is actually true. Indeed, it is *perfectly* good evidence. But that does not mean that His belief *makes it the case* that $2 + 3 = 19$. Suppose that Marion has a perfect thermometer – it is always right about the temperature. Today, it reads 87 degrees Fahrenheit. Given that Marion's thermometer is perfect, then it must be true that it is 87 degrees Fahrenheit outside. But Marion's thermometer did not cause it to be 87 degrees Fahrenheit outside. So, in effect, divine command theory can't use this consideration to argue for the theory that morality depends (in a causal way) on what God believes. Rather, it simply has to be stipulated. But then we get back to something like the Euthyphro problem – if God had just decided to believe that torturing kittens is permissible – well, this still seems pretty awful.

None of these criticisms affect the view that religion and morality are connected. For example, we might hold that what God believes provides the best guidance, and that divine revelation is the best source of moral insight for human beings. For God, belief and knowledge amount to the same thing. This view is not affected by the criticisms of divine command theory.

Another theory that often connects morality to God is called "natural law theory." Thomas Aquinas held a version of natural law theory. This theory is not a variation of divine command theory. It does not hold that God's will is necessary and sufficient to make a particular action right or wrong. However, a very popular version of this theory does hold that God created the universe in such a way that morality is revealed to us in His creation. There are laws of morality in the fabric of the universe, just as there are laws of physics. We need not believe this in order to be natural law theorists, of course – we could have some other basis for thinking that morality is revealed to us, or discoverable to us, by observation or introspection alone. For example, we could believe that natural forces have given rise to an orderly natural system in which beings have developed their own particular functions. The heart, for example, functions to pump blood – that is what its purpose is, and we can discover this by simply observing its operations. We can believe this without believing that God created the heart. However, many religious believers have found this view very appealing, because it has made sense to them that God would have created the universe in this way – with an orderly, purposeful design, bestowing objects with particular functions and purposes – and that He would have created us so that we could have access to these, and to morality, through the operation of our reason.

Aquinas, for example, believed that human beings possessed a social nature as well as their rational capacities. Animals may be social as well, but they lack rationality.

Given this background, and the emphasis on God having created the universe in such a way that moral truth is discoverable by examination of God's creation and rational reflection, we have a view that places enormous emphasis on what is "natural" as opposed to "unnatural." The "natural" is good and the "unnatural" is perverse, or bad – Otherwise, why would God have created the universe that way, since God Himself is good? This view has been used – in various guises – to condemn homosexuality, artificial methods in aid of reproduction, and the use of birth control as "unnatural" and thus "immoral."

Consider the example of birth control. The idea within natural law theory would be that women have reproductive systems for the purpose of producing babies. That is the function of the system composed of the ovaries and the uterus. Thwarting this purpose is unnatural and perverse. Birth control thwarts the proper functioning of the reproductive system, and is therefore unnatural. As something unnatural, it is immoral and people ought not to use birth control.

Such an account puts a tremendous weight on "natural" and "unnatural." What are the criteria for something counting as "natural" and therefore good? The philosopher David Hume (1711–76) pointed out the numerous problems with this approach, noting that "natural" is a term "... than which there is none more ambiguous and equivocal." The general problem is that there are a variety of senses of the term, and people who claim that what is natural is the same as what is good, and that what is unnatural is bad, are often not clear about what they mean. So, for example, we might think of "natural" as simply the same as "what we find in nature without human intervention": then things such as tooth decay are natural – yet, surely, tooth decay is also bad, something that we try very hard to avoid. No one thinks that brushing his or her teeth is immoral.

Hume himself noted at least three senses of the term. The first he refers to is that sense of "natural" that is opposed to the miraculous or *super-natural*. The second sense is that which is opposed to the unusual, or the rare. And the third sense is that which is opposed to artificial, or created by humans. None of these will work, he argues, concluding that:

> ...nothing can be more unphilosophical than those systems, which assert, that virtue is the same with what is natural, and vice with what is unnatural. For in the first sense of the word, Nature, as opposed to miracles, both vice and virtue are equally natural; and in the second sense, as oppos'd to what is unusual, perhaps virtue will be found to be the most unnatural. At least it must be own'd, that heroic virtue, being as unusual, is as little natural as the most brutal barbarity. As to the third sense of the word, 'tis certain that both vice and virtue are equally artificial, and out of nature. For however it may be disputed, whether the notion of merit or demerit in certain actions be natural or artificial, 'tis evident, that the actions themselves are artificial, and are perform'd with a certain design and intention; otherwise they could never be rank'd under any of these denominations. 'Tis impossible, therefore, that the character of natural and unnatural can ever, in any sense, mark the boundaries of vice and virtue.[6]

If our view, then, is that nature or the natural is a guide to what is good and bad because, after all, God created the natural world, then we will run up against these problems of how exactly to understand what is "natural" in a way that can accommodate our views of good and evil. Nature contains a good deal that is bad, and we put a lot of effort into avoiding some of the bad things that can be viewed as "natural" – such as diseases, natural disasters, and inhospitable climates.

Even though the view that morality somehow depends upon God continues to be popular, there are many people who also believe that morals can exist independently of God. In the modern era, philosophers who have tried to develop ethical theories, even those who whole-heartedly believed in a god, thought that they could do so without using "God" as a central component in their theory. In the rest of this book, we will consider some of these theories.

One of the earliest of the modern philosophers to do this was Thomas Hobbes (1588–1679). Hobbes believed in God, but thought that it was possible to develop a political system, or a theory of a just state, based on certain very minimal assumptions about human nature and social

---

[6] David Hume, *A Treatise of Human Nature*, edited by L. A. Selby-Bigge and P. H. Nidditch (Oxford: Clarendon Press, 1978), p. 475.

interactions. Hobbes was in part motivated by certain practical difficulties associated with relying on God's will as a measure of morality. So, for example, a number of religious wars had been raging across Europe, causing misery and social chaos. These wars were at least ostensibly caused by differing interpretations of God's will. Without access to the mind of God, there was a good deal of uncertainty about the contents of God's will, yet it did not stop people from having very strong beliefs about it. Further, the divine right of kings was being challenged more frequently. Many people had believed that kings obtained their authority through God's will. Thus, the king was the unquestioned leader. Yet some kings had engaged in practices that at the very least seemed highly questionable. If kings did not get their authority to rule through God, then, the worry was, society would degenerate. There would be moral chaos. Was there any other source of political authority for a ruler?

On Hobbes's theory, the source of the political authority of a leader did not reside in God's will. Rather, it was located in the need of human beings to create a social order in order to preserve their own lives and well-being. By making a fairly minimal assumption about human nature, Hobbes believed that he could generate a political philosophy, and possibly a moral one as well.

Egoism

> [T]he voluntary actions and inclinations of all men, tend, not only to the procuring, but also to the assuring of a contented life; and differ only in the way: which ariseth partly from the diversity of passions, in diverse men; and partly from the difference of the knowledge, or opinion, each one has of the causes, which produce the effect desired. . . . I put for a general inclination of mankind, a perpetual and restless desire of Power after power, that ceaseth only in Death.
>
> Thomas Hobbes, *Leviathan*[7]

An egoistic view is one that either explains or justifies something in terms of the agent's self-interest. For example, *psychological egoism* is the descriptive view that all human action is motivated by self-interest. *Ethical egoism*, on the other hand, is the normative view that holds that all action

[7] Thomas Hobbes, *Leviathan*, edited by C. B. Macpherson (New York: Penguin Books, 1968), p. 161.

ought to be motivated by self-interest. Ethical egoism is not committed to the truth of psychological egoism. Another view, *rational egoism*, holds that an action is rational if and only if it maximizes the agent's self-interest. The only one of these views that offers a normative *ethical* theory is ethical egoism. Psychological egoism is purely descriptive, and rational egoism offers an account of rational appraisal of actions, which might turn out to be different from moral appraisal of actions.

Psychological egoism offers an account of human nature and is nonnormative. It concerns how people actually behave, not how they ought to behave. If we hold that all human action is motivated by self-interest, we're making a strong, universal claim. We're denying that altruistic actions are ever performed. Altruistic actions are those that are performed for the sake of others – purely for the sake of others. The psychological egoist denies that there are such acts. Some actions may seem altruistic, as when a person donates money to charity. However, this can readily be explained, egoists argue, by the fact that the person is supporting a system that has the prospect of helping her in the future, or she gains by being able to display her financial power, and so forth. This view has a long and proud history – some believe that Thomas Hobbes, for example, held this view and then justified a political system in virtue of the fact that since people were only motivated by self-interest, it made sense for them to accept that system, since it best promoted their self-interest to do so. Thus, some argue that Hobbes's political system, a kind of contractarianism, is based on his view of human nature. We will discuss Hobbes in more detail in a later chapter. For our purposes here, it is sufficient to point out that there is good evidence for holding him to be a psychological egoist. Again, it is important to note that psychological egoism is making a radical and interesting claim about human nature – that all of our actions are motivated by self-interest.

The psychological egoist claim has sometimes been interpreted as *trivial* – as the claim that people just do what they, "all things considered," want to do, and whatever that is just *is* their self-interest. But surely this is not correct. We recognize a distinction between what an agent does and what is in his self-interest, and sometimes they do come apart – and this is true even when we consider what an agent does and what the agent thinks or believes is in his self-interest – soldiers sacrifice themselves for the sake of their friends, parents for the sake of their children.

Aside from a rather cynical reflection on human nature, are there any arguments that we can give in support of psychological egoism? We could imagine a kind of evolutionary argument for a weak form of psychological egoism.[8] It might be the case, for example, that exclusively altruistic motivations are penalized from the evolutionary perspective. Those who run risks, for example, to help others simply for the sake of helping them will tend to end up worse off than those that don't, and they will be less able to compete. This means that they will have fewer offspring, and the genes that dispose them to such behavior will, over time, decrease throughout the population. This doesn't mean that altruistic actions won't be performed anymore – it's just that it's unlikely that we'll see altruistic actions that actually *conflict* with the interests of the agent. On this view, people would still help each other out, but acts of truly heroic self-sacrifice would be rare, and would become increasingly rare over time.

It's also worth noting that we could offer a quite different evolutionary picture as well. For example, Geoffrey Miller argues that moral virtues evolved in response to sexual selection:

> ...human morality is...likely to be a direct result of sexual selection. We have the capacity for moral behavior and moral judgments today because our ancestors favored sexual partners who were kind, generous, helpful, and fair. We still have the same preferences.[9]

Miller has the view that potential mates respond favorably to virtues such as kindness and generosity, and are repulsed by cruelty. We seek the moral virtues and avoid the vices. We need only look at empirical evidence on the characteristics that people cite in choosing mates to get confirmation of this. In one study, for example, discussed by Miller, David Buss showed that a trait such as "kindness" was overwhelmingly selected for – across all 37 cultures that he studied.

Again, it is important to stress here that the explanation we receive from science about how things such as virtues come into existence is not a normative one. It is descriptive. Psychological egoism itself is descriptive, and evolutionary theory can provide evidence either to

---

[8] Indeed, Michael Slote does this in an article "An Empirical Basis for Psychological Egoism," *Journal of Philosophy*, 61, 1964, pp. 530–7.

[9] Geoffrey Miller, *The Mating Mind* (New York: Doubleday, 2000), p. 292.

support it or to disconfirm it. Miller's account of how virtues naturally would be expected to arise in human populations simply explains why we might regard something like generosity as a trait that is attractive in someone we want to live with, and thus it explains why something like altruism would have arisen and would continue to be sustained in human populations. To get normativity we need to claim that generosity, altruism, and the like are morally good, and then we need an account of the good. Off hand, it doesn't look as though evolutionary theory can give us an account of the *morally* good (as opposed to an account of what humans find attractive in mates, for example). But evolutionary theory or other descriptive accounts of what human beings are like and how they developed could give us information about what human beings want and desire, what sorts of preferences they have, and how they came to experience the emotions they experience – including the so-called moral emotions such as love, admiration, contempt, and outrage. Thus, these theories do have some relevance to normative ethics, even if they are not themselves normative.

This relevance can be displayed by looking at one case to be made for ethical egoism. Some writers accept ethical egoism because they find psychological egoism plausible; that is, they think that what we ought to do is promote self-interest because, really, that's all we *can* do. But if we believe that we have a lot of evidence against psychological egoism, this argument won't work, because other options for acting will be open to the moral agent. Evolutionary theory, as well as our other observations of human behavior, can provide this sort of evidence to undercut psychological egoism.

At best, we might be able to develop an evolutionary argument to support a very weak form of psychological egoism, as noted above. But weak forms of psychological egoism are not as surprising, since they allow for plenty of exceptions. Nonegoists are happy to say that a great many human actions are consistent with self-interest, and, in ethical egoism, it is even possible for altruistic actions to be compatible with self-interest. That is not enough to generate the very surprising view of human nature embodied by full blown psychological egoism.

The normative counterpart to psychological egoism is ethical egoism. Again, this is the view that the agent *should* act on his self-interest. Note the difference between this view and psychological egoism. Psychological egoism is a descriptive rather than a normative claim.

Psychological egoism is a theory of human nature that purports to describe what motivates persons to act. Ethical egoism, on the other hand, is normative. It purports to tell us how people *ought* to act. We could be ethical egoists who deny psychological egoism – people ought to act on self-interest, but, sadly, they don't do enough of that. Ayn Rand, for example, believed that we could certainly be motivated by altruism, but that this was destructive and, instead, people should follow self-interest. She is often cited as an ethical egoist who is not a psychological egoist.[10]

One way to formulate an ethical egoism view is to hold something like the following: the right action is that action which promotes the agent's self-interest. There is one important indeterminacy to this formulation. Ought the agent do what she perceives to be in her self-interest, or ought she to do what is actually in her self-interest (i.e., "enlightened" self-interest)? Here's an example that helps to illustrate the difference. Suppose that Mary needs to decide between two different careers. One is a career in journalism and the other is a career in computer science. She believes that the career in journalism is better for her and that it will improve her employment prospects. Suppose, however, that career prospects in journalism are quite "iffy" (though Mary does not realize this) and that, in fact, she is far more likely to get a good job with a higher degree in computer science. On the former egoistic principle – that the right action is the one that the agent perceives to be best for her – she should pursue the career in journalism. However, on the latter egoistic principle – that the right action is the one that really is the best for her, irrespective of how she perceives it – she ought to pursue the career in computer science.

A number of people have been attracted to egoism. One theoretical advantage, at least of the subjective view, is that it is generally thought to offer a solution to the problem of moral motivation. Given that an agent knows what morality demands or requires, why should he or she do it? Why should he or she act morally? Some think that if ethical egoism is the correct view, however, then it seems quite clear why – because it is *rational*. Prudence and morality coincide on this view. However, note the earlier distinction that we made between rational egoism and ethical egoism. This position in favor of ethical egoism is

[10] See Rand's *The Virtue of Selfishness*, co-authored with Nathaniel Branden (New York: Signet, 1964).

assuming the truth of rational egoism, and then drawing an analogy between prudential motivation and moral motivation. Moral behavior is then justified instrumentally; it actually helps us to achieve self-interested goals. Thus there is no mystery to why agents ought to act morally. They ought to act morally just as they ought to eat regularly. It is in their self-interest to do so. But it is not clear that this solves a problem at all. For example, the great nineteenth-century philosopher Henry Sidgwick (1838–1900) turned this question on its head by asking why there isn't a problem explaining self-interested motivation. Why is the motivation problem always framed as a *moral* motivation problem? To Sidgwick, it seemed quite clear " . . . that it is 'right' and 'reasonable' for me to treat others as I should think that I myself ought to be treated under similar conditions, and to do what I believe to be ultimately conducive to universal Good or Happiness." Sidgwick believed that practical reason sometimes involves, under some circumstances, a practical contradiction between pursuit of self-interest and universal benevolence (a concern to promote the well-being of as many as possible). He writes, " . . . in the rarer cases of a recognized conflict between self-interest and duty, practical reason, being divided against itself, would cease to be a motive on either side; the conflict would have to be decided by the comparative preponderance of one or other of two groups of non-rational impulses."[11]

So, it is not clear that ethical egoism can provide a response to "Why be moral?" any better than theories that maintain that we ought to purse the well-being of others as well as our own. The latter seems just as reasonable, if not more reasonable, than the former. Indeed, one of Sidgwick's aims was to show that the only two ethical theories that are reasonable are egoism and utilitarianism. Thus, Sidgwick is rejecting rational egoism, and its use as an underlying justification for ethical egoism.

However, a more serious problem is that, on closer inspection, ethical egoism is highly counterintuitive as a moral theory. For example, this view holds that the fact that a course of action would help others is *not* a moral reason to do it. But "helping others" seems the paradigm of a moral reason. Ethical egoism that is based on psychological egoism makes the claim that altruism is impossible, and we've already discussed

---

[11] Henry Sidgwick, *The Methods of Ethics* (Indianapolis: Hackett, 1981), p. 508.

why this seems counterintuitive. We can easily generate plausible counter examples to psychological egoism. But ethical egoism – even ethical egoism that it not based on psychological egoism – has the problem that is the normative counterpart to this one. It actually condemns altruistic action. Assume that we believe ethical egoism but that we don't believe psychological egoism. We then think that even though altruistic action is possible, it should be discouraged. People should not be altruistic. But this type of ethical egoist also gives a peculiar reason for why we ought not to be altruistic: the reason we ought not to be altruistic is that the altruistically motivated person seeks the good of others, but morality demands that we pursue our own good even at the expense of others. Again, this doesn't accord very well with our moral judgments. A person who devotes her life to helping the poor, even though she would rather have gone to art school, should be praised, not condemned.

If we were to argue (as some who claim to be egoists do) that we ought to pursue our own self-interest because that works out best for everybody, or because it promotes the overall good, then we wouldn't actually be egoists. Again, we would be using a justification that appeals to the good of others to warrant the self-interested behavior. This is a very popular justification for egoism, too, so many people have misunderstood what exactly the theory is committed to. Consider the argument in Mandeville's *Fable of the Bees* (1714):

> ... *Fools only strive*
> *To make a Great an Honest Hive*
> *T'enjoy the World's Conveniences,*
> *Be fam'd in War, yet live in Ease*
> *Without great Vices, is a vain*
> *UTOPIA seated in the Brain.*
> *Fraud, Luxury and Pride must live,*
> *While we the Benefits receive;*[12]

Bernard Mandeville (1670–1733) is arguing that what we commonly term vices – things such as self-indulgence, and lies that are used to avoid unpleasant confrontations with others, or to get our own way, are actually good for society; that without these so-called vices of self-interest, society would wither and fade, and prosperity would be

---

[12] Bernard Mandeville, excerpt from the *Fable of the Bees*; reprinted in *Self-Interest*, edited by Kelly Rogers (New York: Routledge, 1997), p. 116.

lost. Some have interpreted this kind of argument as an argument for ethical egoism, but it is not. Even though it may be an argument for the claim that, given human nature and human society, people ought to pursue their own self-interest, it is not an argument that pursuit of our own self-interest is the very foundation of morals. Instead, there is a different justification provided for why we ought to pursue our own self-interest; that is, if individuals do this, then things work out much better for most people, and society as a whole benefits.

Thus, the arguments purportedly in favor of ethical egoism don't seem to work. Further, there are plenty of reasons for doubting that this theory accounts, at the very least, for some of our deeply held moral intuitions, since it seems to get the point of morality entirely wrong. It's true that if morality and self-interest coincided, then it would be great good news. But in those cases where it does coincide it does so by chance – there is no conceptual connection.

Weaker, and therefore more plausible, accounts of ethical forms of egoism have been proposed. One focuses on virtue and so is a kind of virtue ethical egoism: this form holds that moral virtues promote the well-being of the virtuous individual, and that qualities that fail to do this are not moral virtues. Again, off hand, this seems wildly implausible. Consider extremely generous persons who donate all their worldly goods to charity. This sort of generosity seems inimical to the well-being of the generous individual, though it certainly benefits the recipients of the generosity. However, Rosalind Hursthouse, in her work on virtue, has noted an interesting bit of evidence in favor of a moderate egoism:

> . . . good parents start inculcating the virtues . . . in their children from a very early age, in the belief, conscious or unconscious, that this is indeed preparing them for their lives, laying the foundations that will enable them to live well.[13]

On her view, the morally good life is a "good bet" – it does not guarantee the happiness of the moral individual, but it does make happiness more likely than not. This is making an empirical rather than a conceptual connection between self-interest and happiness and,

---

[13] Rosalind Hursthouse, *On Virtue Ethics* (New York: Oxford University Press, 1999), p. 175.

further, the claim is no longer a universal claim, so it is far more resistant to counterexample.

However, it is important to note that on this view we aren't educating our children, necessarily, to be *motivated by* self-interest. We're simply inculcating virtuous traits, such as generosity, in part because we think that if our child is generous, then that it good for the child too – it will help her in life, others will admire and respect her, and so on. So this isn't a form of *motivational* egoism. Indeed, we might even hold that to be truly virtuous, we shouldn't be motivated by self-interest at all, even though our own well-being is a by-product of moral virtue. But this would be compatible with a kind of enlightened self-interest egoism, since the agent on this view need not be aware of what is in her self-interest; she simply needs to be acting according to it, in order to be acting rightly (or virtuously).

If this is the way we decide to go in developing egoism, we can avoid some of the problems raised for the account. However, this will come at the theoretical cost of losing one of the advantages of the theory. We will no longer have the simple account of why it is rational to act morally.

Egoism is one of the earliest attempts to articulate a normative ethical theory by appeal to human nature. The attraction of this view was that it made ethics an outgrowth of our humanity. But this would introduce an unwelcome contingency problem that naturalistic accounts of morality still confront, and a problem that will reappear throughout the book as we consider alternative views of ethics.

Further reading

Milo, Ronald D. (ed.) 1973: *Egoism and Altruism*. Belmont, CA: Wadsworth.

Quinn, Philip 2001: "Divine Command Theory," in Hugh LaFollette (ed.), *Blackwell Guide to Ethical Theory*. Malden, MA: Blackwell, pp. 53–73.

Chapter 3

Classical Utilitarianism

> The applying a mathematical Calculation to *moral subjects*, will appear
> perhaps at first extravagant and *wild*; but some Corollaries . . . may shew
> the Conveniency of this Attempt, if it could be farther pursu'd.
> > Francis Hutcheson, *Concerning Moral Good and Evil*[1]

There are a great many people who believe that whether an action is
right or wrong depends upon its consequences. So, what makes something like killing another person wrong is that it is an act with a very
bad consequence; what makes torture wrong, again, is that torturing
someone causes them pain and humiliation, and, again, this is a bad
consequence. Bad, immoral actions are those actions that cause bad
outcomes and morally good actions are those that cause good outcomes. When a theory holds that the *only* thing relevant to determining whether or not an action is right are the consequences produced by
that action, the account is *consequentialist*. In Chapter 2, we looked at a
view that is consequentialist in nature – ethical egoism. Recall that
ethical egoism holds that persons ought to promote their own individual well-being. So, the actions that I perform are evaluated relative to
the good *consequences* generated relative to *me*. Further, that is the only
consideration relevant in determining whether or not those actions are
right or wrong. The theory we look at in this chapter is a version of
consequentialism called utilitarianism. Like ethical egoism, it holds

---

[1] Francis Hutcheson, An *Inquiry into the Original of our Ideas of Beauty and Virtue: In
Two Treatises. I. Concerning Beauty, Order, Harmony, Design. II. Concerning Moral Good
and Evil* (London: printed by John Darby for William and John Smith Dublin, 1725).

that we ought to do what has the best consequences, but the utilit-arians believe that the scope of relevant consequences is much broader than do the egoists – the egoist counts only his own well-being, while the utilitarian counts the well-being of *all* persons, or even all sentient creatures, impartially considered. The egoist believes that a morally relevant reason for him to act is agent-relative; that is, it is consider-ations of well-being relative to him. The egoist is not impartial; at least, not impartial in this sense. The utilitarian is impartial – on the stand-ard understanding of the utilitarian theory, moral reasons for action are agent-neutral. That well-being has some connection to me, or someone I love, or . . . whatever . . . invests it with no special normative force.

Utilitarianism is a theory with roots that stretch back into ancient philosophy. Indeed, the theory of value that Jeremy Bentham appeals to – "hedonism" – can be traced back to Epicurus (341–270 BC). Geoffrey Scarre notes that the ancient Chinese philosopher Mo Tzu (c.420 BC) also held a view similar to that of the classical utilitarians, advocating that we judge an action on the basis of how useful it is. If an action produces no benefits, it is to be condemned.[2] A number of early philosophers argued, essentially, that when we evaluate actions or try to decide what to do, we need to consider what would happen as a result of the action – and we need to compare the proposed actions to available alternatives and their consequences. It is sometimes difficult to tell if they are utilitarians, strictly speaking, since they can some-times be interpreted as providing a necessary rather than sufficient condition for right action. However, by the 1700s a number of philo-sophers were articulating a roughly utilitarian approach to ethics. The quote from Francis Hutcheson (1694–1746) shows that the basic idea behind the theory certainly held some sway before the classical utilit-arians began writing in the late 1700s. However, the modern devel-opment of the theory really began with the work of the legal scholar and philosopher Jeremy Bentham (1748–1832). Bentham was the first philosopher to systematically develop the theory, and he is the one who dubbed it "utilitarianism." He also took up Hutcheson's challenge· quite enthusiastically, and believed that some degree of mathematical and scientific precision could be brought to bear in moral decision-making.

---

[2] See Geoffrey Scarre, *Utilitarianism* (New York: Routledge, 1996), pp. 27–33.

Bentham was an unusual person. He was a precocious learner, who entered university at the age of 16 and studied law. However, since he was independently wealthy he did not need to work for a living, and he was able to devote himself to legal research as well as legal and political reform – his passions. His articulation of the utilitarian view owes much to his reformist goals. According to Bentham, the basis for utilitarianism is the principle of utility:

> By the principle of utility is meant that principle which approves or disapproves of every action whatsoever, according to the tendency which it appears to have to augment or diminish the happiness of the party whose interest is in question . . . I say of every action whatsoever; and therefore not only of every action of a private individual, but of every measure of government.[3]

Bentham was quite serious about this – laws as well as individual actions should be scrutinized according to this principle. If a law was useless or harmful, then it should be either reformed or tossed out altogether. Bentham used this commitment to utility to develop a powerful tool for reform, and during his life came up with many proposals for reforming laws, penal systems, and governments. Some of his ideas were adopted, others not, but he was an enormously influential individual, and his views led to a good deal of actual reform.

One of his reform plans in particular has become controversial in the past 30 years or so. Bentham was very concerned with penal, or prison, reform, and he developed a design for a model prison, a "panopticon," which he felt would be far more humane than the prisons that existed at that time in Great Britain.[4] The panopticon would be a circular prison, laid out in such a way that each prisoner would have his own cell and each cell would be viewable by one guard from a central platform. This allowed the prisoners to be punished psychologically by limiting their contact with others, and it allowed for greater efficiency in policing the prison – in fact, Bentham proposed that the guard's platform be surrounded by a translucent screen, so

[3] Jeremy Bentham, *An Introduction to the Principles of Morals and Legislation* (Oxford: Clarendon Press, 1789).

[4] Jeremy Bentham, *Panopticon: or, the Inspection-House* (Dublin: Thomas Byrne, 1791). The Bentham Project at University College London also maintains an interesting website on the panopticon, at www.ucl.ac.uk/Bentham-Project/info/panopticonhtm.htm

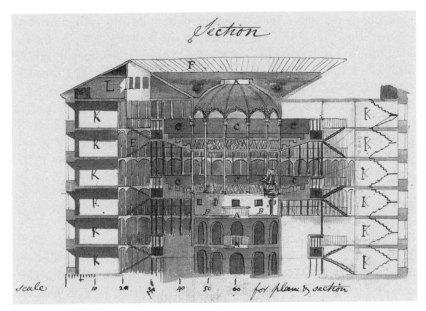

Figure 3.1 Jeremy Bentham's panopticon model prison.
Reproduced courtesy of University College London

that at any given time the prisoners could not tell if they were being watched by a real person. That could lead to even more efficiency! Bentham felt that this was humane as well, though, since it dispensed with physical punishment and allowed for tidier, less chaotic prisons. Some panopticon or panopticon-like prisons were built. Prisons in Great Britain, Australia, and Russia, for example, incorporated some of the features characteristic of the panopticon design – a circular structure, or keeping the prisoners separate and silent, chapels with the seats separated by screens to keep the prisoners focused on the sermon, and so forth.

However, this idea became controversial because it seemed to smack of "Big Brother" – someone watching you to make sure you are behaving – and this seemed an invasion of privacy. Indeed, in Port Arthur, Australia, where a model prison incorporating some panopticon features was built, prisoners would later complain that the psychological punishment was worse than the physical punishment. But the idea of surveillance being used to fight crime is catching on. For example, video cameras are being used to monitor public sites, to discourage crime as well as provide evidence in cases where crimes take place.

Bentham did carry his commitment to utility to rather extreme lengths. Upon his death, he willed that his body be dissected for the sake of furthering scientific knowledge. That is not unusual. But he also willed that his body be placed on public display at University College London. That *is* unusual. To this day, you can see Bentham's body – albeit with a wax head – tastefully displayed in a large Victorian cabinet. The rationale that Bentham gave for this strange bequest is that it would always bring to mind utilitarianism – anyone who saw the body would be curious about it or would have it come to mind. And isn't that something that would help to maximize utility?

The Principle

The principle of utility has two parts. The first part specifies the approach that we are to take to value. In the case of the utilitarians, we are to *maximize* value, to bring about as much of it as possible. The second part is the value-theory part that provides a substantive account of intrinsic value; that is, the value that we ought to be maximizing or promoting. Bentham believed that the morally right action for the individual was that action which produced, on balance, the greatest amount of *pleasure* overall. Like Epicurus, then, Bentham was a hedonist about value. However, he differs from Epicurus in a very crucial respect – for Bentham, the scope of the morally relevant consequences is broader. The right action brings about the most *overall* good, not just the most good for the agent performing the action.

So for the classical utilitarian the basic good is pleasure – that is what has intrinsic value. What has intrinsic disvalue is pain – that is the basic bad. According to Bentham, pleasure is a sensation and can be measured along the following parameters:

1. intensity
2. duration
3. certainty or uncertainty
4. propinquity or remoteness
5. fecundity
6. purity
7. extent[5]

---

[5] Bentham, *Principles of Morals and Legislation*, 2nd edn, ch. IV.

Uncharacteristically, Bentham composed a little poem to help people remember this:

> *Intense, long, certain, speedy, fruitful, pure –*
> Such marks in pleasures and in pains endure.
> Such pleasures seek, if *private* be thy end:
> If it be *public*, wide let them *extend*.
> Such pains avoid, whichever be thy view:
> If pains *must* come, let them *extend* to few.[6]

Some of these parameters, such as intensity and duration are pretty obvious. A pleasure will be better the more intense it is – and how long it lasts, its duration, is significant as well. I may prefer a weaker but longer pleasure to a shorter but more intense one. So, listening to music for an hour may be more preferable to me than eating an ice cream cone. But Bentham included other factors that are relevant in considering pleasures, so the certainty will matter – all other things being equal, we should go for the more certain rather than the less certain pleasure. The pleasure that is closer to me – for example, that I can have now – is to be preferred to a remote pleasure in the future. Further, I should give preference to pleasures that are fruitful, that will themselves lead to more pleasures in the future. Also, pleasures that are pure, or less mixed with pains, are to be preferred, and I must consider scope – How many people will be affected by the action in positive and negative ways? It is possible that some of these could be reduced to others – so, for example, we might think that propinquity can be reduced to certainty, perhaps. But Bentham isolated ways of measuring and evaluating pleasure that allow the hedonist to give plausible responses to superficial problems for the account of value. One superficial problem is the following: Alice could go to a party tonight and have a good time, though that would mean failing to study for her exam tomorrow. We might claim that on the hedonist view this would be good, because she gets pleasure from going to the party. But clearly this is bad for her. Therefore, hedonism is wrong. But Bentham would argue that this is the wrong way to look at it. Hedonism, properly understood, does not commit us to such foolhardy courses of action. Alice may get pleasure from going to the party, but

---

[6] Bentham, *Principles of Morals and Legislation*, 2nd edn, ch. IV, sec. 2.

this is not a very fruitful sort of pleasure, and indeed will lead to pain down the road – the pain of doing poorly in her exams. And that pain is more far reaching and has more serious negative consequences for her. So, hedonism does hold that it is bad for her to go to the party if that means forgoing an opportunity to study for her exam.

Also, some things may be intrinsically bad but instrumentally good. Here's another example. Vaccinations cause pain. Thus it would seem that on this view, vaccinations are bad. But clearly they are good. Therefore, hedonism is wrong. Well, again, Bentham would say that this isn't the right way to look at it: insofar as vaccinations cause pain, they are bad in that respect – however, they lead to protection against disease and the pain associated with disease, so they bear fruit down the road and are instrumentally good.

Bentham had the very egalitarian view that everyone's pleasure basically counted the same, and that the only differences between pleasures was quantitative – all of the factors listed above are quantitative; they simply have to do with *how much* pleasure there is associated with a given action. So Bentham repudiated the view that some pleasures are intrinsically better than others, or superior in terms of quality. Indeed, he famously remarked that "Prejudice apart, the game of push-pin is of equal value with the arts and sciences of music and poetry. If the game of push-pin furnish more pleasure, it is more valuable than either."[7] Bentham's view is that what really matters is pleasure, but he was willing to count a lot of things as pleasures, such as satisfaction, enjoyment, and fulfillment. He was not against the fine arts *per se*, but didn't think them superior in *kind* to other sources of pleasure. So, if people get just as much gratification from viewing bobble-head dogs as they do from gazing at the Mona Lisa, so be it. The pleasures are of equal value. To show any superiority on his account it would have to be quantitative in nature – we would have to argue that gazing at the Mona Lisa generates a more intense or more durable pleasure, for example.

Of course, Bentham's theory came under a good deal of criticism at the time. One problem was that, though egalitarian in that it counted everyone's pleasure the same, some thought it too egalitarian because it would seem to imply that all pleasures are intrinsically the same in kind.

[7] Jeremy Bentham, *The Rationale of Reward* (London: John and H. L. Hunt, 1825).

To many, this seemed to make the theory a kind of "swine morality," advocating that we ought to promote just whatever pleasures are quantitatively greater, even if those should turn out to be the simply sensual pleasures we have in common with lower life forms – such as the pleasures of eating, drinking, and so forth. Further, this account of value would also seem to include animals on the list of beings with moral standing. After all, animals feel pleasure and pain. Now, there is a sense in which this aspect of Bentham's theory provides an advantage. Other theories give no moral weight to animals at all, and this seems too extreme in the other direction. Surely animals must count for something. Isn't it immoral and wrong to torture a puppy just for the fun of it? This seems quite obvious, so Bentham's view has the advantage of giving a theoretical rationale for counting animals in the moral community. However, on Bentham's view, if animal pleasures are similar to ours, they would even have the *same* moral standing as people!

> The French have already discovered that the blackness of the skin is no reason why a human being should be abandoned without redress to the caprice of a tormentor. It may come one day to be recognized, that the number of legs, the villosity of the skin, or the termination of the *os sacrum*, are reasons equally insufficient for abandoning a sensitive being to the same fate.[8]

It is not that people find this odd because they think that animals don't count morally at all. What strikes them as absurd is that animals should count *the same* as people in virtue of their sentience. This is what led some critics to refer to Bentham's theory as a "swine morality." What struck many as lacking in Bentham's value theory was a special place for the rational capacities that mark a difference between persons and animals.

This was one criticism of the theory that Bentham's student John Stuart Mill (1806–73) would attempt to remedy. John Stuart Mill was exposed to the work of Bentham through his father, James Mill, who was one of Bentham's disciples. John Stuart Mill was a brilliant scholar, a compassionate and humane individual, who would become the

---

[8] Jeremy Bentham, *Introduction to the Principles of Morals and Legislation*, edited by J. H. Burns and H. L. A. Hart (New York, Oxford University Press, 1970), p. 283.

greatest British philosopher of the nineteenth century. He had a rather unusual upbringing – his father was assiduous at developing his intellect, but neglected his social and emotional development. This led Mill to have a rather constrained social life until he reached early adulthood, at which time he experienced an emotional breakdown. He recovered, but – he claimed – the experience during his breakdown taught him a lesson about happiness:

> I never . . . wavered in the conviction that happiness is the test of all rules of conduct, and the end of life. But I now thought that this end was only to be attained by not making it the direct end. Those only are happy (I thought) who have their minds fixed on some object other than their own happiness; on the happiness of others, on the improvement of mankind, even on some art or pursuit, followed not as a means, but as itself an ideal end.[9]

Mill went on to not only develop and flourish as a philosopher, but to engage in great public service. He ran for Parliament, was elected, and in 1868 became the first person to present a bill for women's suffrage. Like Bentham, he was influenced by a desire for reform. Harriet Taylor, his wife whom he married rather late in life, supported him in his reforms, and shared his utilitarian views. They both felt that too many laws and social practices reflected ignorance and prejudice rather than reason. Useless and harmful laws should be exposed and abandoned.

Though Bentham was the earlier proponent of utilitarianism, and there is no doubting his influence, it was John Stuart Mill who articulated perhaps the most influential version of the theory, one that provided a foundation for liberal social reforms. In *Utilitarianism*, Mill writes:

> The creed which accepts as the foundation of morals "utility" or the "greatest happiness principle" holds that actions are right in proportion as they tend to promote happiness; wrong as they tend to produce the reverse of happiness. By happiness is intended pleasure and the absence of pain; by unhappiness, pain and the privation of pleasure.[10]

[9] John Stuart Mill, *Autobiography*, edited by J. Stillinger (Boston: Houghton Mifflin, 1969).

[10] John Stuart Mill, *Utilitarianism*, edited by Roger Crisp (New York: Oxford University Press, 1998), p. 55.

As formulated, this principle is rather vague, and not too different from the one articulated by Bentham. However, Mill unpacked the definition rather differently. Like Bentham, the point is to produce the greatest overall good. Like Bentham, he subscribed to a hedonistic theory of value, though for Mill it was a somewhat modified one. It was modified in part to deal with the "swine morality" objection.

Again, one problem with the straightforward hedonistic account of value espoused by both Epicurus and Bentham is that it would seem to give equal *intrinsic* weight to animal experience and the experiences of persons. Thus, while animal pleasures and human pleasures may vary according to circumstantial, or extrinsic, considerations such as those listed by Bentham, and the intellectual pleasures of humans may turn out to be extrinsically better, there is no intrinsic difference between the two. This seems highly counterintuitive. It isn't just that human intellectual pleasure is more fruitful than sensual, animal, pleasure, or more fecund – many have the intuition that it is better *in kind*. Mill noted that people, if given a choice, would choose the life of a dissatisfied Socrates over the life of a happy fool. What this indicated to him is that some pleasures that people experience are better kinds of pleasures – Socrates received a good deal of intellectual satisfaction from his philosophical interests. Such satisfactions are not available to the fool, who may be happy, but whose happiness is derived from trivial pursuits and activities. Thus, while pleasure can be measured quantitatively, pleasures can also be qualitatively compared. As Mill noted:

> Human beings have faculties more elevated than the animal appetites and, when once made conscious of them, do not regard anything as happiness which does not include their gratification . . . It is better to be a human being dissatisfied than a pig satisfied; better to be Socrates dissatisfied than a fool satisfied. And if the fool, or the pig, are of a different opinion, it is because they only know their own side of the question.[11]

Thus, Mill solved the animal problem by noting a distinction between higher and lower pleasures, one that Bentham did not hold.[12] It is important to note that what Mill is saying is that higher pleasures are

---

[11] Mill, *Utilitarianism*, pp. 56–7.
[12] Indeed, Bentham actually repudiated it.

superior in *kind*. They may or may not also be superior in terms of quantity – but the important point for him is one of quality. The life of a dissatisfied Socrates is better than the life of the pleased fool because Socrates's life also has its intellectual pleasures, pleasures that the fool's life lacks. Here's a thought experiment that is intended to show Mill's point. Suppose that you had a choice between living the life of an accomplished artist such as Georgia O'Keefe and living a pleasant animal life. Georgia O'Keefe's is an interesting life, filled with mixtures of pleasure and pain and a good deal of creative satisfaction and pleasure – but it is short relative to the life of, let's say, a turtle. Suppose that the turtle we are talking about lives a safe and secure existence in the South Pacific – swimming in the warm water, occasionally making it to the beach to bask comfortably in the sun, and so on. It lives a life of contentment and pleasure, but possesses no intellectual and creative capacities – and certainly none to rival Georgia O'Keefe. But the turtle lives for a long, long, time – centuries. Who would you rather be? Most would pick a life like O'Keefe's. And that's not to do with quantity: in terms of pure quantity of pleasure, the turtle's life wins, but it is deficient in terms of quality of pleasure.

This distinction between higher and lower pleasures allows Mill to hold that while animals do have moral standing in virtue of their sentience – that is, in virtue of their capacity to feel pleasure and pain, and thus to have both positive and negative experiences – their moral standing is not the same as that of persons who have higher moral standing in virtue of their capacity to experience *higher* pleasures. A person has a better life than that of an animal to the extent that he or she experiences higher pleasures. This argument rests on the claim that the higher are superior to the lower, which in turn rests upon a rather wobbly argument to the effect that of those persons who have experienced both, all prefer the higher to the lower, all agree that the higher are superior. It is important to note that while this distinction does offer a solution to the animal problem, it can have some unpalatable implications, and ones that Mill did not confront head on. For example, will there be a similar distinction drawn between persons as is drawn between persons and animals? So, will the lives of some persons be better than the lives of other persons in virtue of their intelligence? This seems very nonegalitarian. On the other hand, it provides a powerful moral argument for a system of public education that develops the intelligence and intellectual capabilities of as many people as possible and doesn't limit this type of good to those who can afford to pay.

Proving the Principle of Utility

Bentham had said that the greatest happiness principle could not be proven, any more than any other "first" principle can be proven. I can't give a proof that we ought to maximize pleasure any more than I can prove that $1 + 1 = 2$. However, Mill disagreed with Bentham on this issue as well, and attempted a notorious proof of the principle:

> The only proof capable of being given that an object is visible is that people actually see it. The only proof that a sound is audible, is that people hear it: and so of the other sources of our experience. In like manner, I apprehend, the sole evidence it is possible to produce that anything is desirable is that people do actually desire it. If the end which the utilitarian doctrine proposes to itself were not, in theory and in practice, acknowledged to be an end, nothing could ever convince any person that it was so. No reason can be given why the general happiness is desirable, except that each person, so far as he believes it to be attainable, desires his own happiness. This, however, being a fact, we have not only all the proof which the case admits of, but all which it is possible to require, that happiness is a good: that each person's happiness is a good to that person, and the general happiness, therefore, a good to the aggregate of all persons. Happiness has made out its title as *one* of the ends of conduct, and consequently one of the criteria of morality.[13]

Mill then goes on to argue, in similar vein, that not only is happiness one criterion, but that it is the *sole* criterion of rightness. Later, in *Principia Ethica*, G. E. Moore (1873–1958) would criticize the proof by noting that it traded on an ambiguity:

> Mill has made as naïve and artless a use of the naturalistic fallacy as anybody could desire. "Good", he tells us, means "desirable", and you can only find out what is desirable by seeking to find out what is actually desired . . . Well, the fallacy in this step is so obvious, that it is quite

---

[13] Mill, *Utilitarianism*, p. 81.

wonderful how Mill failed to see it. The fact is that "desirable" does not mean "able to be desired" as "visible" means "able to be seen." The desirable means simply what *ought* to be desired or deserves to be desired; just as the detestable means not what can be but what ought to be detested . . . [14]

Put this way, it really does look as though Mill has made a silly mistake. However, many commentators feel that Moore interpreted Mill's "proof" very uncharitably. For example, one thing that Mill was trying to do was to show that how people behave gives some indication of what their values are – Moore claims this is no good as normative evidence, because there is a difference between what people desire and what they *ought* to desire. It would be a mistake for Mill to infer that the "good" just means "what is desired" especially since, when he discusses higher and lower pleasures, he admits that there are many who mistakenly desire the lower pleasures. However, Mill's aim was much more modest – he was simply making the claim that what people desire gives us the only evidence of what is desirable. How good the evidence is could well be open to further argument.

Moore also offered up some pretty compelling criticisms of hedonism.[15] Moore himself would end up adopting a form of ideal utilitarianism, so he was committed to maximizing the good. However, he did not think the good reducible to pleasure. There are other things that we value even if they do not generate pleasure on balance. These things will have intrinsic value. One example of this that he discusses is beauty. He believed that a beautiful thing would have value independently of any pleasure that it might induce. The Mona Lisa, then, is a valuable object because of its beauty and not simply because a lot of people enjoy looking at it. The same applies to a wild flower. He did not mean to deny that people received pleasure from looking at beautiful things, listening to beautiful music, and so forth. Rather, he wanted to say that the value of beauty doesn't depend upon this. The Mona Lisa would be wonderful even if no one could see it.

---

[14] G. E. Moore, *Principia Ethica* (Amherst, NY: Prometheus Books, 1988), pp. 66–7.

[15] See Moore, *Principia Ethica*, as well as his *Ethics* (Oxford: Oxford University Press, 1965).

Moore also questioned whether or not all pleasure really did have intrinsic value. Sadistic pleasure, for example, seems to be completely bad – intrinsically bad. So how can pleasure *per se* be something intrinsically good? If we change our view and argue, let's say, that benevolent pleasure or nonsadistic pleasure is intrinsically good – well, then it looks as though we're offering a trivial account of the good, a vacuous account of the good, by claiming, in effect, that morally good pleasure is morally good. Bentham would have met Moore head on. He believed that malicious pleasure is good unless it *leads to* pain. We have become accustomed to thinking of it as always bad, and intrinsically bad, because it overwhelmingly does involve pain to others, and not simply imagined pain.

Both Bentham and Mill viewed the theory as very common-sensical. Neither Bentham nor Mill viewed the decision procedure afforded by the principle as one that ought to be followed at any opportunity – that would be counterproductive, since the costs of engaging in the calculation itself could be formidable. Bentham wrote that the correct utilitarian decision procedure begins by considering the person most to be affected by the action in question, and then considering the pleasures and/or pains to be felt by that person along the first six parameters listed above; then one needs to sum them, and consider extent as well:

> Sum up all the values of all the *pleasures* on the one side, and those of all the pains on the other. The balance, if it be on the side of pleasure, will give the *good* tendency of the act upon the whole, with respect to the interests of that *individual* person; if on the side of pain, the *bad* tendency of it upon the whole . . . Take an account of the *number* of persons whose interests appear to be concerned; and repeat the above process with respect to each. *Sum up* the numbers expressive of the degrees of *good* tendency, which the act has, with respect to each individual, in regard to whom the tendency of it is *good* upon the whole: do this again . . . in regard to whom the tendency of it is *bad* . . . Take the *balance*; which, if on the side of *pleasure*, will give the general *good tendency* of the act, with respect to the total number or community of individuals concerned; if on the side of pain, the general *evil tendency*, with respect to the same community.[16]

---

[16] Bentham, *Principles of Morals and Legislation*, p. 31.

And then he adds (whew!):

> It is not to be expected that this process should be strictly pursued previously to every moral judgment, or to every legislative or judicial operation. It may, however, be always kept in view: and as near as the process actually pursued on these occasions approaches to it, so near will such process approach to the character of an exact one.[17]

Again, Bentham believed that efficiency was important – this carries over into the actual reforms that he tried to put into place, reforms that would save costs to society through increased efficiency, with the consequence that the funds saved could be used elsewhere to promote human happiness.

Mill also believed that we ought not to calculate constantly. For example, he suggested that we knew what was appropriate in most cases, since history has proven to offer us a guide. In this way, we might argue that there are rules of thumb, the following of which by and large enables us to maximize the good. Candidates for these rules are things such as "Don't steal," "Don't kill," and so forth. But these rules can be overridden in cases in which doing so clearly maximizes the good. They are not absolute rules by any means. And some will find this troubling. They believe that there is something *intrinsically* wrong about stealing, and that its wrongness is not simply a matter of it leading to suboptimal consequences. They feel that the wrongness of stealing extends beyond this consideration. But the consequentialist may argue that, though it could be useful to think of stealing as intrinsically bad or wrong, it is really only wrong given that the consequences of allowing theft would be very bad indeed – bad for individuals and bad for society as a whole.

If you recall from the Introduction, I made a distinction between decision procedure and criterion of rightness. Even if we reject the view that the principle of utility is the decision procedure that we always ought to use, this does not mean that we're rejecting the theory – instead, it can also be viewed as offering a criterion of rightness; that is, a way of evaluating actions, and so forth. Thus, if Sarah decides to save a drowning baby, not because she thought about maximizing utility but just because she felt that it was what she ought to do – well, on the

---

[17] Bentham, *Principles of Morals and Legislation*, p. 31.

utilitarian view she did the right thing even if she didn't follow the principle of utility as a rule. Since her action still promoted the good, and led to the best outcome, she did the right thing.

Mill applied the principle of utility to his thought on other issues, particularly those having to do with the peculiarities of some social and legal norms. For example, he was a vocal proponent of a woman's right to vote, own property, and control her own material resources. He was an articulate and compelling advocate for a very liberal view restricting government and legal intervention – the harm principle. This principle, which he discusses in *On Liberty*, states " . . . the sole end for which mankind are warranted, individually or collectively, in interfering with the liberty of action of any of their number, is self-protection. That the only purpose for which power can be rightfully exercised over any member of a civilized community, against his will, is to prevent harm to others."[18] This principle squarely supports individual liberty of action and expression. He provides compelling and very utilitarian arguments for this principle; for example, if the government interferes in someone's actions in order to protect that person – that is, if the government engages in paternalistic interventions – that will lead to a decrease in happiness. First of all, it is the individual who is in a better position to ascertain what is in his own best interest. The government is liable to make mistakes, even sincere mistakes. But further, the government can also use corrupt reasoning to interfere if given the power to interfere – fascism, for example, claimed to give people what they "really" wanted. Mill felt that it was better by far to allow for freedom of action, and if the individual made a mistake, it was better that he learn by his own mistake.

This, in turn, formed the basis for his advocacy of an open society in which free speech was legally tolerated and individuals were allowed to promulgate ideas that would either die or flourish on the basis of rational argument. This is all in keeping with his perfectionist brand of hedonism. People will achieve the highest degree and type of pleasure through developing their intellectual capacities, and one route to this is through vigorous argumentation. Even things that you are convinced must be true are true for reasons that you should be able to articulate. Taking an opponent's position seriously, rather than

[18] John Stuart Mill, *On Liberty*, edited by E. Rapaport (Indianapolis, IN: Hackett, 1978), ch. 1.

silencing it by making it illegal, forces us to develop and articulate arguments in support of our dearly held convictions. History has taught us that at least some of these convictions turn out to be false – some people believed that slavery was permissible, that women were inferior, that it was appropriate for children to work at dangerous jobs rather than go to school, that homosexuality was wrong, and so forth. For Mill, these views that many took for granted could be criticized, but this was practicable only in an environment in which free speech is tolerated. The moral growth of society depends on questioning "convictions" such as these and this in turn depends upon free speech.

Mill also advocated women's equality and suffrage by questioning the "convictions" of those who viewed women as incapable of using the vote responsibly. Again, in Mill's argument we see a utilitarian guiding principle. On his view, "...the legal subordination of one sex to the other... is wrong in itself, and now one of the chief hindrances to human improvement" and "it ought to be replaced by a principle of perfect equality, admitting no power or privilege on the one side, nor disability on the other."[19] That half the population is disenfranchised has terrible consequences for that half of the population – they are made to be servile and miserable. Their intellects are stunted by neglect. The inventiveness and productivity of which they are capable is denied to society. Further, the dominant half fares poorly when it comes to character, and they are prone to greater abuses, which in turn generate more unhappiness – they have, in effect, been given the power of tyrants over women. (At the time Mill was writing, not only did women not have the vote or the right to hold public office, they could rarely hold property in their own names, they had extremely limited avenues of employment open to them, they did not have equal divorce rights, they lost custody of their children should they leave their spouses, and so forth – the list of inequalities is long indeed.) This power can have a corrupting influence: "In domestic as in political tyranny, the cue of absolute monsters chiefly illustrates the institution by showing that there is scarcely any horror which may not occur under it if the despot pleases, and thus setting in a strong light what must be the terrible frequency of things only a little less atrocious." Again, we see in Mill's practical views the strain of perfectionism

[19] John Stuart Mill, *The Subjection of Women*, in *On Liberty and The Subjection of Women* (Ware, Hertfordshire, UK: Wordsworth Editions, 1996), p. 118.

discussed earlier – our pleasure is morally important, but it's the kind of pleasure that counts too – some pleasures are not befitting human nature, or at least, the best in human nature.

Mill and Bentham shared a commitment to improving society and articulating a principle to guide that improvement. Of course, the theory was not without controversy in its time, not withstanding how influential it was. Part of the controversy turns out to rest on a misunderstanding of the theory, which Bentham regretted later in his life. He had originally wanted to call the theory something like *Eudaimonology*, in reference to the Greek *eudaimonia*, which means "happiness," "well-being," or "well-functioning." But this terminology was not adopted, for which we can perhaps be thankful. However, "utilitarianism" struck many as cold and led to a superficial misunderstanding of what the theory stood for. Bowring writes that a Lady Holland complained to Bentham " . . . that his doctrine of utility put a *veto* upon pleasure; while he [Bentham] had been fancying that pleasure never found so valuable and influential an ally as the principle of utility."[20] The worry that Bentham had was that "utilitarianism" sounds sterile, mechanical, and emotionless, and Lady Holland's comment seemed to confirm that people had that perception. Not having any more details of Lady Holland's misgivings, it is hard to say whether she really was simply misunderstanding the theory as offering cold calculation in replacement of human feeling and pleasure. A more sympathetic construal of what she believed is some version of a fairly serious problem for the theory – its seeming demandingness. If we are to maximize the good, then it looks as though we never get a personal break. There are so many needy persons and other beings out there in the world – Shouldn't we be spending our time and our money helping them? It seems as though my time will *always* be better spent by doing things such as working for Oxfam or Greenpeace. It seems as though my money would *always* be better spent if I sent it to charitable organizations. If I care about doing the right thing, I am never free to just take a break and splurge on a bagel and coffee and watch *The Lord of the Rings*. My view of Lady Holland's remark is that this is the problem she was alluding to, and for many people this is a serious problem for the theory, and one that we will discuss in greater depth in the next chapter.

[20] Sir John Bowring, *The Works of Jeremy Bentham* (Edinburgh: William Tait, 1843).

The views of Bentham and Mill would later be criticized by others who accepted the broad theoretical framework of utilitarianism; that is, some version of maximizing the good as the end of morality. Those critics included the great philosophers Henry Sidgwick and G. E. Moore, and unfortunately space does not allow for a detailed discussion of their views here. Sidgwick, however, pointed out a serious indeterminacy in the formulation of the principle of utility.[21] The basic issue is this: Utilitarianism tells us to "maximize the good," but how should we maximize it? Should we maximize the *total* amount of good, or should we maximize *average* good per person? Some utilitarians have viewed this distinction as one that has little practical significance. But this seems overly optimistic to me. Consider the following, based on some of Derek Parfit's cases: imagine two groups of people – group A and group B.[22] Group A consists of 100 people who are living great lives, while group B consists of 80 people living lives that are significantly less happy. Imagine that these two populations are separated by an ocean, and that they are not aware of each other's existence: the average level of happiness in this world is brought down by group B, yet we do not think that the world is somehow worse for their existence. This may in part be due to the fact that since they are separated populations, no social injustice can be used to explain the discrepancy in happiness levels. It would be wrong to prefer just A to A + B, even though the average level of happiness would be greater if we just had A. So this seems an argument against average utility. Yet going with total utility has problems as well. Suppose two other populations, C and D. In C there are 100 people living wonderful lives, in D there are 5,000 people living lives barely worth living – yet when we add them up, because there are so many more people in D than C, the total happiness for D is greater than for C. Yet most would argue that C is preferable to D. If we go with total utility, we run into the problem of what Parfit terms the "repugnant" conclusion.[23] This conclusion would be that a world of millions of barely happy people is better than a world with fewer, but much happier, people. This clearly goes against our intuitions, since we think that things such as birth control

---

[21] Henry Sidgwick, *The Methods of Ethics* (Indianapolis, IN: Hackett, 1981).

[22] See Derek Parfit, *Reasons and Persons* (Oxford: Clarendon Press, 1984), particularly pp. 388ff.

[23] Parfit, *Reasons and Persons*, p. 388.

to prevent over-population are good – and that it would be bad to bring into the world new people who would live lives barely worth living, while at the same time reducing the overall quality of life. So either formulation, all by itself, seems rather unattractive.

What some consequentialists have done is to try to argue that we should go for total happiness, and yet limit ourselves to considering the welfare of actual, already existing, people – so that we don't worry about bringing more people into existence at a certain level of happiness.[24] We may, if we choose, have children on this view, but it is no moral obligation. Our obligations are restricted to increasing the total happiness levels of existing persons. Thus, if we already have a huge population of persons whose lives are barely worth living, the imperative would be to improve their lives as much as possible. Further, if we add an equality constraint based on diminishing margin of utility, then we could argue for an equal distribution of happiness to get around the problem that, on the total view, we are insensitive to distribution issues.

As we saw earlier, Moore offered devastating criticisms of some of Mill's positions – the hedonism and the proof of the principle, to be more specific. He also challenged the naturalism that influenced Mill's thinking by noting that good could not be a natural property such as, let's say, "yellow" that we can see. If someone were to suggest that good is understood naturalistically, in terms of pleasure, Moore would contend that we could always ask "why," and whether or not something that is pleasant is good is always an open question – just calling x pleasurable does not close the door on explaining or accounting for its goodness. This led some, at the turn of the twentieth century, to regard the classical view of the theory as not only dead but without philosophical influence – indeed, Lytton Strachey (1880–1932) passed this judgment (along with a negative judgment about just about everyone else) when he remarked in a letter that Moore's *Principia Ethica* had demolished "... that indiscriminate heap of shattered rubbish among which one spies the utterly mangled remains of Aristotle, Jesus, Mr. Bradley, Kant, Herbert Spencer, Sidgwick, and McTaggart! Plato seems the only person who comes out tolerably well. Poor Mill has, simply, gone."

As devastating as *Principia Ethica* was, this judgment was quite premature. Even if you reject the proof and reject Mill's brand of

---

[24] See, for example, the work of John Skorupski.

hedonism, the legacy of classical utilitarianism is formidable and noble. Certainly, Mill's use of the theory to argue for women's suffrage and free speech are towering classics of modern liberal thought. Indeed, the present age owes a great deal to classical utilitarianism. The classical version of the theory is no longer widely accepted, that's true, but it has morphed into more sophisticated versions. We will consider that part of the legacy of Bentham and Mill in the next chapter.

Further reading

Scarre, Geoffrey 1996: *Utilitarianism*. New York: Routledge.
Skorupski, John 1988: *John Stuart Mill*. New York: Routledge.

Chapter 4

Contemporary Consequentialism

In Chapter 3 we introduced a consequentialist theory, Utilitarianism, by discussing the classical version of the theory, introduced by Jeremy Bentham and later elaborated and refined by John Stuart Mill. In the previous chapter, we noted some problems for the overall theory as well as some problems for the value-theory portion, hedonism, but left off most critical discussion for this chapter. Here, we will look at how the basic theory has been modified by various writers in order to accommodate and resolve criticisms of the earlier theory. To better accomplish this, we will first go over some of the standard problems raised for classical utilitarianism.

Justice

One potential problem that has received a good deal of attention is the fact that utilitarianism seems incompatible with some of our strongly held intuitions about justice – both distributive justice and retributive justice. Distributive justice is justice concerning the distribution of benefits – such as health care, which would be an economic benefit – and burdens – such as taxation, which would be an economic burden. Retributive justice is justice concerning the distribution of rewards and punishments – such as criminal prosecution and prison terms, or good citizen's awards or court settlements to compensate for a harm.

Consider a problem with distributing resources. Suppose, for the sake of simplification, that we have a population of 100 individuals. Let's also make the empirical assumption that if 75 people were to work really hard in this society, the other 25 people could enjoy lives of luxury and be able to really develop their intellects – they could take extra courses, and continue creative pursuits after college, leaving the drudge work to others. Of course, the 75 drudges would not be unhappy, but they would be a lot happier if they didn't have to work constantly to make the life of intellectual luxury a reality for the 25 happiest people. A utilitarian might have to argue that this is a just distribution of resources and burdens – if the 25 are really, really happy (lets say 100 units of happiness each) and the drudges only somewhat happy (30 units of happiness each), that adds up to 4,475 units of happiness over the entire society. If all were equal, let's say 40 units of happiness each, then the total amount would be 4,000 units, which is less. So it is less in total and less in terms of the average too, since the average level of happiness in the drudge state is 44.75 units. Therefore, it looks as though the utilitarian is committed to viewing this nonegalitarian state as morally superior to the egalitarian state. This, however, seems unfair. Why should we be left much worse off for the sake of making lives better for others – others who are already very well off! John Rawls (1921–2002) notes this problem when he argues against the fairness of a utilitarian account of just distribution: "The principle of utility presumably requires some to forgo greater life prospects for the sake of others . . . ".[1] And he argues that this fails to treat persons as individuals, as ends in themselves. On Rawls's own account, inequalities can only be justified if they benefit the worst-off in society. Rawls does note, however, that some utilitarians will disagree with his interpretation of their doctrine, citing Bentham's classic stipulation "everybody to count for one, nobody for more than one." Yet, for many writers, this problem of how to account for the value of equality in distribution is just more evidence that utilitarianism doesn't respect the distinctness of persons, and the fact that they have rights and duties that don't hinge on calculations of utility. Some utilitarians try to avoid this problem by noting that it is very useful to recognize rights, or protections of individual liberty – John Stuart Mill, discussed in the last chapter, falls into this category. In this case, Mill would appeal to a kind of perfectionist notion of human well-being that is being violated by this unequal distribution – it is not befitting us to take advantage of others for the sake of our own well-being. Another

---

[1] John Rawls, *A Theory of Justice* (Cambridge, MA: The Belknap Press of Harvard University Press, 1971), p. 180.

response to this case, and one appealed to more recently by utilitarians, is to note "diminishing marginal utility" – one unit of utility will mean more to those who are disadvantaged, making it far more likely that the best distribution of goods will be roughly equal. Peter Singer notes this when he writes:

> When compared with giving resources to meet someone's core needs, giving further resources "at the margin" to someone else whose core needs have already been satisfied will lead to diminished utility. Hence a utilitarian will generally favor the worst-off when it comes to distributing resources.[2]

But it is very important to note that if the utilitarian favors equal distribution of goods it is because that is what really does make people happier – that provides the most efficient distribution scheme. On Rawls's view (discussed in more detail in another chapter), equality is to be favored and inequality only justified if it benefits even the worst-off – no matter the *aggregate* utility.

But the problems with justice don't stop with this case. Here's another problematic case – the classic example intended to show that utilitarianism would lead to horrific violations of moral norms and thus cannot be the correct moral theory. Suppose that a terrible murder has occurred in a small town and the townspeople are convinced that a lone drifter who happened to be in town at the time committed the crime.[3] Many of the townspeople form a mob to hang the drifter. The sheriff, however, knows that there is no evidence at all linking the man to the crime and that in all likelihood he is completely innocent. He takes the man into protective custody, but the mob surrounds the jail and demands that the sheriff hand over the drifter. The sheriff realizes that a riot is in the works, and if that were to happen then many innocent people would be killed, including schoolchildren on their way home from school. The phone lines have been cut, so he can't call for help (and he doesn't have a cell phone!). What should he do? Should he hand over the drifter, and thus sacrifice an

[2] Peter Singer, *One World: The Ethics of Globalization* (New Haven, CT: Yale University Press, 2002), p. 42.

[3] This case is based on a famous one first presented by H. J. McCloskey in "Two Concepts of Rules – A Note," *Philosophical Review*, 66, 1957, pp. 466–85.

innocent life to the mob? Or should he keep the drifter in protective custody until help can arrive, and thus let dozens of innocent children be killed by the rioting and stampeding mob? One innocent life weighed against dozens of others – it looks as though the utilitarian is committed to the view that morality demands that he sacrifice the drifter to the mob. But this is clearly incompatible with justice – it would be unjust to do that. And – the criticism goes – if a moral theory requires what is unjust, it cannot be the correct moral theory.

Some proponents of utilitarianism have sought to avoid this problem by noting that there is a distinction between *act*-utilitarianism and *rule*-utilitarianism. The act-utilitarian holds that whenever we are trying to decide how to act, we choose the act that itself has the best consequences. So it would *seem* that, on this view, we ought to hand over the innocent person to the mob.

However, things are different for rule-utilitarianism. This view holds that the right action is that action which is performed in accordance with a rule, or set of rules, the following of which maximizes utility. Thus, consider the rule "Do not hand over innocent persons to mobs." A rule-utilitarian could plausibly maintain that this rule is a good rule because following it maximizes utility overall, even if in some weird and unusual cases it might not. Thus, the rule-utilitarian would hold that the sheriff ought not to hand over the innocent person to the mob, because that would be in violation of a rule that we know to be a good one.

Note that act-utilitarians also recognize the significance of rules – rules are extremely useful tools in guiding action and evaluation. However, for the act-utilitarian, the rules are rules of thumb – they can be overridden by a consideration of consequences when those are clear. Roger Crisp calls Mills's version, for example, a multi-level act-utilitarian view, since the rightness of an action is determined by whether or not it maximizes utility; however, in particular cases, in deciding what to do, we needn't make reference to the principle – instead, we can simply follow the rules of "customary morality," which are rules of thumb.[4] And, indeed, this picture of how people go about and ought to go about making decisions seems about right. The principle of utility provides a criterion for evaluating actions.

---

[4] See, for example, his introduction to J. S. Mill's *Utilitarianism* (Oxford: Oxford University Press, 1998), pp. 18–21.

Decision procedures are the rules of thumb that work in particular contexts. For example, a person tempted to steal should default to the "Do not steal" rule that is generally utility maximizing. However, in cases in which stealing is quite clearly utility maximizing, this wouldn't be the case. So, someone who needs to steal a loaf of bread from a rich person who doesn't need it, in order to feed her starving family, ought to steal the loaf. The rule of thumb can be overridden.

The rule-utilitarian, on the other hand, views the rules – when correctly articulated – as absolute. But the rule-utilitarian, then, looks like an absolutist about rules, and this seems quite inflexible and, for that reason, problematic. If "Don't lie" maximizes utility overall, then it seems like "rule-worship" to simply say that it is wrong to lie even to save an innocent life. On the other hand, if the rule is changed to "Don't lie except to save an innocent person's life, or except to spare someone's feelings, or except when telling the lie maximizes utility!" then the rule just collapses back into act-utilitarianism – and the theory's recommendations are identical to those of the act-utilitarian.[5]

Brad Hooker has recently developed a kind of rule-consequentialism that, he argues, avoids the collapse problem. He calls for a form of rule-utilitarianism based on an ideal code. On his view:

> An act is wrong if and only if it is forbidden by the code of rules whose internalization by the overwhelming majority of everyone everywhere in each new generation has maximum expected value in terms of well-being...The calculation of a code's expected value includes all costs of getting the code internalized.[6]

There's a lot going on here. The theory is rule-consequentialism; it is indirect since actions are evaluated in terms of compliance with ideal rules. So, if I do something that violates a rule that is part of a code of

---

[5] Some spell this out by arguing the flexible, nonabsolutist form of rule-utilitarianism is simply extensionally equivalent to act-utilitarianism, so that there's no practical difference between the two even though how they define "right action" does differ. See, for example, the discussion of this in David Lyons's *Forms and Limits of Utilitarianism* (New York: Oxford University Press, 1965).

[6] Brad Hooker, *Ideal Code, Real World: A Rule-Consequentialist Theory of Morality* (New York: Oxford University Press, 2000), p. 32.

rules that maximizes the good, given that a majority of people internalize that code, then I've done something wrong. Suppose that part of this ideal code – the best code, the code that maximizes the good given that a majority of people internalize it – is the rule "Don't steal except to prevent starvation." This rule is part of a system that, if adopted by all, would maximize the good. If Conrad steals for any other reason than to prevent starvation, he has done something wrong, even if the particular act he performed might well produce more utility – for example, he's stealing a diamond ring from someone who will hardly notice that it's gone, and this will provide the funds he needs to buy a very nice stereo system. This result seems right. Further, Hooker's account avoids the rule-worship criticism by allowing exceptions for disasters, in effect. He allows for a disaster-avoidance rule that can override the other rules; that is, we can violate even one of the ideal rules as long as that is necessary to avoid disaster. So, maybe "Don't kill an innocent person" is part of the ideal code, but Hooker's version allows us to use an appeal to disaster avoidance to override this rule if it is necessary to save half the world's population, or necessary to avoid some devastating catastrophe. So, it doesn't collapse into act-utilitarianism, because it won't allow exceptions for small gains in utility, or intuitively unimportant gains in utility; but it avoids the absolutist problem by allowing that a "disaster-avoidance" rule can override the other rules. Threading this needle allows him to say that the sheriff, in handing over the innocent person to the mob, would be acting immorally, since a rule against this would likely be part of the ideal code. We might argue that a riot is a "disaster" – in which case the rule can be overridden by the disaster-avoidance rule. But that would involve a disagreement about what we are to count as a disaster, not a disagreement with his theory *per se*.

Demandingness

Do you remember the quote from Lady Holland in the previous chapter? My interpretation of her complaint is that she thought of utilitarianism as demanding too much of us, as not allowing for the category of supererogatory act. Here's an example. One contemporary consequentialist, Peter Singer, argues that those living in affluent Western societies have an obligation to give to famine relief to improve the lives of those living in countries where poverty and starvation are endemic. Note how strong this claim is – it is not just that it would be nice for an affluent individual to give, but she has an *obligation* to give. Giving is not supererogatory but, instead, is morally required. To many, this seems too demanding – giving is nice, but failure to give does not entail a *moral* failure.

Thus, critics of utilitarianism argue that the theory conflates the supererogatory with the obligatory or the forbidden. Supererogatory acts are conventionally taken to be acts that are good but not required. So, if Samantha runs into a burning building to save the lives of some children trapped on the second floor, she has done something good – indeed, given that it isn't outright recklessness, she has done something quite admirable – but not obligatory. No one has an *obligation* to risk life and limb to help others. However, the utilitarian would disagree – if my taking that risk generates greater good than not, then I do have an obligation. Similarly, suppose that Samantha decides to do something nice for her husband on his birthday – she decides to knit him an afghan instead of buying one for him at the store. This is very nice, but in no way obligatory. Assume also that she is a poor knitter, that it takes her a good deal of time and effort to knit, and that a better product – one that her husband would, quite frankly, appreciate more – could be obtained at the store. Here, the utilitarian might argue that her supererogatory action – very nice indeed – is actually forbidden, since it fails to maximize the good. Instead, from the point of view of promoting the good impartially considered, it would have been better for her to simply buy the more efficiently produced and better-quality afghan that her husband would use and enjoy more.

These cases may seem "far out"; however, in reality this poses a compelling challenge for utilitarians in the following way. As Singer and many others have noted, it is undoubtedly true that there are very many people in the world who are suffering from malnourishment, unsanitary and debilitating living conditions, and poor health due to lack of medical care. It is also true that there are people who live in relatively affluent circumstances, mainly in the West. These are people who can afford things like nice cars, color TVs, the latest stereo equipment, trips to Disneyland and Cancun, expensive restaurant meals, the very best furniture and carpets, beanie babies – and so on. Many of these people could take the money they spend on amusements and use that money to save lives. Are they obligated to do so? On the utilitarian theory, it would seem that they are. Clearly, a person's life is worth more than a shelf of beanie babies. Again, to many people, this demand seems too much. It would be very nice of someone to forgo collecting stuffed animals and instead send that money to Oxfam to alleviate suffering, but it is not morally required, they believe – it would not be wrong for someone to fail to do this. So, given that utilitarianism holds that it would be wrong to collect stuffed animals rather than save someone's life, utilitarianism is wrong – it cannot be the right moral theory since it gives us the wrong answer in this case. This is because it conflicts with the content of conventional morality, or what people widely believe about the scope and extent of what morality demands of us.

But Singer has a response to this. Conventional morality has problems. There are tensions within it, perhaps even inconsistencies. Deference to conventional morality may simply be deference to biases and prejudices that cannot be rationally supported. Consider the following case:

> ...if I am walking past a shallow pond and see a child drowning in it, I ought to wade in and pull the child out. This will mean getting my clothes muddy, but this is insignificant, while the death of the child would presumably be a very bad thing.[7]

Singer takes this as uncontroversial, and as supporting the principle, which is consistent with at least *some* aspects of conventional morality: "if it is in our power to prevent something bad from happening, without thereby sacrificing anything of comparable moral importance, we ought, morally, to do it."[8] So, it is clearly true that keeping my suit clean does not compare in significance to saving the life of the child. The life of the child is far, far more important. So, I ought to save the child. However, by parity of reasoning, ought I not also forgo buying

---

[7] Peter Singer, "Famine, Affluence, and Morality," *Philosophy and Public Affairs*, 1, 1972, p. 230.

[8] Singer, "Famine, Affluence, and Morality," p. 230. Singer is not actually assuming utilitarianism here – he thinks that even if people endorse a weaker standard, they must view themselves as obligated to help alleviate famine, on pain of contradiction. But certainly the obligation also follows the stronger utilitarian standard that Singer himself endorses.

beanie babies, new stereos, and so on in order to send money to Oxfam to be used to save lives? Yet conventional morality holds this to be supererogatory rather than obligatory. And this conflicts – or seems to – with the view that we ought to save the drowning child. So, conventional morality itself doesn't seem to be a good guide if it gives us conflicting advice in structurally similar cases. Of course, Singer would opt for utilitarianism – we have very good reason to suspect that when conventional morality holds helping the distant suffering to be supererogatory it is mistaken, and in fact, such aid is obligatory. It is worth noting, however, that we need not adopt utilitarianism to reach this conclusion. Though Singer is a utilitarian, he believes that this conclusion is inescapable even if we don't believe that we ought to *maximize* good outcomes. All we need to believe is that if we can easily prevent a terrible thing from happening, we should do so. This is much weaker and less demanding than utilitarianism, strictly speaking – but it is demanding enough to place a heavier burden on the affluent than would raw intuitions based on conventional morality.

Someone who believed that conventional wisdom could be made consistent might argue that the cases are relevantly different – that the baby is right next to you, whereas the starving masses are far away, and we cannot actually see how our sacrifices can make a positive difference to them. But this doesn't seem to withstand scrutiny. Oxfam, for example, is a very reliable charity and we can be confident that our aid will be well spent there, and that it will be used to make life better for people who are starving and suffering from lack of adequate medical care. Why we have the intuitions we do in these cases, intuitions that seem to underlie conventional morality, is an interesting issue. However, though empirical investigation of these intuitions would undoubtedly be interesting, this issue has nothing to do with our normative commitments, in that we must recognize that even if our feelings don't compel us as strongly when the suffering is out of sight, that suffering still matters, objectively, as much as the suffering that we actually see before our very eyes. In these conflict situations, a consistent theory seems to demand that one of the intuitions is wrong – and utilitarianism opts for the more demanding. The alternative, that saving the drowning child at minimal cost is supererogatory rather than obligatory, seems much too cold-hearted; indeed, most of us, I think, would regard the person who would keep his suit clean under those circumstances as a moral monster.

However, one could also hold that empirical facts matter in the following way. That is, one other response to the demandingness objection is to soften the utilitarian commitment to demandingness by arguing that utilitarianism must be sensitive to facts of human psychology. One of those facts is that in order to be productive and happy we need to have incentives for working – and those incentives would include being able to keep a fair degree of our money or other goods to benefit our families and ourselves. A person who donated everything to charity, down to a subsistence-level standard of living, would wind up depressed and apathetic. This person would not be as productive, and would produce less to give away to the needy. This is not maximally good. Therefore, the response goes, utilitarianism would only demand as much as we could give and still remain happy people, and this doesn't seem too demanding at all. However, this line of thought assumes that we are not psychologically malleable. If people can be made or trained to want to be more sacrificing, to take up the welfare of others as a project that brings happiness to their lives, then this appeal to psychological limitations won't work.

The famine relief debate highlights an interesting feature of utilitarianism – the fact that in using this theory in *deciding* what to do, we need to get the facts straight. Further, it is what happens that is relevant to the evaluation of an action or policy. So it is possible to have two theorists who are utilitarian – who accept exactly the same moral theory – yet who disagree about what ought to be done, because they disagree about what the facts truly are. At least one writer has suggested that we ought *not* to give to famine relief, because if we do then the results would be even worse.[9] Note that this view would also conflict with conventional morality, which holds that giving to famine relief is supererogatory. On this view, rather, we have an obligation not to give, so giving would be morally forbidden. The argument is that if we give to famine relief and, as a result, more people in overcrowded countries live to reproduce and have more children, then eventually we will get to the point at which there is not enough food to feed everyone, no matter how generous

---

[9] See Garret Hardin's chapter "Lifeboat Ethics: The Case Against Helping the Poor," in *Morality and World Hunger,* edited by W. Aiken and H. LaFollette (Englewood Cliffs, NJ: Prentice-Hall, 1977).

we are, and even more people will starve to death. We can fail to give now, and five million will starve, or we can give until we can't give anymore, and then 30 million will starve. Thus, using utilitarian reasoning, it's better to let five million starve than let 30 million starve – so we ought not to give to famine relief. However, there are several problems with this argument. The first is that of the empirical assumptions, which are very pessimistic – the argument is assuming that no other factors will be put into place to limit population growth. But another problem is that this isn't an argument against charitable giving altogether, it's just an argument against a particular form of charitable giving. We could still give to family planning programs, for example, or programs that teach farmers how to grow more food on their own, and so forth. So it wouldn't solve the fundamental "problem" of demandingness.

Even though, as we've seen, there are some strategies in place to try to limit how demanding morality would be on the utilitarian theory, most philosophers still believe utilitarianism to be a very demanding moral theory, more demanding than conventional morality. However, advocates will argue that this is the nature of morality – Why should we think it has to be easy? If we reply that easy theories are more likely to actually be followed, then the utilitarian would argue that this has to be factored in, and then we may have to follow more lenient rules to get higher compliance to moral norms – but then we just have a utilitarian argument for why we ought to follow less demanding rules than the greatest happiness principle!

Also, many utilitarians don't view demandingness as a genuine problem for the theory. It's just due to a very uncomfortable fact that there are lots of suffering people in the world, people who need help. The demand is one made by the sad fact of the way the world is.

Integrity and Negative Responsibility

The integrity problem could be viewed as a variation on the demandingness problem. Some have objected to utilitarianism because they believe that it leads to a kind of alienation – the person, the moral agent, is made alienated from her projects and goals. A very famous case, introduced into the literature by Bernard Williams, raises this problem quite vividly.[10] It is the case of Jim, who is forced to decide between killing an innocent person or allowing that person, plus 19 other innocent people, to be killed by someone else. We are asked to imagine that Jim, traveling through South America, stumbles upon a village taken over by an evil man. This evil man has rounded up 20 innocent villagers and intends to execute them as an example. However, once Jim stumbles upon the village, he decides that he would like to do something else instead. This man tells his captain, Pedro, to make Jim the following offer: either kill one of the villagers, and then the other 19 will be spared, or all 20 will be killed. Jim's values would not endorse killing an innocent person, but utilitarianism would demand this, given that killing the one is the only way to save the 19. Would Jim, if acting on utilitarian grounds, and against his deeply held convictions regarding killing, therefore lack integrity? He would be giving up on this norm if he killed the one to save 19. He would not be standing by this value. If integrity consists in sticking to our values, then it seems that he would lack it if he did kill the one to save the 19.

The problem, as Williams sees it, is that utilitarianism is committed to negative responsibility – if we are to maximize the good, then we have an obligation to make sure that the greatest amount of good occurs, if it is within our power to do so. Therefore, I can be held responsible for failures to act, as well as for my actions that directly cause harm. If I fail to save the child who is drowning when I could very easily do so, then I am responsible, at least in part, for that child's death. Because we can be blamed for our inactions, our failures to act in a certain way, this responsibility is called "negative" responsibility. Though Williams thinks it plausible to maintain that Jim ought to kill the one under the circumstances as described, he also thinks that if Jim does not do so, he ought not to be held responsible for the deaths of the 19. Rather, the evil dictator is the one who bears responsibility for this. Insofar as the utilitarian holds that Jim must bear some responsibility for a bad outcome that he could have prevented, Williams holds that it fails to cohere with our views about integrity and identification with normative commitments.

---

[10] Bernard Williams, "A Critique of Utilitarianism," in J. J. C. Smart and Bernard Williams, *Utilitarianism: For and Against* (Cambridge, UK: Cambridge University Press, 1973).

Many utilitarians don't really take this case seriously, because they think that if Jim's values result in the needless death of 19 innocent people, perhaps they ought to be given up. Further, they note that though our intuitions are by no means clear-cut on this issue, we often have a strong intuitive commitment to negative responsibility. Imagine Cynthia, who is conducting some scientific research on a beach, and who sees a nasty man push a toddler into the surf and then run away. She is in the midst of observing a rare starfish in a tide pool, and does not have long to make her observations before the starfish is swept away. Leaving the pool now to save the child would put an end to these observations, for which she has waited so long. Should she save the child? If she does not, if she just remains sitting next to the tide pool, is she in part responsible for the child's death? Many would answer "Yes" to both. She would be held morally responsible, though perhaps not legally responsible. Williams would probably respond that this case is not truly analogous to his – it is not that he is against negative responsibility across the board. Rather, he thinks that people should not be morally required to do things that are normally very, very bad – such as killing innocents – in order to save others. In Cynthia's case, she is simply required to save someone at the cost of her research – but saving people is normally a very good thing to do, unlike killing them.

So, in all probability, Williams would not have disavowed negative responsibility altogether. To avoid the above observation, however, the utilitarian would respond by noting that, intuitively, we think we should do things that are normally bad to avoid much greater harms taking place. So, suppose that Cynthia, to stop the nasty man from drowning the toddler, simply has to run over to him and tell a lie – such as "The police are on their way here right now!" If she fails to tell the lie that would scare away the nasty man, and save the toddler's life, if she fails to do so out of a kind of squeamishness, since she is very against lying in general, would she be held at least partly responsible for the toddler's death? Again, I think that intuitively we would argue "Yes" – the lie is so minor compared to the harm of the toddler drowning. If someone objects that the nasty man has no right to the truth because he is evil, then the scenario can be modified so that we just ask ourselves, suppose she has to lie to an innocent dupe of the nasty man to save the toddler? The answer would be the same.

A better case for Williams might be another one that he discusses, that of George, who is a chemist and needs to decide whether or not to take a job making chemical weapons. On the one hand, he is deeply opposed to these weapons; on the other hand, he knows that if he does not take the job, someone else will – someone more enthusiastic about the weapons and who would actually do a better job at making them more efficiently, so that more of them could be made in the long run. George calculates that if he takes the job fewer people will be killed by the weapons, since fewer weapons will end up being made. What should he do? Williams notes that the utilitarian would advise George to take the job, and thus advise George to act against his deepest convictions, which are against having anything to do with the manufacture of chemical weapons. This result does seem rather counterintuitive – most of us would argue that George is perfectly justified in not taking the job – and, indeed, he really ought not, since chemical weapons are so awful. But, the utilitarian would argue, yes, they are awful, and that is exactly why George should take the job – so that he can very subtly sabotage the chemical weapons effort and make it less efficient. This implies no loss of integrity, since George's basic values – against these weapons – are intact. But, is he responsible for the extra deaths that would occur if he did not take the job? Few would say "Yes." So, how is this case different from that of Cynthia, where we would judge her responsible if she failed to thwart the nasty man's plan to kill the toddler? My view is that often our intuitions tend to be confused, especially in cases that deviate from the norm. In George's case, it would be hard, in the real world, to say for sure what will happen should he take the job. It is also difficult in cases in which we are asked to consider nonemergencies – So, why should George be the one who has to take on the onerous task of subtly undermining chemical warfare? It is also less clear in the real world that he would succeed in this – After all, aren't there people who would check up on him? So, just as these facts are not clear in the real world, the issue of responsibility lacks clarity, and our intuitions tend to be formed by real-world cases with which we are familiar. But if we were to try to correct for this lack of clarity, and specify the case in such a way as to make reference to real life, then I think many intuitions would follow the utilitarian. In World War II, for example, there were many people who found the opportunity to undermine the Nazis, while people who did not do so, but who were in a position to, were often blamed for their passive stance. Some people did tell lies to save people from Nazi death camps. They felt compelled, morally, to do so – if they had not, I'm sure they would have at least felt partly responsible for the deaths of those they could have saved. Clinging to norms that keep our "hands clean," so to speak, is to just to hide behind a kind of moral squeamishness.

Another funny thing about negative responsibility is that there is an asymmetry between the good and bad effects of our actions. Is Chris responsible for Sally winning the tennis match because he could have broken her leg before the match but didn't? This seems totally absurd. If we take this seriously, then what we are responsible for is legion. There are all kinds of things that happen because I don't do x or I don't do y – surely our notions of responsibility can't track all of this!

I think that the consequentialist's best response here is to say there is a difference between being responsible and holding someone responsible – we may indeed be causally responsible for all kinds of things that we are never even aware of. But holding someone responsible for some outcome is like any other act – it can be assessed using the consequentialist criterion. If it pays to hold someone responsible, then it's justified. If it doesn't, then it isn't justified. Now, we may want to supplement this crude principle with some other factors – so, we might hold that causal responsibility is also necessary. But the basic idea is that it doesn't pay to praise Chris for not breaking Sally's leg, at least in the normal case that we can imagine. Also, in the George-type cases, where it is in practice difficult to determine the effects of failing to take on the chemical weapons job, it doesn't pay to hold people responsible. This, at least, can give us some principled guide for laying blame.

However, Williams's scenarios raise interesting problems in cases in which we think someone is not responsible for a failure to act. It may be true that it is very hard to find some principled way to distinguish cases in which people are responsible from cases in which they are not. But Williams's challenge is that there are *some* cases in which we are not responsible, and utilitarianism cannot allow this. And, indeed, this brings us back to the demandingness problem. It seems very demanding to hold someone responsible for the deaths of those he or she could have saved by sending more money to Oxfam, just as it seems outrageous to hold George responsible for those he could have saved by creating less efficient chemical weapons.

We need to distinguish two problems, both of which are raised by Williams's discussion. There is the problem of demandingness – of consequentialism demanding too much in the way of sacrifice, and sacrifice of integrity, of the moral agent. And there is another problem, that of *pervasiveness*. Consequentialism is demanding in that it requires the agent to *maximize* the good. So giving just a bit of money to charity when we have greater resources just isn't enough. Consequentialism is pervasive in that it turns everything into a moral issue – all of our choices, for example, that we tend to intuitively regard as neutral. Normally, for example, what I eat for lunch – if I eat an orange as opposed to an apple, for example – is not considered a moral issue; nor is taking my vacation in Istanbul as opposed to Paris, or deciding to pursue journalism as opposed to civil engineering, and so on. These are personal choices, but Williams's discussion highlights the problem that some have with utilitarianism, or consequentialism – it leaves little room for personal choices and values in *justifying* our actions.

Friendship and Special Obligations

Consequentialism holds that we are supposed to promote value – what some philosophers call "agent-neutral" value. Indeed, though this is somewhat controversial, consequentialism has been standardly understood as a theory that defines right action in terms of the maximization of agent-neutral value. So, on this view, if I break a promise that is bad, and it is no more or less bad than someone else breaking a promise (all other things held equal); friendship is good, and my friendship with someone is no more or less good than someone else's friendship (all other things held equal); and so on. This seems incompatible with the values that we attach to friendship and to our special relationships with family members as well – these seem highly relative and partial. So, my child is special to me in a way that no one else's child is, and this seems entirely appropriate. Yet, again, this seems incompatible with neutral value and impartiality. Utilitarianism demands that we maximize good impartially considered. Thus, I should give a present not necessarily to my own child, but rather to the person who would be made most happy by the gift. Perhaps that is my own child, but it is likely to not be my own child, at least not all the time. This seems highly counterintuitive. It is part of my role as mother that I show special consideration to my children. And surely the role of mother is not incompatible with morality.

And this doesn't exhaust the problem. It seems that the utilitarian is also committed to viewing these close relationships, including friendship as well as love, as having only instrumental value. Thus, friendship can only be justified on the basis of producing pleasure – but this seems quite incompatible with how we are supposed to regard our friends and the friendships that we have. We value our friends, not simply the pleasure that they produce; and, indeed, it is conceivable that a friendship might well be valuable even if it is the source of more pain than pleasure.

How do consequentialists handle these sorts of considerations, ones that seem to show that the good isn't agent neutral? Recall the distinction between decision procedure and criterion of rightness. This has been invoked to argue that special obligations, ones that are partial, need not pose a problem for consequentialism, since they need not be incompatible with the promotion of agent-neutral value. One writer who uses this strategy, or one similar to it, is Peter Railton, who discusses the following case of Juan and Linda. Juan is someone who is committed to consequentialism – he believes that we do have obligations to help those in need. He is married to Linda, toward whom he displays the appropriate sort of partiality, and a friend asks him how this can be compatible with consequentialism. He replies: "Look, it's a better world when people can have a relationship like ours – and nobody could if everyone were always asking themselves who's got the most need. It's not easy to make things work in this world, and one of the best things that happens to people is to have a close relationship like ours. You'd make things worse in a hurry if you broke up those close relationships for the sake of some higher goal..."[11] What Juan ends up saying is that, for the sake of the greater good, it's not always best to think in terms of the greater good. But this in no way means that consequentialism is wrong – it just means that it has limited applicability as a decision procedure. Railton uses a compelling thought experiment to illustrate the basic point:

[11] Peter Railton, "Alienation, Consequentialism, and the Demands of Morality," *Philosophy and Public Affairs* (1984), pp. 134–71.

Imagine an all-knowing demon who controls the fate of the world and who visits unspeakable punishment upon man to the extent that he does not employ a Kantian morality. (Obviously, the demon is not himself a Kantian.) If such a demon existed, sophisticated consequentialists would have reason to convert to Kantianism, perhaps even to make whatever provisions could be made to erase consequentialism from the human memory and prevent any resurgence of it.[12]

Again, just because under this scenario people should adopt Kantian ethics doesn't make consequentialism *false*. Railton notes that to think that this shows the theory to be false is to confuse two different things – truth-conditions and acceptance-conditions. There may be very practical reasons why I ought to accept a falsehood and there may be moral reasons why I ought to accept a falsehood. This is just another way of saying that moral and epistemic norms may not always coincide.

It is also important to keep in mind that the consequentialist approach has advantages that mirror the disadvantages. For example, some don't like the fact that, on the consequentialist view, moral decision-making can become an empirical issue. Recall that two utilitarians who adopt the very same version of the theory could end up disagreeing with each other about what ought to be done – because they disagree about what the consequences of the proposed alternative actions would be. If we think that famine relief only makes things worse, as Garret Hardin did, then we would argue against it. Likewise, when it comes to lying, the act-utilitarian will ask "Well, what are the consequences?" If the consequences are clearly better for lying – for example, we save an innocent person from being killed – then we should do it. Note that this empirical quality – this appeal to what the consequences would be – saves utilitarianism from some of the absurdities we will see when we take a look at Kant's ethics in the next chapter. Of course, the price of this flexibility is plausibility in some other cases. Some things just seem plain wrong to us even if they produce somewhat better consequences overall. Rights violations would be one example of this. It would be just plain wrong to kill one innocent person, even to save five other innocent people from dying. In this case, Kant's view, we will see, seems to give us the right answer.

---

[12] Railton, "Alienation," p. 155.

But again, the utilitarian has responses. First off, a consequentialist could argue that the right thing to do would be to kill the one to save the five, but that we very naturally have an aversion to doing this – and we would be suspicious of the character of someone who could do this sort of thing. This strategy is suggested by some of Railton's remarks about Juan. We could also argue that we are so psychologically constructed, or "hard-wired," that we simply can't ignore special relationships in pursuit of overall good. If so, consequentialists would have to recognize this as a legitimate moral constraint on our actions.

Another strategy is to say that the action is wrong, and then give an indirect consequentialist account of this – in terms of rule violation, if you are a rule-consequentialist, or in terms of character defect, if you are a virtue-consequentialist.

All of these strategies try to reconcile consequentialism to conventional morality, at least to some extent. However, it is important to keep in mind that strict adherence to our moral intuitions may not be desirable. It may be that some of our intuitions are not sound and that we need to turn to theory to help us discover this. If a theory is simply a reflection of our intuitions and adds nothing to our understanding of ethics, then it is an empty theory. Consequentialism provides us with a general criterion for rightness of actions, so it does more than simply reflect our views about particular cases.

Further reading

Hooker, Brad 2000: *Ideal Code, Real World: A Rule-Consequentialist Theory of Morality.* New York: Oxford University Press.

Shaw, Joseph 1999: *Contemporary Ethics: Taking Account of Utilitarianism.* Malden, MA: Blackwell.

Chapter 5

Kantian Ethics

> A good will is good not because of what it effects or accomplishes, nor because of its fitness to attain some proposed end; it is good only through its willing, i.e. good in itself.
>
> Immanuel Kant, *Grounding for the Metaphysics of Morals*[1]

We will be discussing Kantian ethics as a form of deontological ethics – an ethical theory that defines right independently of the good. Some theories are teleological; that is, they define right by reference to the good – usually, the good that the action produces. Utilitarianism, discussed in the two previous chapters, is an example of a teleological ethical theory, since right action is determined by production of the good. Immanuel Kant's theory is perhaps the most well-known exemplar of the deontological approach. As you can see from the above quotation, Kant seems to deny any consequentialist element to his theory. Instead, whether or not a contemplated course of action is morally permissible will depend on whether or not it conforms to what he terms the moral law, the categorical imperative. Our duties can be understood in terms of respecting this imperative, even if respecting the moral law leads to bad effects rather than good ones. For example, we are obligated to keep our promises, even when keeping them results in less good. Suppose that Maria, who is very poor, has promised to pay back a loan she received from Charlotte, who is very rich and who doesn't need the money at all. Even though there is a sense in which more good would be accomplished if Maria could keep

[1] Immanuel Kant, *Grounding for the Metaphysics of Morals*, translated by James W. Ellington (Indianapolis, IN: Hackett, 1981).

the money – since that money would make much more of a positive difference to her than it would to Charlotte – it would still be wrong of her to keep it. One of the ideas underlying Kant's approach is that what makes an action wrong, then, is not the bad it produces, but something else, the kind of action that it is.

Immanuel Kant (1724–1804) is certainly one of the most significant and influential philosophers in the history of philosophy. He was what people sometimes call a "polymath" – very talented in a wide variety of fields. He made significant contributions to science as well as philosophy. The "Kant–Laplace" hypothesis about the formation of the solar system is named in part for him; he was one of the earliest to suggest that the planets of the solar system formed through a rotation of matter around a core such as the sun.

Kant reacted against David Hume's naturalism, and in the area of ethical theory, against the view that morality is based on sentiment rather than reason. Kant believed that morality was *a priori*. He believed that in investigating morals, we need to look at *pure* practical reason. Morality would hold not just for beings with our nature, but for all rational beings. The moral law, then, must be sought *a priori*, independent of the peculiarities of our nature. He writes in the *Grounding for the Metaphysics of Morals*:

> "Thou shalt not lie," does not hold only for men, as if other rational beings had no need to abide by it, and so with all other moral laws properly so called...the ground of obligation here must therefore be sought not in the nature of man nor in the circumstances of the world in which man is placed, but must be sought a priori solely in the concepts of pure reason...[2]

Kant's entire system of morality is based upon a rejection of Hume's claim. For Kant, reason is what makes us capable of morality to begin with. Animals are creatures of instinct rather than reason, and so are not capable of moral action. Hume must be wrong, then, in believing that the authority of morality is simply an outgrowth of human nature.

Kant's theory of morality and his substantive normative theory have had an enormous impact not only in philosophy but in formulating

---

[2] Kant, *Grounding*, p. 2.

policies in applied ethics. His emphasis on autonomy and his anti-consequentialism have, for example, informed a good deal of policy that has been implemented in medical ethics surrounding patient's rights. It follows from Kant's view that lying to patients even for the sake of their own good is impermissible; misleading patients about therapies and experimental procedures, again for the sake of the good, is impermissible, and so forth. The emphasis that he placed on respect for autonomy, as opposed to mere concern for well-being or happiness, can be seen in policies that make clear that the individual has the right to be treated with respect and not simply benevolence.

In the development of our understanding of the status of morality itself, his disagreement with Hume frames one of the most fundamental problems in meta-ethics – Does morality rest on human nature or transcend it? In this chapter we will examine the details of Kant's normative ethical theory, critically discuss it, and then talk about various ways in which modern Kantians attempt to either defend Kant or modify his theory to deal with the criticisms.

Reason

David Hume, who many consider to be a proto-utilitarian, argued that reason was subordinate to feeling in that reason had only an *instrumental* role to play in practical deliberation. It is desire that sets our goals for us – reason simply enables us to choose the means to achieve those goals. When Mary goes to the delicatessen at lunch to get a sandwich, what explains her action? First of all, it is her desire to get a sandwich because she is hungry. She goes to the delicatessen to get it because she judges this the best means to achieve that goal. Her goal is determined by her desire, and reason or judgment determines no more than the best means for reaching that goal. Reason is serving the purposes set by desire – hence the label "instrumental" reason. Hume also believed that the basis for morality could be found in human nature – specifically, our capacity to sympathize with others. Kant denies both of these claims, arguing that reason can set goals and that reason is particularly required in order to set moral goals, which are independent of our desires. Indeed, the very concept of a moral duty must be understood independent of desire – if I make a promise to return a book to the library for you, I thereby take on an obligation or a duty to do so. Morally, I must do it even if I don't want to, or no longer have the desire to. Genuine moral duties are categorical and unconditional. Further, the source of moral authority is not to be found in human nature at all. For example, if moral duty is unconditional duty, then its authority is not contingent on features of our nature, such as our emotions, which can be fickle and unreliable. Rather, the ground of morality is found in pure reason. Animals, for example, lacking reason, are neither bound by nor covered by moral norms of duty or obligation.

Categorical versus Hypothetical Imperatives

What is it to hold that moral duties bind unconditionally? Here, Kant makes use of an important distinction, that between hypothetical and categorical imperatives.

The moral law is categorical rather than hypothetical and it is an imperative. Imperatives are commands or orders. A hypothetical imperative is a contingent command, one that we ought to follow *given* our desires, for example. "Go to the doctor" is a good command to heed if we want to get well. That would be an example of a hypothetical imperative. It only makes sense to go to the doctor, to obey this imperative, if we want to get well. A categorical imperative, however, binds us no matter what our desires are. "Don't just use someone for your own purposes" is obligatory even if we actually have a desire, or want to manipulate someone else. Likewise, we ought to keep promises even when we don't want to do what is required to keep the promise. We ought to tell the truth, even if it is unwelcome, and so on. This is the nature of morality – obligations bind independent of our desires; they are not based in desire but in *reason*.

Duty versus Inclination

Aristotle had argued that the best, most virtuous sort of person is the person who exhibits harmonious psychological functioning. That is, it is necessary for the virtuous person to have the parts of the soul, the desiring and judgment parts, in harmony. If we judge x to be good or right, then we desire it. Persons who lack this are less excellent examples of human beings – the person who desires what is bad but is still able to act rightly has a kind of intermediate good quality on this view – moral strength of will. But his character would be better if he did not have to force himself to act well, if he both understood and desired what was good and right.[3] Thus, what we were inclined to do would be in harmony with our knowledge of what it was right to do, our knowledge of our duty.

But what we have here is an inclination that may or may not be cultivated. Kant believed, however, that when we act well and are solely motivated by good inclination, our actions lack moral worth. Animals, after all, act on inclination. What differentiates us from them is our capacity to use reason, to make rational judgments about what we ought to do. A person can exhibit moral worth while still experiencing psychological conflict. In a famous passage, Kant writes about a person whose mind is:

> ...clouded over with his own sorrow so that all sympathy with the lot of others is extinguished, and suppose him still to have the power to benefit others in distress, even though he is not touched by their trouble because he is sufficiently absorbed with his own; and now suppose that, even though no inclination moves him any longer, he nevertheless tears himself from his deadly insensibility and performs the action without any inclination at all, but solely from duty – then for the first time his action has genuine moral worth.[4]

It is important not to misinterpret what Kant is saying here. He is not saying that it is better to go on duty against our inclination *per se*. Rather, he is simply saying that from the moral point of view, this misanthropic agent is exhibiting as much moral worth as someone who acts from duty, but also consistent with his inclinations. What is important to moral worth is whether or not the sense of duty is what is motivating our action. Inclination can be there too, but need not be. Kant believed that our inclinations are basically just desires that we have, pushing us in a certain direction. These desires are too fickle a basis to provide firm moral motivation. The content of our desires

---

[3] See Book VII of the *Nicomachean Ethics*, translated by Martin Ostwald (New York: Bobbs-Merrill, 1957).

[4] Kant, *Grounding*, p. 11.

changes, but the commands of reason do not. Thus, reason provides moral motivation, since – as we've discussed – morality is by its nature unconditional and not dependent on our desires, or on typical desires, or even the idealized desires of an ideal observer.

Kant goes so far here as to suggest that the *morally* significant sort of love is love that is commanded, or a matter of duty, rather than mere inclination. If a person acts rightly because of duty and not simply because he desires the good, or had an inclination to seek it, then:

> ...for the first time does his conduct have real moral worth. Undoubtedly in this way also are to be understood those passages of Scripture which command us to love our neighbor and even our enemy. For love as an inclination cannot be commanded; but beneficence from duty, when no inclination impels us and even when a natural and unconquerable aversion opposes such beneficence, is practical, and not pathological, love. Such love resides in the will and not in the propensities of feeling, in principles of action and not in tender sympathy; and only this practical love can be commanded.[5]

This degree of psychological hygiene will strike many as rather cold. Critics of Kant will argue that in this respect he demotes some of our most significant emotions – Who wants to be loved *as a matter of duty?*

Michael Stocker has argued that this picture of the finer emotions – love and friendship out of duty rather than desire – is quite noxious. He asks you to consider the following scenario, in which you are visited in the hospital by your friend Smith:

> You are now convinced more than ever that he is a fine fellow and a real friend – taking so much time to cheer you up, traveling all the way across town, and so on. You are so effusive with your praise and thanks that he protests that he always tries to do what he thinks is his duty, what he thinks will be best. You at first think he is engaging in a polite form of self-deprecation, relieving the moral burden. But the more you two speak, the more clear it becomes that he was telling the literal truth: that it is not essentially because of you that he came to see you, not because you are friends, but because he thought it his duty...[6]

---

[5] Kant, *Grounding*, p. 12.

[6] Michael Stocker, "The Schizophrenia of Modern Ethical Theories," *Journal of Philosophy*, 73, 1976, pp. 453–66.

Stocker clearly intends that we be put off by this. What we want in a friend is someone who doesn't regard his kindnesses to us as a matter of duty but, instead, someone who wants to spend time with us, who is inclined to help, irrespective of duty. Anything less than this, the thought goes, is a diminished form of friendship.

Other writers, such as Marcia Baron, defend the Kantian outlook. Baron argues that Stocker has spelled out the case in a way that does not accurately represent how Kant would approach this issue. Stocker's example is open to a variety of interpretations because it can be filled out in different ways, True, if Smith visits grudgingly then that seems bad. But that Smith visits out of duty does not rule out a positive inclination to visit as well. The problem is not that he is visiting out of duty, but that this seems to imply that he is doing so grudgingly or resentfully, and that is what is disturbing. Absent those negative feelings, however, and the case Stocker presents does not seem so objectionable.[7]

One worry that we see in the expression of this example is that Kant is according the emotions only instrumental value, that Kant is operating with a view that the emotions can interfere with moral behavior as much as help it along, and that this results in his failure to recognize the intrinsic value of some of the emotions, such as love.

To be fair to Kant, however, we should be quite clear that he is not saying that these "positive" emotions are in any way bad. Emotions such as pathological love can be very good indeed – but they have no moral worth. We can value them, even if we are not justified in respecting or esteeming them. Further, persons who are naturally benevolent are very nice persons – they just don't behave in a morally admirable way when they act out of this natural benevolence: "...there are many persons who are so sympathetically constituted that, without any further motive of vanity or self-interest, they find an inner pleasure in spreading joy around them...But I maintain that in such a case an action of this kind, however, dutiful and amiable it may be, has nevertheless no true moral worth."[8] So, when someone, for example, overcomes temptation by force of a good will, that is worthy of respect, a special kind of valuing. We more than *like* good wills, we

---

[7] Marcia Baron, *Kantian Ethics Almost Without Apology* (Ithaca, NY: Cornell University Press, 1995), p. 119ff.

[8] Kant, *Grounding*, p. 11.

respect them. On this view, it may make sense to encourage and praise actions that happen to correspond to the dutiful, but such action is not worthy of moral admiration. Here's a distinction that might help – we can note that there is a difference between (1) following a rule and (2) behaving in such a way that our actions happen to conform to a rule. So, consider a rule such as "Don't walk on the grass" and then consider two people, Maria and Carla, neither of whom walks on the grass. Maria stays on the sidewalk because she knows the rule and recognizes that it's her duty to follow it – she would love to walk on the soft, plush, grass, but does not act on this inclination. Carla, on the other hand, may or may not know about the rule, but the reason why she walks on the sidewalk instead of the grass is that she just doesn't like walking on the grass. If she did like walking on it she would walk on it, rule or no rule. The Kantian intuition is that Maria deserves our admiration for not walking on the grass, but Carla does not. And the same insight would apply to following the moral law.

The Categorical Imperative

Given that moral worth consists in following the moral law, the *categorical imperative*, what is it? How exactly do we follow it?

There are a variety of formulations – at least three – that Kant discusses in his *Grounding for the Metaphysics of Morals*. Here, however, we will only consider the best-known formulations.

Formulation one

Kant's first formulation of the categorical imperative is as follows:

> Act only according to that maxim whereby you can at the same time will that it should become a universal law.[9]

Kant argued that in thinking about whether or not to perform an action, we are to first formulate a maxim describing the action. We then test the maxim against the categorical imperative. Roughly, if it fails, then the action is impermissible; if it passes the test, then the

---

[9] Kant, *Grounding*, p. 30.

action is permissible. Different kinds of maxims will fail this test differently. Universalizing some maxims will produce a contraction in conception; others when universalized will produce a contradiction in the will. We discuss these in more detail in the following paragraphs.

Kant goes over a variety of examples to illustrate how this is supposed to work. The one we will focus on is the following – the case of a man who needs to borrow money, though he knows he cannot repay it. He *wants* to promise to repay, even though he knows he cannot. Is this morally permissible? Well, first we need to describe the prospective action from the point of view of the agent; that is, *the agent*, in trying to determine what to do, needs to first formulate a maxim describing the action in question. In this case, the maxim would look something like this (in Kant's words): "...when I believe myself to be in need of money, I will borrow money and promise to pay it back, although I know that I can never do so."[10]

In testing this against the first formulation of the categorical imperative, we then ask, what if this were a *universal* law? What if everybody did this? According to Kant, it is clear that this cannot be universalized. We would get a *contradiction in conception*. In the literature on Kantian ethics, there are two different interpretations of what this means. The standard interpretation, attributed to H. J. Paton, holds that Kant means that we cannot will the universality of lying promises, since this would be *self-contradictory*. That is, we would actually get a logical contradiction. If everyone did this, such promises would not be believed, and instead they would be viewed, in Kant's words, as "vain pretences."

So, we cannot will this to be universal because we *cannot even conceive* of a world in which everyone makes lying promises successfully – universal lying would undermine trust in communication. This is why it is termed a contradiction in conception.

This raises an important interpretive issue regarding how to test the maxim of action against the categorical imperative. Is the right question (1) "Can we will that everyone do this?" or (2) "Can we will that everyone be allowed to do this?" Question (1) just seems wildly implausible – Why should I think that everyone would break their promises? Further, it seems way too broad. For example, suppose that I am considering whether or not to sit in my living room rocking chair

---

[10] Kant, *Grounding*, p. 31.

right now. Can I will that everyone do that? No – it is not possible; there isn't enough room in the chair. Yet it is absurd to suggest that my sitting in the rocking chair is morally impermissible.

But perhaps the correct way to test is suggested by question (2). While it is true that not everyone can sit in the rocking chair, it also seems right that everyone be allowed to – given that it is possible. And while it seems implausible that everyone would break promises, the same imaginative resistance doesn't apply to *allowing* everyone to break promises. However, this version suffers from the fact that it is difficult to see how we can actually get a contradiction. We *can* conceive of a world in which everyone is *allowed* to break promises.

Recently, some commentators on Kant's ethical writings have argued that Paton's interpretation of how the categorical imperative tests maxims is mistaken and that, instead, Kant held the view that all testing using the universal formula rests on testing for a *practical* contradiction, not a logical one.[11] Lying is wrong not because a logical contradiction is generated by trying to universalize the maxim; rather, when an agent tests a maxim and gets a contradiction in conception, the purpose that is undermined by universalization of this maxim is *the purpose that appears in the maxim itself*. The idea is that a maxim will fail the test if universalizing it thwarts the agent's purposes. When those are expressed in the maxim itself, we have the contradiction in conception. Thus, in the lying promise case, the maxim would be something like "I will make a false promise to get a loan I want." When this is universalized, however, people wouldn't be able to get loans because no one would lend them money if they couldn't rely on the promises – thus, the frustration of the agent's purposes. And therein lies the practical contradiction.

Recall that I mentioned there are *two* ways in which we can get a contradiction by testing a maxim against the categorical imperative. We have just discussed two interpretations of the first way we can get a contradiction – the contradiction in conception. However, the universalization test can produce another kind of contradiction, too – Kant calls this a *contradiction in the will*. On the standard Paton interpretation some maxims, when universalized, do not produce logical contradictions

---

[11] For an excellent discussion of this debate, see Christine Korsgaard's essay "Kant's Formula of Universal Law," in *Creating the Kingdom of Ends* (Cambridge, UK: Cambridge University Press, 1996), pp. 77–105.

but, rather, simply practical ones; that is, they produce states that no rational agent would want. The classic case is that of benevolence. Suppose that Robert is considering a donation to charity but is very reluctant, because he would rather spend the money on a new stereo, so he considers a maxim something like "I will not give anything to charity." This is not universalizable because if Robert is rational he will realize that he would not want to live in a world in which no one gave to charity – such a world would be depressing indeed. Further, Robert should realize that he might, himself, come to need the benevolence of others and then would certainly want there to be some charity in the world. Again, on Paton's view, there's no logical contradiction – we could certainly conceive of a world without charity. But there is a practical contradiction in that a rational person could not want this to be the case.

The more recent interpretation of this test of maxims would hold that the contradiction in the will test gives us another way to get a practical contradiction. When an agent tests a maxim that generates a contradiction in the will, the purpose that is undermined by universalization of the maxim is a purpose that is "...essential to the will," rather than a purpose that is actually specified in the maxim itself.[12] Recall that for something like a lying promise we get a contradiction with what is specified in the maxim. But in the case of failure of benevolence it would be different – the purpose that is frustrated is not in the maxim itself, but is understood as essential to the will, something rather more basic. What is essential to the will? This could be answered in a variety of ways – exercise of the will requires the capacity for autonomous decision-making; and it also requires having our basic needs met in order to be autonomous agents. Thus, in the benevolence case we could not will that failures of benevolence be universalized, since that would be like willing a world in which these conditions were not met.

Formulation two

The second formulation of the categorical imperative is the following:

> Act in such a way that you treat humanity, whether in your own person or in the person of another, always at the same time as an end and never simply as a means.[13]

[12] Korsgaard, "Kant's Formula," p. 97.
[13] Kant, Grounding, p. 36.

In spelling out this formulation, we need to understand that the word "simply" is very important. Kant is not saying that we can never use another person as a means to our own ends; he is not saying that it is always wrong to do so. When Melissa goes grocery shopping, she uses the store clerks as means to get her groceries. This is fine, as long as she is not treating them simply, or merely, as means – as long as she is treating them with respect. And what does this entail? It entails a respect for them as autonomous, rational, beings. If the store clerks are working voluntarily, they are freely consenting to be store clerks and to help people acquire their groceries, then Melissa does not violate their autonomy when she uses them to do things such as checking out her purchases, loading up her cart, and so forth.

How does this apply to some of Kant's own cases? Again, consider the lying promise example. If Ann were to lie to Bob, she would be using Bob merely as a means to her own end. This is in clear violation of the categorical imperative.

It is less clear how this works in the case of failures of beneficence. However, Kant writes that in these sorts of cases – where a person fails to give to those in need, for example – he is failing to show them respect in that he is not treating their happiness with sufficient weight in his practical deliberations. He writes: "For the ends of any subject who is an end in himself must as far as possible be my ends also, if that conception of an end in itself is to have its full effect on me."[14]

Perfect versus Imperfect Duties

Again, recall that there are two ways for the maxim to fail the test of the universal law formulation of the categorical imperative. In the case of the lying promise, the test results in logical contradiction. In other cases, the contradiction is a "contradiction in the will"; that is, the result is not logically contradictory, but it is nevertheless something that a rational person could not will to be the case. One case that Kant uses to illustrate this is the case of someone who is considering whether or not to help others who are suffering hardships. He has no

---

[14] Kant, *Grounding*, p. 37.

desire to help them, though. What should he do? We might formulate the maxim in the following way: "I will not help others in need when I have no desire to do so." Now, Kant admits that this is not contradictory when universalized – that is, it is not logically contradictory – people would still survive, and of course there would still be acts of beneficence as long as people felt like it. However, no one could will it because in doing so the will would contradict itself. As Kant writes: "...a will which resolved itself in this way would contradict itself, inasmuch as cases might often arise in which one would have need of the love and sympathy of others and in which he would deprive himself, by such a law of nature springing from his own will, of all hope of the aid he wants for himself."[15] I take it that the idea here is something like the following – a person who formulates the above maxim is someone motivated by the desire to keep his resources and is concerned about his own welfare, but not the welfare of others. But if he were to universalize the maxim, that would involve willing that the world be such as to preclude others helping him out should he need it, and – given the original motive of self-love – this does seem like the will contradicting itself.

So, some duties come about because failure to live up to them would involve a logical contradiction of the universalized maxim; but in other cases the contradiction is one in the will – no rational person would want the maxim to apply universally. These two sorts of duties can be distinguished in the following way – the first are *perfect* and the second *imperfect*.

The duty to tell the truth is perfect – we must always tell the truth on Kant's view; lying is always impermissible. The duty to beneficence is imperfect. We need not be beneficent all the time, on all occasions, and in any way possible. These duties allow for more latitude – we can choose the time and method of our beneficence. So, Robert is never allowed, morally, to lie; but when he decides that he ought to help others, he can have more flexibility about when and how – perhaps he decides to help those in need by donating to charities, or through volunteer work at community service centers, or a combination of both. As long as he is doing something to help, he is fulfilling his imperfect duty of beneficence.

[15] Kant, *Grounding*, p. 32.

Some writers have noted that with this way of classifying our duties, Kant seems to have a problem accounting for supererogatory acts. At least, on his view, which of the benevolent acts that we perform are to count as supererogatory is very vague. We have a duty to beneficence, but it is not perfect. This means that it is permissible for us to choose how to be beneficent and to what extent. So, Sally may decide to work at a soup kitchen once a month and make an annual donation to Oxfam; Constance volunteers at Greenpeace every summer vacation, and on her weekends acts as a "Big Sister" to orphaned children; Robert works for Habitat for Humanity during his vacations and contributes 10 percent of this income to medical charities. Are these people simply fulfilling their duty of beneficence, or are they also doing more than required? If they are doing more than required, how are we to tell when they have fulfilled their duty? Kant offers no guidelines in response to this.

Also, Kant himself believed that the perfect duties were more important than the imperfect, so if ever a conflict between the two arose, we ought to fulfill the perfect one. But this does not accord with some of our intuitions – perfect duties sometimes seem rather trivial in comparison with the imperfect. A promise to take a book back to the library by a certain time can easily be overridden by helping someone in desperate need of help. Yet the first is a duty to keep our promise, which is a perfect duty, and the second is a duty of beneficence, which is imperfect.

Criticisms and Responses

The strictness of perfect duties also led Kant to adopt some counter-intuitive views about how the categorical imperative is to be applied in some cases. So, for example, Kant believed that it was always wrong to lie because it could not be universalized and it involved manipulating another person – a failure to respect that other person (the one being lied to), a failure to respect the autonomy of that person. But suppose that someone wants to tell a lie, not for selfish reasons, but for altruistic ones. Suppose that he sees the lie as the only way to avoid a disastrous outcome. Kant discusses just such a case and even here says that he should not tell the lie:

Truthfulness in statements that cannot be avoided is the formal duty of man to everyone, however great the disadvantage that may arise therefrom for him or for any other. And even though by telling an untruth I do no wrong to him who unjustly compels me to make a statement, yet by this falsification, which as such can be called a lie...I do wrong to duty in general in a most essential point. That is, as far as in me lies I bring it about that statements...in general find no credence, and hence also that all rights based on contracts become void and lose their force, and this is a wrong done to mankind in general...To be truthful (honest) in all declarations is, therefore, a sacred and unconditionally commanding law of reason and admits of no expediency whatsover.[16]

The kind of case discussed by critics of this approach is the following. Suppose a prospective murderer comes to you to find out where your friend is hiding, so that he can kill your friend. Your friend has done nothing wrong whatsoever. He is simply an innocent person who has been targeted, let's assume, for his unpopular political views. Suppose also that you know your friend is hiding in your house. Should you lie to the prospective murderer or should you tell the truth? Kant believes that even in this kind of situation, if you cannot avoid a response, you must tell the truth. This seems completely ridiculous to many people – of course you ought to lie to save your innocent friend's life!

To be fair to Kant, however, I think that he is making a very interesting theoretical point, one that came up earlier in our discussion of utilitarianism. I interpret Kant's position here as a rather strong denial of *negative responsibility*. If we hold someone negatively responsible for an event, then we hold him responsible for an outcome that he could have prevented but did not prevent. The idea is that we can be responsible for passively allowing bad things to happen. So, if Melissa is walking along the beach and sees a toddler drowning in a tide pool, a toddler she could easily save, but she does nothing to help and just walks by, allowing him to drown – well, she's at least partly responsible for the toddler's death, even though she didn't actually push him into the tide pool. She could have easily saved him, but did not.

Now compare this case with the following, adapted from the case by Bernard Williams that we discussed earlier in the book. Suppose that a

---

[16] Immanuel Kant, "On a Supposed Right to Lie Because of Philanthropic Concerns," translated by James W. Ellington and printed in his edition of *Grounding*, op. cit., pp. 64–5.

young man named Jim is traveling through South America where he happens upon a village that has been taken over by an evil man, the Captain. The Captain happens to be in a good mood on the day Jim arrives. He had been planning to execute 20 innocent villagers as an example and warning to those who would oppose his control of the village. But instead of just proceeding with the killings, he offers Jim the following choice: if Jim kills one, he will spare the lives of the other 19. If Jim declines, he will go ahead and kill all 20. First of all, what should Jim do? Well many people would say, probably, that though it would be extremely difficult, Jim probably ought to kill the one – since the one he would kill is doomed to die, and this would result in saving 19 innocent lives. And Williams agrees that this might indeed be the right thing to do. *However*, suppose that Jim declines the offer, and then all 20 villagers are killed. Who is responsible for their deaths? Williams, and many others I suspect, would not want to hold Jim even partly responsible. The responsible person is the Captain – he's the one who actually kills them. The one we hold responsible – that we ought to hold responsible – is the one who actually does the killing. Killing is something that is inherently terrible. So we might want to claim that the difference between the Melissa case and the Jim case is that she's doing something wrong if she fails to aid the toddler, since there's nothing inherently immoral about pulling someone out of a tide pool.

Kant may be drawing on a similar intuition in his passage on lying – though expressing Williams's reservations much more strongly. Kant thinks that not only are you not responsible for the bad things others do, even if you could have prevented them, but in the failure to prevent you have not done anything wrong if prevention involves doing something inherently immoral – such as lying. Some writers view Kant as actually being an idealist on this point – noting that under ideal circumstances one ought not lie. So, one ought not lie. This can be seen as part-and-parcel of Kant's uncompromising view of morality and its demands.[17]

---

[17] Christine Korsgaard develops a similar approach to understanding Kant's position on lying in "The Right to Lie: Kant on Dealing with Evil," reprinted in *Creating the Kingdom of Ends*, op. cit., pp. 133–58. Here, she argues that what Kant is doing is telling us what we should do in ideal circumstances. Of course, in the real world, circumstances are often not ideal – as when one is faced with evil. Under these circumstances we should not allow ourselves to be used by evil, and telling the truth under these circumstances would be to help the evil individual accomplish his goals.

This leads us to note that in applying the categorical imperative a lot depends on how we formulate the maxims. Do the two formulations of the categorical imperative really express the same moral insight?

Here's at least one reason to think not: at least for some cases, application of the different formulations gives you different answers about what is morally permissible, depending on how you formulate the maxim of action. So, for example, if you claim that instead of

(1)   I will lie.

the maxim be formulated as

(2)   I will lie to save an innocent life.

you can see this split. Version (1) fails the test of both formulations; version (2) does not. Maxim (2) can be universalized, so it would seem to pass the first formulation of the categorical imperative. However, it would still involve treating another person merely as a means, by lying to him, and thus would fail the second formulation of the categorical imperative. This seems to offer some indication that they are not, in fact, the same.

On my view, what is appealing about Kant's two formulations of the categorical imperative is that the first appeals to our intuitive notion of fairness. No rational being is any more special than any other rational being. We all count the same, morally speaking. So, if I think that x is fine for me to do under the circumstances, then it is only rational for me to recognize and agree that it would have to be fine for everyone else as well.

The second formulation appeals to our sense that persons, rational beings, are deserving of a special sort of respect and that it would be wrong – across the board – to simply use a person to achieve our goals. As Kant puts it, persons are "ends in themselves." On Kant's view, for example, slavery is just wrong, end of story – and deception and manipulation as well. Thus, Kant's view has often been associated with a kind of absolutism about rights. And this appeals to our view that some things are just plain wrong, period. So, while the two formulations don't really seem to express the same moral insight, they do express the deeply held moral views of many people.

Another appealing feature of Kant's theory, and any theory that diminishes the role that consequences play in moral evaluation, is that the moral quality of a person's action is insulated from moral luck. For someone who holds that the rightness of an action depends on actual consequences (whether these are merely necessary or necessary and sufficient), the evaluations of actions become hostages to fortune. Things may not work out as expected: for example, Sandra may try to save someone's life, but through an unfortunate and unexpected sequence of events, actually end up harming that person. We can think of many cases in which people have good and noble intentions, but the actions just don't work out. On Kant's view, those people have still acted rightly. Their actions are just as good and worthy as those in which well-intentioned agents do manage to actually produce some good outcomes.

Though there is some disagreement among commentators, it is generally agreed that Kant did not think that consequences are weighed in determining the permissibility of an action. Instead, if the maxim of the action involved some sort of contradiction – either a strict one or a "contradiction in the will" – then the action would not be permissible. So, the categorical imperative was supposed to impose a logical requirement on permissibility of actions.

Because he believed that it is our capacity for reason that underlies our intrinsic worth as persons, Kant had his own version of the animal problem. On his view, since animals are not rational beings, they are not worthy of moral respect. They have no moral rights. On this view, then, one cannot behave immorally toward an animal. While most people would not accord equal moral status to animals as they do to persons, they still think that animals have *some* moral standing. How to account for morally appropriate behavior toward animals within the Kantian framework is a problem for Kant. He is aware of this difficulty and tries to deal with it – a bit in the *Grounding for the Metaphysics of Morals*, as well as in his *Lectures on Ethics*:

> ...so far as animals are concerned we have no direct duties. Animals are not self-conscious and are there merely as a means to an end. That end is man...Our duties towards animals are merely indirect duties towards humanity. Animal nature has analogies to human nature, and by doing our duties to animals in respect of manifestations that corres-

pond to manifestations of human nature, we indirectly do our duty towards humanity.[18]

Kant goes on to cite, as an illustration of this, William Hogarth's series of engravings *The Stages of Cruelty.* The idea is that if we are cruel to animals, or display nastiness toward animals, that will spill over into behavior toward persons. We owe nothing to animals, on Kant's view, but we should still moderate our behavior toward them, since it can have an impact on our attitudes and actions toward rational beings.

To many, this misses the point. If someone tortures a kitten, what makes that wrong is that it harms the kitten unnecessarily; it may also corrupt that person's character further, and that is a bad thing too, but that all by itself does not exhaust the immorality of the action. It is wrong because it harms *the animal.* This problem is a fairly significant one for the Kantian.

Some modern proponents of the Kantian approach to ethics accept this aspect of Kant's views and argue that animals do not *deserve* any moral consideration. But they will generally try to soften this by then noting that a nice person is still nice to animals even if animals don't deserve it – just as a nice person will do a favor for someone even if that person doesn't deserve it. Again, this goes some way to dealing with the problem, except that we have to ask – What of the not nice person who is mean to animals, and who displays his cruelty with respect to animals? We should still be able to say that this person is not simply "not nice" or that he exhibits a vice. We could say the same thing of someone who smashes a vase in an angry tantrum – that is "not nice" and exhibits a vice. This explanation does not acknowledge that animals have some kind of morally significant status, and this status, for example, differentiates them from things such as vases and rocks in a morally significant way.

Other proponents reject this feature of Kant's ethics and say that, on this subject, he is wrong. But this does not mean that his entire theory is wrong. For example, Christine Korsgaard argues that, on a broadly Kantian theory, there is more to respect in animal nature than rationality. Animals, like people, display goal-oriented behavior – they

---

[18] Immanuel Kant, *Lecture on Ethics,* translated by Louis Infield (Indianapolis, IN: Hackett, 1980), p. 239.

display behavior that indicates that they matter to themselves. She notes that they certainly do have a natural good and this is something on which we also confer normative value, so "It is therefore our animal nature, not just our autonomous nature, that we take to be an end-in-itself."[19]

There are other options open to someone who wants to adopt a Kantian perspective but still accords rights to animals. Tom Regan, for example, believes that animals have rights – absolute rights – and he appeals to Kantian egalitarian views to justify this. One ought never treat an animal merely as a means to an end.[20] Of course, this doesn't accord with our "conventional" intuitions either – animals may have moral status, but not the same status as people have. While many would think that harming animals is wrong, they might not think it right to go so far as to accord equal respect to animals. For those who want to accord moral standing to animals, and yet hold that persons, in virtue of their rationality, have greater status, this is a difficult needle to thread. Recall that John Stuart Mill tried to do this by citing a distinction between higher and lower pleasures, and noting that only human beings are capable of the higher pleasures.

There are many modern ethicists who have been influenced by Kant's ethical theory, though they reject some of his actual prescriptions. For example, many would argue that his absolutism about duty is too severe. They believe that ethics is duty based, *not* a function of what consequences are produced by a given action. They might, for example, believe that there is a hierarchy of duties, and the possibility that duties can sometimes conflict. Consider the lying case again. We do have a duty to tell the truth, but we could also hold that we have a duty to save innocent life when feasible, and in cases in which there is a conflict between the two – in which we need to lie to save the innocent life – then we should go with the weightier duty, that of saving the innocent life. Recall that this approach tries to distinguish

---

[19] Christine Korsgaard, "Fellow Creatures: Kantian Ethics and Our Duties to Animals," forthcoming in *Tanner Lectures on Human Values* edited by Grethe B. Peterson (Salt Lake City: The University of Utah Press), vol. 25/26, p. 31 (ms.).

[20] Tom Regan, *The Case for Animal Rights* (Berkeley: The University of California Press, 1985).

itself from consequentialism. Given this, there is no way – besides raw appeal to intuitions – to justify one duty being weightier than another. If we appeal to consequences – that, for example, we generate better outcomes by saving the lives of innocents – then we are simply giving a consequentialist account of duty. The challenge to the duty-based approach is to soften absolutism without seeming to reduce itself to just another form of consequentialism.

We have seen that in the philosophical system that Kant develops, emotion is demoted from the place and significance it was accorded by writers such as Aristotle and Hume. This has led some to view Kant's ethics as cold and unemotional. However, this is not true. Kant simply wanted to give emotion a subordinate role, not eliminate it altogether. He felt that morality could not be based upon emotion; otherwise it would lose its authority over our actions. Emotions, unlike reason, are fickle and transitory. They resist the pull of reason. Further, we couldn't explain how it is that persons have morality and animals don't if we viewed the basis of morality as emotion and desire. Animals have desires; they can be happy or unhappy and they desire happiness – they have instincts that allow them to achieve this within their constricted circumstances. Humans, on the other hand, have more than instinct – they have reason. Thus, the point of morality isn't mere desire fulfillment, or happiness. It isn't something that is based for its force or authority on our emotions at all. It is, rather, demanded by reason. Since animals don't possess reason, they can't have a system of morality – they can neither be bound by it, nor can they be the proper subjects of moral consideration and respect.

Kant's ethics has been enormously influential. He is responsible for articulating a vision of morality that captures many of our deeply held views of the status and content of morality. Some of his particular prescriptions seem highly counterintuitive. But again, Kant himself might well have discounted some of these intuitions as being influenced by our desires rather than pure reason. In evaluating his system of ethics, we should keep in mind that it has an admirable theoretical integrity. Further, we can adopt the framework but disagree with Kant in its application (though Kant himself would not agree with this). There are many philosophers writing today who agree with the basics of Kant's theory, but who think him mistaken about its implications in some cases.

Further reading

Baron, Marcia 1997: "Kantian Ethics," in Marcia Baron, Philip Pettit, and Michael Slote, *Three Methods of Ethics: A Debate*. Malden, MA: Blackwell, pp. 3–91.

Hill, Tom Jr. 1992: *Dignity and Practical Reason in Kant's Moral Theory*. Ithaca, NY: Cornell University Press.

Korsgaard, Christine 1996: *Creating the Kingdom of Ends*. Cambridge, UK: Cambridge University Press.

Sullivan, Roger 1994: *An Introduction to Kant's Ethics*. Cambridge, UK: Cambridge University Press.

Chapter 6

Social Contract Theory

> Where there is no common Power there is no Law: where no Law, no
> Injustice. Force, and Fraud, are in warre the two Cardinall vertues.
>   Thomas Hobbes, *Leviathan*[1]

With the failure of divine command theory and the lack of uniform
assurance that the will of God could provide a basis for morality (or
that, even if it could in theory, the practical problems surrounding
which interpretation of God's will to endorse posed too many practical
difficulties), alternative theories came to be adopted that focused on the
connection between morality and its function as a regulator of human
interaction. Utilitarianism and Kantian ethics both provided secular
alternatives, but there are other alternatives as well, and social contract theory provides just such a theory.

Many people restrict social contract theory to political philosophy
and discuss it merely as an account of the source of political obligation
and political authority. However, we can also discuss it as an account
of morality itself – this theory, then, would roughly hold that moral
rules are a matter of agreement between rational individuals, and that
agreement is the source of their authority over our actions. Thus the
basis for morality would be a kind of contract.

Recall that Thomas Hobbes (1588–1679) was a philosopher who
believed that human beings were motivated by self-interest. For this
reason, as we discussed in Chapter 2, most philosophers regard him as
a psychological egoist. Hobbes was also a *contractarian*, who based his

---

[1] Thomas Hobbes, *Leviathan* (Harmondsworth, UK: Penguin, 1988; first published in
1651), p. 188.

political and social philosophy on his theory of human nature. So some forms of contractarianism are not incompatible with *descriptive* egoism at all. It is precisely because human beings are self-interested that they will agree to abide by codes of conduct. Failure to have such an agreement would lead to social chaos, which harms the interests of *everybody*. The laws that govern our behavior are a matter of agreement between rational persons. There is some evidence that he extended this to morality as well.

Again, it is his view of human nature that provides the basis for the contractarian system that he proposes, since he argues that persons who are rational and self-interested will be motivated to pursue the agreement and abide by it. The chaotic state of affairs, the state of affairs in which humans live without rules or laws, is a *state of nature*. In such a state there is no right or wrong, no justice or injustice. But this is a terrible state to be in. A person is subject to the force of others and risks being killed and having her goods stolen. This is clearly not in that person's interest. The fear of death is a powerful motivator – indeed, Hobbes believed it a major motivator for human beings. He writes:

> The Passions that encline men to Peace, are Feare of Death; Desire of such things as are necessary to commodious living; and a Hope by their industry to obtain them. And Reason suggesteth convenient Articles of Peace, upon which men may be drawn to agreement.[2]

Given that life in the state of nature – the state of people living without any rules, laws, or government enforcement of norms – is "nasty, brutish, and short," it is in the interests of individuals to band together and agree to rules of behavior to avoid the state of nature. With minimal assumptions about human nature, such as the assumption that we are all motivated by self-interest, and it being in the individual's self-interest to have a long peaceful life rather than one that is brutish and short, he can account for the motivation to enter into such an agreement. The beauty of this account is that he can explain why people *do* and *ought to* obey rules – so it is not just an explanation of behavior but a justification as well. They ought to obey these rules when these rules maintain order in society. In effect, then, people

---

[2] Hobbes, *Leviathan*, p. 188.

contract to abide by them in order to avoid the state of nature. In the political sphere, too, these rules are enforced by a sovereign power – a government that uses force to make sure that people obey the rules and are punished if they do not. We could hold that some kind of force is also necessary to make sure that people behave morally and don't opt out of the system of rules that they have agreed to. This force could be physical, or it could take the form of social pressure and blame.

So, we *needn't* assume that people are benevolent and self-sacrificing in order to explain moral behavior. That can be explained by the assumption that they are solely self-interested and that it is in their interest to avoid the state of nature. This allows Hobbes to provide a simple theory. It also allows him to hold that the prudential "ought" and the moral "ought" are really the same thing – which in turn helps him to explain moral motivation. We "ought" to be moral just as we "ought" to pursue self-interest. Prudence is not a mystery. If morality and prudence are really the same thing, then the mystery of moral motivation, or why people behave morally, is also no mystery.

There is an ambiguity in how to understand "self-interest." Some theorists make a point of saying that the moral rules are those agreed to by *rational*, self-interested agents. But why make this assumption if one of the motives behind the theory is to explain why people are actually motivated to act morally? Consider the following case:

(1) Alice decides to feed her children only yellow food, because she believes (without any good evidence) that food with other colors is toxic and she does not want to harm her children (which would clearly be immoral).

Let's assume that a diet consisting only of yellow food is, in actual fact, bad for the children. Here, then, Alice is in reality acting against her self-interest, though she doesn't believe that she is. Is Alice doing the wrong thing? Some would argue "Yes," since she is actually harming herself, given the assumption that it is in her interest to have healthy children. On this view, then, the right thing is to act on our *enlightened* self-interest, not our own perception of our self-interest. Since Alice is not displaying the proper sensitivity to evidence regarding nutrition, she is not really being rational, so the action is wrong even though she believes she is doing the right thing.

There is, however, a further indeterminacy. Even rational and reasonably well informed individuals don't get it right – sometimes evidence underdetermines the right answer, for example, or people are reasonably misled by the evidence. Suppose that it turns out that cauliflower is actually a very unhealthy food, though the best evidence currently available indicates that it is an extremely important part of a healthy diet. Would it be wrong to feed cauliflower to our children?

However we understand the self-interest invoked, the problem with this account of human nature is that it seems to go too far in trying to dispel the mystery of how people are motivated to act morally – and this calls into question Hobbes's empirical assumption. Surely there are cases in which morality and prudence do not coincide, cases in which the morally good thing requires a great deal of self-sacrifice. Recall that in discussing psychological egoism we considered such cases. Self-sacrifice may not be required, but most think of it as good (as long as it is not outright foolish); further, people seem to perform such actions and they seem to do so fully knowing that the action requires a good deal of self-sacrifice. Imagine the case of someone who saves the lives of her friends, but at the cost of her own life – this is generally considered admirable and noble.

It also seems odd to regard immoral behavior as *irrational*. Sometimes people who do terrible things can be seen to be acting all too rationally – a person who kills to inherit, for example, and who is confident that he will not be caught. This person is terrible, and has done something dreadful, but there seems to be nothing wrong with his ability to plan and calculate, he is not deluded, and his action is capable of rational *explanation*, though it cannot, of course, be morally justified. So Hobbes's view of human nature seems at odds with at least some our intuitions.

To those who would argue that his picture of human nature is a rather "strange" view of how nature has arranged things, he replies:

> Let him therefore consider with himself, when taking a journey, he armes himselfe, and seeks to go well accompanied; when going to sleep, he locks his dores; when even in his house he locks his chests; and this when he knows there bee Lawes, and publike Officers, armed to revenge all injuries shall be done him; . . . [3]

---

[3] Hobbes, *Leviathan*, p. 186.

Hobbes is using this to argue that his view of human nature is simply realistic, and reflects our experience – we often will take precautions against theft and various sorts of harms. But Hobbes's critic will still note that at best this can show that we do believe that people are motivated to some extent, maybe even to some large extent, by self-interest – but it doesn't show they are solely motivated by self-interest. Indeed, one problem with this approach is that it is difficult for Hobbes to explain how obligations can continue to bind us when we calculate that they don't promote our self-interest. It might seem that a clever person will honor the rules only to the extent that they help him. Yet again this seems quite contrary to moral norms. We must obey the rules, even in situations in which we may not be maximally profiting from the rules. However, Hobbes rejects this as a potential problem for his view. Indeed, he calls the position sketched above the "foole's" position:

> The Foole hath sayd in his heart, there is no such thing as Justice; and sometimes also with his tongue; seriously alleaging, that every mans conservation, and contentment, being committed to his own care, there could be no reason, why every man might not do what he thought conduced thereunto: and therefore also to make, or not make; keep, or not keep Covenants, was not against Reason, when it conduced to one's benefit.[4]

The "foole" believes that we should abide by agreements only to the extent that the agreements benefit us. So, Hobbes is clearly rejecting the view that we can opt out of agreements if those agreements don't suit us. But this is puzzling – on his view, if we are motivated only by self-interest, and if, indeed, this is what gets us to enter into the initial agreement in the first place, then why shouldn't we, on this view, just opt out when we reasonably perceive an agreement not to be in our own self-interest? His response to this challenge is as follows:

> He...that breaketh his Covenant, and consequently declareth that he thinks he may with reason do so, cannot be received into any Society, that unite themselves for Peace and Defense, but by the errour of them that receive him; nor when he is received, be retayned in it, without

---

[4] Hobbes, *Leviathan*, p. 203.

seeing the danger of their errour; which errours a man cannot reasonably reckon upon as a means of his security: and therefore if he be left, or
cast out of Society, he perisheth;...[5]

The basic idea is pretty simple. Hobbes is asserting that a "foole" who
breaks his promise by violating norms will be left out – others will not
interact with him or, if they do, it is only because they are making
some sort of mistake. And it would not be reasonable to expect people
to make that mistake – so the best bet for any individual concerned to
promote his self-interest is to behave morally and abide by the agreement.

This doesn't completely solve the problem. Suppose that we have an
agent who decides that he doesn't want to interact with others – he's
perfectly fine living by himself, and, in fact, wouldn't even mind going
to prison. Would it be acceptable for him to opt out, and then behave
immorally as long as it suited him? Hobbes might argue that such a
person is foolish indeed, since this behavior leaves him quite vulnerable. However, there does seem to be a difference between being foolish
and being bad, or immoral, which the Hobbesian system seems to
conflate.

Hobbes believed the system to be maintained – the rules formulated
and enforced – by a sovereign body. This sovereign could be one person
or a group of people, in principle, though Hobbes himself believed that
the sovereign should be a monarch. He felt that a divided sovereign
would only result in debilitating logistical problems for the government, that there would be too many disagreements and resulting
inefficiencies. Therefore, it was necessary to have one powerful individual in charge, who would command obedience.

The type of social contract approach associated with Hobbes is
contractarianism. Persons agree to abide by various rules in order to
avoid falling into a state-of-nature situation, or social chaos. Those
rules are formulated and enforced by the sovereign, to whom the
individuals have ceded their natural rights. A major problem with
this approach has to do with how we are to understand the nature of
the contract or agreement that these individuals make – Is it *actual* or
hypothetical?

---

[5] Hobbes, *Leviathan*, p. 205.

It seems wildly implausible to hold that the contract is actual, if by "actual" we mean "explicitly agreed to." First of all, we have no record of human beings as a group coming together to make such a contract. Indeed, Hobbes himself did not think that the state of nature in its pure form really existed between individuals; though he did suggest that it existed between kingdoms that constantly seemed to be at war and prepared for war, since they were not answerable to a higher secular authority. He also thought that such agreements were necessary to avoid degeneration into a kind of civil war. This led him to view revolutions as very rarely ever justified. This is because in order to justify the revolution you'd have to think that the government was so bad that it was almost as bad as the state of nature itself – since without the government in place we would be reverting to a state of nature, at least for a time. And, indeed, Hobbes had plenty of empirical evidence that revolutions frequently resulted in chaos for a time. So, we would have to be living under a government that did not protect us – that either had weak laws, weak enforcement, or both. It is hard to think of a modern revolution justified on the basis of citizens truly living in fear of their lives because the government was so corrupt or inept.

But, more importantly, *even if* this agreement had taken place, it seems irrelevant to the norms that we, today, are bound by. Just because ancestors of ours made an agreement, it does not follow that those of us living today are bound by the agreement. If Robert's grandmother contracts to pay a certain amount of money each year for heating oil for her family, Robert himself is not bound by the contract unless *he* agrees. No one else can agree on his behalf. Attempts to avoid these problems have led people to postulate that we implicitly agree to the rules of the society that we are voluntarily living in – otherwise, we could just leave. However, given the fact that today there is really no place to go to escape government altogether, this approach rings a bit hollow. Further, if we are to imagine that moral norms do not exist prior to agreements, then what those norms turn out to be seems rather arbitrary – What if we live in a society in which it is agreed by the majority that persons of a certain religious background should not be eligible to hold public office or to leave the society to set up their own society? This seems immoral, even though agreed to by a majority. Political systems based on social contract generally do assume that there are preexisting moral norms in order to avoid this kind of problem. But then, of course, that means that the contractarianism provides only an account of political obligation rather than moral obligation.

Again, one could argue that the agreement, though actual, is not explicit. Rather, people – by living in a given community or society – are tacitly agreeing to abide by the norms of the community. This view doesn't commit us to the implausible historical claim that humans explicitly agreed to the norms underlying morality, or even simply norms of justice. It also avoids the problem of being bound by agreements of our ancestors, since the agreement on this model is actual, and present – just tacit rather than explicitly made. However, while some and even most people in a given community may well be tacitly agreeing to the norms, it again seems implausible that all are agreeing – indeed, for any given norm that we could specify, there will be some people who do not agree, probably. But surely they are still bound by the norm in spite of the fact that they do not agree. For example, there may be someone who thinks that parking downtown should be free, and who does not agree to the provision in the town charter that allows the town to collect fees for parking. It seems that *simply because* he disagrees he cannot opt out, and he ought to pay for parking just like everyone else. It might also be the case that we think it is occasionally fine to "opt out," but only when we think there may sometimes be a fundamental injustice involved in some of the accepted norms – some accepted norms may be unjust, such as norms of the past that didn't allow for equal treatment of women in society. But what is wrong with them isn't that they weren't agreed to, or not simply that they weren't agreed to – there is some injustice that is more basic than this, which underlies our judgment of unfairness.

To avoid these problems, one could also argue that the contract is not actual, but is, rather, hypothetical. So, the rules we ought to adopt are those that *would be* agreed to under certain circumstances. For example, you could argue that the moral principles are those that all rational persons would agree to – or, all rational persons who are unaware of their specific place in the society. The point would be to make the agreement relativized to certain idealized circumstances that are intended to rule out factors that distort our moral judgment – factors such as stupidity or self-interested bias. The problem with this approach is that it is difficult to understand how a hypothetical agreement could have any binding force at all. So what if I would have agreed to x, or would not have agreed to x under certain circumstances? Consider the following case used by Ronald Dworkin:

> Suppose I did not know the value of my painting on Monday; if you had offered me $100 for it then I would have accepted. On Tuesday, I discovered it was valuable. You cannot argue that it would be fair for the courts to make me sell it to you for $100 on Wednesday. It may be my good fortune that you did not ask me on Monday, but that does not justify coercion against me later.[6]

But, even more fundamentally problematic is the issue of why we should abide by any agreement to begin with. Again, Hobbes tries to assimilate the moral "should" to the prudential "should." Only a "foole" opts out, since this would leave that person in a very undesirable state. However, we have some reason to doubt this. For example, some people do immoral acts and don't get caught, and there is no negative impact on them. Further, there are very many people who "free ride" on what others in the system do. They opt out in a passive sort of way, by failing to contribute to the common good. In some cases this opting out is met with blame and condemnation, but other times not – or, at least, not in any way that seems to harm the free rider, all things considered.

These sorts of considerations have led critics to hold that the "ought" of "One ought to keep one's agreement to abide by the rules" must be a distinctly moral ought – one that obtains even against the individual's rational self-interest. So, the fact that by making an agreement I seem to have put myself under a moral obligation indicates that there are some moral norms operating prior to that agreement, norms of the sort "One ought morally to keep one's agreements."

One modern contractarian is David Gauthier. On Gauthier's view, it is rational to agree to abide by moral rules of justice.[7] That is, he believes that rationality and justice go hand in hand. A rational person recognizes that he ought to conform his behavior to principles of

---

[6] Ronald Dworkin, *Taking Rights Seriously* (Cambridge, MA: Harvard University Press, 1977), p. 152. Dworkin uses this example as part of his case arguing that John Rawls is best not interpreted as a social contract theorist.

[7] David Gauthier, *Morals By Agreement* (Oxford: Clarendon Press, 1986).

justice; those principles themselves are determined by what rational individuals within a society would agree to given their perception of the rules that they would adopt from the state of nature. He recognizes that Hobbes' Foole is a problem for this account since it looks, on the face of it, as though if we are concerned to maximize self-interest we ought to opt out of agreements when they don't seem to be in our interest – And isn't that unjust? For example, if Samantha promises to pay back money she has been loaned, we have the very decided intuition that if she doesn't pay it back then she's behaved very badly – she's not treating the person who loaned her the money fairly.

Yet, it seems that it might well be in her self-interest, and rational, to not pay it back. After all, she could do something else with the money. At the moment, she is deciding whether or not to pay it back, and calculating what is in her own best interest – what maximizes the good *for her*. It seems quite plausible that if all she considers is her own interest, then she should keep the money and use it for something she wants.

Gauthier's solution to this problem involves making a distinction between *straightforward* maximization and *constrained* maximization. The Foole is someone who adopts the strategy of straightforward maximization in interactions with others. She calculates, on the basis of each individual interaction, which of her options maximizes good for her on that occasion, and then acts to promote her own good without factoring in how she can generate good for others too – that is, she doesn't give any weight to cooperative goods, goods that may sometimes go against her own specific interests on a given occasion, for example, but benefit others or benefit the collective. Thus, she is a person who is not willing to genuinely cooperate with others, unless that cooperation just happens to coincide with what she would do anyway.

The constrained maximizer, however, will adopt strategies that maximize her overall good, given that others cooperate; or, more precisely, given that she expects cooperation from others. Thus, the constrained maximizer can gain advantages that are possible only through cooperation. The straightforward maximizer might be able, on occasion, to take advantage of those willing to cooperate, but by and large she will be shut out of the advantages of cooperative goods, since others will be reluctant to trust her. They will be able to detect the unwillingness she has to advance cooperative interests if they conflict with her own.

Gauthier's argument relies on the view that people are "translucent" to each other; that is, that we have the ability to understand each other and detect the motivations and intentions of others. Thus, cooperators will be able to detect noncooperators and respond appropriately by withholding benefits of cooperative interaction. This is a portion of his argument that can be attacked. In fact, as far back as Plato it has been suggested that someone could gain the benefits of cooperation by not actually being cooperative if only he *seems* to be cooperative. He would then be trusted by others even though he is not trustworthy. But Gauthier would deny that this is typically the case – noncooperators get found out, and then they suffer the consequences. It is better to be a cooperator and thus avoid the risk of detection.

Other contract theorists take Kant, and the idea that each rational individual is of supreme moral worth, to be their inspiration. These writers are called "contractualists," to distinguish them from the contractarian approach to contract theory inspired by Hobbes. Both John Rawls (1921–2002) and Thomas Scanlon have offered views in which a contractualist model can provide guidance in determining principles of justice for a given society, or rules by which people ought to live in a given society and how a government should distribute benefits and burdens.

John Rawls's account is the most famous, and I cannot stress enough its importance to the development of contemporary political philosophy and moral theory. In *A Theory of Justice*, Rawls sought to provide an account of the principles of *justice* that would be at the foundation of a just state.[8] Thus, his project was not to account for all of morality, but only one aspect – that of just political and social arrangements. Still, this is a significant portion, and other writers have thought Rawls a bit modest in his stated aims.

Rawls famously argued that if we want to decide fair principles we must think of how to do so under conditions of fairness. These are conditions that rule out or minimize distortions of impartial judgment. We would like to see biases and prejudices of various sorts ruled out in the agents that are party to the agreement on the fundamental principles of fairness. For example, it wouldn't be fair to decide these principles on the basis of race or religious affiliation. We also don't

---

[8] John Rawls, *A Theory of Justice* (Cambridge, MA: The Belknap Press of Harvard University Press, 1971).

want people to be making the judgment on the basis of their own particular interests. In order to accomplish this, he suggests we consider what principles would be chosen in what he terms "the original position," where the choosing agents are behind a "veil of ignorance" – that is, where they are unaware of factors such as their own social standing, race, and so forth that might have a distorting impact on their judgments of what is fair and just. These agents are rational and self-interested as well. We can see in Rawls the move to an idealized understanding of the agents in the agreement – so idealized, in fact, that writers such as Ronald Dworkin have pointed out that it is a mistake to even view Rawls's theory as a contract theory. We really just need to have one rational agent who is unaware of distorting factors, and this agent will be able to decide on the principles without bargaining: the bargaining is unnecessary since all other potential agents will be in the same position – fully rational and absent distorting influences on their judgment. The contract imagery in Rawls is then really just a heuristic that helps us grasp why Rawls views this procedure as arriving at the heart of fairness. Rawls also uses the process of *reflective equilibrium* to justify his view. This is the process by which we compare intuitions and principles to arrive at settled judgements.

Under these circumstances, and given the additional condition that people will tend to "play it safe" under these conditions and be risk averse in this sort of context of tremendous uncertainty about where they actually are in the economic and social hierarchy, Rawls argues that the principles chosen for institutions would be something like the following:

First Principle
Each person is to have an equal right to the most extensive total system of equal basic liberties compatible with a similar system of liberty for all.
Second Principle
Social and economic inequalities are to be arranged so that they are both:
(a) to the greatest benefit of the least advantaged, consistent with the just savings principle, and
(b) attached to the offices and positions open to all under conditions of fair equality of opportunity.

He then offers some priority rules to adjudicating between the principles, and then the following:

General Conception
All social primary goods – liberty and opportunity, income and wealth, and the bases of self-respect – are to be distributed equally unless an unequal distribution of any or all of these goods is to the advantage of the least favored.[9]

Unpacking these principles and a complete discussion of their application is not feasible in a book of this size. The basic idea behind Rawls's approach is that liberty should be as expansive as possible; that is, to the extent that it is compatible with liberty for others. In a just society there could still be inequality of resources, but only if the system is one that benefits those who are least well off in that society. So, for example, it is possible to justify disparities of wealth as long as the system is one that also benefits those who are not wealthy. Perhaps, as in the United States, there is a system of taxation, for example, that redistributes wealth and makes sure that basic services are provided to those who could not otherwise afford them.

People are to have as much liberty, or freedom to do as they please, as is consistent with the liberty of others and does not interfere with their primary goods. So, liberty does not entitle someone to violate the rights of someone else, for example. All are free to worship as they please in the just society, or not worship at all. However, someone could not use religion to violate someone else's rights – so a practice such as human sacrifice would not be allowed in the just society, even if it was part of someone's religious beliefs.

That is a rather extreme example. But other examples would include issues such as the obligation to provide for the satisfaction of social primary needs – this will be important in a just society. There is the obligation to alleviate poverty and ignorance and make sure that people have enough goods to ensure that they can develop their basic capacities, which in turn will ensure that they have what is necessary for self-respect and a decent life.

Why would people want to agree to a system like this – one in which the least well off are guaranteed consideration in the distribution of benefits and burdens? Rawls believes that in the original position, under conditions of extreme uncertainty, people will tend to be risk averse because they will be choosing principles under very extreme

---

[9] Rawls, *Theory of Justice*, pp. 302–3.

conditions of uncertainty – they have no idea whether they are rich or poor, what racial group they fall into, or what their religious beliefs are. They will thus want a system that maximizes the minimum – that is, maximizes the good for the least well off in the society – just in case they happen to fall into that group. But they will also want to allow for rewards for initiative, hard work, and merit – since these rewards are incentives to productivity within a society that potentially can benefit the least well off as well by, for example, generating more tax revenues to be redistributed, or creating more jobs and more economic opportunities.

This view has come under considerable attack. Robert Nozick (1938–2002), a libertarian, has argued that Rawls's view is actually incompatible with liberty, since it would provide justification for redistributing wealth, which is tantamount to stealing money and goods from some people to give to others, and thus violates their freedom to do with their goods what they will.[10] If a rich person wants to give her money to the poor, fine and well. But she should not be forced to do so by the government, he argues. That is unjust, but it is a scheme that would be allowed and justified on Rawls's theory. On Nozick's view, redistribution is a matter of charity, not justice. Vast differentials in wealth can still be quite just even if these disparities don't themselves benefit the worst-off in society. The issue of justice has to do with how the disparities came about – if there was no fraud or coercion involved, then they were just. He illustrates this point by using a well-known example – that of "Wilt Chamberlain":

> ...suppose that Wilt Chamberlain is greatly in demand by basketball teams, being a great gate attraction...He signs the following sort of contract with a team: In each home game, twenty-five cents from the price of each ticket of admission goes to him...The season starts and people cheerfully attend his team's games; they buy their tickets, each time dropping a separate twenty-five cents of their admission price into a special box with Chamberlain's name on it...Let us suppose that in one season one million persons attend his home games, and Wilt Chamberlain winds up with $250,000, a much larger sum than the average income...Is he entitled to this income? Is this new distribution...unjust?[11]

[10] Robert Nozick, *Anarchy, State, and Utopia* (New York: Basic Books, 1974).
[11] Nozick, *Anarchy*, p. 161.

Nozick's point is that all of the spectators paid the money quite willingly – they wanted to see Wilt Chamberlain and seeing him was worth the extra twenty-five cents. They were not defrauded, they were not coerced in any way. So isn't Wilt entitled to a salary that is much larger than anyone else's? Nozick argues "Yes" – no liberties are being violated at all, and, indeed, they are being supported. Nozick argues for the following slogan: "*From each as they choose, to each as they are chosen.*"[12]

On this view, the role of government is quite minimal. The government should make sure that people are not defrauded and coerced, thereby ensuing free rather than unfree social interactions.

Nozick is not without his own detractors – many find the view that he seems to have of the "just" society very unappealing. It has been called "the night watchman" approach. If we give priority to this conception of liberty, then why not go back to a night watchman state in which people pay for their own basic services, and the only thing the government does is make sure that people are free from fraud and coercion? Even this, he notes, required some redistribution and so must be morally justified somehow – if some are made to pay for the protection of others' rights, that itself has to be justified. But even if this is successful in showing how the minimal state – which requires some to pay for a police force, for example, that would help even those who couldn't pay – could be morally justified, many would say that it doesn't go far enough. Certainly, a utilitarian would argue that Nozick is ignoring responsibilities to generate benefits for others as well. The government should work to provide things such as public education that is open to all, even those who could not pay for their own education and do not themselves pay taxes to support education. This helps to highlight a serious problem with Nozick's account, since it is difficult to see how he can account for the rights of children. Children, by and large, have very little in the way of income, yet a child who is not provided for by parents should be provided for by the government – by, in effect, those who can afford to pay collectively making contributions that can be used to care for the vulnerable. I think that most people would find it plausible to hold that if the government fails to feed the child and fails to provide him with clothing and a basic education, then the child is entitled to complain. A liber-

---

[12] Nozick, *Anarchy*, p. 160.

tarian view would have this child's welfare depend upon the charity of individuals who might or might not happen to be moved by his plight. Both Rawls and the utilitarian can provide arguments that show that we ought to care for the child (not just that it would be nice for individuals to engage in charity toward the child – which is true too, but not enough).

Gerald Cohen brings up another criticism – one that attacks the intuitive plausibility of the Wilt Chamberlain example. Cohen believes that we could make a case for Nozick's Wilt Chamberlain example being importantly underdescribed. While it is true that the people going to the game are excited to see him play, it may also be true that they are not reflecting significantly on the disparity of income that is the result of their collective willingness to pay extra to see him. In the actual world there is already a good deal of inequality – paying extra to see Wilt play doesn't change that. So that may affect our intuitions on this case. But if we think that equality takes priority, and we think that what is just is something other than what we see now in the real world, then our views about this case may be very different indeed. He argues that people who prize equality and have egalitarian values will be reluctant to contribute to a system in which one person such as Wilt Chamberlain amasses disproportionate wealth and power:

> *For all that Nozick shows*, a socialist may claim that this is not a bargain informed people in an egalitarian society will be apt to make: they will refrain from so contracting so as to upset the equality they prize, and they will be especially averse to doing so because the resulting changes would profoundly affect their children.[13]

Cohen is not making the implausible claim that paying an extra twenty-five cents to see Wilt Chamberlain is going to make things worse for your children; however, he does believe that such could be the outcome if we endorse such "contracts" generally – in other words, that is what the general effect of such transactions would be. And it is not clear that we could endorse that. Maybe we could, but Cohen tries to show that the Wilt Chamberlain case is not at all decisive on this.

[13] Gerald Cohen, *Self-ownership, Freedom, and Equality* (Cambridge, UK: Cambridge University Press, 1995), p. 25.

Inclusion and Contracts

Feminist writers have noted that there is an inclusion problem that the theory suffers from – those not party to the agreement are left out.[14] Those left out are then left without recourse on the basis of justice, which seems very counterintuitive. In fact, we might argue that leaving out people in a seemingly arbitrary way is itself unjust. However, contract*ualist* accounts, those which present the agreement as one that would be made between rational beings, or that would be agreed to by all rational beings, on the basis of mutual respect, do not have this particular defect. Yet they may suffer from another inclusion problem. Some beings are not capable of entering into agreements. So, there needn't be any moral duties toward animals, for example, if that is not something that is agreed upon (or would be agreed upon, and so on). Yet, intuitively, we think that animals have some moral standing independent of what people happen to agree on. Contractualists will argue that they are presenting a narrow, restrictive account of morality – it is not intended to cover all the moral territory. For example, a contractualist might claim that he is giving an account of justice and that's it.

Thomas Scanlon, who has also developed a contractualist account – a contractualist account of wrong action – adopts the narrow scope. On the account he presents:

> . . . an act is wrong if its performance under the circumstances would be disallowed by any set of principles for the general regulation of behavior that no one could reasonably reject as a basis for informed, unforced general agreement.[15]

According to Scanlon, we want people to think about right and wrong – and it is important for us to be able to live with others under circumstances they could not "reasonably reject" – so it is very important for us to try to figure out what others could not reasonably reject as a basis for a moral guide. This consideration motivates us to

[14] See, for example, the work of Susan Moller Okin; for example, *Justice, Gender, and the Family* (New York: Basic Books, 1989).

[15] Thomas Scanlon, *What We Owe to Each Other* (Cambridge, MA: The Belknap Press of Harvard University Press, 1998), p. 153.

act rightly (or, at least, not wrongly). This in no way means that others must actually accept those principles – unfortunately, people can sometimes be unreasonable and reject what they shouldn't.

But the problem with this is that the definition doesn't seem to be doing any work. Instead, it is those features of the act (whatever they are) that the rational person is picking up on which renders it impermissible. Critics have called this the *redundancy* objection. If the contractualist describes what is right or wrong as what reasonable people who are reasonably well informed, and so forth, would agree to (or would disagree with, or at least would not find reasonable in the case of wrongness), then the agreement *per se* looks entirely unnecessary – rather, what determines rightness or wrongness are those features of the action that the reasonable persons are picking up on and to which they are responding appropriately.

Further, animals can still be treated badly, though not unjustly, on this account. This offers a response to the inclusion problem, but not a very satisfactory one. This is because if there is some account of why it is bad or wrong in some sense to mistreat animals, then why does this account need to be treated separately from the account of justice? Thus, even if we idealize the agreement so that it is what all rational persons would agree to, so that no rational persons can be excluded, we still have a version of the inclusion problem. The response that Scanlon offers is that his account is narrow in scope, and thus does not account for all of morality – but again the ethical theorist will want to know the fundamental ethical theory. If utilitarianism, for example, can account for the rightness and wrongness of actions – and not just what makes one action just and another unjust – then that theory seems to have a significant theoretical advantage.

The general problem is that, even if we think this a plausible account of how we might go about determining just rules of the political state, it seems inadequate as a basis for a moral system. It either suffers from an inclusion problem that makes it highly counterintuitive or a redundancy problem that makes it *unnecessary* to understanding moral norms. Some of these problems remain even if we view the account as simply a narrow one, covering justice only, and not moral norms in general. The account nevertheless appeals to many peoples' intuitions about morality – that it is fundamentally conventional, and that there is no basis for it beyond human convention. It is committed to the view that we – or at least idealized versions of human beings – determine the content and scope of morality. But the more idealized the agents become, in order to avoid relativistic problems, the less conventional the account seems to be. On Rawls's view, in fact, when the contract image is viewed as a heuristic, the contract itself is not at all the basis for viewing the principles of justice as the right ones. So it isn't really convention, here, that is doing the work of arriving at a moral theory. This isn't a problem for Rawls's account at all – I merely use it to make a point about the attractiveness of the general approach. Leaving it up to pure convention raises the specter of relativism; idealizing the context in which the principles are arrived at, however, makes it seem completely unconventional.

The next philosophical perspective that we look at disagrees with the contractualist approach. Intuitionism has as its historical basis a variety of approaches to ethics – natural law theory, as well as the intuitionism of those who believed that careful reflection would reveal moral truth. On this approach, which is considered in the next chapter, the truth is *out there* already. It is not manufactured by human beings.

Further reading

Daniels, Norman 1989: *Reading Rawls: Critical Studies on Rawls' A Theory of Justice*. Stanford, CA: Stanford University Press.

Kymlicka, Will 1990: *Contemporary Political Philosophy*. Oxford: Clarendon Press.

Chapter 7

Intuitionism

While Kant's ethics is, for many, the paradigmatic example of a deontological approach to ethics, there are many other approaches out there that fall into this category. One is contractarianism, which we discussed earlier. There are other deontologists who approach ethics from the standpoint of "common sense"; that is, they believe that there are principles that can be used to guide and evaluate action, and that those principles are accessible to us by reference to our intuitions about particular cases and dilemmas.[1] For this reason, these approaches tend to be labeled "intuitionistic." These approaches historically have arisen out of the natural law tradition, discussed in Chapter 2, as well as from the work of philosophers who were critical of utilitarianism. The idea is that – contra utilitarianism – there is no one principle that can be used to justify our actions. Indeed, there are a plurality of principles that govern various aspects of our lives – principles of just distribution of goods within a society, for example, principles that specify the circumstances under which killing may be permissible, and principles that indicate when we ought to help the needy, and so forth. For these deontologists, there may well not be anything deeper to moral theory than these principles; that is, no deeper rationale tying them together as ways of justifying behavior.

---

[1] There are a variety of ways in which one can be an intuitionist. For example, one could be an intuitionist simply about the rightness and wrongness of actions in particular cases, and reject intuitionism about principles. However, the version that I focus on in this chapter will be intuitionism about principles.

Again, deontologists are united in that they all reject a consequentialist approach to ethical theory. They believe that there are deontological constraints on action that undermine consequentialist justifications. These constraints are common-sensical. They note that some actions are just wrong, even if they maximize the good. For example, it is wrong to kill an innocent person even to save the lives of 10 other innocent persons. It is wrong to tell a lie even for a good end. The basic idea is that some things are just plain wrong even if they produce the maximally good result, and that consequentialism doesn't recognize this important moral fact. Instead, consequentialist accounts treat rightness and wrongness as instrumental – actions are not intrinsically wrong. If they are wrong it is because of the bad consequences that they generate. It is important, however, to note that many deontologists are not absolutists – they do believe that even though some actions are wrong in most normal contexts, there will be extraordinary circumstances that might warrant killing an innocent person. For example, it would be permissible if the number of people to be saved were large enough. However, they are reluctant to specify the cutoff at which killing an innocent person becomes permissible in order to save lives. Still, many deontologists do not commit themselves to the sort of absolutism that seems to have been adopted by Kant.

Though this approach has been associated with a religiously based natural law tradition, more recently writers have attempted to defend these principles without appealing to any particular religious tradition, or even without appealing to a deeper metaphysical underpinning for them. Instead, they want to show that the moral commitments underlying these principles reflect our common-sense views about what is, and what is not, morally permissible.

It is sometimes necessary to make decisions that involve imposing harms on some people in order to aid others. Ethical theories that try to provide a guide to action will try to give the agent some principle to use in making the decision of how and upon whom the harm is imposed. For example, the consequentialist is supposed to consider the effects of alternative actions in nondefault situations and then perform the action with the least bad effects (overall). But, as we have discussed, there are many theorists who reject consequentialism because they believe that it condones and even recommends unjust actions – such as sacrificing the welfare of an innocent person to save the lives of others.

There are many people who have the view that this kind of sacrifice is fundamentally unfair and wrong – and that it cannot be justified by considering consequences, or at least by considering *only* consequences. Many will argue that consequences of an action of course do matter morally, but that they are not the only things that matter to the justification and moral evaluation of an action. They may also reject the other standard approaches as simply failing to reflect our deeply held moral convictions. Instead, they may try to distill those convictions, or intuitions about what is right and wrong, into principles that map out our views about what is and is not morally permissible. These principles can take the form of recognizing *constraints* on what we are permitted to do, as well as *prerogatives* regarding what we are allowed to do, even when this involves failure to maximize utility. The consequentialist would not allow these, since they are in effect exceptions to the commitment to maximizing the good.

These principles, then, will be the proper guide to our action, and will provide what is necessary to evaluate actions. Some of these principles have been in the philosophical literature for quite some time. Within the tradition of Catholic ethics, in particular, one finds debates on deontological constraints on action. Again, there is also a tradition in secular ethical theory, often referred to as *intuitionism*, which holds that the basis for correct moral practice is a set of a plurality of principles that cannot be reduced to a single principle. In both of these traditions, one sees a discussion of nonconsequentialist constraints and prerogatives for morally appropriate action.

Prerogatives

Prerogatives allow individuals to act in certain ways that do not maximize the good, impartially considered. This might involve – as Bernard Williams's cases discussed in Chapter 4 show – allowing "moral space" for agents to pursue their own projects. It seems, intuitively, quite permissible for Monica to spend some time on the weekend visiting the Metropolitan Museum of Art rather than working the phones at Oxfam. Surely, at least sometimes, this kind of activity is perfectly permissible. Yet, there is no doubt that Monica is not using her time efficiently to promote impartial good – more good could be accomplished working for Oxfam as opposed to contemplating Flemish masterpieces. We discussed how a consequentialist would try to accommodate this insight in Chapter 4, and I won't repeat the discussion here. However, deontologists are skeptical of consequentialist maneuverings. They believe (here following the Kantian intuition about the special status of persons) that morality is about showing respect for persons, and this need not involve maximizing impartial good – particularly when that comes into conflict with allowing persons to pursue enriching projects.

Constraints

Constraints prohibit individuals from acting in certain ways – even if this means that the good will not in fact be maximized. There are certain things that are wrong to do – even if they happen to generate more good, impartially considered. For example, a fairly common intuition is that it is wrong to kill in many circumstances even when the killing would bring about a greater overall good. To consider a classic case, it would be wrong to kill one person in order to harvest his organs even if that were required to save the lives of six other people. It would be permissible – and, indeed, *better* – to allow the six persons to die rather than to kill the one person in order to save them. This demonstrates an intuitive morally relevant distinction between *doing* something and *allowing* something to happen.

The Doctrine of Doing and Allowing

Consider two cases, first presented by Philippa Foot: Rescue I and Rescue II.[2] In the case of Rescue I, our options are to either save five people from drowning in one place or save one person from drowning in another place. We cannot save all six. In Rescue II, the only way to save the five who are drowning is to quickly drive over to where they are located. However, this necessitates running over a person in the

---

[2] Philippa Foot, "Killing and Letting Die," reprinted in Bonnie Steinbock and Alastair Norcross, *Killing and Letting Die* (New York: Fordham University Press, 1994), pp. 280–9.

road, thereby killing him. If we stop to pull him off the road, then by the time we get to them the five will have drowned. Most people have the view that it would be best to save the five in Rescue I, but quite the opposite in Rescue II. The challenge, then, is to explain the disparity in intuitions in a way that would also justify the saving of the five in Rescue I, but would rule out the saving of the five in Rescue II. The distinction between *doing* something and *allowing it to happen* is supposed to underlie the intuitions in these cases. The idea is that there is a morally relevant difference between doing something that harms or benefits someone as opposed to simply allowing it to happen. In the case of harming, it is considered worse to actively harm than to allow a harm to happen. Thus, in Rescue I, when we save the five as opposed to the one, we are not harming the person who is not saved – we simply allow him to die. However, in Rescue II, if we have to run him over to save the five – that is much worse, because we are actively harming him, and not simply allowing him to die. He would not have died but for our intervention. The moral relevance of this distinction is often taken as evidence against consequentialism – the charge is that the consequentialist is committed to regarding Rescue I and Rescue II as morally equivalent – so if we save the five in Rescue I then we save the five in Rescue II. Thus, if they really were not morally equivalent, then this would seem to count against the consequentialist. Foot's own analysis is not that doing/allowing *per se* is relevant, but that we need to make a distinction between negative and positive duties and rights to understand why there is a morally relevant difference between the two sorts of cases. Negative rights are rights to noninterference from others, for example, and positive rights include the right to be aided – what she terms the "rights to goods or services..."[3] Negative rights are weightier than positive rights, so more is required to justify interfering with someone than is required to justify a failure to render aid to him. In the case of Rescue I, we have two positive rights that conflict; thus, saving five takes precedence over saving one. However, in Rescue II there is a conflict between a positive and a negative right; and since negative rights are weightier, we ought to avoid harming the one even if that means that we fail to aid the five.

The philosopher Warren Quinn (d.1991) analyzed these types of cases in a similar way, also noting a distinction between positive and

[3] Foot, "Killing and Letting Die," p. 284.

negative rights. Again, the positive right to be aided is more easily overridden than the negative right not to be harmed by another person. Quinn's analysis rests on the idea that this distinction is morally significant because respect for negative rights is very important to a person's sense of moral autonomy. It is very important to human dignity that we recognize a person's right to not be interfered with mentally or physically, even for the sake of the greater good. Decisions relating to personal harm must be the potentially harmed agent's to make. Otherwise, we have a serious violation of the agent's autonomy and personal dignity.[4]

Some writers have regarded the doctrine of doing and allowing as underlying another distinction – that of *killing* versus *letting die*. Intuitively, there does seem to be a morally relevant difference between actually killing someone as opposed to letting the person die. Killing seems worse than merely letting die. Since consequentialists will generally deny this, because they are committed to negative responsibility, this is often taken as a problem for consequentialism. If I kill someone, then I intend for that person to die; whereas if I simply don't act so as to save someone, I don't necessarily intend that person's death – I merely foresee it. There is something much worse about actually pushing someone over a cliff and killing him than watching him fall off the cliff without trying to save him. Both actions may be bad, but the first seems worse (even though the effects of the action and inaction are the same – the person is dead).

But, as James Rachels (1941–2003) has pointed out, this asymmetry may simply be an illusion caused by the fact that when we think of people killing others we think of people with horrible motives and intentions; whereas when we think of people as letting others die we tend to think of passive people who have no active interest in bad things happening. But this is to think of the distinction without holding the factors in the cases constant – a methodological error. Rachels asks us to consider two contrasting cases in which relevant factors are held constant:

[4] Warren Quinn, "Actions, Intentions, and Consequences: The Doctrine of Doing and Allowing," *The Philosophical Review*, 99, 1990, pp. 131–55; reprinted in *Ethics: Problems and Principles*, edited by John Martin Fischer and Mark Ravizza (Orlando, FL: Harcourt Brace Jovanovich, 1992), pp. 145–61.

In the first, Smith stands to gain a large inheritance if anything should happen to his six-year-old cousin. One evening while the child is taking his bath, Smith sneaks into the bathroom and drowns the child, and then arranges things so that it will look like an accident.

In the second, Jones also stands to gain if anything should happen to his six-year-old cousin. Like Smith, Jones sneaks in planning to drown the child in his bath. However, just as he enters the bathroom Jones sees the child slip and hit his head, and fall face down in the water. Jones is delighted; he stands by, ready to push the child's head back under if it is necessary, but it is not necessary. With only a little thrashing about, the child drowns all by himself, "accidentally," as Jones watches and does nothing.[5]

As Rachels notes, in the first case Smith kills, whereas in the second case, Jones lets die. Yet we don't want to say that Smith acted less badly than Jones. What these cases show is that our intuitions are affected by whether or not the agent has bad motives or intentions, or plans to carry out his intentions, and so on. Thus, there is no morally relevant distinction between killing and letting die *per se*. This would have implications for medical practice. As Rachels points out, many people are opposed to voluntary active euthanasia, but not to voluntary passive euthanasia. Active euthanasia involves actually killing the sick individual, whereas passive euthanasia involves simply letting the person die – not treating the person, failing to act so as to prolong that person's life. Many people think that killing someone is always worse than simply letting someone die, and this is why active euthanasia is wrong even though passive euthanasia can be permissible under some circumstances. But if the above cases are taken seriously, then it looks as though this does not hold up to careful scrutiny. In genuine cases of euthanasia, the motive for killing is humanitarian – it is to spare the patient much unwanted suffering. This is surely a good motive. Further, if we view the end as a good end – that is, if we think it good that the patient got what he wanted and was spared the suffering – then it seems as though voluntary active euthanasia would be justified in cases in which we think voluntary passive euthanasia would be justified as well. Indeed, given that passive euthanasia will often involve

[5] James Rachels, "Active and Passive Euthanasia," *New England Journal of Medicine*, 292, 1975 (January 9).

allowing patients to starve themselves to death, or experience more suffering before they die, active euthanasia may even be morally preferable to passive euthanasia in some circumstances.

Other writers have attacked Rachels's claim. Warren Quinn points out that this type of case only works to show that harming and allowing harm can both be bad – even extremely bad – but that this doesn't undercut the asymmetry since the distinction has to do with degrees of badness. So most might still regard the cousin with murderous intentions who actually murders as doing something that is worse than the cousin with murderous intentions who allows his intended victim to die, though this is really horrible as well.

But it has also been pointed out that there are situations in which letting die is equivalent to killing, morally. John Harris notes that if a physician were to fail to treat a patient, thus allowing the patient to die, that would be the same as killing.[6] Is it as bad as some other form of killing that is more active? Maybe not. However, the fact that we view some lettings die as killings does serve to undercut the basic distinction. Then, the issue of how bad a particular action is can be ascertained on other grounds.

The Doctrine of Double Effect

To what extent should our choices be guided by our perception of what will happen as a result of our actions, even if we don't *intend* those effects? Answers to this question have serious implications for moral practice. Another principle relies on a distinction between what an agent intends and what an agent foresees. This is the *doctrine of double effect* (DDE). The actions that we perform tend to have more effects than those that are intended by us. Sometimes we can foresee these unintended effects, or "side-effects," of our actions. The DDE recognizes a morally relevant distinction between what we intend to do and what we merely foresee will happen as a result of our actions. Intending to harm someone may be morally impermissible,

[6] John Harris, "The Survival Lottery," *Philosophy*, 50, 1975, pp. 81–8; excerpt reprinted in *Utilitarianism and its Critics*, edited by Jonathan Glover (New York: Macmillan, 1990), pp. 123–30.

for example, while simply foreseeing the very same harm as a result of our actions may be permissible. This may be because intending a harm may be worse than simply foreseeing that a harm will result from our actions. Consider cases that commonly come up in war. Suppose that a general wants to knock out a munitions factory that is producing weapons for the enemy. He will be deploying aircraft in the region to drop bombs on the factory to destroy it. He does not intend to kill any innocent civilians. However, he knows that it is impossible to rule out civilian losses in these cases – he knows that some innocent people will die as a result of the bombing. Should he go ahead and bomb, or not? Most people do think that there are some circumstances that might justify loss of innocent life, but is there an intuitively plausible principle that underlies this conviction? The principle usually cited in these cases is the DDE, which holds – very roughly – that it may sometimes be permissible to perform an action with bad effects as long as those effects are not intended, but instead are merely foreseen. Weaker versions of the doctrine just hold that intended harms are worse than merely foreseen harms. Thus, if the general truly does not intend to kill innocent civilians, but merely foresees that some will die as a result of his actions, he has done nothing wrong: his action in dropping the bomb under those circumstances is permissible. Of course, some qualifications on this will be in order. Suppose that Maria intends to heat up some water for her tea, and to that end she wants to plug her teakettle in and turn it on. However, suppose she is also aware that a mad scientist has hooked up the outlet so that if she were to turn the teakettle on and get her hot water, as a side-effect she would electrocute 10 innocent people. Is it permissible for her to go ahead and turn the teakettle on? Clearly the answer is "No,"even if she is not intending and merely foresees the deaths. Because of this sort of problem, a constraint of *proportionality* has to be placed on the DDE.

The constraints that are generally placed on double effect are the following:

1 The agent acting must have good intentions and be trying to achieve a good end.
2 The agent does not want the bad consequences that he foresees; if there were any way to achieve the good end without generating the bad consequences, the agent would choose that way.

3   The bad consequences that the agent foresees are not sought by the agent, either as an end or as a means to the agent's good end.
4   The good end is in proportion to the bad consequences the agent foresees as a result of pursuing the end.[7]

The first is justified by noting that good intentions are often taken as absolutely necessary to right action.[8] The second offers a test that the act must pass – we can tell that an agent sincerely does not intend the effects if he would try to avoid them or mitigate them when possible or realistically feasible. The third constraint is intended to rule out impermissible "using" of another person. Suppose that I see a car getting ready to hit two people who are crossing the road, and I know that if I push the person standing next to me into the road, the car will hit him instead and spare the other two. I cannot appeal to double effect to justify this. I cannot say "I did not intend to kill him, I only foresaw that would happen; if there were some other less harmful way to save the two lives I would have done that instead." The third constraint will rule out that kind of rationale because I am *using* the bystander as a *means* to save the lives of the other two people, and that is impermissible. Given these sorts of constraints on the doctrine, we can see that actually applying it (as opposed to using it as a *post hoc* justification) will be tricky. One way to mark the distinction between intention and foresight is to argue that when we actually intend to harm someone we are displaying an "attraction" to badness – a desire for it, whereas when we simply foresee bad side-effects of our actions, there is no such implication.

But many philosophers have pointed out that the DDE doesn't seem to really capture our common-sense intuitions in a range of cases. For

---

[7] For a discussion of these types of constraints on the doctrine, see Nancy Ann Davis's "The Doctrine of Double Effect: Problems of Interpretation", *Pacific Philosophical Quarterly*, 65, 1984, pp. 107–23; reprinted in *Ethics: Problems and Principles*, edited by John Martin Fischer and Mark Ravizza (Fort Worth, TX: Harcourt Brace Jovanovich, 1992), pp. 199–212.

[8] Not everybody agrees. An objective consequentialist might argue that the agent's state of mind is not relevant, at least subjectively. If we interpret "good intention" objectively, then subjective theorists might not agree. So point 1 is open to some interpretation.

example, consider the well-discussed contrast between the two cases "Transplant" and "Hospital."[9] Most people would agree that killing one person to transplant his organs into five other people who need them, in order to save their lives, is impermissible. It is wrong even though we are killing one to save five. It is wrong because – to appeal to one insight embodied by the DDE – in this "Transplant" case we are intending to kill the one; we are using his death as a means of saving the other lives. However, contrast this case with "Hospital." Five people are in the hospital awaiting a cure for an illness that, untreated, would kill them. The medicine they require can only be manufactured in the hospital. However, a byproduct of the manufacturing process is a toxic gas, and in this case the toxic gas would leak into the room of a nearby patient, killing him (he cannot be moved). Again, most would argue that it would be impermissible to create the medicine, even though we are merely foreseeing that an innocent person will die in the process. It would seem that the DDE would justify the death, however, so critics argue that it cannot be right.

Thus, we may not recognize a morally relevant distinction between intention and foresight. A consequentialist will argue that foreseen consequences have the same moral weight. Even for the person who accepts the DDE, they have *some* weight – otherwise we wouldn't need the proportionality condition. But perhaps we could argue that the morally relevant distinction lies between intended consequences and foreseen but undesired ones. But this can be tricky to disentangle too. For example, Alison McIntyre considers a case in which we must choose between letting a train go down a particular track, which results in the destruction of an almost extinct variety of wildflower, versus diverting the train, which would save the flower but kill someone working on the other track. If we were to choose to save the flower, she notes that it seems just as reasonable to say of this case that we intend to harm the worker because we value the flower and want to save it (as a member of an almost extinct species). So, it isn't clear that we merely foresee the death of the workman as opposed to

---

[9] These cases are used by Philippa Foot. See her "The Problem of Abortion and the Doctrine of Double Effect," in *Virtues and Vices and Other Essays in Moral Philosophy* (Malden, MA: Blackwell, 1978), pp. 19–32; the examples are used at different points throughout the chapter.

intending it because we want to save the wildflower. This undercuts the intention/foresight distinction as well.[10]

For these reasons, the DDE is generally considered deeply problematic.

Other principles have been suggested as a way of providing conditions to regulate harm-doing. Some deontologists argue that the central problem with consequentialism is that it does not regard persons as fundamentally *inviolable*. We can call this approach *inviolabilism*. For example, Frances Kamm, in her work, has stressed inviolability as a way to ground constraints on maximizing the good. She offers the Principle of Permissible Harm (PPH):

> . . . it is permissible for (i) greater good and (ii) means that have greater good as their noncausal flip side to cause lesser evil, but not permissible to (iii) intend lesser evil as a means to greater good or to (iv) intend means that cause lesser evil as a foreseen side effect and have greater good as a mere causal effect unmediated by (ii). By "noncausal flip side," I mean that the greater good occurring is, in essence, another way of describing the situation in which the means occur.[11]

Consider "Hospital" again. The PPH could be used to show why manufacturing the medicine to save five at the cost of one life is not permissible. Even though saving five is a "greater good" numerically, this greater good is a "mere causal effect unmediated by (ii)." The PPH does allow harm under some circumstances, so one advantage of this principle is that it is not implausibly absolutist about duties to refrain from harming others.

Why do persons have this special status? After all, it is perfectly fine to destroy a rock to save a person, or even to save another rock. In fact, it is probably permissible to destroy a rock just for the fun of it (given that it doesn't belong to someone else, and so on). Many people also agree that it would be permissible to kill an animal, or perhaps even any number of animals, to save a person's life. Rocks and animals don't seem to have the same status as persons. Recall that a conse-

---

[10] Alison McIntyre, "Doing Away with Double Effect," *Ethics*, 111, 2001, p. 236.

[11] Frances Kamm, "Nonconsequentialism," in the *Blackwell Guide to Ethical Theory*, edited by Hugh LaFollette (Malden, MA: Blackwell, 2000), p. 214.

quentialist such as John Stuart Mill would argue that there is a morally relevant difference between rocks and animals, since rocks are not sentient. Further, there is a morally relevant difference between animals and persons, in that the quality of experience for persons is higher than that for animals. But the consequentialist would typically not hold persons to be completely inviolable: there will be circumstances under which it is morally justified to violate the right to life of an individual – to use the individual as a means of saving the world, for example.

Deontologists tend not to pick sentience as the morally relevant difference that underlies inviolability.[12] Instead, they tend to focus on Kantian views on the nature of worth and its connection to autonomy of the will. Persons are autonomous; they deliberate and make choices about what they are going to do. They respond to reasons. Rocks simply respond to physical causal forces; and animals are creatures of instinct only. Only persons reason and deliberate – and it is this that underlies their freedom. It also provides the basis for the respect that is owed to persons and which underlies their inviolability. The fact that persons have autonomous wills makes them the appropriate objects of this sort of respect.

It is quite true that persons are distinct from animals in that they have reasoning capacities that animals lack, and a consequentialist also would recognize that this underlies a distinctive sort of respect for persons. But the consequentialist would question whether that is enough to provide inviolability.

This approach to normative ethics has been criticized for relying on uncritical intuitions. This is because there is no underlying theory, no underlying explanation for the principles. Suppose that Martha has a crystal that turns red whenever she thinks about doing something wrong, and green whenever her intended action is permissible.[13] She thus employs the following principle of action: "When the crystal is red, the action is wrong; when the crystal is green, the action is permissible." She may be able to use the crystal and this principle as

---

[12] This is not universally the case. Tom Regan offers a deontological approach to animal rights in "The Case for Animal Rights," in *In Defense of Animals*, edited by Peter Singer (London: HarperCollins, 1985), pp. 15–26.

[13] I thank Keith DeRose for this example.

a guide to action, but she lacks any understanding of what makes the contemplated action either wrong or permissible. It would be odd to call this a theory, since a theory is supposed to provide a deeper understanding of justification of action. To justify the action by saying "The crystal was green" seems somehow unsatisfying. What was the crystal responding to? Why did it turn green? In the same spirit, we might ask about some of the suggested principles – What makes one kind of cause bad, and the other permissible?

To be fair, deontologists try to meet this challenge in ways suggested earlier in the chapter – by noting that the values that underlie deontological principles are respect for autonomous agency, and so forth. But unless these underlying values can be made clear, we simply get a mysterious principle supported by even more mysterious concepts.

Another problem has been to point out that this same reliance on intuitions – or, rather, an uncritical reliance on intuitions – is problematic since many of our intuitions seem inconsistent or incoherent. We are often affected by things that really don't seem morally relevant at all. This line of criticism has been influenced by work in psychology that demonstrates that a person's response to cases is heavily influenced by framing effects. The term "framing effects" refers to effects of context, or how a question is posed or worded to the agent who is being called upon for the intuitive response. So, for example, if extra payment for being late on your bill is framed as a "discount on the price if you pay on time," rather than as "interest on the late payment," then people generally find it more appealing, although the two may amount to the same thing. But framing a payment as just not getting the discount seems less upsetting than framing it as being charged interest.

Framing effects undoubtedly do influence our intuitions. And philosophers have all along noticed curious asymmetries in our intuitive responses. One classic example is one that Peter Singer uses to motivate his view that we have obligations to contribute to famine relief, and that such aid to the needy is a matter of duty, not charity. Singer asks us to suppose that we are walking by a puddle where a baby is drowning – surely we have an obligation to save the baby.[14] The

---

[14] Peter Singer, "Famine, Affluence, and Morality," *Philosophy and Public Affairs*, 1, 1972, pp. 229–43.

cost to us is very small, and the benefit to the baby is enormous. Most will agree with Singer here. Yet, in a similar case – where low cost can bring about great benefits – we seem to come to other conclusions. Most people also view giving even small amounts of money to help buy food for starving people as supererogatory, not obligatory. This is puzzling. Singer, of course, believes that we should reconcile these intuitions by appeal to utilitarian theory – so we do have obligations to the needy on his view. But intuitionistic approaches have no such theory to appeal to. It is for this reason that many ethicists favor the more theoretical approaches that can provide an underlying justification to our responses to these sorts of cases.

In the next chapter, we'll be taking a look at a tradition in ethical theory that has experienced a resurgence in the past couple of decades – virtue ethics. This approach treats virtue concepts as central to ethical theory in that a person's actions need to be evaluated in terms of either the persons' virtues or in terms of what a virtuous person would do. This makes character, rather than action, the central focus of the theory.

Further reading

Darwall, Stephen (ed.) 2003: *Deontology*. Malden, MA: Blackwell.

Fischer, John Martin and Ravizza, Mark (eds) 1992: *Ethics: Problems and Principles*. Fort Worth, TX: Harcourt Brace Jovanovich (this volume contains a full range of articles in this tradition).

Chapter 8

Virtue Ethics

Sometimes, in deciding on what we ought to do, we first consider how we ought to be. For example, if faced with a situation that involves social injustice, we might pick someone whom we admired and wanted to be like – Gandhi, let's say, or Mother Teresa – and then ask "What would Gandhi do?" This doesn't give us a rigid formula or decision procedure to employ. Instead, it asks us to consider a virtuous person, to consider his or her virtues, and then ask what behavior people with these good traits and dispositions exemplify. Some writers have thought that a picture like this better reflects how people should go about making their moral decisions. They should do so on the basis of concrete virtue judgments instead of abstract principles, such as "Maximize the good" or "Never treat another person merely as a means," and so forth.

Recall also that some writers found Kant's view of the role of emotion in moral life to be rather antiseptic. While Kant does regard the emotions as sometimes morally significant, they are only instrumentally significant on his account. Cheerfulness in doing our duty is good, but good only because it makes us more willing to do it – it makes duty come more easily to the virtuous person. Also, in spite of the work of Peter Railton and others, critics of consequentialism still view that theory as committed to the view that friends ought to view each other's value instrumentally – as a means of promoting the overall good. These are additional considerations that lead many writers to be unhappy with Kantian ethics and consequentialism.

This dissatisfaction with abstract principles that seem difficult to apply in practice, as well as theories that don't seem to allow room for emotions, or for norms of ethics that are partial rather than impartial, have led some contemporary writers to try to develop an alternative ethical theory that focuses on virtue evaluation – on evaluating the agent, and not merely the agent's actions. Of course, theories such as Kantian ethics and utilitarianism offer accounts of virtue evaluation, so what would make virtue ethics truly distinctive is the claim that virtue evaluation has *primacy* – that is, the normative concepts in the theory are defined in terms of virtue – so that, for example, right action is defined in terms of virtue, rather than virtue being defined in terms of right action.

Other writers have felt that we should turn to ethical practices of the past to find a theory that could be used to bring together disparate traditions and practices – and virtue ethics has actually been around in one form or another for thousands of years. Current virtue ethicists in fact tend to take their inspiration from Aristotle (382–322 BC), who was a student of Plato (428–348 BC), and certainly one of the greatest philosophers in the history of philosophy. Aristotle wrote the *Nicomachean Ethics*, which – as an aid to his son – spelled out the steps to a good life. Of course, "good" is a bit ambiguous – Is that morally good, or prudentially good, or intellectually good, or all of the above? Well, for Aristotle, the good human life had all these ingredients. A good human being was virtuous in the sense that he embodied all the excellences of human character.

So, Aristotle is often held up as a paradigmatic virtue ethicist. Again, though there is some lack of clarity about what exactly virtue ethics is committed to, it is generally agreed that virtue ethics maintains that character, human excellences, *virtues* are the basic modes of evaluation in the theory, as opposed to act evaluations such as "right" and "wrong." It is important to note that many virtue ethicists do not believe the theory to be *incompatible* with act evaluation at all.[1] Rather, act evaluation is to be understood *in terms of* character evaluation. Virtue is the primary mode of evaluation, and all other modes are understood and defined in terms of virtue. Thus, one popular version of virtue ethics defines right action in terms of virtue, rather than defining virtue in terms of right or good action. For example, Rosalind Hursthouse offers the following:

---

[1] The "eliminitavist" strategy is more associated with "anti-theory" or the view that we should do without moral theory altogether.

(RA) An action is right iff [if and only if] it is what a virtuous agent would, characteristically, do in the circumstances . . . [2]

This is a virtue ethical characterization of "right action" because the rightness of the action is explained in terms of virtue, and not the other way around. Most of the theoretical weight is therefore borne by the account of virtue provided in the theory. To unpack this account of right action, we need to know what the virtuous agent would do. We need to have an account of virtue that will give us some way to approach this issue.

Hursthouse herself adopts a broadly Aristotelian account (with some qualifications). On Aristotle's account of virtue, virtue is seen as a quality that leads to *eudaimonia*, or human well-being. Aristotle discussed two types of virtue: intellectual and moral virtue. Intellectual virtues are virtues conducive to certain kinds of knowledge, and there are two main intellectual virtues: theoretical wisdom and practical wisdom. *Practical* wisdom is important to our project here because Aristotle understood it to be necessary for moral virtue – moral virtue involves activity that leads to well-being and it is practical wisdom that enables the agent to figure out how to act well: " . . . a man of practical wisdom is he who has the ability to deliberate . . . it is a truthful characteristic of acting rationally in matters good and bad for man."[3]

Virtue is a mean state, which means that it does not exhibit excess. And practical wisdom comes into play since it is crucial for the virtuous person in choosing the mean:

> . . . virtue or excellence is a characteristic involving choice, and . . . it consists in observing the mean relative to us, a mean which is defined by a rational principle, such as a man of practical wisdom would use to determine it.[4]

There is a lot to unpack in this account. The virtuous agent chooses virtue and chooses to perform the virtuous action. Not only this, but

---

[2] Rosalind Hursthouse, *On Virtue Ethics* (New York: Oxford University Press, 1999), p. 79.

[3] Aristotle, *Nicomachean Ethics*, translated by Martin Ostwald (Indianapolis, IN: Bobbs-Merrill, 1962), pp. 152–3.

[4] Aristotle, *Nicomachean Ethics*, p. 43.

the virtuous agent in choosing exhibits practical wisdom, knowledge of what he is doing and why it is good. This entails that the virtuous agent cannot act out of ignorance; otherwise, he would not be genuinely choosing and would not be exhibiting practical wisdom. The virtuous agent has to be aware of the nature of the choices that he is making. Here's an example to help illustrate what Aristotle believed: Suppose that there are two individuals, Al and Barb. Al is a naturally good person who enjoys helping others – he isn't too bright, but his nature is such that he ends up helping people simply out of the kindness of his heart. This kindness on his part is not cultivated; it is just part of his personality, his basic nature. Barb, on the other hand, is also a kind person, but someone who has worked at it by developing good habits. She is good because she chose to be – she rationally and reflectively endorsed virtue and set out on a path to be virtuous. She might have been helped along by having good parents who instilled good values, but still the choice was hers to make when she grew up, and was able to rationally reflect on her own character and make decisions about what to endorse and what to work on improving. On Aristotle's view, Al is someone who has natural goodness, but no true virtue. Barb, on the other hand, has genuine virtue because she has chosen virtue; she has displayed practical wisdom. Al has not, and so his goodness, in a way, is accidental. It may have turned out that Al just happens to be nice and does nice things for others, but without the guidance of practical wisdom and common sense, Al is operating by a kind of mindless instinct that is actually dangerous:

> ... it is true that children and beasts are endowed with natural qualities or characteristics, but it is evident that without intelligence these are harmful... as in the case of a mighty body which, when it moves without vision, comes down to a mighty fall because it cannot see... just as there exist two kinds of quality, cleverness and practical wisdom, in that part of us which forms opinions... so also there are two kinds of quality in the moral part of us, natural virtue and virtue in the full sense.[5]

The analogy with vision is important. One way to understand Aristotle's account of how the virtuous person, as opposed to the nonvirtuous

---

[5] Aristotle, *Nicomachean Ethics*, pp. 170–1.

person, arrives at correct moral judgments is via *perception* of what is morally relevant in the context of making that judgment. On this view, Aristotle is a kind of particularist about moral judgment – about how reasons work in justifying our actions. The person who is well trained, or who has been brought up well by her parents and received the right sort of education, will have developed this perceptual capacity. She will be able to see that a given course of action is wrong, or inappropriate, in much the same way that an interior designer can look at some rocks and tell the difference between granite and slate, and that one is good for countertops and the other for mud rooms.

Practical wisdom is good deliberation that ends in judgments, well-considered judgments, of what we ought to do and how we ought to live. That is why it is termed "practical" and is generally contrasted with "theoretical wisdom," which is wisdom that does not concern action, but rather contemplation – figuring out interesting abstract problems, for example – or understanding, which has to do with comprehending something that has been written or what someone has said, but does not itself result in a judgment of action, a judgment about what we should *do*. This is important because on Aristotle's view virtue crucially involves activity. The brave person chooses the path between rashness and cowardice and acts accordingly – he doesn't simply pass judgment on what we ought to do in his circumstances – that judgment results in action. Otherwise, persons who are weak-willed, who believe or know what they ought to do but fail to do it, would count as virtuous.

Aristotle famously believed in the claim that virtue is a mean state, that it lies between two opposed vices. This is referred to as the doctrine of the mean. The basic idea is that virtue will tend to lie between two extremes, each of which is a vice. So, bravery lies between cowardice and foolhardiness; temperance lies between gluttony and abstinence; and so forth. Some virtues can be hard to model on this view. Take honesty. Of course, failure to tell the truth – telling a lie – would be one extreme, but is there a vice of telling too much truth? Maybe . . . though I suspect there might be some disagreement over this. Part of the mean state concerned our emotions, however, and not just our actions. The virtuous person not only does the right thing, but he does the right thing in the right way – in the right sort of emotional or psychological state. Our emotions can be excessive or deficient as well. The person who runs into the battle to fight, but who is excessively fearful, is not fully virtuous. The truly well-functioning person is able to control and regulate his feelings and emotions, as well as act rightly.

Aristotle's picture, then, of the virtuous person is the person who functions harmoniously – his desires and emotions do not conflict with what he knows to be right. They go together. This leads him to view a person who acts rightly, but who feels badly about it, as not being virtuous. This person is merely "continent" – this person can control his actions, but needs to work on bringing his emotions in line with what reason tells him is the right and appropriate thing to do. So the excellent human being is not conflicted; he does not suffer inner turmoil and the struggle between reason and passion.

As a matter of historical fact, Aristotle's account of virtue suffered from prejudices that were rampant in Ancient Greece. He believed that slaves and women, for example, being defective reasoners, could not possess full virtue. They might possess imperfect forms of virtue, appropriate to their station in life, but not full human excellence:

> In the soul the difference between ruler and ruled is that between the rational and the non-rational. It is therefore clear that in other connexions also there will be natural differences. And so generally in cases of ruler and ruled; the differences will be natural but they need not be the same. For rule of free over slave, male over female, man over boy, all are natural, but they are also different, because, while parts of the soul are present in each case, the distribution is different. Thus the deliberative faculty in the soul is not present at all in a slave; in a female it is inoperative, in a child undeveloped. We must therefore take it that the same conditions prevail also in regard to the ethical virtues, namely that all must participate in them but not to the same extent, but only as may be required by each for his proper function.[6]

Modern Aristotelian virtue ethicists such as Hursthouse reject this feature of Aristotle's theory. It is anachronistic and completely misinformed. Slavery and the inherent inferiority of some persons on the basis of race, nationality, and gender are rejected by neo-Aristotelians. Everyone has the same chance at goodness, limited only by, perhaps, things such as the circumstances under which they were raised and the sort of moral education they received as children. But, they argue, the

---

[6] Aristotle, *Politics*, translated by T. A. Sinclair (Harmondsworth, UK: Penguin, 1962), pp. 51–2.

broad framework set up by Aristotle is still correct. Rational excellence is crucial to *eudaimonia* and to moral virtue. From a certain perspective, we can see why this feature would be appealing. After all, when we look at what separates humans from animals, it is the capacity for reason – this is a sort of "functioning" that seems unique and distinctive to humans. So shouldn't reasoning excellence be part of human excellence and thus a crucial component of moral virtue? This reflects a strong strain of naturalism that runs through Aristotle's philosophy. If we look at human nature, and what marks us off from the rest of nature, we see that we have this capacity that other animals lack and that is of crucial importance to our concept of being a good person, a person who functions well and realizes the full potential of his or her distinctive capabilities. And he is right that most people do think that we ought to work at developing our intellects: education, intellectual self-improvement – these are viewed as good things. On the Aristotelian view, they are good because they improve our lives by making us better people. Note the similarity with John Stuart Mill's modified hedonism. Like Aristotle, Mill placed a premium on the development of the intellect – however, his rationale was somewhat different. On his view, this would lead to better sorts of pleasures. Still, some have argued that what Mill had been adopting in his own theory was a sort of Aristotelian *perfectionism*, and that he really wasn't a true hedonist. Aristotle's account is called "perfectionist" because it treats the good for humans as a perfection of their distinctive capacities – in his case, their rational capacities. The brand of perfectionism favored by Aristotle has been subject to considerable attack. It depends upon holding the view that there is a human nature and that what is good for humans depends upon developing our natural and distinctive capacities – our "essential" features, if you will. But that we have such "essential" human natures, and that it is somehow developing them that makes our lives go well, both seem rather dubious. Perhaps if we understood the essentialism in extremely general and vague terms it might be right, but then has very little content. But even if we accepted this, many would challenge the claim that developing our essential human capacities makes us good – including morally good. So, for example, suppose that "jealousy" is an essential human emotion – indeed, it is hard to imagine a person who does not ever experience it under completely understandable circumstances. We still might disapprove of it and its expression on moral grounds.

Virtue Ethics

On the Aristotelian view, moral virtue is chosen, virtuous acts
themselves are the result of deliberation and choice, and the agents
so deliberating are good deliberators – they possess practical wisdom
that allows them to make the correct decisions about what they ought
to do. In spelling out Aristotle's view, some writers have made use of a
perceptual analogy: morally virtuous agents are correct perceivers –
they are the ones to correctly see what is morally relevant in a given
context, and they act according to the perceptual knowledge they have
acquired. So it is really clear that on Aristotle's view there are a lot of
psychological requirements for moral virtue.

One controversial feature of tying practical wisdom so closely to
virtue is that it seems to commit the account to a *unity of the virtues*
thesis. Practical wisdom is sufficient for being virtuous and it is also
necessary: anyone who truly possesses the ability to deliberate well
about practical matters and correctly figure out what he ought to do,
and when, has moral virtue. Further, anyone who does not have this
ability does not have true virtue – he may have some kind of imperfect
virtue, or "natural" virtue, but is not true moral virtue. But what this
means is that if someone has one virtue, through practical wisdom,
then he's going to have all of them, because the same good deliberation
that underlies one virtue will underlie all of them. If practical wisdom is
necessary and sufficient for one virtue – such as kindness – it will be
sufficient for all of them. So the kind person will also be courageous
and just and exhibit the proper amount of pride, and so on. This is the
unity of the virtues thesis – that they go together, they are united, and
to have one virtue is to have them all. Thus, there are no courageous
thieves and liars. There are no generous people who are cowards.
There are no irresponsible, but noble and self-sacrificing, individuals.
And therein lies the oddity.

Aristotle also developed an account of friendship that has been very
influential. He incorporated into this account of friendship elements of
his view of moral virtue. He claims that there are basically three
distinct types of friendship: (i) friendship based on utility; (ii) friendship
based on pleasure; and (iii) friendship based on virtue. Type (i) is the
sort of friendship we might have with a business acquaintance, for
example. It survives as long as the business relationship survives, but
its purpose is simply to facilitate the business – we don't have an
interest in this sort of friend for his own sake. Type (ii) is closer to
what we think of as friendship. This friendship is the sort we have with

someone who is fun to hang out with – maybe he has a great sense of humor, or maybe he always has good tickets to the opera. In any case, the reason for the friendship is simply that it is pleasurable and if that were to cease, the friendship would cease. It is type (iii) that constitutes perfect friendship, and this sort of friendship can only exist between perfectly virtuous individuals. We need to accept Aristotle's unity of the virtues claim in order to find this picture of friendship at least initially plausible. This is because, on his view, having one virtue means that we have practical wisdom, which means that we have all the virtues. Thus, on his view, the issue of partly virtuous friends does not arise. But for this very reason the account seems implausible upon reflection, because most of us are familiar with virtuous people who are good friends with only partly virtuous people. You may, for example, have a friend with character flaws, but who also has very admirable quality traits – perhaps he's too gruff with people, for example, but you know that when they really need help he's always there to help them. Though you see room for improvement, this does not get in the way of the friendship, and your desire for that person's good. Aristotle might respond that this is really one of the other sorts of friendship – based on utility or pleasure. But those relationships are not marked by desire for that sort of friend's good for its own sake. So, at the very least, Aristotle's classification of friendships does not seem exhaustive or complete.

At the opening of this chapter, I noted that many people were attracted to virtue ethics out of dissatisfaction with impartialist ethics. So, what advantage here does virtue ethics offer? Well, there's no foundational commitment to impartiality. There will be virtues of friendship – appropriate traits to embody in the context of friendship, just as there will be different virtues appropriate to judges, or members of juries, or politicians. Not all virtues need embody impartiality to have moral worth and significance. On Hursthouse's view, if I want to know what to do as a good friend I ask myself what the virtuous person would do in the circumstances – visit the friend in the hospital as opposed (let's say) to working on the Oxfam phone line, which might actually promote more impartial or neutral good. This does raise a tricky issue about conflicts among the virtues – Doesn't the friendship virtue conflict with the civic virtue? In which case, how do you choose? I believe that Hursthouse's answer to this is that either action would be right – so there can be many "right" actions in a given context.

A number of other problems have been raised for the Aristotelian and neo-Aristotelian account of virtue. First of all, it is certainly a highly intellectualist account of virtue. If we view virtue as necessarily involving *correct* perception of what is morally relevant, then some traits that we intuitively think of as virtues would not qualify. Think of a trait such as *modesty*. Surely *sometimes*, anyway, people are modest because they lack a full and correct understanding of how good they are, or how skilled they are, or how significant their research is. Albert Einstein, for example, apparently had a relatively modest view of his own accomplishments. Though he thought well of his work, of course, there were others he thought superior. This seems a case of modesty where the person is making a mistake, an epistemic error – that is, an error in belief about how well his work stacks up against others. Since this would involve a failure of reason – a failure to perceive correctly, on Aristotle's account – it could not count as a moral virtue.

Further, the correct perception requirement raises the issue of whether or not anyone has ever really been virtuous – Isn't it reasonable to assume that we all make moral mistakes of some sort?[7] For example, the Ancient Greeks seemed to believe that slavery was morally permissible and that women should be sequestered. These are clearly moral errors. Does this mean that no Greeks were ever virtuous *at all*, or in any respect whatsoever, because they lacked correct perception in some area, and thus lacked true practical wisdom? This seems rather harsh. Indeed, this has led some commentators on virtue ethics to note that virtue ethics isn't very practicable in a heterogeneous society.[8] Suppose that Sheila and Ron are arguing about – let's say – capital punishment. Sheila favors it, but only for the punishment of the most heinous crimes. Ron is against it altogether, arguing that it is cruel and unusual punishment, and that the state should not be involved in administering death under any circumstances whatsoever. Each has arguments to support his or her view. There is no doubt that their opinions on this matter are quite different, and yet, at least in contemporary liberal discourse, we wouldn't want to say that either was unreasonable, even if one of them at least must surely be mistaken.

---

[7] Michael Slote makes this kind of argument in "Is Virtue Possible?" *Analysis*, 42, March 1982, pp. 70–6.

[8] J. B. Schneewind makes this argument in "The Misfortunes of Virtue," *Ethics*, 101, 1990, pp. 42–63.

Aristotle's correct perception view of virtue would make it the case that at least one of them – the one who fails to see some morally relevant consideration with respect to capital punishment in a particular case – must lack virtue. And thus, each person, convinced that he or she is right, if they accept this view, must regard the other not only as mistaken but as also lacking in virtue. Again, this seems rather harsh. Ron may think Sheila to be misguided, and perhaps as someone who puts a bit too much weight on deterrence arguments – and still view her as a good and virtuous person who is, in good faith and responsibly, trying to decide on a complex issue of justice.

These sorts of cases make a more fragmented view of virtue a bit more appealing. People may have moral blind spots, but they can still possess some virtues. So, for example, a man may be insensitive to his children, and thus not be a good father, and yet still be generous in helping the poor. Most of our experience of the people around us is like this. We rarely will have experience of anyone who we think is morally perfect.

Of course, the virtue ethicists could still maintain this very intellec-tualist view and hold that virtue ethics offers us an ideal to strive for, even if it cannot realistically be obtained. But we might instead try to soften the Aristotelian picture and not have such stringent require-ments for the virtuous person.

Recall that Rosalind Hursthouse has offered an account of "right action" that is Aristotelian. She is one modern theorist who is sensitive to some of the problems raised for the Aristotelian account and wants to offer a version that can avoid some of them. For example, she believes that the view can in fact guide our actions by providing a decision procedure as well as a criterion for act evaluation. The right action is the one the virtuous person would perform. However, a standard problem for her account of right action via virtue has to do with giving an account of why the virtuous agent would do what she does. Is it simply the case that whatever the virtuous agent character-istically does is right, which seems capricious, or is it the case that the virtuous agent picks up on reasons that are morally significant and that justify the action in question – in which case it is those reasons that determine the moral quality of the action, and appeals to the virtuous agent are redundant? Recall from Chapter 2 that divine command theory suffered from a similar problem. Surely the virtuous person is responding to reasons that make one act morally preferable over the other available options – perhaps considerations of human dignity and respect, or considerations of good consequences, or a mixture of different reasons, weighed appropriately. In any case, it is these reasons that justify the action as right – it is not that the virtuous agent wills them to be right by fiat. So, these justifying reasons make up the raw materials for a normative ethical theory and we can bypass theoretical appeals to the virtuous agent altogether. Here's an analogy. Suppose that we accept the following for water safety: "Safe water is water the Environmental Protection Agency (EPA) says is fine to drink." It may be good for me to abide by this and only drink water that meets EPA standards, but the EPA does not will water with a certain composition safe or unsafe. Instead, the EPA monitors contaminants in the water and studies their toxicity levels, and on that basis decides what is safe and what is unsafe. The true account of water safety, then, involves an account of these contaminants and their toxicity levels for humans – it need make no reference to the EPA at all.

Humean Virtue Ethics

Until a few years ago, this chapter could have been titled "Neo-Aristotelian Ethics," since virtue ethics seemed to entirely draw its inspiration from Aristotle. This, however, has recently changed. David Hume (1711–76) was another philosopher who wrote on virtue and some recent virtue ethicists have looked to his work for ideas about how to develop a virtue ethics. Hume's account differs from that of Aristotle in that Hume views virtues as mental qualities that are pleasing; and they are pleasing (at least in part) because they are conducive to social utility in some respect. Thus, he places no heavy psychological requirements on virtue. Having a virtue just means that one has a pleasing quality (with certain caveats on what counts as "pleasing"). The virtuous person needn't have wisdom or intelligence, though they themselves will count as intellectual virtues because they are pleasing and useful qualities. Hume's account does depend upon a certain view of human nature; the view that we are the sorts of creatures moved by feelings of sympathy for others, as well as concern for ourselves. He rejects the Hobbesian view of human nature that is egoist. In the *Treatise*, Hume writes of selfishness:

I am sensible, that, generally speaking, the representations of this quality have been carried much too far; and that the descriptions, which
certain philosophers delight so much to form mankind in this particular,
are as wide of nature as any accounts of monsters, which we meet with
in fables and romances. So far from thinking, that men have no affection
for any thing beyond themselves, I am of opinion, that tho' it be rare to
meet with one, who loves any single person better than himself; yet 'tis
as rare to meet with one, in whom all the kind affections, taken together,
do not over-balance all the selfish.[9]

Hume believed that people are motivated by self-interest, but that they
are also motivated by love and sympathy for others. It is this sympathy
that forms the basis for morality. We judge things to be morally good or
bad, virtuous or vicious, on the basis of our sympathy with others. The
pain of another person is bad, and when I see this I react sympathetically to the person. For example, I would probably feel pity for a person
I saw in pain. Suppose that I saw someone evil in pain, someone who
had tortured thousands of innocent people. Wouldn't I feel pleasure
rather than pity in this case? Perhaps so, but Hume could explain this as
a product of my sympathy for his victims. That feeling would depend on
the extent to which I thought he deserved the pain he was feeling.

Hume also believed that when we make moral evaluations of people,
what we are concerned most about are their motives. A person's
actions just give us evidence of the person's motives. Some have
interpreted Hume as arguing that the primary focus of moral evaluation is motives – internal states of the agent associated with virtue, or
having good character traits. The pleasing motives are the virtuous
ones; the ones associated with sympathy, directly or indirectly. For
example, when Arthur helps his elderly neighbor with groceries, we
might naturally infer that Albert is motivated by benevolence and
kindness – we find this pleasing, out of sympathy with the elderly
neighbor who is being helped. On Hume's view, if we had no sympathy
at all with others, we would not be capable of moral judgment. So his
view of moral judgment is dependent on assumptions about human
nature. Recall that Kant had a very different view: moral judgment is a
matter of reason – if anything, sympathy can get in the way.

[9] David Hume, *Treatise of Human Nature*, edited by L. A. Selby-Bigge and P. H.
Nidditch (Oxford: Clarendon Press, 1978), pp. 486–7.

One contemporary virtue ethicist, Michael Slote, picks up on this feature of Hume's account to argue for a kind of virtue sentimentalism. On his view, the wrong action is the one that is not properly motivated. An action must be motivated by warm benevolence to be motivated properly, and a failure to be so motivated makes the action wrong.[10]

One appealing feature of this approach is that it can be used to provide a theoretical underpinning to a care approach in ethics (to be discussed further in Chapter 9). While this work was pioneered by feminist writers, Slote believes that the theoretical framework of this approach can be articulated with virtue ethics, so that ethics of care could be formulated along virtue-ethical lines. Since Hume seems to hold the view that as a matter of our nature we are benevolent beings, and that we also make moral judgments based on this – since our sympathy is responsible for the benevolent motives we have – this means that our caring for others is part of our nature as well. And, on a Humean view, it is the part of our nature associated with morality. The worry, I think, for anyone attempting to derive an ethics of care from Hume, however, is that Hume himself was well aware of the dangers of too much partialism. On his account, correct moral judgment is not simply given in our emotional responses to others – true, we need those to begin with, to even get started in making moral judgments, but these responses need to be corrected in order to give us reliable judgments. Hume suggests that this correction takes place when we regard the trait we are judging from "the general point of view" and not simply from our own particular situation. Thus, I may actually be alarmed and upset when I see how brave my enemy is – but, *from the general point of view*, abstracted from my own interests, I can see that this bravery is indeed admirable. However, it would be possible to reject this feature of Hume's analysis and still retain some of the structure of his account of virtue.

Criticism

Many challenges have been posed to virtue ethics in general, as well as to the specific approaches outlined in this chapter. One *general* criticism of the whole approach is that it fails to conform to what we know

---

[10] Michael Slote, *Morals from Motives* (Oxford: Oxford University Press, 2001).

about how best to explain human behavior in light of recent experimental findings in psychology. This is a very exciting area in philosophy today. It is interesting in part because we can see how experimental evidence can be brought to bear in either shoring up or ruling out certain normative ethical theories. Although this is highly controversial and the subject of much current debate, one such challenge is that posed by situationism in social psychology.

This is the view that the best explanation for the virtuous behavior we observe someone perform is the situation the agent finds herself in, not her "character traits," or at least character traits of a robust sort that can span widely varying contexts.

For example, researchers have found "...subjects near a fragrant bakery or coffee shop more likely to change a dollar bill when asked than those near a neutral-smelling dry goods store."[11] Whether or not we are smelling something nice is seemingly irrelevant to justification of our benevolent action, yet is causally responsible for the benevolent action. So, some people just smell a lot more cookies than others and they act more nicely – Is the best explanation for their behavior a virtue, or the fact that they live above a bakery? It looks as though situational circumstances are much better predictors of behavior – so that seems to be bad news for virtue. If we don't need to appeal to virtues to explain behavior, they don't serve any theoretical function. We have no reason to believe that they actually exist either, since all the behavioral regularities that we observe in people can be better explained in terms of consistent situational factors. If there are no virtues, it looks as though there can't be any virtue ethics – it would be a bit odd to base our normative ethical theory on appealing to normatively significant things that don't actually exist. This is the view that Gilbert Harman endorses.[12] A virtue ethicist could respond in a variety of ways. The first is to accept the evidence of social psychology and claim that virtue ethics offers a "regulative ideal" of behavior. Even if no one is really virtuous, the virtuous ideal can still

[11] John Doris, *Lack of Character: Personality and Moral Behaviour* (Cambridge, UK: Cambridge University Press, 2002), p. 31.

[12] Gilbert Harman, "Moral Philosophy Meets Social Psychology: Virtue Ethics and the Fundamental Attribution Error," *Proceedings of the Aristotelian Society*, 99, 1999, pp. 315–31.

guide us in our actions. For example, someone might think that it would be impossible for a real person to be like the fictitious accounts of heroes that we read about in comic books, or the gods of Greek mythology – and yet argue that, to the extent that we can, we should use these paradigms as guides to our actions.

Another strategy is, of course, to deny the significance of this research to virtue ethics. We could try to point out methodological problems with the experiments. However, there are so many different experiments that it becomes difficult to knock them all out on methodological grounds.

We could also try to argue that the evidence provided is not sufficient for the radical conclusion that Harman wants to draw. But this could still pose some difficulties for virtue ethics. For example, John Doris proposes that the globalism of traditional virtue ethics be rejected.[13] There is no one "honesty" trait, for example. Instead, we may have 50 or more "honesties"; that is, narrowly circumscribed traits or dispositions to tell the truth. So, Joe might not have honesty 1, which is the disposition to tell the truth about how well he does on exams, but he might have honesty 34, the disposition to tell the truth about how tall he is. So, Doris thinks that Harman's view – that situationism provides evidence that character traits don't exist – is too radical. However, he does think that the experimental evidence supports the view that there are no robust traits; that is, traits to tell the truth over all or even most contexts or situations. And this is a problem for a virtue ethics that understands virtue as a "stable" or "reliable" character trait.

Another challenge has been that virtue ethics doesn't provide a guide to action. "Be nice, dear" – Well, what is nice, and what are the circumstances under which I should be nice? That's what we really want to know. This shows that it is these other reasons that actually justify our behavior. This has been raised as a very standard problem for the theory, but virtue ethicists have spent a good deal of time trying to show how their theories could be applied. Michael Slote, for example, has argued that we need to look at what motivates a person's actions to determine the action's moral quality – so my guide will be what I consider proper motivational structures. Rosalind Hursthouse

[13] Doris, *Lack of Character*, p. 64 ff.

has argued that we can get perfectly serviceable rules from virtue ethics, what she terms the "v-rules" – such as "Be honest" or "Be kind." Further, this objection is no more a problem for the virtue ethicists than it is a problem for the consequentialist who offers an evaluative criterion rather than a decision procedure (though at least the consequentialist does give us a way to evaluate decision procedures).

This challenge can be expanded by noting that virtue ethics has trouble telling us the right thing to do in conflict situations, where two virtues may conflict, and thus the corresponding rules – such as "Be honest" or "Be kind" – may conflict. But some virtue ethicists think that this is simply the way morality is – it is messy, and for any situation there may be more than one right answer. Insisting that morality is neat and tidy is simply to impose a misleading clarity on moral decision-making.

Virtue-based theories, however, face another practical problem. Recall that if we adopt the Aristotelian view that virtue involves "correct perception" of what is morally relevant, then we are committed to the view that those who disagree with us are lacking in virtue. In a heterogeneous society, this view would lead to lack of respect between people who disagreed with each other on important social issues. This seems rather alien to our outlook today. Rather, it seems quite possible that two people could disagree about something, and yet both are virtuous. Further, if we really do think that something like correct perception is crucial, then it becomes difficult to figure out how anybody is virtuous. Was Aristotle himself virtuous? Well, he certainly had false and appallingly bad views of women – and yet it seems a bit odd to say that because of this he had no moral virtues whatsoever.

Still there are a variety of formulations of the theory that we could adopt that would avoid these implications. We could, for example, soften the psychological requirements that Aristotle places on the possession of virtue. And a Humean account would not be subject to these objections. This is because on Hume's view, virtues are simply mental qualities that are found pleasing from the correct perspective. This does not place undue psychological requirements on the possession of virtue. Virtue ethics remains an interesting alternative approach to moral evaluation and moral guidance.

Further reading

Crisp, Roger (ed.) 1996: *How Should One Live?* New York: Oxford University Press.

Crisp, Roger and Slote, Michael (eds) 1997: *Virtue Ethics*. Oxford: Oxford University Press.

Hursthouse, Rosalind 1999: *On Virtue Ethics*. New York: Oxford University Press.

Slote, Michael 2001: *Morals from Motives*. Oxford: Oxford University Press.

Chapter 9

Feminist Ethics

Feminist philosophy has given rise to a host of different approaches to core areas in philosophy – ethics included. The approach that is taken within feminism is distinctive methodologically as well as substantively – that is, from the methodological point of view many feminist writers will point out that earlier theorists used very biased samples in gathering "data" for their theories, and they also used biased interpretations in explaining the data and in using the information as the basis for a system of normative ethics. This, I believe, is the hallmark of psychologist Carol Gilligan's interpretation of her teacher and colleague Lawrence Kohlberg's work. Feminist writers will also criticize the standard theories – such as the ones we have discussed so far in this book – not only for methodological failings but also for substantive failures of content; that is, the actual content fails to reflect experience that is typical of women's lives, and, indeed, can even often discount that experience as trivial and not worth accounting for. And Carol Gilligan's positive claims about moral thinking can be seen to fall into this category – her research suggests that the content of morality may be substantively different if we take into consideration and take seriously how women respond to moral problems. One of the aims of this chapter is to explore the impact that Gilligan's work has had on feminist ethics, and to also discuss how feminist ethics has grown and developed in the years since Gilligan's initial research. Important though her work is, it no longer forms the central core of feminist ethics.

Background

Utilitarianism and Kantian ethics both advocate an *impartial* moral system. Feminist philosophers have attacked this. The mode of criticism will depend upon the fact that utilitarianism, for example, tends to ignore the significance of special obligations – such as family obligations, which weigh more than obligations to strangers. Feminists have also criticized contractarianism for failing to take adequate account of the rights and entitlements of those with disabilities, or those who are vulnerable, such as young children and the mentally impaired. Some feminists have argued that what is needed is a wholly alternative theory – that the old stand-bys just can't be patched up to adequately reflect legitimate moral practice. Carol Gilligan's work helped set the stage for one form of this alternative approach – the ethics of care.

The Ethics of Care

Until recently, feminist ethics was centrally associated with Nel Noddings's *ethics of care*. Noddings believed that a distinctly moral attitude to others required receptiveness to their needs and desires, to the point of not focusing on the self. She did suggest, however, that this relationship is not complete unless the person who is cared for recognizes the attention.

Carol Gilligan's work on how girls tended to think about morality is most commonly thought to provide the basis for the care approach, though Noddings is the one who developed the normative ethical theory itself. Gilligan's important and provocative research seemed to show that girls tended to think differently than boys about moral issues and problems.[1] This had been noted by earlier researchers such as Jean Piaget (1896–1980) as well as Lawrence Kohlberg (1927–87), both of whom seemed to view the male "justice" perspective as superior – and this is something Gilligan took issue with.

---

[1] Carol Gilligan, *In a Different Voice: Psychological Theory and Women's Development* (Cambridge, MA: Harvard University Press, 1982).

Piaget studied the development of perspective taking in young children, among other issues.[2] He noted that children start off as very egocentric, and it is only over time that they develop the ability to adopt the perspective of another – a crucial component of empathic connection with others and moral development. But this is just one stage. As the capacity for abstract thought develops, people become more and more able to formulate and actually follow rules. This is important to understanding justice, which involves adherence to the moral rules. Kohlberg, building on Piaget's work, would note this as a higher stage of moral development. Piaget himself also noted that girls tended to be much more flexible about rule-following, so much more accommodating about exceptions to the rules.[3] Girls lacked the legalistic sense of the importance of rules and procedures, and Gilligan notes that for Piaget this sense was "...essential to moral development."[4] Of course, it would then follow that girls have a less developed sense of morality than boys. Gilligan would take exception with this work, as well as that of Kohlberg, which seemed to suggest that girls and women were stuck at an intermediate stage of moral development; that they were, in effect, morally immature. It is easy to see why this finding would be disturbing to many, and ironic as well. Women had been made to work very hard indeed to overcome the Victorian stereotype of permanent and childish immaturity.

Another Victorian stereotype was that women were the morally superior, the nice ones, as opposed to males who were supposedly inherently rough and aggressive. The work of psychologists such as Piaget and Kohlberg seemed to reinforce the first stereotype while at the same time undermining the second! This finding did not at all seem to accord with everyone's view of the weight that should be placed on the way women go about making moral decisions. Girls exhibited more flexibility, but that did not make their caring perspective less truly moral than the male way of adhering to rigid rules.

[2] Jean Piaget, *The Moral Judgment of the Child* (New York: The Free Press, 1965).
[3] See, for example, Lawrence Kohlberg, *The Philosophy of Moral Development: Moral Stages and the Idea of Justice* (San Francisco: Harper and Row, 1981).
[4] Gilligan, *In a Different Voice*, p. 10.

Kohlberg interviewed over 80 boys over a period of 20 years in order to get his data on moral development. Kohlberg listed six stages of moral development:

1. Punishment and Obedience: the stage at which one obeys the authority figure in order to avoid being harmed by punishment
2. Individual Instrumental Purpose and Exchange: making deals with others for mutual benefit; reciprocity relationships
3. Mutual Interpersonal Expectations and Conformity: respecting trust and loyalty
4. Social System and Conscience Maintenance: subordinate one's own desires or personal relationships for the sake of the group norms or maintaining group rules
5. Prior Rights and Social Contract or Utility: personal relationships subordinated to justice
6. Universal Ethical Principles: adhering to principles with universal validity[5]

It turns out that women seem to be stuck at the third level. They seem to place far greater weight on relationships than on formal systems for social justice. There is a classic thought experiment – or hypothetical dilemma – devised by Kohlberg that illustrates this lesson: "... a man named Heinz considers whether or not to steal a drug which he cannot afford to buy in order to save the life of his wife." The question is then asked, "Should Heinz steal the drug?"[6]

A boy, Jake, aged 11, says that Heinz should steal the drug, and proceeds to give an argument to that effect, relying on appeal to the fact that most people would regard this as the reasonable thing to do; Heinz's wife is worth more than the money that the druggist could expect to get.

However, a girl, Amy, also aged 11, provides evasive answers to the question. She tries to redescribe the case so as to avoid the dilemma altogether – for example, "I think there might be other ways besides stealing it, like if he could borrow the money or make a loan or something...".[7] So, it looks as though Amy is placing more weight

---

[5] Kohlberg, *Philosophy*, p. 96.
[6] Gilligan, *In a Different Voice*, p. 25.
[7] Gilligan, *In a Different Voice*, p. 28.

on working around things, on preserving relationships, and so forth. Does this mean that she is morally less developed? A Kohlberg analysis would be committed to this – Jake is somewhere around stage 4 or 5, Amy is stuck at stage 3.

Gilligan challenged these findings: just because there seems to be a progression in males from 1 to the other stages, to 4 or 5 or 6, it does not follow that the progression indicates any improvement or advancement of ethical views and practices. Her interpretation of the data is that perhaps there is a female way of looking at moral issues that is distinct from the typical male way, and the female way is not a lower stage of moral development. Indeed, it could well be the case that the *caring* attitude that tends to be exemplified by the female subjects is a much better guide to behaving morally than abstract and rigid rules. But it is very important to point out here that Gilligan did not think that males and females thought about morality differently in any *essential* way. That is, there will be many males who reflect the "female" or "care" voice and many females who reflect the "male" or "justice" or "rights" perspective. They tend to get labeled in gendered terms because the empirical evidence seems to show that females tend to adopt the care perspective, while males tend to adopt the justice perspective. The evidence suggests that there are different ways of thinking about moral issues, the justice way being merely one. Study of the others, such as the care perspective, should not be ignored because there is the assumption that the rights perspective represents the pinnacle of moral development.

Gilligan interprets Amy as putting more weight on relationships rather than rules, and that is one feature of the females' moral voice. She notes that in her research, which involved studying the diaries of girls, and interviewing women about moral dilemma situations, her take is that:

> The moral imperative that emerges repeatedly in interviews with women is an injunction to care, a responsibility to discern and alleviate the "real and recognized trouble" of this world. For men, the moral imperative appears rather as an injunction to respect the rights of others and thus to protect from interference the rights to life and self-fulfillment.[8]

[8] Gilligan, *In a Different Voice*, p. 100.

158

Virginia Held echoes this by noting that for some feminists the self is understood relationally, and this is reflected in the moral ways of thinking that Gilligan posits to the female subjects of her studies. Held writes:

> ... Gilligan valued tendencies found especially in women to affiliate with others and to interpret their moral responsibilities in terms of their relationships with others. In all, to value autonomy and individual independence over care and concern for relationships was seen as an expression of male bias.[9]

This observation further becomes a nexus for criticism of contractarianism, in which the basic system of rules is established by agreement between fully autonomous individuals. If moral reality is instead "relational" and many agents, if not all, in some way depend on others, then this ideal of fully autonomous agents is a false ideal. Instead, we want a system that reflects and accommodates the dependencies and vulnerabilities that are a part of our real lives.

Gilligan's research has been attacked as empirically flawed. It relied on small and possibly biased samples. Whatever the flaws of her own methodology, however, she did make the very interesting observation about the available data that it is open to interpretation. One person's evidence of progress is another person's simple sign of change – and not necessarily change in the better direction. Further, there is no doubt that it suggested to many feminist writers a way of going about ethics that bypassed adherence to rules, and was based simply on adopting an attitude of benevolence and caring toward others. Again, contractarians fare poorly, since their view suffers from the inclusion problem, which seemed to leave out a whole host of persons who we intuitively regard as having moral standing, though not capable of entering into fully autonomous agreements. Indeed, the ethics of care has been very popular in nursing ethics – the paradigm case of care is care toward the vulnerable.

Other writers, such as Nel Noddings, picked up on Gilligan's research and sought to develop accounts of the caring perspective that

---

[9] Virginia Held, *Feminist Morality: Transforming Culture, Society, and Politics* (Chicago: University of Chicago Press, 1993), p. 60.

could be applied.[10] On Noddings's view, caring involves a receptivity to the needs and desires of *others*. But "others" is to be understood particularistically, within a particular relationship with the caring agent. So, for example, a mother will care for *her* child, a husband for *his* wife, a friend for *her* friend, and so on. Thus, caring is not impartial. Further, this receptivity involves a feeling of concern for others that is not bound by rational adherence to principles of ethics. There is a one-on-one response to those calling for a caring response; and ideally that response is reciprocated.

This approach rejects rule-following as a moral guide. Moral judgment does not depend upon following moral principles. Nor, on some interpretations of this view, can moral judgments even conform to moral principles. Moral reality is too rich and complex to be captured by general principles. Morality is *particularist*. The morally good person who has inculcated moral norms simply responds appropriately. She is not applying general rules; she is not appealing to general reasons. Further, there are no general reasons that can be given in support of her response. As in the case of some of the virtue ethicists, the care ethicist views the generalist approach to ethical decision-making and evaluation as far too simplistic to accurately represent moral reality. Highly general claims such as "Pleasure is good" are false if understood as applying across contexts, for example. The pleasure of a sadist is not good. The morally sensitive individual knows when pleasure is a good, but not in any way that can be completely articulated in a principle. It is, however, a knowledge that can guide her action in concrete situations.

This focus on the significance of relationships, and on decisions based on particular features of context rather than following the rules, in turn was adopted by other contemporary philosophers – virtue ethicists as well as feminists – who felt that impartial ethics failed to reflect the caring dimension so crucial to ethics. Further, taking a leaf from Gilligan's research, this was no surprise: men had been the architects of earlier theories, so it was no wonder the female sensibility was not reflected.

However, while this view dominated feminist ethics for more than a decade, in recent years it has been criticized and rejected by feminist

---

[10] Nel Noddings, *Care: A Feminine Approach to Ethics and Moral Education* (Berkeley: University of California Press, 1984).

moral theorists. Indeed, some have expressed the worry that Nod-dings's work simply reinforces pernicious old stereotypes of women as sensitive and emotional but fundamentally nonrational. This re-minds us of the challenge faced by early feminists such as Mary Wollstonecraft (1759–97). In her classic *A Vindication of the Rights of Women*, published in 1792, she wrote that

> It would be an endless task to trace the variety of meannesses, cares, and sorrows, into which women are plunged by the prevailing opinion, that they were created rather to feel than reason, and that all the power they obtain, must be obtained by their charms and weakness...that is the condition for which woman was organized, has been insisted upon by the writers who have most vehemently argued in favor of the superiority of man; a superiority not in degree, but essence...man was made to reason, woman to feel... [11]

Of course we don't want to present a false dichotomy – and Wollstone-craft is careful to point this out. Sentiment can well be regulated by reason. Indeed, if we look back to the work of the David Hume – who died less than 20 years before Wollstonecraft's book was published – we see this very point made as well. The basis for our moral judgments is sentiment – the feelings that we have for the well-being of other people. But this sentiment is corrected by the exercise of reason.

The worry being expressed recently in feminist ethics is that the ethics of care approach is really reactionary. It recalls images of the "angel of the house" or the Victorian ideal of womanhood that was so damaging to female accomplishment.[12] The angel is one who is totally self-abnegating and dedicates herself to the care of others. According to Virginia Woolf (1882–1941), the angel was "...intensely sympa-thetic. She was immensely charming. She was utterly unselfish...She

---

[11] Mary Wollstonecraft, *A Vindication of the Rights of Women: With Strictures on Political and Moral Subjects* (London: printed for J. Johnson, 1792), pp. 61–3.

[12] See Jean Hampton's discussion of this issue in "Feminist Contractarianism," in *A Mind of One's Own*, edited by Louise Antony and Charlotte Witt (Boulder, CO: Westview Press, 1993), pp. 227–55. Hampton discusses the angel of the house example and its relevance to understanding some criticisms of an over-emphasis on partiality in ethics.

sacrificed herself daily. If there was chicken, she took the leg: if there was a draught, she sat in it . . . "[13] The angel then looks rather like the paradigm of the ethics of care approach.

Virginia Woolf wrote that fighting the angel was a necessity for self-fulfillment. Indeed, the Victorian ideal of the woman whose domain was that of the home, in contrast with the man, who was the family member who went outside the home to earn and govern, is one that has been used to deny equality to women. It provided one argument against extending suffrage to women, since voting is a political act, not a domestic one, and thus was thought by some to be inappropriate for women. So, Woolf's connection between the angel of the *house* and a stumbling block in the path to freedom for women certainly has some truth to it. There is no doubt that caring for others in our family – our children and spouses, for example – is extremely important in the moral dimension of our lives; and this is true for men and women alike. But it needs to be tempered or mediated by some other goals as well, so as not to become simple self-abnegation. Here, as Jean Hampton suggests, we might note an important role for impartiality in ethics, and we shouldn't be too quick to dismiss it as cold and unfeeling, leaving no room for special obligations. Hampton's work on contrac-tarianism and feminism helped show that impartiality is actually something that is quite amenable to feminist concerns. Indeed, anyone who has raised small children knows that the issues of "justice" and "fairness" frequently come up, and parents are often in a position of having to mediate disputes fairly and justly. These norms are quite familiar in the domestic setting.

Noddings, however, did note that on her view the best relationships will be those marked by reciprocity of caring. Thus, the angel of the house is not one who embodies this ideal. Clearly, those she defers to are not returning the regard.

Other feminist writers have pointed out that the private/public dichotomy that this picture presupposes is a false one. Susan Moller Okin, for example, discusses how this dichotomy was thought to have been supported using naturalistic, functionalistic arguments that noted the biological and emotional differences between women and men – woman have the angelic, caring natures and men the aggres-

[13] Hampton, "Feminist Contractarianism," p. 231.

sive, dominating ones. Women, in virtue of their biologically determined roles as mothers, are properly within the domestic nurturing
sphere. Men, who are not emotionally suited to childrearing, will do
better outside the home in earning money for the family, farming, and
governing. The nineteenth-century philosopher Arthur Schopenhauer
(1788–1860) believed that women were suited solely to childbearing
and the rearing of very young children, because women were themselves childish in nature. And Schopenhauer was by no means alone in
this belief. Many believed that women lacked the judgment for anything more serious. We needn't have Schopenhauer's dismissive attitude toward the female character in order to believe in the dichotomy
underlying different spheres for men and women. But this view of
different spheres, in which, again, women are seen as the caring and
nurturing ones *by nature*, has been attacked by feminist writers such as
Susan Moller Okin. There is nothing that renders men by nature
unsuitable to rearing children and sharing in that responsibility. She
writes that when it comes to the socialization of young children,
traditionally, of course, this has been the female's task:

> . . . the structure of the family that has predominated throughout history
> must change radically if women are to achieve equality with men . . . We
> must aim toward a time when child-rearing will be equally shared
> between the sexes.[14]

Even if we think that the domestic/political or the public/private
dichotomy holds, there is nothing that makes each side of the dichotomy gendered in a particular way.

Of course, we can also attack the dichotomy altogether as false.
There is no sharp, principled, distinction between public and private
spheres – at least to the extent that concerns in one are irrelevant to
concerns in another. For example, there is plenty of legislation that has
an impact on the family. In our own society there are laws that
encourage home purchases, for example, which certainly has an impact on the family. A person within a family is not thereby insulated
from the rest of the world. The family is one aspect of the world at
large. Further, Okin does a wonderful job of showing how public

[14] Susan Moller Okin, *Justice, Gender, and the Family* (New York: Basic Books, 1989),
pp. 300–1.

functions can be skewed out of "consideration" for the "private" functions associated with women's domestic roles. For example, jury composition will be skewed toward males if women are given automatic exemptions from performing this public service out of consideration for their private roles as wives and mothers.

The ethics of care approach could make use of this point – and, indeed, there is some evidence that care theorists would be in favor of holding the emotions regulated by reason. The main theoretical difficulty with this way of viewing the theory, however, is that it then seems to lose its distinctive character. If the point is simply that emotional responses have a proper place in normative ethical theory, then the list of targets for the approach grows much smaller. A good many traditional theorists would be happy to concede this. Even Kant believed that emotion was something that could prove instrumentally very valuable – for example, we ought to be cheerful in doing our duty, since that makes it much easier to accomplish the appropriate ends, and this is something the morally good person should care about.

But perhaps – as some, such as Virginia Held, argue – what Gilligan's research has shown is that women don't use rules: this is not the same as using raw emotion divorced from reason. This criticism, the argument goes, fails to hit a genuine target: the target is really a rule-based, formalist system of morality that leaves no room for things such as exceptions – even reasoned exceptions. To this, the rule-based theorist would respond that she is not advocating rules as mechanical decision procedures. The proper application of rules will require sensitivity, since she will have to be able to pick out the instances in which certain rules appropriately apply.

A recent trend in feminist ethics is to show how other theories can accommodate the cases raised by feminist theorists as problems for the more traditional approaches. For example, Jean Hampton and Marcia Homiak try to do this for contractarianism and Aristotelian virtue ethics, respectively.

Jean Hampton, as mentioned earlier, believed that there is a role for impartiality in feminist ethics – indeed, not just a role for it but a genuine need for it – and this need is reflected in what people have referred to as "women's" experiences. So, women have by and large, at least until recent history, been relegated to the domestic sphere, and have been responsible for nurturing and sustaining family relationships and fulfilling family needs. Within this sphere, true, there is a need for expression of care. However, there is also a need for justice and the impartial administration of rewards and punishments. Any mother who has had to adjudicate disagreements between siblings sees the truth of this. Indeed, to go too far in the care direction is to invite legitimating arrangements that have been really abusive of women in the past. Hampton discusses Woolf's angel example to illustrate the need for something like impartiality (or perhaps a kind of balanced partiality). The angel may exemplify an attitude of caring, but she is also being taken advantage of by others, and this is not right. It is not right because it is not *just* – she has moral claims on others as well, claims to be treated with respect and as an autonomous individual. Surely this must be reflected in ethical theory and, if so, it is the care approach that comes up deficient.[15]

Aristotelians would also like to show how their approach can accommodate feminist concerns. While the basic structure of Aristotle's virtue approach is sound, they will, of course, reject his false and archaic views of gender and race. The argument that Marcia Homiak presents is that the rational ideal for human beings presented in Aristotle does not exclude emotions and emotional responses to others from the good life, and it also offers a model of a life of reason that should be appealing to men and women alike. She notes, as Hampton did, that an unrestrained kindness or attitude of caring can actually be very destructive: "By showing kindness and compassion when other responses might be more appropriate, the kind person can act to sustain oppressive and unhealthy ways of relating to others."[16] This isn't to say at all that the Aristotelian is against kind responses to the needs of others – rather, it simply means that those responses should be regulated by reason. If they cannot be rationally endorsed, then they should be rejected. This seems quite sensible. If Alice's dead-beat cousin asks her for a loan, she may feel very sorry for him and really want to help him, but also realize that it would be foolish of her to give him money since he would not spend it wisely. So she realizes that

---

[15] Hampton, "Feminist Contractarianism," p. 231. This issue, as well as a consequentialist account of this challenge, is discussed further in Julia Driver, "Consequentialism and Feminist Ethics," *Hypatia*, 20, Fall 2005, pp. 183–99.

[16] In Marcia Homiak's "Feminism and Aristotle's Rational Ideal," in *A Mind of One's Own*, edited by Louise Antony and Charlotte Witt (Boulder, CO: Westview Press, 1993), pp. 1–18; see p. 15.

giving the money to him is not really a good thing. In doing this, she is exercising her rational capacities to help regulate her emotional response and provide a check on meeting indiscriminate appeals for help.

Recall also our discussion of contemporary consequentialism – if we adopt the objective approach favored by writers such as Railton, we could argue that partial norms can themselves be justified impartially, so that these norms are not at all incompatible with a higher-level impartiality. This "sophisticated" consequentialist would try to fold feminist insights into her theory. I ought to love my husband in a noninstrumental way, because this is what is conducive to overall happiness. A world without special attachments of this sort would be a much less happy place.

Again, a consequentialist who wanted to discount the angel of the house as a moral exemplar would be able to argue that it is not good to inculcate these sorts of norms, since they lead to passivity and lack of self-determination – and this will have detrimental effects. For the consequentialist, of course, the case rests on empirical factors: What really does lead to the best outcomes? But, presumably, if we really do think that there is something lacking in the angel of the house, then we wouldn't think it good to encourage people to be like that. Perhaps what is lying behind this is a kind of Millian perfectionism – it is demeaning to be the "angelic" sort of person who allows herself to be taken advantage of. In any case, if we have the intuition that Woolf's case is meant to elicit, we can, again, fold that into the consequentialist framework.[17]

So, feminist ethics has moved beyond its early identification with Gilligan's work and Noddings's ethics of care. One of the features of this diversification is that specialized topics are being analyzed from the feminist viewpoint. Some of the really exciting work has to do with relational features of the self – another topic that grew out of dissatisfaction with Rawlsian contractarianism. Recall that Rawls had argued that the principles of justice be derived from agents reasoning in the "original position," where they are unaware of things such as their own race, gender, social status, and so forth. Thus, his heuristic relied on a very stripped down notion of the self.

---

[17] Again, for more details on such a strategy see Driver, "Consequentialism and Feminist Ethics."

But for many feminist writers this heuristic would be very misleading, since one cannot think of the self in this light. Carole Pateman writes that "Rawls' original position is a logical abstraction of such rigor that nothing happens there."[18] Yet, she notes, there is no denying, even here, the roles that individual people play. They have descendants for which they will care, for example. This sort of information is very important in understanding motivations – Why would someone care about, for example, preserving the environment if she did not care what happened to people who existed in the future? These kinds of carings – and this is just one example – help to configure a person's identity. An individual's identity is often dependent on relations with others – someone may think of herself as a daughter, or a mother and as part of a certain sort of community – and if these relations are stripped away there is no "self" that is the same as before. The feminist idea, then, is thought to be similar to the communitarian view that we are not isolated individuals, that the worth and value of our lives is not understood in terms of individuality and the pursuit of individual perfection at the cost of the community. Instead, we are embedded in communities and families and friendships that are crucial to our self-understanding. If we look at things this way, it is often argued, we can look at issues such as well-being more holistically – so, the individual needs to be sensitive to community and relationship goods. The good of the community may not be a simple compilation of the goods of members understood completely individualistically. Jeremy Bentham would have disagreed – see to the individuals' well-being and you've seen to the community's as well. But many feminists would disagree, because there are connections between individuals that can't be accounted for this way. There is a character to the whole community that gets lost in this kind of translation.

Further, these connections may be voluntary – but again, they may not be. A person does not choose his or her parents, for example, and yet there is a consensus that children have special duties toward their parents – such as duties of care and support. So not only are there feminist writers who oppose the kind of individualism they see as underlying much of the methodology in normative ethics; they also

[18] Carole Pateman, *The Sexual Contract* (Stanford, CA: Stanford University Press, 1988), p. 43.

oppose the view that things such as duties and obligations are acquired voluntarily. Again, that seems to be making a contractarian assumption that we all somehow agree to take on certain obligations. But this seems false, as many family relationships can demonstrate. Sometimes we just find ourselves with obligations that we did not seek. The fact, for example, that an infant is vulnerable and needs help may be enough to impose on the parent an obligation to provide that help – even if the person has not sought parenthood.

But the idea that the self is relational in this way doesn't mean that people have to, or are morally required to, accede to whatever roles fate sends their way. One feature of traditional liberalism is the importance placed on rational self-determination. A person who is truly autonomous will be able to rationally endorse – or not – her roles. But the idea is that even if we want to change ourselves into what we think of as better human beings, we will still be the sorts of creatures that get some satisfaction from relationships with others. That is very important to the moral dimension of our lives. The goal is not to be completely and totally self-sufficient, both materially and emotionally. The goal, rather, is to be able to reflect on our lives and make choices about them, including choices about what sorts of relationships are healthy and good for us and for others. So the relations are not simply accepted as a given that cannot be altered. Of course, this leaves us with the task of developing an account of how we evaluate purported "goods" – Which relationships are good, and which not? And here the feminist philosopher is free to adopt the host of theories out there – some of which have been discussed earlier in this book.

Feminist ethics has also been deployed to understanding issues of relevance to political philosophy – again, generally in counterpoint to contractarianism. For example, much of the work done in understanding concepts such as "power" and "oppression," and "respect" and "self-respect," is done by writers working in the feminist tradition. Indeed, Samantha Brennan takes the study of oppression, and a theoretical understanding of it, to be of central importance to feminist ethics[19] – not only understanding it, but also working to end it. And this is where some of the traditional theories come up short – most

---

[19] Samantha Brennan, "Recent Work in Feminist Ethics," *Ethics*, 106, 1999, pp. 858–93.

glaringly, utilitarianism. This is because it is theoretically possible on the utilitarian view to justify the subordination of women (it is possible, theoretically, to justify the subordination of anyone, actually). If we could show that this subordination would result in more happiness overall, then it would be justified on utilitarian grounds. Yet, this seems manifestly wrong and unfair. Thus, utilitarianism is inimical to concerns central to feminist ethics. Further, it doesn't do to just say that experience has shown us that equality for women does in fact lead to greater happiness – that gives us the right answer, but not for the right reason. An adequate theory, from a feminist point of view, would have to show that it is intrinsically bad – and wrong – to subordinate women, not just instrumentally bad. Kantian ethics would have no problem with this, since failure to treat women with respect is intrinsically wrong, a clear violation of the categorical imperative. But if this is taken as a desideratum of an adequate feminist ethics, it is quite true that utilitarianism will have trouble meeting it. The best I think that could be achieved is to hold that the utilitarian must – but for instrumental reasons – be committed to holding certain things intrinsically bad and wrong; that, in other words, the utilitarian must be committed to rights that are absolute and that protect individual liberties. This, I believe, would be close to John Stuart Mill's position. And we know that Mill was a major proponent of women's rights.

The common theme running through feminist ethics is the effort to correct for male biases in theory formation, biases that tended to find their way into the dominant theories because those theories were in many cases initially formulated by men. How this correction takes place makes for interesting and lively discussion of our older theories, as well as of concepts central to normative ethics and political philosophy.

Further reading

Calhoun, Cheshire (ed.) 2004: *Setting the Moral Compass: Essays by Women Philosophers*. New York: Oxford University Press.

Held, Virginia (ed.) 1995: *Justice and Care: Essential Readings in Feminist Ethics*. Boulder, CO: Westview Press.

Walker, Margaret 1998: *Moral Understandings: A Feminist Study in Ethics*. New York: Routledge.

Chapter 10

Moral Nihilism

One knows my demand of philosophers that they place themselves *beyond* good and evil – that they have the illusion of moral judgment *beneath* them. This demand follows from an insight, first formulated by me: *that there are no moral facts whatever.*

Friedrich Nietzsche, *Twilight of the Idols*[1]

In Chapter 1, we discussed one challenge to morality, moral relativism. We discussed some of the problems associated with a naïve form of this view. We then spent the other chapters discussing different ways in which theorists have tried to spell out the content of morality. In this chapter, we turn to another challenge to morality, *nihilism*.

Moral nihilism is the view that there are no moral facts. It is a metaphysical view about what is out there in the world, about what exists or does not exist. Nihilism holds that moral facts do not exist. There is a distinction between moral nihilism and moral skepticism. Again, nihilism is a metaphysical claim about what does or does not exist. Skepticism is epistemological – it is concerned with what we can be justified in believing to be the case. Thus, you could reject nihilism, believe that there are moral facts, and yet be a skeptic by noting that you are not justified in believing in them. Skepticism about morality is not the same as nihilism, because the recognition that we don't know whether or not moral facts exist does not commit us to the denial of their existence. The Stoics, for example, believed that "The number of stars in the universe is even" was either true or false, but that we would not ever be in a position to know. It does not follow from this, however, that I am justified in believing that

---

[1] Friedrich Nietzsche, *Twilight of the Idols*, translated by R. J. Hollingdale (Harmondsworth, UK: Penguin, 1968), p. 55.

the number of stars in the universe is not even. Their number could be even, but the evidence that would make me justified in that belief is unavailable to me, and unless we are wrong about the laws of physics, it will remain unavailable. So, strictly speaking, nihilism is not the same as skepticism about morality, though you will often hear people speaking as though nihilism is just another kind of skepticism. But nihilism is the very strong view that moral facts don't exist, not the view that we're not justified in believing in their existence.

However, we do often speak *as though* moral facts exist. What's going on, then, with our moral language? On this view, it would follow that when we make moral claims, when we use moral terms to make claims, we are not saying anything that is true. There is no truth to morality at all. This is very different from relativism. Relativism holds that moral claims are true or false; it's just that their truth-value is relative. But if we accept moral nihilism, then it would seem to follow that our moral language doesn't actually pick out anything and, as such, claims incorporating this language lack truth altogether.

There are two groups who deny truth to moral claims: (i) those who believe that all moral claims are false, the "error theorists"[2]; and (ii) those who believe that moral claims are not the sorts of things that can be either true or false, the "noncognitivists."

Error theorists get their name from the fact that they think we are systematically mistaken, or in error, when we believe that claims such as

(1)   Killing innocent persons is wrong.

are true claims. One type of error theory is moral fictionalism. On this view, (1) is on a par with

(2)   Sherlock Holmes smoked a pipe.

Claim (2) is, strictly speaking, false. It is false because there is no such person as Sherlock Holmes. Of course, there is a story in which Sherlock Holmes is a character, but it is fiction. Similarly, we might think that we have a story of morality and moral norms, so most of us would be like someone who believes that Sherlock Holmes exists and

---

[2] Richard Joyce is an error theorist who believes that moral claims can be truth apt, but, strictly speaking, neither true nor false.

utters (1) believing it to be true, when in fact it is not true. The moral fictionalist thinks that most people do believe that (1) is true, and true in a much more robust way than (2), but they are wrong, since properties such as "right" and "wrong" don't actually exist out there in the world, anymore than Sherlock Holmes does. There is no *objectivity* to morality, in the sense that there is nothing out there in the world that constitutes morality. It is entirely a human invention, like a work of fiction.

Those who hold (ii), noncognitivism, disagree with the error theorists. They think that claims such as (1) are not true, but neither are they false. They lack any truth-value at all. On this view, when someone utters (1), that is like expressing an emotion or attitude. It's like saying "Killing innocent persons – boo!" or "Yuk!" What you are doing when you say "Murder – boo!" or "Charity – yay!" is providing an expression of emotion about the various acts in question. Expressions of emotion are neither true nor false. They may be appropriate or not appropriate. But since you are not making a genuine statement, the utterance cannot have truth-value.[3]

Noncognitivists note, again, the distinction between prescription and description. Descriptive statements such as "Wombats are mammals" do have truth-values, since they're making claims about something in the world – they are reports, or attempted reports, of facts. Moral claims, however, are not reports of facts. They're attempts at persuasion, or an expression of an attitude, or a form of advice, or a kind of cajoling. If Kelly says "Don't hurt the kitten," she is not reporting a fact; she is trying to protect the kitten. "Don't hurt the kitten" is not the sort of utterance that can have a truth-value; it is neither true nor false. And that's what utterances such as "Hurting kittens is wrong" amount to – utterances intended, for example, to express an attitude of disapproval toward hurting kittens.

The following table maps out the various positions:

		Are any moral judgments...	
		True?	False?
Nihilism {	Error theories	No	Yes
	Noncognitivism	No	No
	Skepticism	Don't know	Don't know

[3] Other examples: commands, questions.

Why do some writers find nihilism about morality plausible? One purely sociological explanation would appeal to empirical evidence. That is, if we look at human history, we see a seemingly endless procession of atrocities and horrors – human beings killing each other, or being killed in earthquakes, tsunamis, and hurricanes, or by disease and famine. How can this be if there is a god? These events have caused some to question the existence of God and, for some people, questioning God's existence leads to doubts about morality, since they cannot imagine another objective basis for moral norms. We've spent a good deal of this book, however, demonstrating that we can develop a system of morality without depending upon God. We don't need a god for there to be moral norms. But, just as a sociological explanation, this may account for why some people develop nihilist leanings. We can certainly see these leanings in the work of Friedrich Nietzsche (1844–1900), though for somewhat different reasons. Nietszche challenged conventional Christian morality. He called it "herd" morality and seemed to view what most of us would think of as "morality" as hopelessly wrong-headed, a force for human mediocrity. Nietszche charged the Christian Church with having corrupted men – in particular, of having corrupted "the noble Teutons," under the guise of improving them through the force of Christian morality:

> But what did such a Teuton afterwards look like when he had been "improved" and led into a monastery? Like a caricature of a human being, like an abortion: he had become a "sinner," he was in a cage, one had imprisoned him behind nothing but sheer terrifying concepts...There he lay now, sick, miserable, filled with ill-will towards himself; full of hatred for the impulses towards life, full of suspicion of all that was still strong and happy. In short, a "Christian"...[4]

In a way, Nietzsche was a nihilist, and in a way not. He certainly believed that conventional morality – the morality that honored the humble and extended compassion to the weak – was a fiction that had been foisted upon the strong in order to control them through guilt and bad conscience. In his *Genealogy of Morality*, he describes the birth of morality as springing from a slave mentality, as a device the weak use to justify their weakness. He writes in a famous passage:

---

[4] Nietszche, *Twilight of the Idols*, p. 56.

That the lambs feel anger toward the great birds of prey does not strike us as odd: but that is no reason for holding it against the great birds of prey that they snatch up little lambs for themselves. And when the lambs say among themselves "these birds of prey are evil; and whoever is as little as possible a bird of prey but rather its opposite, a lamb, – isn't he good?" ... To demand of strength that it *not* express itself as strength, that it *not* be a desire to overwhelm, a desire to cast down, a desire to become lord, a thirst for enemies and resistances and triumphs, is just as nonsensical as to demand of weakness that it express itself as strength.[5]

What conventional morality does, on this view, is twist a defect – weakness – into a virtue and make strength and power into vices. Thus, what according to "master" morality is wonderful about human beings is corrupted. The weak resent the strong, and it is through this *ressentiment* that values of weakness are born and propagated. In the twisted system of conventional morality, merit is conferred to the *weak* in virtue of their very weakness. Nietszche believed that to confer merit on the basis of weakness was wrong-headed.[6]

Thus, it also seems that Nietzsche did believe in a value-system, though one that would strike many of us as perverse and one that he would not wish to call a *moral* value system. One plausible interpretation is that human beings need to break free of the dichotomy presented by different conceptions of morality. We need a new ideal, one that transcends morality.

Even though Nietzsche has been viewed as a nihilist, and there is a good deal of textual support for that interpretation, one could also view him as either a relativist – believing that the truth to morality is variable – or as a kind of moral elitist, offering an alternative view of morality that rejects values such as equality and compassion. Nietzsche believed that human beings could be perfected by developing their wills. The best sort of person is one who creates himself. One of Nietzsche's primary examples of this act of self-creation was Johan Wolfgang Goethe, the great German writer:

Goethe conceived of a strong, highly cultured human being, skilled in all physical accomplishments, who, keeping himself in check and having reverence for himself, dares to allow himself the whole compass and

---

[5] Friedrich Nietzsche, *On the Genealogy of Morality: A Polemic*, translated by Maudmarie Clark and Alan J. Swenson (Indianapolis, IN: Hackett), p. 25.

[6] Nietzsche, *Genealogy of Morality*, p. 26.

wealth of naturalness, who is strong enough for this freedom; a man of tolerance, not out of weakness, but out of strength, because he knows how to employ to his advantage what would destroy an average nature; a man to whom nothing is forbidden, except it be *weakness*, whether that weakness be called vice or virtue.[7]

Nietszche does offer a positive model of self-creation, though one that disdains the conventional virtues of compassion and kindness. These are weaknesses. The "modern idea" of "equality for what is unequal" has simply led to mediocrity and the *exaltation* of mediocrity, and a rejection of human greatness and strength.

The nihilism we see in the writings of Nietzsche is the result of his view that the adoption of conventional morality has been destructive to human excellence. As such, what most people consider morality is false or utter nonsense.

But there are also seen to be some very compelling metaphysical considerations in favor of nihilism. For example, if there are objective properties of "right" and "wrong," or "good" and "bad," out there in the world, that are not the mere reflections of human nature – Well, where are they? We can't see them like other properties of things. We can see shape, we can see size, and so on – but we can't simply look at an action and see "right" or "wrong." A famous quotation from David Hume illustrates the point:

> Take any action allow'd to be vicious: Wilful murder, for instance. Examine it in all lights, and see if you can find that matter of fact, or real existence, which you call *vice*. In whichever way you take it, you find only certain passions, motives, volitions, and thoughts. There is no other matter of fact in the case. The vice entirely escapes you, as long as you consider the object. You never can find it, till you turn your reflexion into your own breast, and find a sentiment of disapprobation . . . [8]

This passage from Hume's *Treatise* has been taken to support a range of positions on the objectivity of evaluative terms. One way to interpret Hume's point is to note that in making our judgments of virtue and vice, or right and wrong, we are projecting our feelings about things onto the world. Aesthetic judgment would work the same way: if I note

[7] Nietzsche, *Genealogy of Morality*, p. 103.
[8] David Hume, *Treatise of Human Nature*, edited by L. A. Selby-Bigge and P. H. Nidditch (Oxford: Clarendon Press, 1978), pp. 468–9.

that "The fungus is disgusting," I don't note an intrinsic property of the fungus. Its disgustingness is completely a matter of my reaction to it. If I were to insist that the fungus *really is* disgusting in itself, then I would simply be objectifying that response. Alice, in *Alice in Wonderland*, noted that she was very happy she didn't like beets, because if she liked them she would eat them. This is funny because we note that there is nothing objectively disgusting about beets – if you like them, *go ahead* and eat them – but Alice has objectified her revulsion to them.

Another way to express Hume's lesson is to note that when we are describing the world and the things in it, we need make no use of evaluative terms in order to come up with a complete description. Thus, moral terms have no essential descriptive significance or content. Some writers, such as Gilbert Harman, have gone further to claim that not only do they lack descriptive significance, but they are explanatorily impotent as well.[9] If they are explanatorily impotent – if we do not need them in constructing an explanation of, for example, why a certain person died, or why the spoons went missing, then – due to considerations of simplicity – we have no reason to think that moral facts exist, that the moral terms actually pick out anything.

Of course, this chain of reasoning can go too far. Can't I explain, for example, why a glass falls over when I bump it without appeal to my elbow? – By talking about atoms and their trajectories, and so forth? But surely my elbow exists. Or, if this kind of argument gives me reason to doubt the existence of my elbow . . . well, I'm not going to worry too much about this line of reasoning. Not only do we end up with moral nihilism, we end up with elbow nihilism as well.

Moral nihilism was widely seen as promoting moral vacuum, and the philosopher Jean Améry (1912–78) believed that it was this vacuum that allowed for the atrocities of World War II, a "festival of cruelty" that must be condemned and not simply shrugged off as an alternative way of life. In his wonderful book *Humanity*,[10] Jonathan Glover notes that Améry believed that the challenge expressed in Nietzsche's nihilism about morality had to be met by civilized thinkers. He quotes Améry: " . . . the man who dreamed of the synthesis of the brute with the superman . . . must be answered by those who witnessed

---

[9] Gilbert Harman, *The Nature of Morality* (New York: Oxford University Press, 1977).

[10] Jonathan Glover, *Humanity: A Moral History of the Twentieth Century* (London: Jonathan Cape, 1999).

the union of the brute with the sub-human; they were present as victims when a certain humankind joyously celebrated a festival of cruelty, as Nietzsche himself has expressed it." What response can we give? There are at least three ways to go here.

One way to go is to note that nihilism is not warranted. At most, what is warranted is skepticism about moral facts, the acknowledgment that they may exist, but we have no way of knowing whether or not they do. This may seem cold comfort as a response to nihilism. However, it might be possible to argue that skepticism about moral facts is helpful because it allows us to reject nihilism, and then we could develop a line of argument that would justify *belief* in moral facts on grounds other than evidential grounds for their actual existence. Perhaps, for example, belief in moral facts is necessary for successful and happy human interactions, without it there would be social chaos, and so forth. This response, however, could also be used to justify a *belief* in Santa Claus, if it turned out that such a belief had socially significant positive effects.

Another way to fight the nihilistic tendency is to note that even if you are a nihilist about moral value, it needn't follow that anything is thereby as justified as anything else. So, it may be true that Nietszche's views may well be subject to Améry's concerns, whether or not you consider him a nihilist. But a simple acceptance of moral nihilism as I've described it here need not lead to moral chaos. Even if there is no truth to morality, there may still be *a point to it*. Just to use one example, an expression such as "Murder – yuk!" can have guiding force just as "Spinach – yuk!" might have guiding force. The authority of the claim would depend upon truths about human beings even if the utterance itself was neither true nor false. Thus, philosophers who adopt this approach tend to use the word "apt" instead of "true." Given facts about human psychology, for example, "Murder – how wonderful!" just would not be *apt* or appropriate. We might believe that this kind of expression is not apt because humans find this type of action repellant, they try to avoid it, and they discourage others from doing it.

It is true that you could be a nihilist and yet still think that utterances we consider moral have a point and can serve to encourage people to act appropriately. But the problem is that the status of these claims is questionable. Recall the example from *Alice in Wonderland*. Is "Murder – how awful!" on a par with "Beets – how awful!" supposing even that someone had an overpowering revulsion toward beets? This doesn't seem right, at least not if we're concerned with defending the traditional view of moral practice as having a weight and significance that transcends taste.

Another approach is to argue for realism or "objectivism" for moral values. I believe that numbers exist even though I don't see them. What about our moral language? Moral truth can have a basis similar to mathematical truth. I can't see $2 + 2 = 4$; I know it to be true nevertheless. When I see four apples grouped out there in the world, I know "There are four apples" is true, even though I don't see a big fat "4" flashing over them. Am I justified in believing in moral facts? If I am justified in believing in numbers, this line of reasoning goes, then yes. The skeptical arguments that cite the lack of descriptive content to moral facts go too far. However, this example can be countered by noting the distinction between description and explanation. It may be true that numbers cannot, even in principle, be seen out there in the world. Thus, they do not figure essentially into descriptions. However, they are crucial to explanation – it would be difficult indeed to imagine, for example, doing science without mathematics. If I need to explain why the Earth's rotation wobbles ever so slightly, for example, the fact that it has *one* moon as opposed to two might be crucial to that explanation. But, as writers such as Gilbert Harman have noted, moral terms do not serve such explanatory purposes when it comes to understanding the natural world; thus there is a crucial difference between mathematics and morality when it comes to assessing their reality.

It may be that the best counter to skepticism about morality is the view that it is simply psychologically untenable. One cannot but help making judgments that are morally evaluative. This may be due to the fact, as we mentioned earlier, that such evaluations are a crucial part of social interactions for humans, that without them we *cannot* explain why we should stay away from bad people and encourage good people, or why we ought to be benevolent as opposed to vicious. Indeed, we opened the book with just such an observation – that moral evaluation is quite important to our interactions, and affords us with valuable information and insight into how we should conduct ourselves. The exact basis for the "should" remains somewhat mysterious. That, however, is the basis for further reflections on the nature of moral reality. The focus of this book has been on spelling out different moral theories, and the different ways in which writers have attempted to spell out the content of morality.

As we come to the end of this book, after looking at a variety of different moral theories, different candidates for spelling out the content of morality, we may come away with a sense of skepticism. How can we know what the right one is, if any? This is the opportunity for further reflection. It is import to recall, also, that when it comes to many concrete issues the different theories will agree on the actual prescriptions – that stealing is wrong, for example, except under certain unusual circumstances. The disagreement is at the basis of justification, at the basis of the values that render or explain why that action is wrong. But that people disagree here is not a sufficient reason to give up thinking about it or reflecting on our fundamental values. It is exactly this sort of reflection, in my view, that has led to moral progress. John Locke (1673–1704) on inalienable rights, Jeremy Bentham on useful as opposed to useless laws, and Immanuel Kant on categorical imperatives – all of these thinkers have proposed systems that have had a positive impact. The values identified by them as fundamental deserve further reflection – and that's the task of continuing education in moral philosophy.

Further reading

Glover, Jonathan 1999: *Humanity: A Moral History of the Twentieth Century*. London: Jonathan Cape.

Joyce, Richard 2001: *The Myth of Morality*. Cambridge, UK: Cambridge University Press.

Mackie, J. L. 1977: *Ethics: Inventing Right and Wrong*. Harmondsworth, UK: Penguin Books.

Shafer-Landau, Russ 2004: *Whatever Happened to Good and Evil?* New York: Oxford University Press.

Index

Index

Index

Index

DATE DUE

DEMCO 38-296

Founded in 1972, the Institute for Research on Public policy is an independent, national, nonprofit organization. Its mission is to improve public policy in Canada by promoting and contributing to a policy process that is more broadly based, informed and effective.

In pursuit of this mission, the IRPP
■ identifies significant public-policy questions that will confront Canada in the longer term future, and undertakes independent research into these questions;
■ promotes wide dissemination of key results from its own and other research activities;
■ encourages non-partisan discussion and criticism of public policy issues by eliciting broad participation from all sectors and regions of Canadian society and linking research with processes of social learning and policy formation.

The IRPP's independence is assured by an endowment fund, to which federal and provincial governments and the private sector have contributed.

INSTITUTE FOR RESEARCH ON PUBLIC POLICY

iRPP

INSTITUT DE RECHERCHE EN POLITIQUES PUBLIQUES ■

Créé en 1972, l'Institut de recherche en politiques publiques est un organisme national et indépendant à but non lucratif.

L'IRPP a pour mission de favoriser le développement de la pensée politique au Canada par son appui et son apport à un processus élargi, plus éclairé et plus efficace d'élaboration et d'expression des politiques publiques.

Dans le cadre de cette mission, l'IRPP a pour mandat :

■ d'identifier les questions politiques auxquelles le Canada sera confronté dans l'avenir et d'entreprendre des recherches indépendantes à leur sujet;

■ de favoriser une large diffusion des résultats les plus importants de ses propres recherches et de celles des autres sur ces questions;

■ de promouvoir une analyse et une discussion objectives des questions politiques de manière à faire participer activement au débat public tous les secteurs de la société canadienne et toutes les régions du pays, et à rattacher la recherche à l'évolution sociale et à l'élaboration de politiques.

L'indépendance de l'IRPP est assurée par les revenus d'un fonds de dotation auquel ont souscrit les gouvernements fédéral et provinciaux, ainsi que le secteur privé.

INSTITUTE FOR RESEARCH ON PUBLIC POLICY

INSTITUT DE RECHERCHE EN POLITIQUES PUBLIQUES

CHILD SUPPORT: THE GUIDELINE OPTIONS

BY

ROSS FINNIE

AND

DAVID M. BETSON

ELKE B. KLUGE

ELLEN B. ZWEIBEL

———

PART OF A SERIES OF MONOGRAPHS

ON SOCIAL POLICY

PUBLISHED BY

THE INSTITUTE FOR RESEARCH ON PUBLIC POLICY

L'INSTITUT DE RECHERCHE EN POLITIQUES PUBLIQUES

reserved

Canada

ɔnale du Québec
al 1994

in Publication Data

ᴵ ᴵᴵᴵᴵᴵᴵᶜ, Ross
Child support : the guideline options

(IRPP monograph series on social policy ; 2) Includes bibliographical references.
ISBN 0-88645-157-4

1. Child support—Canada. I. Institute for Research on Public Policy. II. Title. III. Series

HV745.A6F55 1994   346.7101'72   C94-900499-5

Marye Bos
Director of Publications, IRPP

Series Editor
Elisabeth B. Reynolds

Monograph Editors
Elisabeth B. Reynolds
Michel Leblanc

Copy Editor
Mathew Horsman

Design and Production
Schumacher Design

Cover Illustration
Sylvie Deronzier

Published by
The Institute for Research on Public Policy (IRPP)
L'Institut de recherche en politiques publiques
1470 Peel Street, Suite 200
Montreal, Quebec H3A 1T1

Distributed by
Renouf Publishing Co. Ltd.
1294 Algoma Road
Ottawa, Ontario K1B 3W8
For orders, call 613-741-4333

2

There is growing concern in Canada about the increasing number of poor single-parent families in our society. A large proportion of single-parent families are living in poverty and, subsequently, the proportion of children growing up poor is increasing. Clearly, Canada is not alone in this: the problem is equally prevalent in the US and Great Britain. Policy makers, advocacy groups and the concerned public in Canada are searching for ways to remedy the situation. But before we look to traditional policy mechanisms to assist these families, we must first ensure that both parents are taking financial responsibility for their children.

Over half of lone parents in Canada (82 percent of whom are women) are either divorced or separated, and another 20 percent have never married. Ensuring the adequate and consistent payment of financial child support by non-custodial parents is the first priority in addressing the problems facing single-parent families.

In this monograph, the second in IRPP's series on social policy, Professor Ross Finnie evaluates child support guidelines, the most recently developed approach to regulating child support. Experiments with guidelines in the US and UK have had mixed results. While guideline reforms in the US have lead to an overall increase in child support awards and have been viewed positively by custodial parents, reforms in the UK have sent angry non-custodial fathers into the streets complaining that they are being left impoverished by new child support legislation. Finnie presents a thorough analysis of the guideline options and recommends a clear policy for Canada to adopt. In addition, he presents what I consider a most original and wise idea: the establishment of contracts between couples *before* they embark on parenthood. This seems, to my mind, the most sensible type of insurance against future break-ups that any of us could buy.

This monograph comes at a timely point in Canada as governments review the current child support system and discuss replacing it with a more coherent and consistent policy. IRPP is very pleased to be publishing important work that we believe will inform policy makers and the public and lead to the adoption of a better framework for improving the fortunes of single-parent families in Canada. Finally it should be noted that the opinions expressed in this study are the responsibility of the authors and do not necessarily reflect the views of IRPP or its Board of Directors.

Monique Jérôme-Forget
President

CONTENTS

A C K N O W L E D G E M E N T S

A N D   D E D I C A T I O N

I am grateful to many individuals for help with this monograph. Irv Garfinkel and David Betson have taught me much about guidelines through their writings and conversations, and Garfinkel also provided comments on the discussion paper from which this project originated. Elke Kluge was patient and generous in offering insights on how child support works in reality, and properly scolded me to attend divorce court so that I could gain a better understanding of how things actually operate; indeed, it was fascinating. Ellen Zweibel provided lively discussion on numerous occasions, and I look forward to any future opportunities we might have to exchange views on guidelines and related issues; there probably remains much that each of us can learn from the other. Carolina Giliberti has been a useful sounding board on much of my writing, has taught me a great deal about divorce and child support in Canada and has continually tried to inject a modicum of *realpolitik* into my thinking — even as I typically resist.

Elisabeth Reynolds and Michel Leblanc of IRPP were always supportive and encouraging, provided very useful comments, and generally made the whole project run smoothly from the beginning to the end. They also helped make it fun, and I am most grateful for their generosity of spirit in agreeing to forsake the convenience of their offices on Peel Street to instead meet me at the Brûlerie St. Denis on a number of occasions; thanks for the *cafés allongés*. Mathew Horman's editing was excellent in every respect, carried out with a demeanour both professional and pleasant. Gordon Betcherman was particularly helpful when I was trying to nail down an introduction that was both fun and interesting, although I hardly hold him responsible for the final result. Daniel Stripinis co-authored the discussion paper from which this project originated and has been a close colleague on a number of related projects; his views are sometimes off-beat, sometimes provocative, often dead-on right and always intelligent and interesting.

I am also very grateful to my colleagues at Université Laval for permitting the leave at Statistics Canada during which this project was carried out, and the latter for providing this opportunity. Special mention must go to Pierre Frechette of Laval and Garnett Picot, John Leyes and Gordon

Brackstone at Statistics Canada, who seem to be in the business of figuring out how to make things work rather than explaining why they cannot.

And finally, the volume is dedicated to my parents, Don and Joan Finnie, and my daughter, Kalla Richards-Finnie, who puts everything in perspective and from whom I have learned the most important things of all.

CHILD SUPPORT:

THE GUIDELINE OPTIONS

BY

ROSS FINNIE

I just wanted a coffee. But then as I settled in to enjoy my *espresso allongé* it dawned on me what the people at the next table were talking about — *child support*.

"I think the children's costs should be split fifty/fifty. Why not? After all, they're half yours and half hers," said one. Fair enough, I thought. "No, the one who earns more should pay more," demurred another. I again found myself in agreement. "Just make it so that nothing changes for the kid," suggested a third. Once more the notion was appealing. Of course the problem was that, while all were stating reasonable positions, they were obviously contradictory. Tough problem. That's the child support debate.

It is no wonder that people talk about child support. Up to one-half of those who marry now wind up divorced, and a similar proportion of children born today are likely to live at least a part of their childhoods in a single-parent family. For all of these reasons, getting child support right is central to ensuring economic justice between the divorced parents and vital to the economic well-being of the children involved.

Child support is currently in a period of major change in Canada. Most provinces have recently adopted enforcement programs to help ensure that non-custodial parents make the payments due; the case law regarding the determination of award quantums has been moving toward a more formulaic splitting of the costs of raising the child in proportion to the parents' incomes and continues to evolve; and the current tax treatment of child support — a deduction for the payer and payable for the recipient — has been successfully challenged in court.

Probably most importantly of all, however, it is very possible that there is likely soon to be radical legal reform regarding the procedures used to determine the level of child support awards in Canada. A Federal/Provincial/Territorial Family Law Committee has recently been commissioned to study the possibility of replacing the current case-by-case budget-based system with a set of guidelines according to which awards would be calculated on the basis of a few key variables such as the number of children involved and the parents' incomes. The committee's report is currently pending, but it is anticipated that its recommendations will lead to the introduction of legislation which, if adopted, would make child support guidelines the law of the land within a year or two.

Why Child Support Guidelines?

One principal goal of child support guidelines is to reduce the arbitrary variation in awards that many observers believe characterizes the current system. A second often-cited goal is not just to standardize awards, but also to increase their average amounts. A third point in their favour is that individuals would have a much better idea of what their post-divorce economic situations were going to be, and could plan accordingly. Fourth, it is sometimes alleged that, under the current system, child support awards tend to impose too heavy a financial burden on low-income non-custodial parents while not demanding enough of those with higher incomes; guidelines could smooth out any such inconsistencies. Fifth, guidelines could reduce the financial and emotional costs of divorce by immediately resolving the important child support question and preventing it from being dragged, pawn-like, into other aspects of the settlement.

Guidelines thus look very appealing on paper. But how likely are they to actually deliver on these promises, and at what cost? In particular, the relatively simple rules which characterize guidelines are in contrast to the enormous variation in the particular circumstances faced by different families — variation that would not be taken into consideration. For example, some families spend more on their children than others, and this would typically be captured to at least some degree in the current budget-based system, whereas a guideline would impose a uniform award across all families of the same broad type.

More generally, under the current system child support is often integrated into a broader settlement that represents a full weighing of property settlements, access to other resources, special needs of the parents and children and so on. Guidelines would, on the other hand, remove child support from these global ponderations, to be decided with a simple formula based on the basic characteristics of the situation. Some custodial parents and their children would benefit from this uniformity, but others would likely lose, with a similar group of winners and losers on the non-custodial side.

The possibilities for raising custodial families' incomes through guidelines should not be inflated either. While guidelines could indeed lead to higher — as well as more standardized — awards, the child's standard of living ultimately depends on the *total* income of the custodial family, not just child support *per se*. In particular, the gender earnings gap means that most custodial parents and their children would continue to suffer large income drops at divorce, and many would still fall into poverty.

Guidelines have already been introduced in several other countries. While they seem to be working reasonably well in some jurisdictions, the results appear to be fairly disastrous in others. These experiences suggest that while guidelines can offer the hope of certain improvements, they are not the panacea some might hope for, and their success is anything but guaranteed. In particular, the specific form of guideline chosen would be an important factor regarding its success or failure, and implementation issues are of the first order of importance.

A Contribution to the Debate

In short, there appears to be a general feeling that "something needs to be done about child support," and guidelines have many supporters — for good reasons, especially in terms of the uniform justice they can offer divorced families. But it is at the same time, a sort of *rough* justice. The final evaluation of these trade offs will probably depend on one's assessment of how bad a job the courts are currently doing, *versus* the characteristics of the particular guideline under consideration.

13

The purpose of this volume is therefore to help inform the debate on child support guidelines. This is done by documenting the economic consequences of divorce, describing the current system of child support in Canada, explaining what guidelines are and how they work, presenting simulations of the outcomes that different guidelines generate and providing an overall evaluation of the various guideline options.

In the end, the author advocates the adoption of a child support guideline based on a fixed percentage of the non-custodial parent's income. Such a guideline would have the advantages sketched out above, while its simplicity would make it feasible and efficient in practice. It is also suggested that such a guideline be adopted in parallel with a widespread movement that would see couples working out their own contingent contractual arrangements early in their relationship — when divorce presumably seems entirely unlikely and when a fair and reasonable agreement could be amicably concluded. Such a system would allow individuals to reach the arrangements best suited to their own particular circumstances and then to live their lives with a good understanding of the likely economic consequences of their major decisions regarding marriage, childbearing and — in the event — divorce.

The monograph is laid out as follows. The following chapter provides the evidence on the economic consequences of divorce in Canada; chapter 3 is a review of the current system of child support; the fourth chapter is an explanation of the various approaches to child support guidelines in terms of their construction and implementation; in chapter 5, the relationship between child support and the economic well-being of the two households is addressed; the sixth chapter contains a discussion of a number of implementation issues; chapter 7 provides simulations of the various guideline approaches in terms of awards quantums, economic well-being and the associated implicit tax rates; and there is a concluding chapter where some specific policy recommendations are offered.

The Economics of Divorced Families

in Canada

Child support is an issue of ever-increasing importance primarily because there continues to be a steadily growing number of divorced families, characterized by significant differences in the standard of living of the two households and high poverty rates for the resulting single-parent families. In this light, many of those who support guidelines are motivated by a desire for greater economic justice in the sharing of the costs of the divorce between the two households, as well as by the hope for a reduction in the economic deprivation of custodial parents and their children.

This chapter provides a view of the current situation regarding the increased numbers of divorced families and their incomes. It begins with a few statistics on divorce rates. Next, it presents some conventional income comparisons based on the standard cross-sectional databases available in Canada. The results of an analysis of the economic consequences of divorce carried out by the author using a recently available longitudinal database (where the same individuals are followed over time) are then presented. The chapter thus provides a useful empirical background to the discussions of child support guidelines that follow.

THE RISING INCIDENCE OF DIVORCE

It is sometimes easy to forget just how much social change there has been in the past couple of decades, and divorce is a good case in point. Up until the introduction of the Divorce Act in 1968, there were only a few thousand divorces per year in Canada. After the major reforms of that year, however, which included the introduction of marital break-down as sufficient grounds for divorce, rates rose steadily to just over the 60,000 mark by 1985. In that year the law was reformed once again, and marital breakdown became the sole ground for divorce, with separation for a period of not less than one year sufficient to meet this condition. After another rise following the 1985 changes, divorce rates are steady at around the 80,000 level.*

These divorce rates can be compared to marriage rates, which cur-rently number just under 200,000 per year. In 1951, one couple divorced for every 24 who married; in 1987, when marriages dipped and divorce peaked, there was one divorce for every two marriages, meaning that the ratio of divorces to marriages had changed by a factor of 12; and in 1990 the ratio stood at one divorce for every 2.4 marriages. In terms of divorce rates per capita, Canada moved from having one of the lowest rates among industrialized nations in the mid-1960s to one of the high-est by the late 1980s; only the United States has a higher rate.

These divorce rates are for all couples, including those without chil-dren. Unfortunately, there appear to be no reliable statistics for the num-ber of divorces specifically involving children — that is, those where child support is relevant. Furthermore, these statistics do not include break-ups of common-law marriages, many of which involve children and child support. Nevertheless, the above figures give a good indication of how family break-ups have gone from being rare to ubiquitous in the short span of approximately one generation. Hence the rising importance of the issue of child support.

---

*Vanier Institute of the Family, Profiling Canadian Families (Ottawa: Vanier Institute, 1994), which is the source for the following paragraphs as well. (Note to readers: footnotes will be indicated by asterisks; endnotes, reserved for references, are numbered consecutively and the full list is located at the end of the text).

COMPARING THE INCOMES OF TWO-PARENT AND LONE-PARENT FAMILIES

Given the heavy barrage of statistics faced daily, most individuals probably have the impression that we know a great deal about how incomes change at divorce. Unfortunately, this is not really the case. To give an idea of the current state of knowledge and to set the stage for the alternative analysis based on longitudinal data which follows, this section presents some income figures taken from a recent Statistics Canada publication.[1]

Before proceeding, it needs to be understood that the Survey of Consumer Finance (SCF), the principal source for many income statistics, does not actually identify divorced individuals; instead, there is a more general category of separated, divorced *and* widowed persons. Furthermore, the commonly published income statistics typically compare two-parent *versus* lone-parent families, where the latter include never-married as well as previously married parents; while all "unattached individuals," including never-married and widowed as well as separated and divorced individuals, are similarly lumped together. This means that i) published statistics are actually quite limited in terms of what they tell us about the incomes of divorced *versus* married persons and ii) comparisons are problematic even if one goes back to the raw SCF data, due to the imprecise identification of marital status. We proceed with these *caveats* in mind.

Table 1 presents various income measures for families with children. The first column shows that mean incomes of two-parent families are more than two and one-half times those of lone-mother families, and more than one and one-half times the level for lone-father families. Poverty rates are even more divergent — just under 10 percent for two-parent families, 21 percent for lone-father families and approaching 60 percent for lone-mother families. The third column shows that mother-only families also comprise a large *share* of all families in poverty, approaching that of two-parent families, even though there are many fewer lone-mother families in the population. On the other hand, father-only families make up only a very small share of all poor families, due to their small numbers and their only moderately high poverty incidence.

Deeper probings of the underlying income distributions are presented in the last two columns of table 1. At the lower end, average poverty

Table 1:
Selected Income Statistics For Families With Children By Family Type, 1992

Family Type	Mean Incomes ($1992)	Poverty Rates[c] (%)	Poverty Shares[d] (%)	Poverty Gap[e] ($1992)	Surplus Income[e] ($1992)
Husband -Wife [a]	62,050	9.6	35.2	8,340	38,830
Lone-Parent - Father [b]	38,780	20.9	1.4	10,950	25,190
Lone-Parent - Mother [b]	24,080	57.2	30.1	8,270	16,140

[a]"Husband-wife families with single children only" (i.e., extended families excluded).

[b]"Lone-parent families with non-elderly head and children under eighteen" (i.e., extended families excluded). Note the slight inconsistencies in the categorization of two-parent and single-parent families in terms of the age of the head and children which characterize these published statistics.

[c]"Poverty" status is defined according to the Statistics Canada 1992 Low-Income Cut-Offs (LICOs). Although Canada has no official definition of poverty, the LICOs are the most commonly used standard.

[d]Represents the proportion of all families (including the family types not shown) in poverty.

[e]"Poverty Gap" refers to the differences between the family's income and the relevant LICO; the figures shown represent the mean gap for families in poverty. "Surplus Income" is the amount by which the family's income exceeds the relevant LICO; the figures shown are the means for families above the poverty line.

SOURCE: Statistics Canada, *Income Distributions By Size in Canada,* 1992, Catalogue 13-207 Annual, 1993: table 16 (p. 86) for column 1; table 67 (p. 169) for column 2; table 68 (pp. 166-69) for column 3; table 69 (pp. 170-75) for column 4; and table 71 (pp. 178-79) for columns 4 and 5.

Table 2:

Poverty Rates and Poverty Shares By Family Type Over Time

Family Type	Poverty Rates (%)			Poverty Shares (%)	
	1982	1989	1992	1982	1992
Families With Elderly Heads	12.0	11.3	6.3	20.4	8.0
Non-Elderly Headed Families: Married Couples (Only)	7.9	7.9	8.0	11.4	13.8
Husband-Wife Families With Children[a]	11.2	9.2	9.5	38.5	31.6
Married Couples - Other	4.7	3.6	5.5	3.2	4.7
Lone Parent - Male Head[a]	22.9	18.0	18.5	0.9	1.3
Lone Parent - Female Head[a]	55.1	52.8	54.8	19.4	31.6
Other	18.4	16.1	19.3	6.3	9.0
				100.1	100.0

NOTE: Poverty status is defined with respect to the Statistics Canada 1992 Low-Income Measures (LIMs). LIMs are based on different methods than the LICOs reported in the previous table, and the classifications by family type are also slightly different in the two sets of figures, but the comparable poverty rates are quite similar in the two tables. (Compare the results for 1992 for the family types which appear in both tables.) LIMs — rather than LICOs — are employed here due to their availability in times-series form in the source publication.

[a]With children less than 18 years of age.
SOURCE: Statistics Canada, *Income Distributions By Size in Canada,* 1992, Catalogue 13-207 Annual, 1993: Appendix Table 3 (pp. 192-93).

gaps are similar by family type, but these translate into larger per-capita gaps — deeper impoverishment — for the smaller lone-parent families. As for non-poor families, two-parent households are clearly much better off, with average incomes almost $39,000 above the poverty line, *versus* the average margin of just $16,000 for non-poor lone-mother families.

Table 2 focusses on low-incomes, showing the evolution of poverty rates from 1982 to 1992, with 1989 included to reflect a particularly good year just before the current recession. For purposes of comparison, all family types are shown (unattached individuals are ignored). The first point to note is how well the elderly have fared. Their poverty rates have dropped in half, from 12 percent in 1982 to just over six percent 10 years later, and are among the lowest of all family types.* Second, poverty rates for two-parent families with children have actually fallen as well — from 11.2 percent in 1982 down to 9.5 percent a decade later. The third and most important point is that poverty has, in contrast, remained essentially unchanged for lone-mother families, and their rate of 54.8 percent is well over double that of any other family type.

The second portion of table 2 shows the shifts in the composition of the population of poor families over time. The dramatic movements of elderly couples are seen again; they made up over 20 percent of the poor families in 1982, but just over eight percent in 1992 — despite the fact that their share of the population rose. This may again be contrasted to the rise for lone-mother families, who by 1982 made up a hugely disproportionate one-third of all poor families.

Problems with the Standard Income Measures and a New Approach for Studying the Economic Consequences of Divorce[2]

Besides the specific problems noted above regarding the SCF-derived statistics, there are certain fundamental shortcomings of all stud-

---

*The elderly would be seen to be doing even better if we accounted for in-kind benefits and the imputed value of owner-occupied housing. On the other hand, a fair percentage of the elderly population lay quite near the poverty line, and the 1982-92 improvement in poverty rates includes a significant number who shift from being just below the poverty line to just over. It should also be noted that unattached elderly persons — who are disproportionately women — have poverty rates considerably above those of elderly couples.

ies of divorce based on cross-sectional data. Because divorce is an event whose consequences unfold over time, it requires similarly dynamic (i.e., longitudinal) data to be properly analyzed. This section includes a discussion of the problems with cross-sectional data and the general advantages of using longitudinal data to study divorce outcomes. It also includes a discussion of the "LAD" database used in the analysis of divorce outcomes presented in the next section.

Many readers might be inclined to run, not walk, from any serious discussion of databases, especially one which compares the relative merits of two broad types of data to address a specific problem. Such a reader probably wants — *at most* — a bare-bones and, if possible, lively presentation of the results of the analysis. However, any reader who surveys the brief points which follow should be rewarded not only with a much better understanding of the measurement of divorce outcomes, but also an accessible discussion which breathes life into statistical issues applicable far beyond the topic at hand.

The first major limitation of cross-sectional data is that only the incomes of currently married and currently divorced individuals can be compared, and this may not accurately represent the income changes associated with divorce for given individuals. For example, if lower-income couples are more likely to divorce, cross-sectional married-*versus*-divorced comparisons will confound these initial income differences with the effects of divorce *per se*.

Second, cross-sectional data usually preclude the classification of post-divorce outcomes by the pre-divorce characteristics of the individual and his or her family. For example, the experiences of divorced men and women who come from families with children cannot be compared because only the post-divorce presence of children is usually known.

A third problem is that cross-sectional data veil the evolution of the post-divorce situation over time, since the year of any split is not typically given. It would be very useful to know, for example, if women tend to first suffer sharp drops in income followed by a period of recovery, or if they hold steady at some new low level after divorce; that is, we would like to track divorce outcomes in a year-by-year framework. Cross-sectional data lack this time dimension, thereby limiting the analysis to a calculation of an average of post-divorce outcomes. The average depends on how currently divorced individuals are distributed across the post-divorce years in the sample.

A fourth consideration is that cross-sectional data typically do not identify remarriage status, and therefore the remarriage event and remarried individuals themselves are precluded from any analysis. While it would be interesting to know how divorced men's and women's incomes change with remarriage and to factor these outcomes into any general analysis of what happens to the population of people who divorce, this is not possible. It turns out that remarriage typically results in improved standards of living for both men and women, but especially for the latter, while men are more likely actually to get remarried. This means that cross-sectional studies not only do not enable us to analyze the income changes at remarriage *per se*, but are also likely to make the economic consequences of divorce appear worse than they really are, and distort gender comparisons.

Finally, although the categorization of common-law relationships is inevitably somewhat problematic, associated "divorces" are often not identified in cross-sectional data, thus making it impossible to analyse them.

The Longitudinal Administrative Database (LAD)

By contrast, the research presented here provides the desired dynamic perspective through its use of the Longitudinal Administrative Database (LAD) file. Specifically, there is direct comparison of post- *versus* pre-divorce income levels for given individuals; outcomes are classified by a number of important pre- and post-divorce characteristics; individuals are tracked in a year-by-year time framework following the split; the years leading up to the split are studied; remarriages are identified and play a central role in the analysis; and common-law divorces are included. The following LAD-based analysis thus provides an original and very useful empirical foundation for understanding the effects of divorce on the economic well-being of men, women and children.

The original LAD file upon which this work is based was constructed from Canadian income tax files and comprises a large (10 percent) representative sample of Canadian adults followed as individuals from 1982 to 1986 and matched according to family unit so as to provide key family-level information. Most importantly, the longitudinal aspect of the LAD file permits the identification of those who divorce — defined here as separations or divorces with respect to legal or common-law marriages — over the 1982-86 period, and the opportunity to follow these individuals up to, at the point of and following the split. The LAD thus provides, for the first time, a Canadian database suitable for the study of the economic consequences of divorce, while the LAD-derived sample of marital splits is unequalled *anywhere* in terms of its size and representative nature.

There are two principal limitations to the data. First, social assistance (SA), or "welfare," is not included in the income totals. Checks performed with the Quebec data in the LAD, for which SA income was included, indicated that first, poverty incidence is barely affected by the exclusion of SA income and second, that incomes of single-parent families are probably understated by 15-20 percent due to the missing SA data, while other groups (unattached individuals and two-parent families) are only marginally affected.*

The second major limitation of the LAD data is that while spousal and child support payments are included in the income of recipients (although they are not separately itemized), they are not deducted on the payer's side; furthermore, direct spending on the children relating to joint custody or visitation is not taken into account. (In these data, custody is defined by determining who declares the child as a tax deduction.) These factors will tend to leave fathers' incomes overstated, but probably by no more than 10 percent due to the omitted child support deductions, while the adjustment for their direct spending on the children would be even smaller.[3]

THE ECONOMIC CONSEQUENCES OF DIVORCE[4]

This section presents the findings of the empirical analysis of the economic consequences of divorce carried out with the LAD database. Post-divorce changes in income are presented in three ways. First, the ratios of total (post-tax) family income in the years following the break-up to the level which held in the last year of the marriage are shown. Ratios greater than one therefore represent increases, while ratios less than one reflect declines. These income measures are not, however, good

---

*Martin Dooley of McMaster University has found similar results in unpublished work based on the SCF.

Table 3:

Income Changes at Divorce

Measure and Group	First Year	Second Year	Third Year	Fourth Year
1. Number of Observations:				
Men				
Not remarried, no children	1,650	1,225	875	475
Not remarried, children	975	750	500	250
Remarried, no children	525	250	150	75
Remarried, children	75	100	100	75
	100	125	125	75
Women				
Not remarried, no children	2,000	1,525	1,075	600
Not remarried, children	275	250	175	100
Remarried, no children	1,600	1,125	750	400
Remarried, children	-	-	-	-
	100	150	150	100
2. Post- Vs. Pre-Divorce Total Family Income:				
Men				
Not remarried, no children	.73	.78	.79	.80
Not remarried, children	.65	.69	.69	.63
Remarried, no children	.78	.82	.80	.87
Remarried, children	1.21	1.11	1.14	1.22
	1.23	1.22	1.27	1.13
Women				
Not remarried, no children	.42	.49	.53	.52
Not remarried, children	.37	.42	.47	.47
Remarried, no children	.41	.47	.48	.45
Remarried, children	-	-	-	-

3. Post- Vs. Pre-Divorce Adjusted Family Income:

Men	1.18	1.28	1.30	1.26
Not remarried, no children	1.30	1.38	1.39	1.22
Not remarried, children	1.01	1.07	1.13	1.18
Remarried, no children	1.67	1.58	1.71	1.87
Remarried, children	1.20	1.23	1.22	1.21
Women	.57	.66	.71	.70
Not remarried, no children	.72	.77	.78	.82
Not remarried, children	.52	.60	.61	.56
Remarried, no children	-	-	-	-
Remarried, children	.94	1.03	1.06	1.10

4. Post-Divorce Poverty Rates:

Men	.17	.15	.15	.17
Not remarried, no children	.18	.16	.18	.21
Not remarried, children	.16	.16	.11	.10
Remarried, no children	.03	.07	.04	.09
Remarried, children	.16	.13	.15	.15
Women	.52	.46	.43	.42
Not remarried, no children	.30	.32	.27	.20
Not remarried, children	.59	.53	.53	.55
Remarried, no children	-	-	-	-
Remarried, children	.15	.22	.15	.22

NOTES: See the text for a description of the data and explanations of the measures employed.
To conform with Statistics Canada confidentiality rules, the numbers of observations are rounded to the nearest 25.
SOURCE: Tabulations by the author using the LAD-derived sample of divorces.

indicators of changes in actual economic well-being because they don't take into account the different needs of families of different sizes.*

Thus a better measure of the family's standard of living is the income-to-needs ratio (INR), which is defined as the ratio of total (post-tax) family income to the poverty line (LICO) for that family. This is an established method of adjusting family income for needs based on the principle that LICOs vary with family size. (Larger families are calculated to have greater needs, but also to enjoy certain economies of scale.) INR values below one thus indicate that the family is in poverty, while values greater than one reflect proportionately higher levels of well-being.

The tables present the changes in adjusted income (INR) in the same manner as for total income: the ratio in the years following the divorce to that in the last year of marriage. Change ratios greater than one therefore indicate improvements in the standard of living relative to the last year of marriage, while ratios less than one reflect declines. (The tables report median changes, these being more stable than means.) Poverty rates in the post-divorce years are also reported.

To begin, table 3 presents income changes by remarriage status and the presence of children after the split (i.e., the custody arrangements). The first section of the table shows how custody usually goes to the woman, and that remarriage rates are low, especially at first, meaning that most of the men are in the first category ("not remarried, no children"), while most women are in the second ("not remarried, children").**

The second panel of table 3 shows that those who do not remarry experience drops in total family income — men and women alike. This

---

*Total family income includes all family members of the current household, including new spouses in the case of those who remarry.

**There is some misallocation of the children in the first year of divorce in the data because the higher-earning parent (normally the father) is permitted to declare children as dependents even when he does not have custody at the year's end. This results in a general over-representation of the number of custodial fathers and an underestimation of their economic well-being in the first year and, at the same time, an under-representation of the numbers of custodial mothers and an overestimation of their well-being (although it is less clear how INRs within each sex-remarriage group are affected). Various checks indicate, however, that while the distribution of the sample across the custody categories is clearly affected, the income patterns shown are robust. The years beyond the first year of the break-up are not affected by this problem.

is hardly surprising, since the break-up of the family means that family incomes are also split. The drop is much greater for women than men due to men's typically higher earnings. Interestingly, those who do remarry have, in contrast, not just steady family incomes, but *increases* — suggesting a sort of "trading up market" of spouses. This is especially true for men, who are generally thought to have an easier time remarrying than women. Men's remarriage *rates* are also much higher than those of women — 32 *versus* 16 percent by the third year after divorce. (First panel of figures.)

We now turn to adjusted incomes — the preferred measure of well-being — which are shown in the third panel of table 3. Men's ratios are everywhere greater than one, indicating increases in measured economic well-being for all the remarriage-children groupings shown. The immediate gains are as high as 67 percent for remarried non-custodial fathers. ("Remarriage" includes common-law relationships). The modal group is non-custodial fathers who have not remarried, and these men enjoy a rise of 30 percent at the median. Unremarried fathers with custody have stable standards of living across the split. In summary, men's economic well-being is generally either stable or rises significantly with divorce when children are present in the marriage, and this finding would not be overturned by the missing support payments.

For women, it is the polar opposite, with drops in adjusted income in the first year of divorce for every children-remarriage group. The worst situation is for unremarried custodial mothers, who immediately fall to just .52 of the pre-divorce standard of living — and these single mothers represent a full 80 percent of the women in the table. The poverty rates show a similar story; in particular, 59 percent of the single mothers are in poverty in the first year of divorce, in contrast to rates ranging from three to 18 percent for their ex-spouses. While the missing social assistance income and support payments would change these outcomes to some degree, undoubtedly narrowing the gap, the major results would not change.

Furthermore, these patterns are roughly stable over time. For example, in the three years following the divorce, the modal group of single mothers continues to have family incomes less than one-half the pre-split level, adjusted incomes of .55 to .60 of the pre-divorce mark and poverty rates of 50 to 55 percent. Thus, while there are moderate improvements over time for these women *as a group*, these are almost entirely due to

Table 4:

Divorce Outcomes by the Number of Children in the Pre-Divorce Family

Number of Children Pre-Divorce	Adjusted Income		Poverty	
	Men	Women	Men	Women
No Children	.90	.63	.17	.25
One Child	1.13	.64	.15	.40
Two Children	1.22	.54	.14	.57
Three Children	1.22	.49	.25	.67
≥ Four Children	1.26	.45	.26	.75

NOTE: Results shown are for the first year of divorce only, but similar results generally hold over time.
SOURCE: Calculations performed by the author using the LAD-derived sample of divorces.

remarriage rather than any significant improvements in individuals' situations within any of the children-remarriage categories.

Regarding custody of the children *per se*, table 3 shows lower adjusted incomes for custodial parents than non-custodial parents for every gender-remarriage group. In short, those who keep the children of the marriage seem to pay for this with lower post-divorce standards of living — men and women alike. This lower standard of living is then of course shared with the children.

Finally, table 4 provides a summary view of divorce outcomes by the presence and number of children in the pre-divorce family. The changes in adjusted income and post-divorce poverty rates show that the male-female divergence widens not only with the presence of children but also with the number. In the larger families, men's adjusted incomes rise on the order of 25 percent overall, while they drop by more than one-half for women. Poverty rates show similar disparities, with women's rates peaking at a full 75 percent for the largest families.* What is not shown is that *pre*-divorce incomes and INRs are also lower for the larger families. The total effect is a very strong correlation between the presence/number of children in the pre-divorce family and the woman's post-divorce economic well-being and the male-female gap.

THE UNDERLYING CAUSES OF THE INCOME PATTERNS

The proximate causes of these income patterns can be easily summarized. First and foremost, female-headed households have lower family earnings because women generally have lower earnings than men and this gap is greater for those with children — which is, in turn, at least partly due to the different family responsibilities typically assumed by men and women. Second, having custody of the children of the marriage drives post-divorce needs up, and therefore economic well-being — as measured by adjusted income — down. Finally, child and spousal support payments are insufficient to overcome the earnings disadvantages and greater needs that characterize the women's post-divorce situations. It is all very simple arithmetic: lower earnings plus greater needs plus

---

*Adjustments for the missing welfare payments and child support deductions would make the greatest difference in these cases. Nevertheless, the male-female patterns would still clearly be very divergent, and the "pre-transfer" figures presented here are interesting in themselves.

insufficient support equals a lower standard of living for women and their custodial children.

SUMMARY

The evidence on the rising incidence of divorce and the incomes of divorced families may be summarized as follows:

- Divorce has gone from being quite a rare occurrence to a commonplace over the course of a generation. During the same period, there have been two major revisions of divorce law. These have reduced the grounds for divorce to simplify the breakdown of the marriage, with separation of one year or more sufficient cause. Canada now has one of the highest divorce rates in the industrialized world, with one divorce for every 2.4 marriages on an annual basis.

- Cross-sectional data indicate that lone-parent families have much lower incomes and higher poverty rates than two-parent families, while the former's increasing numbers mean that they comprise an ever-increasing share of families in poverty. There are, however, a number of important limitations to all studies based on cross-sectional data.

- An analysis carried out with the "LAD" longitudinal database demonstrates that there are wide divergences in the incomes of the custodial and non-custodial households at divorce. In most cases, the children are with the mother, and suffer large drops in standard of living, including poverty rates of around 60 percent in the first year of the split, whereas non-custodial fathers enjoy significant improvements in their standard of living. This divergence widens with the number of children present in the marriage. Remarriage is strongly associated with post-divorce well-being, especially for women.

- There are some moderate improvements in the post-divorce period but, three full years after the split, unremarried women remain well below their own pre-divorce levels as well as the current levels of their ex-husbands. Furthermore, most of the gains that do occur over time are due to remarriage rather than improvements in individuals' own situations.

THE CURRENT SYSTEM OF CHILD SUPPORT

Before talking about child support guidelines, it is useful to have a good understanding of the current system of child support. This chapter contains a description of the actual procedures used to determine child support awards and a consideration of a number of issues relating to the actual payment of awards and how these relate to the incomes of the payers and recipients.

One theme of this chapter is that we really know very little about the current child support awards. For example, there is only fragmentary evidence regarding award levels and payment rates, and thus we really don't know how much of the current child support problem is due to these two different components. It could in fact be that current award levels are fine, that the bulk of the problem is the nonpayment of awards and that the current push for higher and more standardized awards is therefore entirely unwarranted. On the other hand, there is currently a will to act and an unwillingness to await a better understanding of the current situation. Here, then, is what we know — and what we don't.

How Child Support Awards Are Currently Determined[5]

Under the current system, child support awards are determined as follows. First, the custodial parent prepares a household budget from which the child's needs are determined. Next, the estimated child costs are split between the two parents, with the non-custodial parent's share becoming the child support award. Finally, the taxes payable on the award are taken into account by grossing the payment up so as to leave the appropriate net amount after taxes.

It all sounds fine and fair. Who could argue with such a system? The problem is that the actual implementation of these methods leaves a great deal of room for arbitrary variations across different cases; meanwhile, some argue that awards do not generally cover the true costs of raising a child. What are the merits of these two principal criticisms of the current system?

First, consider the estimates of the child's costs. It is often quite a difficult exercise for custodial parents to estimate household spending and then disentangle the childrens' costs from their own; but this is precisely what is required, and a fair award obviously depends on this being done with a high degree of accuracy. Some items, such as the child's clothing, are quite straightforward but other aspects are much more difficult. For example, what are the total housing costs, and what is the child's share of these costs? Not only should actual current costs be estimated and allocated, but in some cases it should even be taken into account that the custodial parent might be living in a quite different type of housing or in a different neighbourhood in the absence of the child. What percentage of the utilities bill goes to the child? What about spending on food or transportation? The family pet? Holidays? Estimating spending on the child is thus often a daunting task on both conceptual and practical levels.

Furthermore, the custodial parent might have greater personal expenses due to the presence of the child. For example, perhaps there is a greater cleaning bill because of the messes that are a part of living with younger children or because meeting the needs of the child does not leave enough time to do washing and ironing for oneself.*

---

*A practising lawyer cited the example of higher dry cleaning expenses relating to a child's tendency to spew up over her mother's work clothes.

Finally, it is especially difficult to construct these budgets amidst the dislocation that often accompanies divorce. Many costs might be changing and it is necessary to make the spending estimates before it is even clear how much money will be available — which in turn cannot be known until the child support issue is decided.

In reality, lawyers have different approaches to help their clients produce the family budget required by the courts and to generate estimates of the child's costs. For example, some lawyers assign a certain percentage of housing costs to the child, while others use a different rate, and still others do it on a case-by-case basis. Different shares for different numbers of children also vary in an arbitrary fashion. The same holds for the other major spending items.

In short, estimating the child's expenses — upon which the support award is based — is as much art as science. Expense estimates are often characterized by a large arbitrary component and a significant margin of error and, therefore, often become a common source of sharp disagreement between the two parties.

Once the expenditures on the child are determined, there is the issue of sharing the estimated costs between the parents. Since the well-known *Paras* v. *Paras* case,[6] there seems to have been a general acceptance that the child costs should be split in proportion to the parents' incomes. This sounds quite straightforward, and many will find that this approach rings fair. But which definition of income? Some lawyers use pre-tax income, others after-tax; some subtract certain other deductions before doing the shares (e.g., payroll savings plans or insurance payments where the child benefits), while others do not; there is an emerging trend toward having a "set-aside" for one (or both) of the parents, whereby any income below the basic level needed to look after the parent's own needs does not enter the sharing formula, but there are no clear conventions on this as yet, and so awards can be affected very unevenly.*

Again, art rather than science. No clear rules. Lots of room for different approaches. Lawyers can be made to confess that they actually do the calculations in a variety of ways, and then choose the method that works best for their client. So the result is once again arbitrary differences in outcomes, and conflict for the divorcing couple.

---

*These descriptions are based on conversations with various lawyers and are meant to be illustrative rather than exact and exhaustive.

Thus, determining the child's financial needs and how they should be shared is no easy task. Furthermore, there is also enormous uncertainty on the side of the bench. For example, certain judges are reputed to follow a particular set of procedures, such as paying great attention to the submitted budgets and to favour awards of a certain magnitude; other judges, meanwhile, have different procedural styles, such as minimal interest in the budgets and a tendency to much higher or lower awards. Indeed some individual judges and certain jurisdictions have the reputation of largely ignoring the evidence regarding the particular case and operating instead with a particular award formula, such as a fixed percentage of the non-custodial parent's income.

All lawyers seem to have stories of how the judge ignored some carefully prepared budget document or how a demand for an award was slashed in half after the judge mumbled something about it being impossible that a child could cost as much as is alleged. One lawyer spoke of a meeting of the family law section of a Canadian Bar Association meeting in British Columbia in the early 1980s, where a number of judges were given (in writing) the details of some hypothetical divorce cases and asked to arrive at spousal and child support awards. Returning from their private deliberations, the judges announced greatly varied decisions for the identical cases.

One hears reference to the process as a lottery, or Russian roulette, and in this climate most lawyers advise their clients to settle out of court if something close to a reasonable agreement can be obtained. This is obviously a sad comment on the determination of child support awards: that is, rather than being told to have confidence that one will receive a fair hearing and obtain a just award, the general advice is to avoid the system because anything can happen. It is no wonder that guidelines seem attractive in comparison.*

ENSURING THE PAYMENTS

The determination of child support award levels is one issue; their payment is quite another. It is now common knowledge that many non-custodial parents make their child support payments late, irregularly or

---

*It would be interesting to compare court-determined *versus* out-of-court decisions, but the author is aware of no research of this type, nor of any data which would facilitate such an analysis.

not at all. As a result, all provinces have recently established programs to address this problem. These mechanisms take different forms but typically involve a central registry of existing divorce awards; the payment of awards by the non-custodial parent to the agency, which in turn disburses the money to the custodial parent; and the pursuit of nonpayers, including the prompt garnishment of earnings if necessary. (Other enforcement measures currently under consideration include the suspension of nonpayers' driving permits, the suspension of professional licences and so on.)

The word on the street is that the programs have been quite successful in increasing the child support payments due. Unfortunately, they are too recent to have permitted a rigorous analysis of the full extent of their effects or the determination of which program seems to be the most effective in ensuring payments. Furthermore, there are no historical data for comparison.

AWARDS UNDER THE CURRENT SYSTEM — WHAT WE WOULD LIKE TO KNOW

What are the current levels of child support awards, and how do awards figure in the total incomes of the custodial and non-custodial households? How has the level of awards changed over time? What percentage of awards actually gets paid, and with what frequency? Having the answers to these and related questions would obviously be very useful in the child support debate. In particular, such information would help identify which particular aspect of "the child support problem" is of greatest importance and most amenable to policy action.

For example, consider the goal of raising the average level of child support awards, motivated by the perception that current payments are simply too low. (Note, in the preceding sentence, the reference to *awards* as the policy instrument to deal with the *payments* problem.) It could be that nonpayment of awards and the erosion of the value of awards over time due to inflation — as opposed to the actual level of awards — have actually been the primary reasons why child support payments are too low. If so, the adoption of guidelines could be quite the wrong policy initiative, and it would be more appropriate to protect awards further against inflation and ensure delivery of the payments due. We need data to make this assessment.

Furthermore, information on current awards together with the characteristics of the family would permit the comparison of current awards with those simulated according to the various guidelines under consideration.

Unfortunately, the data required for such analysis do not exist.

CURRENT AWARDS — WHAT WE DO KNOW

Let us consider for a moment what the requisite data would look like. There would need to be information on the level of awards, the amounts actually paid and the principal socio-economic characteristics of both households (family structure, incomes etc.). Of course the sample would have to be representative and large enough to do proper analysis. Finally, individuals would ideally be tracked over time, starting at the point of divorce, so that the evolution of the situation could be studied in terms of the level of awards (i.e., variations) and actual payments, and how these relate to changes in income, family situation and other aspects of the situation. (In the absence of the preferred longitudinal data, a well-designed cross-section would suffice.)

As opposed to this ideal, what data actually exist, and what do they tell us about the current child support situation? A short survey follows.

Diane Galarneau has used tax-based data to study support payments and receipts for the year 1989. She found that combined child and spousal support averaged $4,900 per year, or about $400 per month, amounting to 14 percent of recipients' average family incomes of $35,300, and nine percent of payers' mean family incomes of $55,400. While these are very interesting results, they are also quite limited: in the source data, spousal and child support are treated together, rather than separated out; individual recipients and payers are not matched with their ex-spouses; the year of the divorce is not known; and there is no identification of divorced individuals who do not make or receive payments.[7]

As part of its review of the 1985 Divorce Act reforms, the Department of Justice collected two samples of recent divorces in the mid-1980s (pre-and post-reform), based on court records and follow-up interviews. The analysis revealed that there were court awards in 68 percent of the cases involving dependent children, and that awards averaged around $500 per month, with average payments per child declining with the number of children involved. Awards averaged 16-18 percent of the individual's income on the payer's side, and 34 percent (pre-Divorce Act) and 24 percent (post-Act) of income on the recipient's side. More precisely, awards followed a strong "upside-down-U" pattern in terms of the percentage of income they represented for recipients — that is, first rising, and then falling off; whereas on the other side of the ledger, payments represented a continually declining percentage of payers' incomes.[8]

It was also found that only two-thirds of these awards were paid regularly — and this less than a year after the split, whereas it is well-known that payments tend to drop over time. Separate spousal orders were rare, written into only six percent of the cases involving children, which shows how intertwined child and spousal support are under the current system. The samples were not, however, fully representative of the underlying population of divorces: the couples were, again, not matched; and the results obviously provide no information on how the situation evolved over time.

The Department of Justice has recently compiled another database of divorces involving children in late 1991 and early 1992. The data come from divorce court records and include information on award levels, family structure, incomes and other useful information. Unfortunately, these data have not been released to the public and so no analysis has been possible. Furthermore, even when the database is released, it will have certain limitations. In particular, it is not clear how representative the sample is, and it is obviously restricted to a snapshot of the situation as of the point of divorce.

Other snippets of information regarding child support can be found, but they tend to be of very limited use due to the specific nature of the underlying samples, the limited information they contain, restricted time frames and so on.

One final potential data source is the LAD database used for the empirical analysis presented in chapter 2. The LAD is, like Galarneau's sample, based on tax files, but has numerous advantages over the cross-sectional file she used. Most importantly, the LAD database permits the identification of all divorces — not just those where support is paid — and the tracking of divorced individuals over time. The database thus provides a more complete sample, allows for the matching of specific couples for purposes of direct comparison and offers the desired dynamic framework. Unfortunately, the original LAD file does not give the actual award level, and contains information on support (child plus spousal support together) as a separate item only for 1986, the last year covered by the sample, thus limiting the analysis. Also, the data are beginning to be a little out of date.

Looking to the future, the best data would almost certainly come from a special survey designed specifically to address divorce and related issues, including child support. Failing that, the LAD file has just been completely reworked and brought up to date (currently up to 1990, with 1991 and 1992 to be added in the months to come). This would provide a good sample of divorces with very accurate income information in a dynamic context, and would facilitate the pursuit of most of the questions sketched out above. However, while such a project offers an interesting option for the future, this helps us little in the present.

Finally, it should be understood that it is difficult even to imagine a database which would allow us *fully* to assess current awards in terms of arbitrary *versus* appropriate case-to-case variation. For example, even if awards were related to the two parents' incomes, the number of children involved, property settlements or other financial aspects of the divorce and so on, any remaining variation could still be either appropriate due to some unobserved factor, such as the spending patterns of the family, or arbitrary — that is, "good" or "bad" variation. Without this information, it would remain difficult to assess guidelines in terms of their capacity to improve an injustice *versus* the danger that they will run roughshod over a careful weighing of all factors. This is perhaps disappointing, and even troubling, but it is always good to keep in mind the limits of what data can tell us.

Summary

The current method of determining child support awards, and our understanding of the resulting levels of awards and amounts paid, may be summarized as follows:

- Awards are currently determined by estimating the expenditures on the child and then splitting these between the two parents, with the non-custodial parent's share becoming the child support award.
- Estimating the expenditures on the child is often a difficult task on two levels. First, it can be a challenge to identify and itemize accurately all the relevant budget items at the family level; and second, it is often very difficult to separate the child's share of

total spending from that of the custodial parent. The problem is further exacerbated by the various dislocations that typically accompany divorce (e.g., moves, a general decline in the standard of living), and the more fundamental problem of trying to estimate expenses before knowing how much money is going to be available (which can only be known once the award is actually determined).

- Splitting the child's expenses between the parents is perhaps fairly straightforward in concept, but again runs into problems in practice, especially concerning the concept of income that should be used (pre- *versus* post-tax, etc.).

- Differences in approaches and opinions on the part of courts and individual judges add a further element of arbitrariness to the determination of awards.

- The end result is probably a great deal of arbitrary variation in awards for a given set of circumstances — a principal criticism of the current system — and perhaps a general underestimation of child costs as well. As a result, many individuals choose to settle out of court, which is perhaps the most powerful comment regarding the current system —that is, the legal system is seen as a last resort rather than as a place to seek a fair hearing and obtain a just award. To a large degree, however, this is a comment on the inherently difficult nature of determining fair child support awards, and not just an indictment of the alleged failings of the legal system.

- Many provinces have recently instituted programs to ensure the payment of the child support payments due; yet while there is an impression that they have been generally successful, there has been no hard analysis of their effects to date.

- There is some information on the level of child support awards and actual payments, but this is far from complete, and there is no database that would permit the full analysis of the current system or a rigorous comparison with the various guidelines proposed.

CHAPTER FOUR

THE   DIFFERENT   APPROACHES   TO

CHILD   SUPPORT   GUIDELINES

Child support guidelines are not generally well understood. They are often associated with notions of "cost sharing," and "standardized treatment" and so on, but it is crucial to understand what exactly these concepts mean and how radically the guideline approach differs from the current system before they can be properly evaluated. In short, guidelines are not at all the case of taking what exists currently and making it work better, but rather the wholesale replacement of one system with another.

The current case-by-case budget-based approach to child support awards has been explained above: the financial needs of the child in the post-divorce situation are estimated, and these are then apportioned between the two parents in the manner deemed most fair (usually in proportion to their incomes). In complete contrast, guidelines take a few key characteristics of the family — principally the parents' incomes and the number of children — and compute awards directly; in particular, there is no consideration of the individual spending habits or other aspects of the individual family, and no attempt is made to tailor the cost-splitting to the specific situation beyond the broad rules given in the guideline.

In short, guidelines replace the process of estimating child expenditures and dividing these between the two parents on a case-by-case basis with general formulae that reflect spending estimates and sharing rules on a broad level. Guidelines are thus intended to incorporate rules deemed to be fair on average, which are then applied uniformly to all individuals.

Most importantly, two families with the same broad characteristics (number of children, incomes) will have the same awards, whereas under the current system the awards would depend on the prepared budgets and negotiations regarding the shares of these expenses on a case-by-case basis, and would generally vary from one family to another — sometimes by a little, in other times by a great deal; in some cases appropriately, in others arbitrarily. The hope is that the gains from replacing the arbitrary variation of the current system with the consistency and the other advantages of a guideline will outweigh the disadvantages of ignoring the specificity of each situation.

Up to this point, child support guidelines have been discussed as a generic concept, but they actually come in numerous shapes and forms. Any child support guideline may be usefully conceptualized as consisting of two components: i) the estimation of expenditures on children; and ii) a rule for apportioning these expenditures between the two parents. Various guidelines are thus differentiated by their alternative uses of the expenditure estimates and the choice of apportioning rules. They may be grouped into three major categories: Income Shares, Fixed Percentages of Income and Standards of Living.

In this chapter, we first describe the three types of guidelines in terms of their construction and basic characteristics and then explain the procedures used for generating the child expenditure estimates underlying the guidelines. The next chapter goes beyond pure description of the guidelines to a discussion of their implications for the economic well-being of all parties involved; this is followed by a treatment of implementation issues and the presentation of simulations demonstrating the different outcomes obtained with various guidelines.[9]

THE INCOME SHARES APPROACH

The Income Shares approach to child support guidelines, which has been adopted in many US jurisdictions, is predicated on the principle that the financial contribution of the non-custodial parent should be maintained at the level it would be were the family still together. The guidelines consist of formulae based on econometric estimates of the costs of children in two-parent families and a division of these estimated expenditures in proportion to the incomes of the two parents, with the non-custodial parent's share becoming the child support award.

For example, suppose there is a family with two children, the man and woman having incomes of $30,000 and $20,000 respectively, and the woman gets custody of the children. The first step is to go to the estimates of the expenditures on children in intact families to read off the amount for families with incomes of $50,000; suppose it is $15,000. The next step is to split these estimated expenditures in proportion to the two parents' incomes, which results in shares of $9,000 and $6,000 respectively. The custodial parent's share is assumed to be met in the course of living with the child; the non-custodial parent's share is the child support payable.*

Note in particular that it is *pre*-divorce expenditures on the children which are estimated and shared, and not actual post-divorce spending. This follows from the underlying principle of the Income Shares approach — maintaining the non-custodial parent's financial support at the level it would be were the family still together. *Ergo*, an Income Shares guideline differs from the current system in two key respects: it replaces the case-by-case budget-based procedures for arriving at awards with a general formula uniformly applied to all situations; and it shifts the underlying principle for determining the non-custodial parent's financial responsibility for the child from a sharing of the actual post-divorce expenditures on the child to maintaining the non-custodial parent's financial contribution at the level it would be were the family still together. Some may find this guiding principle appealing, others may not.

THE FIXED PERCENTAGES OF INCOME APPROACH

The second major type of child support guideline is a system of Fixed Percentages of Income. This approach has also been adopted in many US jurisdictions, and has come to be most closely associated with the State of Wisconsin, where it was adopted as part of a more general "Child Support Assurance System." This system, as envisioned by Professor Irwin Garfinkel (then at The University of Wisconsin -

---

*In the actual implementation of the guideline, there might be a single step whereby the two incomes are read in and the award is given directly. That is, the two components can be reduced to a single formula. The key point is that the two steps described here underlie the final result, regardless of the actual mechanics observed by the user.

Madison, now at Columbia University) and his colleagues, was also intended to incorporate automatic withholding *via* the tax system and a minimum level of support payable to all single-parent families from a special child support fund. (To date, the withholding provision has been adopted but the assurance aspect has not.)[10]

The fundamental characteristic of the Fixed Percentages of Income approach is that the non-custodial parent pays a percentage of his or her income according to established scales, and payments do *not* depend on the custodial parent's income. In principle, a Fixed Percentage of Income guideline can be based on any number of factors relating to child expenditures, incomes, standards of living and so on. In practice, the approach is usually roughly grounded in the Income Shares approach, but takes those child expenditure estimates and related income shares only as a starting point, after which other factors are also taken into consideration to construct the schedule of payments.

For example, those charged with devising the Wisconsin plan first analyzed the entire existing literature on the costs of children. They threw out estimates which seemed to have clear shortcomings of any sort (e.g., a faulty theoretical approach, data problems) and then selected a somewhat subjective mid-point of the remaining estimates. Most importantly, while their choice seemed reasonable and to enjoy some support, they recognized the inherent margin of error in the exercise, and accepted the fact that another set of estimates might be as reasonable. Next, they calculated the shares of income these costs represented as a point of departure for arriving at a set of fixed percentages.

The Wisconsin architects then took into account various factors that might suggest payments should be higher than the straightforward percentage calculations indicated (e.g., the decline in the child's well-being associated with the loss of economies of scale due to the break-up of the household) *versus* those that would indicate payments should be lower (e.g., the fact that non-custodial parents no longer have the benefit of living with the child, visitation costs, a desire to keep nonpayment rates low by not pushing awards too high).

Thus, the determination of a set of percentages — that is, the guideline — was seen to be an art as well as a science. As Professor Garfinkel writes, "none of these reasons [noted above] for expecting nonresident parents to share more (or less) income with their children suggests an exact amount or percentage. Ultimately, the decision about how much the nonresident parent should pay depends upon value judgements about how to balance the objectives of child support. Establishing a child support standard cannot be a purely scientific exercise."*

In principle, the percentages of income to be paid can either vary with the non-custodial parent's income, or be constant across income levels. (Of course a single fixed percentage translates into higher payments at higher income levels, while varying the percentages by income level affects the *rate* at which payments increase.) The system can also incorporate a set-aside, whereby non-custodial parents with incomes below a certain level pay nothing. In short, the schedule of payments may be quite simple or fairly complex. To repeat, the distinguishing characteristic is that payments depend only on the non-custodial parent's income (as well, of course, as the number of children), and do not vary with the custodial parent's income.

The Wisconsin plan itself is of the simpler variety: non-custodial parents pay a fixed percentage of 17, 25, 29, 31 or 34 percent of gross income, depending on the number of children (from one to five or more). So, for example, the non-custodial parent with two children earning $30,000 in our example would pay $7,500 (25 percent of gross income), another with an income of $40,000 would pay $10,000 and so on.

THE STANDARDS OF LIVING APPROACH

The third major category of guideline is the Standards of Living approach. It is conceptually very simple: objectives are set in terms of the post-divorce standards of living of the custodial and/or non-custodial households, and support payments are then calculated to achieve these targets. While this approach has a certain allure, it has never been adopted in practice, for reasons that will become more clear as we proceed.

---

*Irwin Garfinkel, *Assuring Child Support: An Extension of Social Security* (New York: Basic Books, 1992). In chapter 5, he writes "...we sought to balance the objectives of providing for the children, being fair to the resident parent, minimizing public costs, and retaining incentives and a decent standard of living for the nonresident parent. Our final recommendation to the state was that the sharing rate for non-resident parents with one child be [a little less than the point estimate of the econometric models, reflecting] the view that the reasons for having a lower sharing rate for nonresident parents compared to that for resident parents outweighed those for having a higher sharing rate." See also Garfinkel and Marygold Melli, "The Use of Normative Standards in Family Law Decisions: Developing Mathematical Standards for Child Support," in Irwin Garfinkel, Sara S. McLanahan and Philip K. Robins, *Child Support Assurance: Design Issues, Expected Impacts and Political Barriers as Seen From Wisconsin* (Washington, DC: The Urban Institute Press, 1992), chap. 5.

The best known of the Standard of Living guidelines is probably the Equal Standards of Living (or "Cassetty") formula.[11] Under this approach, child support awards are calculated to leave the non-custodial parent and the custodial household at the same standard of living, measured by adjusting total family income for the different needs of families of different sizes with established "equivalence scales." For example, the equivalence scale underlying the Statistics Canada Low-Income Measures (LIMs) incorporates the judgement that a family of two requires 1.4 times as much income as a single adult to be as well off, a family of three requires 1.7 times as much, a family of four 2.0 as much, and so on. This is sometimes referred to as the "40/30" scale. By this measure, a two-person family is assumed to require an income 40 percent higher than that of a single individual to leave the two households equally well off. Another way of saying this is that the second person (a spouse, or the child in a single-parent family) requires .40 times the income of the first. Beyond this, each additional person is expected to require .30 times as much as the first person: thus 1.4 plus .3 equals 1.7 is the relative income requirement for a three-person family, an additional .30 for a total of 2.0 is required for a family of four, and so on. Dividing family income by the equivalence scale yields the adjusted income figures used to establish the award.

Returning to the example and using the LIMs as an equivalence scale to adjust family income, an award of approximately $11,500 would be required to equalize the two households' standards of living. This would leave the non-custodial parent with an income of $18,500, and the mother and children with a total income of $31,500, but the same adjusted income as the non-custodial parent (i.e., $31,5000 divided by 1.7 equals $18,500).

Another variant of the Standards of Living approach embraces the "maintenance" principle, whereby the award is set to maintain the children at the pre-divorce standard of living. In the example, the pre-divorce standard of living, as measured by adjusted income, is $25,000 (i.e., $30,000 plus $20,000, divided by 2.0). To maintain the children at this level would require a child support payment of $22,500 (i.e., $20,000 plus $22,500, divided by 1.7, equals $25,000). Note that the non-custodial parent would be left with just $7,500 in this case.

In general, any number of objectives in terms of standards of living may be defined and implemented in a similar fashion. For example, standards of living in the two households might be set as equal to the ratio of the parents' own incomes. Again, the general procedure is to determine the objectives in terms of adjusted family incomes, and set child support awards to achieve this. Of course the objectives must be internally consistent. For example, the levels of the custodial and non-custodial families could not *both* be maintained at the pre-divorce level, because this would require more money than is available (unless the parents increased their earnings after the split).

As the examples demonstrate, a Standards of Living guideline can result in extremely high awards. This is because the principle underlying the Standards of Living approach is fundamentally different from that of the Income Shares and Fixed Percentage of Income approaches. The Standard of Living approach is *outcome*-based, and obviously focussed on the post-divorce situation, whereas the others are based on the notion of a fair contribution on the part of the non-custodial parent. The different approaches clearly have grossly different implications for both the well-being of the custodial and non-custodial parents. These issues will be returned to later.

OTHER TYPES OF GUIDELINES

There are other specific types of guidelines, but they may all be seen as consisting of various components of the major three types just described. There may be some sort of splitting of costs (Income Shares), a schedule of payments that depends only on the non-custodial parent's income (Fixed Percentages of Income), or consideration of the well-being of one or the other households (Standards of Living).

For example the "Delaware Melson" formula embodies, interestingly, elements of each of the three major types.* First, there is a set aside for each parent, whereby individuals with incomes below a certain level are not expected to pay anything towards the support of the child (Standard of Living). Second, the child's minimum means are established in a similar manner, and the parents share the responsibility of meeting these needs in proportion to their "surplus" incomes (Income Shares). Once this minimum is met, the non-custodial parent pays a certain percentage of income (Fixed Percentages of Income). Other classifications can be found in the literature, but the triad employed here is simple and useful.

---

*This formula was named after Judge Elwood F. Melson, who devised it in 1979 in Delaware Family Court. The original guideline was revised in 1990. It has been adopted in three states: Delaware, Hawaii and West Virginia.

ESTIMATING EXPENDITURES ON CHILDREN — THE
METHODOLOGY

It has been explained above how every guideline can be thought of
as consisting of two components: estimates of the expenditures on children and a rule for apportioning these expenditures between the two
parents. Having described the three major approaches to child support
guidelines in terms of their use of a given set of child cost estimates, we
now turn to the child expenditure estimates themselves.* This section
contains a discussion of expenditure estimates from a methodological
perspective, while the following section provides a suggestion as to the
choice of a particular set of child cost estimates for the construction of
child support guidelines.

At the outset, it should be understood that the expenditure estimates are clearly of fundamental importance to child support guidelines.
For example, a difference in estimates of, say, 30 percent (which is easy
to find in the established literature), is going to change awards — *all*
awards — by a comparable magnitude. While the issues of child expenditure estimates are often complex and technically difficult in terms of
the underlying economic theory and econometric issues, the essential
points can be explained in nontechnical terms which permit the reader
to understand the key points and make informed judgements.[12]

It is appropriate to begin by identifying precisely the term "the costs
of children" as it is used in the economics literature, as it does not conform to common usage of the term. In fact, there are a number of different concepts of "the costs of children" but the one probably most widely
employed is based on the simple idea that children reduce the amount of
money parents have available to spend on themselves and can be defined
as the dollar amount by which *total family income* would have to rise to
bring the *parents* in families with children up to the same standard of living they would have in the *absence* of children. Each particular method of
estimating the costs of children then differs in how this concept is put
into operation.[13]

Note that this definition of "costs" is a hypothetical construct
derived from economic theory and intended to permit comparisons of
well-being across different types of households. Most importantly, it

---

*Note that the expenditure estimates are used in different ways — in a direct man-
ner for the Income Shares approach and most Fixed Percentage of Income guidelines, and indirectly, *via* the construction of equivalence scales, for the Standard of
Living approach.

does *not* generally represent actual spending on children — which is probably the layperson's notion of the costs of children. For example, if a couple has a certain level of income, decides to have a child, maintains family income at the original level and then spends this income on themselves and — naturally — their child, by the above definition the "cost of the child" is the increase in income which would be needed to bring the parents back up to the pre-child level of spending on themselves, and not what is actually spent on the child.*

The best-known approach to the estimation of child costs is probably the traditional Engel method, which is founded on the assumption that a family's well-being can be summarized by the proportion of its total income which is spent on food: equal proportions spent on food across families are deemed to indicate equal levels of well-being, while a higher proportion indicates lower well-being. The underlying idea is that families who are forced to spend more of their income on this most basic of necessities are materially worse off than others who spend a lower proportion on the basics (and therefore have more money left to spend on luxuries).

The empirical procedures essentially consist of, first, using econometric models to estimate the average difference in the expenditures on food in families with children and childless couples; then using these estimates to determine the additional income the families with children would need to make their expenditures on food amount to the same proportion of family income as that which holds for childless couples. This estimated amount is deemed "the costs of the children." The exercise is carried out for families with different numbers of children to get the costs of families of different sizes, and can be done across other dimensions of family structure, such as for two- *versus* one-parent households,

---

*Martin Browning concludes his report for the Federal/Provincial/Justice Committee by asserting that rather than the "iso-welfare" question, just described, which is generally what interests economists most and where most research has been targeted, "I believe that it is the *costing* question that is of importance when we consider child support." In other words, how much actually gets spent on children? Thus most of the research on child costs is perhaps not even directed at what we need to know to construct child support guidelines. See Martin Browning, "Measuring the Costs of Children in Canada: A Practical Guide," Technical Report prepared for the Federal/Provincial/Territorial Family Law Committee, TR1991-13a, January 1991.

the age of the children and so on.*

For example, if it was determined that couples with incomes of $40,000 spent, on average, $10,000 on food (25 percent), while couples with two children at the same income level spent $15,000 on food, the larger families would be said to require an income of $60,000 to bring their expenditures on food down to the same percentage as the childless couples, thus leaving them as well off (by the assumptions of the approach). The estimated cost of the two children is, then, the additional family income required to maintain that same level of well-being, or $20,000.**

Note that expenditures on food are used only as an *index* of well-being, and that the resulting cost estimate does not represent actual expenditures on the children, neither in terms of food nor any other specific bundle of goods. It is a rather more specific concept, worth restating: an increase in total family income to make the actual spending on food in the family with children an equal proportion of family income as for childless couples would, by the assumptions of the approach, leave the families equally well off.

The basic Engel approach is well-known, fairly easy to understand, and nicely illustrates the specific notion of the costs of children that typically underlies the econometric estimates used in guidelines. Other methods of estimating child costs are fundamentally quite similar, and most are based on the same underlying concept described above.

The Extended Engel or "Isoprop" approach departs from the basic Engel method by using a broader definition of "necessities" (e.g., food, shelter and clothing); the adult goods or "Rothbarth" approach turns the Engel method upside down to use a package of goods that *only* adults consume as the indicator of well-being; while the Blackorby-Donaldson and consumption techniques allow for greater flexibility in consumption patterns, but rely instead on assumptions about the precise form of families' preferences and the maximizing nature of their behaviour to make comparisons of well-being and thereby derive cost estimates. There are

---

*These concepts are described quite well in many places, but Betson is particularly clear, aided by a nice graphical presentation. See David M. Betson, "Alternative Estimates of the Cost of Children From the 1980-86 Consumer Expenditure Survey," *Institute for Research on Poverty Special Report*, no. 51 (Madison, Wis.: University of Wisconsin - Madison, 1990). Note that the whole exercise can also be framed in terms of total family expenditures, rather than income.

**Certain important technical points are fudged here in order to simplify the presentation and leave the reader with a good intuitive understanding of the procedures.

still other ways to estimate the costs of children which need not be discussed here.[14]

CHOOSING A SET OF EXPENDITURE ESTIMATES

Each of the different methods of estimating the costs of children has certain attributes to recommend it, but each also has certain weaknesses in terms of its theoretical underpinnings and/or the demands it puts on the data. There is, therefore, no compelling reason to choose one method over the other for theoretical reasons.* Furthermore, there are always data limitations in terms of the actual estimation, and a margin of error relating to the fact that the estimates depend on statistical models, even if everything is done right. Finally, there is the question of whether or not the existing estimates pertain to the notion of child expenditures which is most relevant to child support guidelines.

In short, it is very difficult to choose among the wide range of existing child expenditure estimates or to know how close the best one might be to the truth.[15] In one of his reports for the Federal/Provincial/Territorial Committee, Martin Browning, one of the world's foremost authorities on these issues, opens with a sobering proviso: "It cannot be emphasized too strongly that this is an area of considerable controversy." After seventy pages, he concludes: "...all we can honestly hope to do is make an informed choice of method that minimizes the bias in estimating the cost of children."[16]

Now recall the previous statement that any substantial difference in child cost estimates is going to result in similarly divergent child support awards. In other words, we know that the choice of child expenditure estimates will have a large impact on the magnitude of awards, yet there is a wide range of estimates to choose from, with no obvious

---

*In Browning's authoritative review of the literature, fundamental problems are found with each method. See Martin Browning, "Children and Household Economic Behaviour," *Journal of Economic Literature*," Vol. 30, no. 3 (September 1992), pp. 1434-75. Regarding the Engel method: "...the method does not seem to have any virtue, except that it is easy to implement." (p. 1443). For the adult goods approach: "Once again, I find it is difficult to see why this commands any widespread attention." (p. 1443). As for the technically more sophisticated Blackorby-Donaldson technique, it is grouped with others of the same general type of which it is said: "...utility methods have not made much progress" (p. 1444) and "[a]t the moment no single [utility] method commands widespread support." (p. 1445). Browning has more recently said in conversation, however, that he has great hope for the Blackorby-Donaldson method in general.

choice. What is to be done?

First, it is important to accept the fact that there is going to be substantial uncertainty attached to any set of child cost estimates; to support a guidelines approach is to accept this uncertainty. That is not, however, to say that guidelines should therefore necessarily be scrapped. After all, it has already been discussed how the current system of determining child support awards is itself replete with uncertainties, margins of error and other arbitrary aspects, *albeit* of different types. It is a question of tradeoffs and relative preferences for one approach over another.

The best strategy might therefore be to rely on the accumulated work on child cost estimates carried out over the years in Canada. In particular, it seems wisest not to embrace the research commissioned by the Federal/Provincial/Territorial Committee too closely, as it has been tested neither by the passage of time nor the thorough scrutiny of peer review.

A natural choice might be the Statistics Canada Low-Income Cut-Offs (LICOs), which incorporate child cost estimates in their adjustments of income for family size. LICOs have been developed over many years, and have the considerable merit of having gained a certain support as being reasonable. An even better alternative might be the Statistics Canada Low Income Measures (LIMs), which are close cousins of the LICOs. Their added advantage is that they reflect not only the econometric evidence embodied in the LICOs but also careful consideration of other scales currently in use in Canada and abroad, as well as extensive consultations with a wide range of advocacy groups.

Perhaps the principal drawback of the LICOs and LIMs is that they are tailored to represent child costs at a very particular point — the low income line — and not necessarily at higher income levels. Child expenditures based on LICOs or LIMs will be estimated to rise with family income, but they are constrained to represent the same *ratio* of family income across the income distribution. For example, the LIM's "40/30" scale implies that about 17.6 percent of family income goes on a first child (30 percent divided by the sum of 100, 40 and 30).* Therefore, if child costs actually rise or fall more than proportionally with income, this could present a problem; fortunately, looking across the full set of child expenditure estimates suggests that child expenditures are in fact

---

*See the previous discussions where the "40/30" equivalence scale and its use for generating child cost estimates are explained.

approximately proportional to income.*

Moreover, any legislation should explicitly address the issue that child expenditure estimates are very likely to change over time, as actual costs change and as estimation methods continue to improve. A review every four years or so might be appropriate, as this could coincide with the general reviews of the Statistics Canada LICOs (based on the FAMEX database, compiled every four years). There then needs to be some sort of established mechanism for revising guidelines and perhaps even existing awards in the light of any significant changes in child cost estimates.

It might be unsettling for some to think that child support awards could potentially shift around depending on the most recent estimates of child costs coming from Statistics Canada or some other group of economists charged with this task. This is, however, inevitable with a guidelines approach.

Finally, some readers might be somewhat disillusioned at this point. One of the major attractions of standardizing awards through guidelines is to avoid the difficulties of estimating expenditures on children at an individual level. Yet now it seems that there has simply been a substitution of uncertainty at the individual level with uncertainty at a broader level, and it is not even clear that this will result in generally better cost estimates. Do we trust economists and their econometric estimates more than individuals' abilities to estimate expenditures regarding their own

---

*Analysts at Statistics Canada again set a useful standard. After having reviewed the accumulation of evidence, they assume linearity of child costs — that is, that spending on children is approximately a constant proportion of family income across different income ranges — when they calculate adjusted family income measures. (For further discussion, see See Michael Wolfson, John M. Evans and Brian Murphy, "Low Income Statistics: Methodological Issues and Recent Experience in Canada," Statistics Canada Labour and Household Surveys Analysis Division Discussion Paper, 1990.) A guideline could, however, incorporate an adjustment built in at very high income levels on the grounds that families spend smaller proportions of their income on children in these ranges.

Similarly, some might feel that payments should vary with the age of the children. This is an interesting point because many individuals instinctively feel that younger children cost more (due largely to day care costs) while others seem to think the opposite (due to teens' elevated clothing and entertainment needs, etc.), and there are econometric estimates to match these conflicting opinions. Once more Statistics Canada sets a useful standard: in the absence of any particularly persuasive evidence in either direction they make no adjustment for children's age in their standard equivalence scales.

children? Again, guidelines are not magic, and might well be an improvement over the current situation, but there is also the element of a tradeoff that must be accepted — or refused.*

A NOTE ON CHILD COSTS IN TWO-PARENT *VERSUS* ONE-PARENT FAMILIES

When are the estimated costs of children in two-parent families needed, and when are costs in single-parent families the relevant consideration? It is important to recognize that this depends on the specific guideline approach in question. For example, the Income Shares approach is based on estimating the financial contribution of the non-custodial parent as if the family were still intact, and thus it is clearly the costs in two-parent families that are relevant. On the other hand, a Standards of Living approach is likely to involve comparisons of adjusted incomes in the two post-divorce households and perhaps a comparison of these with adjusted incomes in the pre-divorce situation, thus implicating the costs of children in both single-parent and two-parent families. In short, determining which expenditure estimate is appropriate depends on the principles of the particular guideline in question.

SUMMARY

The major points regarding the construction of child support guidelines are summarized here.

- ■ The different approaches to guidelines can be classified under three broad headings:
  - *Income Shares*. This is based on setting the non-custodial parent's financial contribution at the level it would be were the family still together; it consists of estimating what total expenditures on the children would be were the family still together and then splitting these in proportion to the two parents' incomes.
  - *Fixed Percentages of Income*. This can be based on a number of different underlying principles, but usually is derived from an Income Shares starting point; the key characteristic is that the

---

*Of course many guideline advocates see the principal problem with the current system as being their perception that the courts are unwilling to set awards that adequately reflect the child cost estimates arrived at under any particular method, rather than the accuracy of the cost estimates themselves.

award depends on the non-custodial parent's income and the number of children but not on the custodial parent's income.

- *Standards of Living:* This is based on targets regarding post-divorce standards of living, such as equalized standards of living for the custodial household and the non-custodial parent, or maintaining the child at the pre-divorce standard of living.

■ Child cost/expenditure estimates enter all of these approaches: directly, for the Income Shares approach; indirectly *via* the construction of equivalence scales for the Standard of Living approach; and potentially in a variety of ways for the Fixed Percentages of Income approach.

■ Estimating expenditures on children is a difficult task, and there is a wide range of estimates in the literature with no obvious way of choosing among them. A case can be made for using an established set of estimates, such as those incorporated in the Statistics Canada LICOs or LIMs.

■ Nevertheless, there is still a substantial margin of error attached to any set of child cost estimates, and this has to be accepted if a guideline approach is chosen. The type of error and uncertainty is very different from that of the current case-by-case system, but it is difficult to say which will be more accurate on average.

■ Child expenditure estimates will change over time, due to changes in actual expenditures, and also due to improvements in estimation procedures. Any legislation should address what is to be done with such updates in terms of the guidelines in general, as well as for specific awards.

CHILD SUPPORT AND ECONOMIC WELL-BEING

The major types of child support guidelines have been described in terms of their underlying principles, construction and general characteristics. An important issue remains, however: what standards of living do the different types of awards generate?

There are, in fact, some widely held misconceptions in this regard. For example, many individuals seem to think that a child's welfare will be maintained at the pre-divorce level if awards are set equal to the non-custodial parent's share of the estimated expenditures on the child in the pre-divorce situation, as with the Income Shares approach. This is, however, not at all the case; in fact, Income Shares guidelines do not ensure *any* particular standard of living for the child — nor for either of the parents.

It is obviously important to have a good grasp of the relationship between guidelines and economic well-being before passing judgement on child support guidelines in general, or evaluating one specific approach *versus* another. Furthermore, these issues are entirely pertinent to one's understanding of the current system of child support.

This chapter begins with discussions of how families function as economic units, with an emphasis on intra-household sharing and how child support payments fit into this model. In particular, it is explained that child support payments should not generally be thought of as going only to the child and ensuring some particular level of well-being for the child in isolation to the custodial parent or any other custodial family members; instead, child support payments are best seen as contributing to the total income of the custodial household, across which a common standard of living is then shared. After establishing these broad principles, the different guideline approaches are reviewed in terms of the resulting standards of living, followed by some related issues regarding the relative well-being of the custodial and non-custodial households.

INCOME SHARING WITHIN HOUSEHOLDS

By way of introduction, recall that the methods of estimating the costs of children described in the previous chapter are all indirect, in that they do not constitute an attempt to simply identify and add up all the spending on children but instead consist of studying the spending patterns of families of different sizes and structures to *deduce* the costs of children.

Such indirect approaches are employed principally because it is very difficult to separate spending on children from spending on adults, due to the joint nature of consumption within families. For example, housing, transportation and food constitute the major spending categories, and are difficult to separate out in terms of the cost shares belonging to each family member. In fact, very few family budget items can be clearly identified as constituting spending on children alone, and any items which can be so identified (e.g., clothing, toys, school supplies) are certainly not going to represent anything like the major part of spending on children. It follows that any attempt to estimate the costs of children by identifying spending on children apart from spending on the parents with whom they live is going to run into significant problems — hence the indirect approaches.*

But what does this discussion of the estimation of expenditures on children have to do with assessments of the economic well-being of post-

---

*An alternative approach to estimating the costs of children is to define certain bundles of goods ("necessities") and then determine how much it costs to provide these items to families of different sizes using actual information on prices. For some recent developments on poverty lines using this approach, see Trudi J. Renwick and Barbara Bergman, "A Budget-Based Definition of Poverty," *The Journal of Human Resources*, Vol. 28, no. 1 (Winter 1993), pp. 1-24. For Canadian work of this type, see David P. Ross and E. Richard Shillington, *The Canadian Fact Book on Poverty - 1989* (Ottawa/Montreal: The Canadian Council on Social

divorce households? Quite simply, once the principle of joint consumption is accepted, not only must we abandon the idea of measuring the costs of children directly, we must also accept the corollary that the material well-being of the children and parents is inherently and inextricably entwined. That is, it is most instructive to think of all family members sharing a common standard of living, with this level determined by the total amount of income available to the family *versus* the needs of the family as summarized by the number of family members.**

In particular, child support payments should not be thought of as providing for spending on the child alone, or raising the child's well-being in isolation to the custodial parent (or any other members of the household). Instead, support payments should be seen as increasing the custodial family's *total* income and spending, and lifting the well-being of *all* members of that household commensurately.

A critic might respond that this is simply not how child support payments work, and that the money *is* in fact specifically targeted on the

---

Development, 1989). These approaches remain "indirect," in that one cannot observe the consumption of the children separately from that of the parents. Such methods are not widely used, however, for a variety of reasons. For further discussion, see Martin Browning, "Children and Household Economic Behaviour," *Journal of Economic Literature*, Vol. 30, no. 3 (September 1992), pp. 1434-75.

**It is worth noting that most economists use as a working hypothesis the idea that parents make spending decisions to balance the needs of all the family members, meaning that the well-being of each individual is functionally related to that of the others. In economic jargon, income is assumed to be spent so as to maximize family utility by equating the marginal utility of expenditures across family members. Any change in spending is shared across all family members so as to keep the marginal utilities of spending equalized, and family utility maximized, thus assuring the well-being of all family members integrally. Thus, economic theory can be added to our understanding of the logistics of (joint) family consumption and empirical observations of consumption patterns to instruct us to think in terms of a common level of well-being for the family.

On the other hand, this is in fact only theory, and while it has some appeal, there are obviously many cases where this is not how things work. In fact, there is currently a great deal of interest on the part of economists in putting this theory to the test empirically. For a recent paper regarding issues of intra-family sharing of income and well-being, see Reuben Gronau, "The Intrafamily Allocation of Goods — How to Separate the Adult From the Child," *Journal of Labour Economics*," Vol. 9, no. 3 (July 1991), pp. 207-35.

child and gets spent accordingly. But for the most part this is simply not possible, for the reasons described above. How, for example, could spending ostensibly targeted on the child's housing, transportation or food be separated from what the custodial parent spends on himself or herself in this regard? How can the child's material well-being be increased while the custodial parent's remains fixed? *Even if* all parties agreed that the support payments should cover only the costs of the child, this would be impossible to actually implement.

Suppose, for example, that the parents decided on a certain standard of housing to be provided for the child; the child lives with the custodial parent, and their consumption of housing is therefore unavoidably linked: one cannot think in terms of a certain standard of living for the child without implicating the situation of the custodial parent as well. For example, the child cannot live in a nice house while the custodial parent has shabbier surroundings. Or suppose that the parents decide at some point that the child should have *better* housing — this would presumably take the form of a nicer house and perhaps a better neighbourhood, and *not* just improvements in the child's own room; this cannot be done for the child in isolation, precisely because the child and custodial parent's consumption of housing are fundamentally inter-dependent.*

Furthermore, even when support payments *are* explicitly targeted on specific types of spending on the child, such as clothes, toys or special activities, the reality of the economic functioning of a household is that this frees money to be spent elsewhere. Such directed spending is therefore largely a charade played out by the parents, and the custodial family's spending patterns are not likely to be very different from what they would be were support payments given without any direction. There may, of course, be exceptions to this rule, but the general principle holds.

---

*Of course one can think in terms of what it would cost to bring the child up to a certain standard of living already established by the custodial parent, but this changes nothing in terms of the present discussion. That is, any transfer short of this specified amount would lead to a reduction of the standard of living of both the custodial parent and the child, and any payments beyond this would have the opposite effect.

WHAT LEVEL OF WELL-BEING DO CHILD SUPPORT PAYMENTS GUARANTEE?

It has just been argued that the principles of within-household joint consumption and income sharing mean that child support payments cannot be separated out as going to the targeted child in isolation to the custodial parent. On the other hand, the payments clearly raise the material well-being of the child and custodial parent together and lower the net income of the non-custodial parent making the payment.

One might then ask: can anything be said about the precise level of the child's post-divorce standard of living when support awards are based on the sharing of the estimated pre-divorce costs of children, as in the Income Shares approach, or the related types of guideline based on the payer's income such as the Fixed Percentages of Income? It should now be evident that the answer to this question is no, because the child's standard of living depends on the *total* amount of money available to the custodial family, and not just the amount received in child support payments.

Specifically, recall that the Income Shares method is based on the principle of maintaining the financial contribution of the non-custodial parent at the level it would be were the family still together. This is very different from calculating awards based on how much money would need to be transferred to ensure that the child's standard of living was maintained at the pre-divorce level — or indeed any other specific level; this would require ensuring that the custodial *family* had enough money to lift it up to the target level — that is, a Standards of Living approach. It would certainly be *easier* if we could treat the child in isolation to the custodial parent and any other custodial family members, but we cannot.

Let us consider an extreme case as an illustrative example of the loose relationship between the level of award and the post-divorce standard of living that characterizes the Income Shares approach to guidelines. Suppose the custodial parent had no income of his or her own, and therefore the non-custodial parent's share of the estimated expenditures on the child was 100 percent, which was duly transferred to the custodial parent, ostensibly to be spent on the child. If there were no spousal support, this would be the total amount of money the custodial household would have. *Even if* the support money *was* actually spent entirely on the child — an impossible notion, because the custodial parent would literally not survive, and also in defiance of the principles of family sharing which have been established above — this would *still* not maintain the child at the pre-divorce standard of living. This is because the money would be spent on the child *as an isolated individual*, leaving him or her at a lower standard of living than when the money was spent at the margin with the parents already provided for.

As an aspect of this example, consider the problem specifically in terms of housing. The estimated child costs are what it might take to provide the *additional* space for the child, with housing sufficient for the parents already in place; starting the child from scratch would obviously yield less housing for this same amount of money. This result is grounded in the simple and fundamental principle of joint consumption, as established above.

Furthermore — and again appealing to the principles of within-family income sharing — it should be presumed that the custodial parent and child would share the *total* income available to the custodial household, which, in our example, consists only of the child support payment. The child's well-being, as measured by adjusted family income, would now be seen as being *much* lower than the pre-divorce level — even though the non-custodial parent is paying the full "child costs" as support payments. Again, this is because those payments are based on estimates of what it would cost the couple to maintain the child at the margin in a two-parent family, whereas those monies now comprise the total amount of income available to support the entire custodial family. Again, this example illustrates the general principle that the child's standard of living will depend on the *total* income in the custodial family *versus* its needs, and not just on what has been specified as a support payment based on the estimated costs of children in the pre-divorce situation.

While the above example is a bit extreme, in that the custodial parent was presumed to have no income (apart from the child support payment), it is worth emphasizing that under an Income Shares or related type of guideline the child will typically be left at a lower standard of living than in the pre-divorce situation. The only exception will be where the custodial parent's own income is high enough that it combines with the support payments to maintain the smaller custodial household at the pre-divorce level. Note, again, the importance of the custodial parent's own income to this result.

An extreme case illustrating the rare conditions under which the child's well-being would actually improve in the post-divorce situation under an Income Shares guideline would be where the custodial parent had the *entire* family income in the pre-divorce situation. The child support contribution of the non-custodial parent would be zero, but the custodial family would have the same income as before, while the smaller size of the household (minus the non-custodial parent) would leave the child (and his or her custodial parent) better off than in the pre-divorce situation. (The non-custodial parent would be left with nothing.) Once more, the general principle is that the child's standard of living depends on the income of the custodial parent as much as it depends on the support payments of the non-custodial parent.

CUSTODIAL *VERSUS* NON-CUSTODIAL HOUSEHOLD WELL-BEING

It should now be clear that Income Shares or related guidelines are likely to leave the child and custodial parent at a very different standard of living from that of the non-custodial parent. In particular, if the non-custodial parent has a higher income than the custodial parent, he or she is likely to be left relatively better off — again, *even if* the child costs are correctly calculated and duly transferred in the form of child support. This is basically because these are *child support* awards, and thus represent the portion of the non-custodial parent's income shared with *the child*, whereas there is also sharing *between the parents* in a marriage that is not taken into account in these transfers.

In general, if there is no explicit spousal support reflecting the interparent sharing of incomes that existed during the marriage, the divorce will tend to leave the higher-income parent relatively better off than the other, since the income previously shared with the spouse is now kept for himself or herself. The child's well-being is obviously affected, with his or her standard of living tending to be higher or lower depending on which parent the child remains with — the one who has the advantage or disadvantage with regard to his or her own earnings.

Of course in the majority of actual cases, the child remains with the mother, who is the lower-income parent, thus leaving the child in the relatively disadvantaged household — even with the full payment of child support. It needs to be emphasized that it is *relative* well-being that is at issue here, since *both* households may be worse off than in the pre-divorce situation due to the loss of economies of scale associated with the family break-up.

A specific example should again help illustrate these points. Suppose the intact family has an income of $50,000, and child costs are estimated to be 20 percent of this total. Now, assume that the non-custodial parent earns the entire family income, therefore bears the full responsibility of the child costs and makes payments in this amount. This means the custodial household will have an income of only $10,000, while the non-custodial parent is left with $40,000.

The post-divorce income differences come from the fact that the non-custodial parent was presumably also sharing income with the ex-spouse during the marriage. In other words, the custodial parents were sharing what did not go towards the children, a sum of $40,000 in this example — and there is no accounting for this in the child support transfers; instead, the non-custodial parent has the use of that entire $40,000. In short, divorce leaves the custodial parent cut off from the portion of the non-custodial parent's income that was shared during the marriage. This obviously affects the income level of the custodial family, and therefore the well-being of the child. On the other hand, if the child remains with the parent with the higher of the parental incomes, the result is reversed. Of course, spousal support might leave the custodial parent with a share of that $40,000 but that is another issue — even as it affirms how tightly related the issues of child and spousal support inevitably are.

The child's post-divorce level of well-being is thus again seen to depend on the economic situation of the custodial parent, and cannot be split apart and treated in isolation. The general result is that, in the absence of an integration of child support with spousal support, there will be differences in the post-divorce standards of living of the two parents —that is, between the custodial and non-custodial households. The greater the income inequalities between the two parents, the greater the resulting parental and household differences, and the more the child is also affected. As long as the child remains with the lower-income parent, he or she will suffer the relative disadvantages of that parent.

This likely inequality of household income is inherent in the Income-Shares approach, precisely because this guideline type is entirely founded on the determination of a fair payment on the part of the non-custodial parent in terms of supporting *the child*, with no regard for the intra-couple sharing that also occurred during the marriage and the fact that the custodial parent's income is a principal determinant of the child's post-divorce level of well-being. Dropping the gender neutrality of the above presentation, it is clear that the gender earnings gap has much to do with determining the post-divorce relative standards of living of the two households, and while the standard guidelines do take this into account when determining the shares of *child support per se*, they do not address the further implications of the children living with a parent who has much lower earnings than the other.

A RECONSIDERATION OF THE STANDARDS OF LIVING APPROACH TO GUIDELINES

To return to an earlier theme, if full support payments based on the estimation and sharing of child costs within the marriage are not generally going to bring the child up to the pre-divorce standard of living, or any other particular level, how can this goal be achieved? More generally, if the objectives are in terms of *outcomes* — such as a target standard of living for the child, or perhaps a certain relationship in standards of living between the custodial and non-custodial families — how can these be achieved? The answer: a Standards of Living approach to guidelines.

The Standards of Living approach has been explained above: objectives are set regarding post-divorce standards of living and support payments are established accordingly. Two specific variants of this approach have been described and are worth looking at again in terms of the resulting standards of living in the two households.

With a Maintenance guideline, support payments are set so that the custodial parent's own income plus the support payments leave the custodial family's adjusted income equal to the pre-split level. The custodial family requires less total income than the intact family, since it is smaller, but this method will generally result in *very* large support payments, especially in the typical case where the non-custodial parent earns more than the custodial parent. This means that the non-custodial parent will generally be left at a standard of living which is well below that of the custodial family, and therefore also obviously well below the standard of living in the pre-divorce situation. This is because the non-custodial parent is effectively left with an income approximately equal to the *marginal* cost of a family member, but must maintain his or her independent household on this relatively small sum. In this sense, the non-custodial parent bears the *entire* economic costs of the divorce (as well as very high implicit tax rates, as will be discussed further below).

For example, suppose we again employ the Statistics Canada LIMs as an equivalence scale (a two-person family requires 1.4 the level of income of a single person, a three-person family 1.7 as much and four people 2.0 as much), and assume a pre-divorce family of four had income of $50,000, made up of $30,000 earned by the non-custodial parent and $20,000 earned by the custodial parent. This family of four, earning a total of $50,000, is judged to have the same standard of living as one person earning $25,000 ($50,000 divided by a factor of 2.0). Thus, $25,000 represents the pre-divorce adjusted income of the family. To maintain this level of adjusted income in the post-divorce three-person custodial family, the base level of $25,000 is multiplied by a factor of 1.7 (translating the base level into the equivalent income level for a three-person family), which equals $42,500. The difference between $42,500 and the custodial parent's income of $20,000 becomes the child support payment, which is $22,500. Thus, out of the non-custodial parent's income of $30,000, he or she is left with just $7,500. This figure is precisely the marginal cost of the last person in the intact family: $50,000 times .3 divided by 2.0 equals $7,500. The custodial family will therefore have a standard of living which is 3.33 times as high as the non-custodial parent.

In short, a maintenance approach will guarantee the children and their custodial parent the pre-divorce standard of living but will also result in a very low standard of living for the non-custodial parent. While protecting the children's well-being is desirable, the extent of the resulting inequality in standards of living between the two households will probably strike most as being unfair — especially in terms of the difference for the two parents. This issue will be discussed further below.

As for the Equalized Standards of Living approach, the two households — and therefore all family members — share equally in the decline in the standard of living which results from the breakup of one household into two. Continuing with the example and again applying the LIMs as an equivalence scale, instead of adjusting total income by the 2.0 value associated with the pre-divorce two-parent/two-child family, income is divided across one household with a scale value of 1.0 and another with a scale factor of 1.7. This means that the post-divorce standard of living will be at 2.0 times the sum of 1.0 and 1.7, or about .74

of the pre-divorce level. Recall that it was previously calculated that a payment of approximately $11,500 would be required to leave the custodial family with a total income of $31,500 and an adjusted income of approximately $18,500, which is the amount with which the non-custodial parent would be left as well. This $18,500 adjusted income level is precisely .74 the pre-divorce level of $25,000.

IMPLICIT SPOUSAL SUPPORT, THE PARENTS' WELL-BEING AND BALANCING THE INTERESTS OF ALL PARTIES INVOLVED

In the preceding sections we have seen that the fundamental principle of intra-household sharing means that child support awards affect the standards of living of all parties involved — the father, the mother, the child. In particular, each additional dollar of child support decreases the material well-being of the non-custodial parent and increases the standard of living of the child and the custodial parent. In this sense, every *child* support award carries with it implicit *spousal* support as well, although the precise identification of this implicit spousal support is not at all obvious.

This suggests that when evaluating a child support system, we should take into account the resulting standards of living of the parents as well as what happens with the children, and judge these against some established principles of how the costs of the divorce should be shared among all three parties. After all, we surely care about the parents as well as the child, and how can we ignore the relative standards of living of the man and woman when the payments of one contribute to the well-being of the other?*

The problem is that it is difficult to balance the various principles that might guide an assessment of the post-award standards of living of the children and the parents. In particular, various appealing notions of fairness could be found to be mutually inconsistent. For example, one commonly held position is that the child should be maintained at the

---

*This is not to imply that these spousal benefits leave the custodial parent in some advantaged position — indeed, far from it. Further, the custodial parent might well be worse off for having custody of the child even with the support payments. But this does not change the basic fact that, dollar for dollar, support payments decrease the standard of living of the non-custodial parent and improve things for the custodial parent — all other things being equal.

pre-divorce level of well-being to the degree possible, while the economic burdens of the divorce should be shared equally by the parents. Yet this position is inherently contradictory, in that each dollar transferred to maintain the child's well-being will increase the well-being of the custodial parent relative to the non-custodial parent as well — meaning that, to the degree one principle is pursued, the other is contravened. Indeed, certain contradictions are apparent in the Divorce Act of 1985 (see Appendix, p. 131).

There is no easy solution to these problems; tradeoffs are necessary, and will sometimes be uncomfortable. These difficulties do not, however, change the fact that implicit spousal support, inter-spousal comparisons of well-being and the relationship of the child's *versus* the parents' well-being will indeed be *determined* by the guidelines, and should thus be taken into account when choosing among the options available. In fact, such evaluations are probably made when a set of guidelines is evaluated — although perhaps often in a more *ad hoc* and less explicit fashion.* For example, such considerations surely underlie the typical rejection of the Maintenance principle, since (among other problems) it leaves the non-custodial parent at an extremely low standard of living relative to the custodial parent and child, which would seem unfair to most observers.

Thus, when making such evaluations, we are at least *implicitly* taking the well-being of all parties into account and balancing the interests of the child and the two parents. Taking *explicit* consideration of these issues would allow the relevant issues to become better identified, the debate more focussed and the resulting judgements clearer.

The final complication regarding the evaluation of guidelines in terms of the resulting standards of living of the children and the two parents is that there are many different situations that we might wish to judge differently. For example, in balancing the relative outcomes for the two parents, the assessment might be affected by how long the couple was married, yet this factor is never taken into account with guidelines — presumably because such factors have nothing to do with the standard of living to which the child should be entitled.

---

* Garfinkel discusses how these considerations were explicitly taken into account when designing the Wisconsin system. See Irwin Garfinkel, *Assuring Child Support: An Extension of Social Security* (New York: Basic Books, 1992).

All this is simply to say that child support awards affect all parties involved; the relative outcomes for the children and the two parents should probably enter into any assessment of a set of guidelines; and that the issues are often very hard ones.

NON-MONETARY COSTS AND BENEFITS OF CUSTODY

In continuing with the consideration of the well-being of the parents, two factors loom very large in this comparison: the non-monetary costs and the benefits associated with having custody of the child. In terms of costs, the principal element is the time involved in being the primary care-giver for a child, which is obviously predominantly borne by the custodial parent. If translated into dollar terms using some sort of hourly rate, the amounts would in most cases dwarf the direct financial costs upon which the guidelines are established, and might suggest that awards should be increased commensurately.

But while there are these great "costs" in time and money associated with having the custody of the child, there are also the benefits of being able to live on a full-time basis with one's children. These benefits are — as with the costs just mentioned — experienced primarily by the custodial parent. The value of these, too, will generally be very large and, following a similar logic, the custodial parent should perhaps be expected to compensate the non-custodial parent for this advantage — although in practice it would be very difficult to know what a fair payment would be.

These two factors — the non-monetary costs and the benefits of having custody of the child — thus trade off against each other, and it is not generally possible to know who, in the end, should compensate whom. The problem is especially difficult given how hard it is to classify much of the time spent with the children in terms either of "work" or "pleasure." For example, is meal preparation work? If so, we might expect a transfer of funds in compensation for the relevant time costs. But what if the child is present and the activity takes on a significant element of "play," or the child actually begins to aid constructively in the preparation? Compensation might be expected to begin to flow in the *other* direction. These are hard problems with no simple answers — and certainly none that lend themselves to a guidelines-type formula.

It might be instructive to put these factors into the context of the decisions taken when the child was born. The couple clearly faced the relevant monetary costs, non-monetary costs and benefits involved in having a child and, in deciding to have children, clearly believed (at least implicitly) that the benefits outweighed the costs.* This reasoning might initially lead one to think that the custodial parent would be in a similarly net advantaged position after the divorce, meaning that compensation should flow from the custodial parent to the non-custodial parent, thus cutting into the child support payments *per se* (to the degree interspousal comparisons of this nature were taken into account). The "revealed preference" of the pre-divorce situation cannot, however, be directly applied to the post-divorce circumstances, since the costs and benefits change in the post-divorce situation.**

In the end, the relevant calculations regarding the non-monetary costs and benefits of having children are, in a practical sense, impossible. Architects of a system of guidelines would therefore be best advised to leave these issues aside, and presume that the factors roughly balance out. It is worth noting that, to date, compensation for non-monetary contributions have not been included in a single jurisdiction where child support guidelines have been adopted.

Summary

The relationship between child support guidelines and the resulting standard of living of the children and parents may be summarized as follows:

- Families are best conceptualized as sharing income and having a common standard of living. This means that child support awards cannot be thought of as going to the child in isolation, or being used to maintain any particular standard of living for the child independent of the standard of living of the custodial parent or any other members of the custodial family.
- As a result, Income Shares guidelines, in particular, do not guarantee any specific standard of living for the child. The child's

---

*This assumes a rational approach to child-bearing.

**Custody battles can actually be revealing in this regard, as each parent reveals that he or she would prefer to have the child, even *with* the associated non-monetary costs and benefits (and perhaps some anticipated child support payments). On the other hand, the issue is more complicated than this. Other factors such as concern for the *child's* well-being can enter into the struggle, as well as pure vitriol and the lust for battle between the parents in certain cases.

economic well-being will instead depend on the total amount of income available to the custodial family *versus* the needs of that family (i.e., the number of members of the household). This is true even if awards reflect the non-custodial parent's full share of the estimated costs of the child in the pre-divorce situation.

■ The child's standard of living will be directly affected by the relative incomes of the two parents as well as the child support award. In the absence of spousal support, children who go with the lower earning parent will tend to have a lower standard of living than those who go with the higher earning parent — even if spousal support is paid in full.

■ These findings also hold with other guidelines which, like the Income Shares approach, are based on the determination of a fair contribution on the part of the non-custodial parent. Most Fixed Percentages of Income approaches therefore have similar implications for the post-divorce standard of living of the child.

■ Standards of Living approaches will of course ensure certain standard of living outcomes. The maintenance principle will result in no change in the standard of living for the child from the pre-divorce situation, but a huge decline for the non-custodial parent. The equal standards of living approach will obviously lead to equal declines for all family members.

■ Every dollar of child support payment increases the standard of living of the child and custodial parent and decreases the well-being of the non-custodial parent. With these transfers occurring, it makes sense that the relative well-being of all parties involved should be addressed when evaluating any set of child support guidelines. Unfortunately, the principles we might wish to bring to bear regarding the well-being of the child and the two parents are often contradictory, especially when they are meant to apply to a wide range of different situations.

■ The non-monetary costs and benefits of the custody arrangement are potentially of huge importance, but extremely difficult to quantify or make operational. As a result, they should probably be ignored, as has been done in every other jurisdiction where guidelines have been introduced.

CHAPTER SIX

THE IMPLEMENTATION OF CHILD SUPPORT

GUIDELINES: PRACTICAL ISSUES

The reader should now have a good understanding of child support guidelines in terms of their underlying principles, their primary characteristics and the mechanics of their construction. The discussion now turns to the actual implementation of child support guidelines. Such considerations are extremely important, because a guideline that looks good on paper might be rather clumsy, and therefore ineffectual, in practice; or it might not adapt well to more complex situations, such as significant changes in the work situation or remarriage. In treating these implementation issues, the discussions should also shed additional light on the various characteristics of each of the different types of guideline.

INFORMATION REQUIRED FOR THE IMPLEMENTATION OF CHILD SUPPORT GUIDELINES

One key aspect of the implementation of child support guidelines is the amount of information required to calculate awards, and one key demarcation in this regard is between guidelines where payments depend on both parents' incomes and those which require information on the non-custodial parent alone.[17]

Fixed Percentages of Income guidelines are of the second, simpler type. As a result, child support payments are very easy to determine initially, which keeps the associated court costs — in terms of time, money and emotional anguish — to a minimum.* Second, this simplicity can make awards relatively easy to collect, monitor and update. In particular, a Fixed Percentage of Income guideline would be extremely compatible with automatic deductions at source and payment to the sort of central bureau that is now in place in most provinces. Ideally, the child support award would simply comprise an additional standard deduction along with UI, CPP and so on. A particularly desirable characteristic of such a system is that any changes in the payer's income could immediately, and even automatically, translate into higher child support payments. In fact, it would even be easy to move toward a system of "smart" social insurance cards which had the appropriate deduction coded directly into the card, or otherwise be electronically linked to an administrative database containing awards.**

The simplicity of a Fixed Percentages of Income guideline would also facilitate financial planning, since it would be easy to calculate awards even in advance of a divorce. Finally, the simplicity could also contribute to the functioning of the system by creating a sense of fairness, since individuals could plainly see how the system operates, and how it works equally for all.***

Compare these attributes to the information required and mechanics involved with an Income Shares guideline. First, both parties' incomes

---

*This discussion leaves the issue of who exactly would be doing these calculations open, but presumably they would be carried out by a government "child support commission" of some type, or simply the courts themselves.

**Some of the centralized systems of collection have come under criticism of late (see "Ontario Crackdown Shows Cracks," *The Globe and Mail*, March 31, 1994) but this should not be seen as evidence that such a system cannot work. In fact, a Fixed Percentages of Income guideline, where updates were effectively automatic, would probably work better with such a system than the current child support regime, where each significant change in economic circumstances requires a court-determined variation of award. It is better to think in terms of UI or CPP/QPP contributions, where there are rarely errors in deductions and income changes result in automatic changes in payments. There is no reason that a system of child support deductions could not be made to work as efficiently and seamlessly as this.

***Of course to the degree the formulae were seen as unfair this would work in the other direction; which is only to say that the system should indeed be fair.

must be ascertained and verified and the appropriate formula then applied. Then, whenever there was a significant change in the earnings of *either* party, the calculations would have to be done again, the support order updated and the new amounts collected. This would be especially problematic in the case of individuals with unstable employment patterns — of whom there are many, especially in the typically unstable period following divorce. The alternative would be to update only for "large" changes in income, but this would leave a substantial margin of error in many current awards. In any event, there would almost certainly be delays involved in updating awards. Needless to say, financial planning would also be more difficult than in the case of a Fixed Percentages guideline, since awards depend on the use of more variables to make a more complicated calculation.

A Standards of Living guideline would require about the same information as the Income Shares approach, although this information would obviously be used in a different manner, since awards are based on adjusted incomes. In addition to the need for information on both parents' incomes, a Standards of Living guideline might also be the most difficult to understand, which could further cut into individuals' ability to plan and perhaps therefore undermine support for it.

In summary, the Fixed Percentages of Income approach has distinct advantages over the Income Shares and Standard of Living approaches in terms of implementing and updating awards, and these could be very important factors in the ultimate success of any set of child support guidelines.

ECONOMIC INDEPENDENCE AND CHILD SUPPORT

It is only right, of course, that non-custodial parents should share in the financial support of their children. On the other hand, it is desirable to allow the divorced parents to go their own ways after the split. There is, therefore, tension between maintaining the responsibility for the well-being of the children and allowing for the independence of the ex-spouses inherent in the issue of child support in general. In fact, this tension is enshrined in the Divorce Act of 1985, which lauds "the clean break" (between the parents) as one of four primary principles, even as the other three address what might be termed the maintenance of the standards of living of the two adults and any children involved. Alternative approaches to child support guidelines generate different tradeoffs in this respect, which are the subject of this section.

Income Shares guidelines require, first, that earnings information on both parents be kept up to date, probably through mutual updating from time to time and perhaps a formal exchange of tax forms at year's end. Thus there would be continual involvement of an administrative/financial nature between the two ex-spouses, even if it was largely or even completely mediated by some appropriate government agency. Second, the child support payments themselves could change whenever there was a significant change in either of the parents' economic situations, which means that the ex-partners' economic situations would remain correspondingly intertwined, with an associated element of uncertainty and loss of independence which neither parent could escape.

For example, if the *custodial* parent decided to take a lower paying job, the *non*-custodial parent's payments could rise — or fall, depending on the particular formula — even though his or her capacity to pay had not changed (and the true pre-divorce conditions obviously remained constant as well). Such entanglement of the divorced couple's economic lives would last until the children of the marriage reached adulthood, or even beyond, to the completion of post-secondary education, presuming that awards were kept "current," as is generally proposed.

In the case of the Standards of Living approach, the implications for the loss of economic independence are even more profound. For example, under a Maintenance formula (where the child's well-being was to be maintained at the pre-divorce level), any drop in the custodial parent's income would oblige the non-custodial parent to increase his or her payments sufficiently to bring the entire custodial household back up to the established standard.

While guaranteeing the child's (and custodial parent's) standard of living at a particular level is laudable, this would clearly be an enormous financial responsibility for the non-custodial parent, and would obviously build a great deal of uncertainty into his or her life. Financial planning — and associated *life* planning — would be very difficult in such circumstances. For example, it would probably be very difficult for such a non-custodial parent to qualify for a mortgage, feel financially secure enough to start a new family, or know what sort of savings would be necessary for retirement. Equalizing the standards of living of the two households would have similar implications, if not quite so extreme.

By contrast, the Fixed Percentages of Income approach allows for significantly greater economic independence of the two parents. First, there would not be the same need for the continual exchange of income information. Second, payments would actually change only with movements in the non-custodial parent's income. This would leave the non-custodial parent economically independent of the custodial parent, which may be considered a good thing. The custodial family would, however, see its payments rise or fall with the economic fortunes of the non-custodial parent, thus leaving a dependence in this regard. However, awards would not change with the custodial parent's own income, thus preserving this element of independence; in particular, while awards would not rise in the face of any declines in the custodial parent's income, neither would they be diminished when the custodial parent began to earn more.

In summary, the Fixed Percentages of Income approach again has certain advantages over the Income Shares and Standards of Living approaches in that it requires less exchange of information and leaves the economic situations of the two parents more independent. In short, the financial contribution of the non-custodial parent remains at what is determined to be a reasonable level of financial responsibility in terms of the child's needs and the non-custodial parent's capacity to pay.

THE LOGIC OF AWARDS OVER TIME

Now let us consider an implementation issue of another sort — that is, how the underlying principles of the different approaches to guidelines stand up over the post-divorce years. Beginning with the Income Shares approach, recall that this type of guideline is based on the principle of estimating the financial contribution that the non-custodial parent would be making toward the child were the family still together. At the time of initial separation, this may (or may not) be a reasonable basis for determining an award, but the hypothetical construct becomes increasingly strained over time, especially given all that can happen in the lives of each of the parents, including changes in employment, remarriage and even the start of another family.

For example, if the custodial parent dropped out of the labour force to have a child with a new partner, it would seem unreasonable to base any change in child support upon the notion of estimating what the level of spending on the couple's child would have been given their two incomes and splitting the shares appropriately. In short, the parents' incomes have less and less relation to the original marriage, and instead increasingly reflect events and decisions pertaining to their post-divorce lives.

This devaluation of the basic premise is even greater in the case of awards based on the Standards of Living approach. For example, while it *might* seem fair to have the child kept at the pre-divorce standard of living initially (although the great drop suffered by the non-custodial parent as a consequence would have to be rationalized) it seems much less appropriate to fix the child's well-being at that precise level for as long as fifteen years or more after the split. Or, alternatively, while it could appear reasonable to maintain the two households at the same standard of living just after the break-up, it would seem to make much less sense to do so many years later — again, especially in light of all the major changes that could occur in the life of one parent or the other.

These situations can be contrasted with the simpler Fixed Percentages of Income approach. With such a guideline, there is typically no single underlying principle, except that the schedule of payments is deemed to be reasonable in terms of the non-custodial parent's level of financial responsibility to the child and his or her capacity to pay. These general principles would seem to stand up well over time. In particular, payments are not linked to any actual or imaginary pre-divorce situation, nor is there any forcing of the two households' standards of living into any particular equality at any point in time.

Furthermore, there is the issue of how a factor that enters into the determination of awards might make sense at the point of divorce, but not in terms of updating the award over time. For example, with an Income Shares guideline, a higher income on the part of the custodial parent could result in a higher payment by the non-custodial parent, rationalized on the grounds that the child needs to be maintained at a higher standard of living; whereas it seems much less reasonable that payments should be *increased* if the custodial parent begins to earn *more* income *after* the divorce. In other words, it doesn't seem fair to see the non-custodial parent's well-being decline as he or she makes greater payments to a custodial family whose situation is anyway improving. Yet the Income Shares approach can generate such results.

In summary, it is important to think of how the factors affecting awards will operate over time, including various associated changes in earnings, family status and so on. Once again, the simpler underlying principles of the Fixed Percentages of Income approach would seem to present advantages over the more complicated Income Shares and Standards of Living approaches.

CHILD SUPPORT AND NEW FAMILY FORMATION

Continuing on the same theme, it is important to consider explicitly how a guideline will work when either of the parents remarries, and/or has more children. For example, consider the Income Shares approach, which uses both parents' incomes to estimate what would be spent on the child were the family still intact, and then divides these hypothetical expenditures in proportion to the parents' incomes. Now think of the implications of remarriage in this approach.

For example, it has been described above how a decision on the part of the custodial parent to remarry and stop working (perhaps to have another child) could result in an increase in child support payments. In other words, there would be a change in circumstances in which the non-custodial parent played no part and had no say; which had nothing to do with the original marriage; and which might even carry few consequences for the children of the original marriage; and yet support payments would be affected all the same. This hardly seems fair. On the other hand, such changes could result in a *reduction* in payments instead — which seems equally inappropriate. Finally, the same situation also holds in reverse, in that the non-custodial parent could remarry and experience an associated change in earnings which could similarly affect the child support payments.

The Fixed Percentages of Income approach has similar characteristics to the Income Shares approach in this regard, but only in one direction. If the non-custodial parent remarried and this led to a change in earnings, child support payments could change; but since payments are independent of the custodial parent's income, any changes on that side would not have any effects on payments.

The issues become considerably more complex and problematic in the case of a Standards of Living approach. Suppose it was decided to adopt the Equalized Standards of Living formula, with these measured in the usual manner of adjusting family income for the size of the family. It is not at all clear how this would be done in the face of remarriage and new family formation. Should a new spouse's income be included in the family total? Whose presence should be considered when adjusting family income for family size? In the extreme, both parents might remarry, have step-children, and then have additional children with their new partners. It is difficult to imagine a Standards of Living approach even beginning to make sense in such a situation. It is this author's opinion that these problems alone render a Standards of Living approach completely unworkable.

In short, the more a guideline depends on the incomes or standards of living of the two parents, the thornier the problems in terms of actually implementing the guideline. And these are not isolated circumstances; for example, the author has found in his own research that 23.1 percent of the women and 35.5 percent of the men in his sample of divorces remarry by the third year after the split.[18]

Here again, the Fixed Percentages of Income approach has an advantage. As was just explained, while payments do vary with any changes in the earnings of the non-custodial parent, which could in turn result from remarriage or the birth of a new child, they are unaffected by changes in the custodial parent's situation. In short, the non-custodial parent's contribution will not change due to events that are beyond his or her control and that have no impact on his or her pre-existing responsibility to help support the child.

Finally, there seems to be some disagreement as to whether or not payments should be reduced if the non-custodial parent starts a new family. One opinion holds that awards should indeed be adjusted down, out of respect for the needs of any additional children and a belief that the new family should be given a better chance to thrive and prosper. Another opinion, however, and one shared by this author, is that any pre-existing child support responsibilities should be lived up to, and that non-custodial parents and their prospective partners simply need to take these responsibilities into account when making decisions. In other words, it should not be possible to remarry or procreate one's way out of existing child support obligations, which should be treated on the same footing as an outstanding loan or any other financial commitment.

ACCESS COSTS AND JOINT CUSTODY

The discussion thus far has implicitly assumed that one parent has sole custody and bears all the costs related to the child. However, there are obviously many cases where the child spends a substantial amount of time with each parent through visitation or joint physical custody. Such co-parenting will typically lead to increased total expenditures on the child, and direct payment of a portion of the child's costs by the non-custodial parent. This should in turn lead to adjustments in child support payments. There is really no complicated theory to consider here: it is more in the nature of an accounting exercise, with some extra costs to be added in and a redivision of the total costs between the two parents to be calculated.

The extra costs relate primarily to the fact that the child has a second residence, with the extent of the costs depending on how elaborate the arrangements are. These might be minimal, such as the child sleeping on a pull-out bed or in a guest room from time to time, to full accommodation in terms of a separate bedroom, play space and so on. There might also be extra clothes, books, toys and so forth. Travel costs also need to be considered, including any costs incurred by the parents themselves in getting the child back and forth between the two residences. Once these full costs are determined they need to be shared between the two parents. The net effect of the exercise will typically be to reduce the child support payment for the obvious reason that the "non-custodial" parent is now picking up certain costs directly.

These principles are general and could pertain to any type of child support regime. With the current system, the budget upon which the award is based would presumably reflect the specific custody arrangements and related costs, with the shares calculated accordingly. With guidelines, one solution would be to follow faithfully the general spirit of the guideline approach by building certain assumptions regarding the amount of time spent in the two households into the formulae, to produce the result of different payments for different types of custody arrangement.

However, a better approach would probably be to calculate the recommended payment where there was sole custody with no visitation or joint custody costs, also provide the payment where custody was evenly shared, and perhaps give information on yet another situation where custody was split, say, 75/25. The award could then be fine-tuned across these reference points according to the specific custody arrangement of each situation, perhaps with the aid of a set of general suggestions as to what sort of adjustments should be made for different situations.

A final point pertains to whether or not there should be a certain minimum below which there would be no consideration of the shared costs relating to visitation or joint custody. While such a cut-off would make awards easier to calculate, it would also be extremely unfair for a number of reasons.

Suppose, for example, the cut-off point was 25 percent, meaning that there would be no consideration of the costs borne by the non-custodial parent in cases where the child spent fewer than 25 percent of the nights (or total time) in his or her care. First, there would be an unfairness between non-custodial parents who spent a significant amount of time with their children and those who spent little or no time, in that the former would incur the expenses related to the time spent with the child, but would have to make the same payments as the latter. Second, there would be a large shift in payments at the cut-off point, whereby those just below the mark would get no financial break for their direct support of the child, while those just above would benefit from the appropriate adjustment. Finally, there would obviously be an inequity between the two parents, in that the "non-custodial" parent would be bearing a disproportionately large share of the child costs.

Ignoring the non-custodial parent's expenses and direct payments at points below any arbitrary cut-off point would not only be unfair, but might also make it financially difficult for many non-custodial parents to provide for the child. For example, if the non-custodial parent is not given a break on child support as a result of providing a room for the child, it might make the provision of that room difficult to manage.

In short, adjustments for direct spending on the child by the non-custodial parent should begin where any significant expenses are incurred, rather than at some artificial cut-off point, such as a set number of days spent with the non-custodial parent.

How a Fixed Percentages of Income Guideline Can Resemble an Income Shares Guideline

It is clear that the Fixed Percentages of Income approach has many important advantages over the Income Shares and Standards of Living approaches in terms of implementation. The Fixed Percentages of Income approach is also based on the appealing principle that payments should reflect a reasonable sharing of income with the child, taking into account the child's needs and the parent's capacity to pay. All the same, the most common criticism of this approach is that payments do not take into account the custodial parent's income, as is the case with the Income Shares approach. This is, however, not as important a factor as might seem on the surface, due to the perhaps surprising fact that a Fixed Percentages of Income guideline can in fact produce awards which are very closely to what an Income Shares guideline would produce in similar circumstances.

In fact, under certain general conditions, a Fixed Percentages system can generate *exactly* the same awards as those of an Income Shares guideline. This stems from the fact that if child costs are determined to be a fixed proportion of family income, the payments from an Income Shares system will in fact turn out to be this same constant percentage of the non-custodial parent's income.

A simple example will illustrate the point. Suppose child costs are determined to be 20 percent of family income, and a family has a total income of $100,000. Assume, initially, that the non-custodial parent has the family's entire income, and thus a standard Income Shares approach generates a payment of the full $20,000 — which is of course 20 percent of his or her income. Now suppose instead that the family's income is split 50/50 between the two parents, giving the non-custodial parent a proportional 50 percent share of the $20,000 costs. This results in a payment of $10,000 — which is again 20 percent of the non-custodial parent's income! Now consider a case where the custodial parent earns only $30,000 and the non-custodial parent still earns $50,000. The child costs are estimated to be $16,000 (20 percent of the $80,000 total), with the non-custodial parent's share being five-eighths of this, which is $16,000 — once again 20% percent of the non-custodial parent's income!*

Thus in this example the Fixed Percentages approach generates exactly the same awards as an Income Shares approach, and by both systems the awards do not actually vary with the custodial parent's income. Therefore the criticisms that the Fixed Percentages system is less fair than an Income Shares approach in how it shares the child costs and in not having payments vary with the custodial parent's income are basically illusionary. Although the Income Shares approach might intuitively *seem* to be more fair, in reality it is not.

---

*Taxes could enter these calculations, but would not change the basic point being made here.

This means that, while an Income Shares approach is much more difficult to implement in practice, these hindrances have no real offsetting advantage relative to the simpler Fixed Percentages approach — except perhaps that the Income Shares approach might — falsely — *seem* fairer. It would appear preferable to adopt the simpler, better Fixed Percentages approach and educate the public about the associated advantages of that simplicity, *and* to make clear that the system is as fair as the more complicated Income Shares option, rather than pander to some false, and costly, notion of fairness.*

CHILD SUPPORT, IMPLICIT TAX RATES AND ASSOCIATED BEHAVIOURAL RESPONSES

Child support payments obviously affect the amount of income the two households have to spend, and therefore enter the "implicit" marginal tax rates of the two parents. This is most clearly the case for non-custodial parents. It is, however, also true for custodial parents, since payments can lead to reductions in certain benefits offered to low-income families or push them into a higher tax bracket; in addition, the fact that the custodial parent's own income enters the Income Shares and Standards of Living guidelines strengthens the implicit tax effects in these cases. In fact, with certain guidelines, the implicit tax rates from support payments and actual taxes can become exceedingly high, approaching 80 percent and even beyond, as will be seen in the following chapter. This section provides a discussion of the possible effects of these high implicit tax rates.

It is hard to say precisely, but one likely possibility is that the labour supply of both parents will decline wherever high implicit marginal tax

---

*The numerical example given is not a mere coincidence, nor the result of finding a trick example that happens to work. On the contrary, the general condition is that, to the degree child costs are estimated to be a constant proportion of family income, the two methods will generate the same results. On the other hand, to the degree child costs are not linear in family income, this equality will not hold exactly. In reality, child costs are typically found to be very close to proportional over income, meaning that the two approaches can generally be made to produce similar rewards.

rates are faced.* Second, non-custodial parents will have increased incentives to hide their income to reduce child support assessments, while custodial parents might do the same to obtain higher awards (depending on the type of award). Such evasion could come in the form of increased informal labour market activity; receiving more income in-kind, through benefits or in some sort of deferred manner; and so on. Finally, default on the support payments themselves could rise, and even with stricter enforcement mechanisms, collection is always going to be easier when there is less resistance to the payment.

Thus, through their effects on implicit tax rates, guidelines will likely affect labour supply and the general efficiency of the economy, income tax revenue, the actual level of child support awards (since awards depend on observed income) and compliance with those awards. One implication is that, in an effort to generate higher awards, the net effect of a guideline with high implicit tax rates could actually be to produce lower payments — thus possibly leaving the intended beneficiaries worse off than before. Finally, a set of guidelines could be politically undermined if public opinion held that the resulting implicit marginal tax rates were too high.

It should be noted that the current system has a major advantage in this regard. Awards are effectively fixed in most cases, and therefore there are no implicit marginal tax rates associated with child support payments and hence no incentives to adjust work, earnings and so on. One compromise solution might be to use a set of guidelines to establish initial awards and then fix awards at this level, much as in the current system. There might still be initial behavioural responses to the awards, but there would be no continuing incentives to change behaviour at the margin. On the other hand, such a compromise would defeat much of what guidelines are intended to achieve.

Furthermore, there is the possibility of strategic behaviour in response to the incentives created by the child support guidelines leading up to the divorce. For example, if the guidelines stipulated that the child's pre-divorce level of well-being was to be maintained, the parent who anticipated having custody of the child might try to push family

---

*One of the reasons why it is difficult to know what the labour supply responses will be is that the changes in effective tax rates are very large, whereas existing labour supply estimates are generally based on smaller (marginal) changes. Furthermore, the reaction to paying one's income out as child support might be different to the response to taxes — with some perhaps more willing to make the payments and others less so.

income up just before the divorce to have the reference level of well-being — and therefore payments — pegged at a higher level. The partner would have the opposite incentives.

Finally, the behavioural responses might extend even further than labour market and related responses. In particular, any significant alterations in child support could change the costs and benefits of marriage and child-bearing in a fundamental way. It seems impossible to predict the net effects, but declines in marriage and fertility rates seem most probable.* On the other hand, if this is the result of simply making people financial responsible for their actions, that is perhaps a good thing.

In summary, the evaluation of any set of child support guidelines should include consideration of the implicit tax rates and the range of associated behavioural responses that might result — from the amount of market work, to dodging the income reporting system, to the effects on marriage and having children.

THE TREATMENT OF TAXES UNDER CHILD SUPPORT GUIDELINES[19]

Thus far, there has been no mention of how taxes are to be treated by the guidelines, but there are some important issues in this regard. This section includes consideration of some of these so as to provide an introduction and place them on the agenda, while leaving their more detailed treatment for another day.

By its very nature, the Standards of Living approach works best by calculating post-tax incomes, adjusting these incomes for the needs of the family using an equivalence scale and setting the award so as to achieve the standards of living target that characterizes the particular guideline being implemented. Thus, the treatment of taxes is integral to the determination of awards, rendering the calculations quite complex. In practice, the calculation of an award would probably require running the relevant information regarding family structure, incomes and so on through a specially designed computer program on a case-by-case basis,

---

*The net outcome is difficult to predict because guidelines could improve post-divorce outcomes for certain groups and worsen them for others, depending on the particular guideline chosen. The full effects on marriage and fertility thus depend on individuals' responses to these income effects. Such an analysis is clearly beyond the scope of the present research, and the mentioned decline is only speculative.

thus placing the calculations beyond the reach of the average person, making planning fairly difficult.*

Conversely, Income Shares and Fixed Percentages of Income guidelines can typically be based on either pre- or post-tax incomes, but the pre-tax approach obviously has significant advantages in terms of implementing the guideline; related advantages hold for any guideline that obviates the need to gross awards up to take account of taxes payable.

Specifically in terms of an Income Shares approach, any case-by-case consideration of taxes would obviously complicate the calculations, especially in a dynamic context. In other words, any significant change in either parent's income would require not only the recalculation of estimated expenditures and shares but also a reconsideration of the relevant tax implications. Indeed, the tax effects could actually be quite difficult to assess at any given point in time, especially if incomes and payments were changing.** Thus, any tax gross-up procedure would make Income Shares awards more difficult to calculate initially, and could seriously compromise the capacity of the guideline to allow for adjustments to awards in changing circumstances.

As for a Fixed Percentages approach, the principal advantage of being able to calculate awards based on the non-custodial parent's income alone would be sacrificed with the inclusion of any tax gross-up procedure. The other problems just mentioned in the context of the Income Shares approach would also apply.

Furthermore, any guideline requiring tax gross-ups can result in some very strange adjustments in awards over time. For example, an increase in the custodial parent's earnings could bump him or her into a higher tax bracket and therefore result in an increase in payments, since the same net payment could require a greater gross-up. In such a case, as

---

*A Standards of Living approach could in fact be based on pre-tax income and pre-tax equivalence scales, but these would constitute less reliable indicators of actual well-being. Given that the calculations are already quite complex, it makes little sense to not do things properly, with post-tax incomes.

**To put this another way, taxes are paid on an annual basis, whereas incomes can obviously change from month to month or even more frequently than this. What is to be the basis of the tax calculations over the course of the year? Note that under the income tax system, current income levels are assumed to have been maintained throughout the year, but with a settling of accounts at year's end. It is less obvious how a child support guideline would work in this regard.

the custodial parent's standard of living rose, payments would also rise, and the *non*-custodial parent's standard of living would be driven down in consequence. This would probably strike most people as unfair.

In short, a consideration of implementation issues suggests that any Income Shares or Fixed percentages of Income guideline should be based on pre-tax incomes with no separate tax gross-up requirement. Furthermore, such an approach would also conform more closely to the underlying principle guiding the Income Shares approach, and upon which the Fixed Percentages of Income approach is typically founded as well. (This point is discussed in greater detail in the appendix to this chapter.)

A CONSIDERATION OF CHANGES IN THE TAX TREATMENT OF CHILD SUPPORT AWARDS

Since the 1940s, child support payments have been deductible for the payer and taxable for the recipient. This "deduction/inclusion" treatment has, however, come under increasing criticism of late, as evidenced by the well-known Thibaudeau court case in Quebec. In fact, just as this volume was going to press the Quebec Court of Appeals decided that Thibaudeau should not have had to pay taxes on the child support she received.*

The Thibaudeau decision is, on one level, of little importance to the general discussions of this volume because the different types of guidelines can be constructed to take account of a variety of tax treatments. For example, if the current tax deduction/inclusion rules were reversed (which the Thibaudeau case might lead to), payments under an Income Shares system would be adjusted downward to generate approximately the same post-tax outcomes as those obtained with the current tax treatment; a Fixed Percentages of Income guideline would have its percentages adjusted downward in a similar fashion; a Standards of Living approach would simply take the different tax regime directly into account; and so on. In short, any guideline would be specific to a particular tax treatment of

---

*"Ironically" (in the court's own words) the court also recognized that awards are currently supposed to include a gross-up which takes the tax consequences of the payment into consideration, thus leaving the custodial parent with the correct post-tax payment; and that Thibaudeau's gross child support award might therefore be revised downward in light of their decision. In other words, while Thibaudeau seems to have won the right not to pay taxes on the child support she receives, there is likely to be a corresponding adjustment in the award which might leave her with no more money to spend on her children than before.

awards and would have an appropriately revised schedule of payments under a different tax treatment.*

On the practical level, however, changes in tax treatment would change the amount of post-tax income available to the ex-partners and thereby generally affect award levels. These effects are potentially quite large. For example, the Federal Department of Finance has estimated that a reversal of the current deduction/inclusion system would increase the taxes paid by the two parents by some $330 million annually, due to the typical shifting of the tax burden from the lower-earning to higher-earning parent that would result.**

The determination of a child support award is generally a process of assessing the needs of the child, calculating what resources are available to meet these needs and determining what a fair payment would be. While many have argued — and often in a convincing manner — that the tax gross-ups are sometimes not made or are incomplete, and that the joint tax benefits of the existing deduction/inclusion system often accrue to the non-custodial parent more than the custodial household, the guideline approach affords the opportunity to ensure a fairer sharing of advantages of the current system. However, a reversal of the current deduction/inclusion system would clearly cut into the amount of disposable income available to the divorced households and, in consequence, reduce child support payments relative to what could be obtained with the current tax treatment.

In short, guidelines could be designed to take advantage of the current tax system, but it could turn out that they will be introduced just as those substantial benefits are being forfeited due to the failings of the

---

*See Ross Finnie and Daniel Stripinis, "The Economics of Child Support Guidelines," *Cahier de recherche*, no. 93-03 (Quebec: GREPE, Département d'économique, Université Laval, 1993) for discussion of the relevant tax issues.

**See Martel, Nathalie, Affidavit submitted to the Federal Court of Appeal, Court Case # A-1248-92, *Thibaudeau* vs. *The Queen*, heard at Québec, Québec, February 28 and March 1, 1994, judgement rendered at Ottawa, Ontario, May 3, 1994. See also Ellen B. Zweibel and Richard Shillington, "Child Support Policy: Income Tax Treatment and Child Support Guidelines," paper prepared for the Policy Research Centre on Children, Youth and Families, Toronto, 1993, which challenges Finance's estimate of the number of "winners" under the current system. Their work, however, is based on a database that is older, less representative, much smaller and that has greater quality of information problems than the database used in the Finance estimates; their methodology is also different.

current system in this regard. It would surely make better sense to make the changes necessary in order to profit from the advantages offered by the current system than to simply hand these revenues back to the government. Why take a substantial step backward in terms of reducing the income available to divorced parents before trying to move forward in terms of a better sharing of post-divorce incomes? One rarely sees such a clamour to turn money back to the government by the parties who could potentially benefit most from its *largesse.**

SUMMARY

The Implementation issues may be summarized as follows:
- The Fixed Percentages of Income approach has clear advantages over the Income Shares and Standards of Living approaches in terms of requiring less information and being easier to monitor and update. In particular, the simpler system would work much better by having deductions at source, whereby child support payments could become almost as easy and automatic as other standard deductions such as income tax, unemployment insurance premiums and CPP/QPP deductions.
- For similar reasons, divorced parents are left with more economic independence at divorce under a Fixed Percentages system.
- The underlying principles of the Income Shares and Standards of Living approaches can be appealing at the point of divorce, but become much more strained over the post-divorce years. They become especially problematic in cases of remarriage and/or new children. The Fixed Percentages system is based on a looser principle of an appropriate amount of sharing relative to the capacity of the non-custodial parent to pay, and thus stands up better over time and across changes in the individuals' situations.
- Access costs need to be taken into account with guidelines (as with the current system), and should begin to be considered as

---

*Note that such improvements could be realized even without the implementation of guidelines. For example, the courts could be more meticulous in ensuring that the appropriate tax gross-ups be made, and it would be relatively easy to devise formulae for sharing out the tax advantages of a given award. This has all been made much easier of late with the advent of computer programs which do the relevant tax calculations or which sometimes even calculate the award with the tax advantages figuring directly in the calculation of the award.

soon as they become significant rather than when the time spent with the non-custodial parent passes some arbitrary threshold.

■ While the Fixed Percentages approach benefits from its ease of implementation, it is often criticized because the custodial parent's income is not taken into account, as is the case under an Income Shares guideline. It turns out, however, that any set of awards generated by an Income Shares guideline can be very closely approximated — or, in the extreme, perfectly replicated — by a Fixed Percentage guideline. This perhaps surprising result thus tilts the advantages heavily towards a Fixed Percentages of Income approach.

■ Guidelines affect the implicit marginal tax rates for both parents and could therefore influence a range of labour market decisions, as well as marriage and fertility rates themselves. While the likely responses to different guidelines are difficult to estimate in a precise fashion, any guideline under consideration should be evaluated in terms of its likely effects in this regard.

■ Tax issues are relevant to the ease of implementation and the degree to which a specific set of procedures conforms to the underlying principles of a given guideline approach. The Income Shares and Fixed Percentages approaches can be based on either pre- or post-tax income, but are obviously easier to implement with the pre-tax measures and without a gross-up; such an approach is also more consistent with the principles underlying these guidelines. Standards of Living approaches are properly done with post-tax incomes, thus making the calculations one step more elaborate.

■ Proposed changes in the tax treatment of child support payments would, if made permanent, require associated adjustments in the structure of any guideline so as to leave the individuals with approximately the same net incomes. The reversed tax treatment would, however, actually lead to lower net awards in the end, due to the loss of the joint tax savings that exist under the current tax regime.

BASING AWARDS ON PRE-TAX INCOME
WITH NO TAX GROSS-UPS

This appendix explains how an Income Shares or Fixed Percentages of Income guideline can be based on pre-tax incomes and not require any explicit case-by-case gross-up to take account of the taxes payable on the award. This makes the guidelines easier to implement and also conforms more closely to the underlying principle of the Income Shares approach as well as any Fixed Percentages guideline based on Income Shares. Furthermore, the gross income approach also tends to work to the advantage of custodial parents and the children.

The issues are considered by way of a concrete example. Suppose the non-custodial parent has an income of $50,000, that this comprises all of the family income and that there are two children involved. Now let us use the Statistics Canada LIMs as an equivalence scale — based on pre-tax income — to estimate expenditures on the children. The children's share of the family's gross income is 60 divided by 200, or .30 of the $50,000; that is, $15,000.*

Being in gross income terms, however, this does not represent actual spending on the children. One way to see this is to also consider the shares of the two adults: 100/200 and 40/200. All the shares taken together, including the children's, comprise 100 percent of gross income — but actual disposable income is much less than this, principally due to taxes and savings. To simplify the example, let's say taxes and savings are 50 percent across the board. The $50,000 gross income translates into $25,000 net, and the children's share of $15,000 translates into $7,500. Furthermore, the non-custodial parent might be thought of as keeping his or her gross income minus taxes, savings and the spending on the children, or $17,500 in the hypothetical situation where the family is still together.**

Suppose now that the non-custodial parent pays the gross share of

---

*Recall that the LIMs presume that two people cost 1.4 times as much as one, and that each of the two children pushes the family's needs up by an additional .30. That leaves the chidren's share of the spending as .60 divided by 2.00, or .30 — their combined shares of the family total.

**That is $50,000 minus $25,000 taxes and savings, minus $7,500 actual spending on the children.

$15,000 as child support, as would be the case under an Income Shares or perhaps a Fixed Percentages guideline based on using the Statistics Canada LIMs to estimate spending on children. Under the current tax system, these payments would be a deduction, leaving the remaining $35,000 to be taxed, thus generating a tax bill of $17,500.* Net income is then gross income less taxes and the award, or $17,500. The key point is that this net amount available to the non-custodial parent for spending on himself or herself is the same as in the hypothetical "still married" situation, as calculated above, thus reflecting the underlying principle of the Income Shares approach. In other words, awards can indeed be based on gross income and require no case-by-case tax gross-up, with all the associated advantages in terms of implementation.

What if one was to look at the Income Shares principle from a slightly different perspective, and claim that it should result in a constant amount of income going to the children, rather than in the maintainance of the non-custodial parent's contribution (and net income) at the pre-divorce level? In terms of gross income, this is obviously the result just described, since the same $15,000 goes to the children in both situations. In net terms, however, it depends on the taxes paid by the custodial parent. If the custodial parent is in the same tax bracket as the non-custodial parent, net income available for the children will be exactly what it was in the hypothetical pre-divorce situation — that is, $15,000 less the taxes makes the same $7,500 in both situations. The Income Shares principle still holds.

However, what happens if the custodial parent's marginal tax rate is different from the 50 percent of the non-custodial parent? In the majority of cases, the custodial parent has lower earnings and therefore faces a lower tax rate, and this will work to the advantage of the custodial family. Consider the extreme case, where a zero marginal tax rate is faced. In such a situation, the custodial parent receives the same $15,000, and has the entire sum to spend. In the opposite case where the marginal tax rate faced by the custodial parent is greater than that faced by the non-custodial parent, the reverse result holds.**

---

*Savings are being fudged here so as to keep the example as simple as possible, but this does not affect the results in any significant way.

**Of course, implicit tax rates pertaining to the loss of government support should also be considered in such calculations, and not just explicit tax rates alone. Such considerations are especially important at lower income levels.

Thus an Income Shares award can indeed be based on gross incomes and not require any tax gross-ups, which makes implementation easier. Furthermore, this result also holds for any Fixed Percentages system with an Income Shares underpinning, which means that all the associated advantages of constructing a guideline based solely on the non-custodial parent's income alone can be realized.

Of course other approaches are possible. For example, gross income could be translated into net income in the first step, and the income shares calculated in terms of actual spending, and then grossed back up for taxes. But such procedures would be much more complicated and difficult to implement, without any obvious advantages in terms of either conforming to underlying principles, or the awards generated.

GUIDELINE SIMULATIONS

Having discussed guidelines from a theoretical perspective, we now turn to the outcomes they actually produce when applied to a range of hypothetical situations. This simulation approach is necessitated by the lack of a suitable database of real divorces, as discussed in chapter 2, and means that we are unable to predict the effects of one guideline *versus* another in the actual population. On the other hand, there is some advantage in being able to analyze outcomes across a range of precisely specified hypothetical cases.

For the simulations, we consider a family with two children, with different combinations of parental income from $10,000 to $50,000. To simplify the tax treatment and the calculation of awards, it is assumed that all income is from wage and salary earnings and there are no payroll deductions apart from taxes, CPP and UI. The 1992 tax system is used, with Ontario residency assumed. Social assistance is ignored, to allow us to focus on the child support system *per se*, whereas actual final incomes would reflect those additional transfers for low-income households. (Refundable tax credits within the tax transfer system are, by contrast, taken into account.) Outcomes are presented in terms of the levels of awards, adjusted family income and implicit tax rates faced by the two parents.*

The first part of this chapter contains an explanation of the choice of the equivalence scale used in the simulations, and how it has been employed to generate expenditure estimates and an adjusted family income measure. This is followed by a description of the guidelines which are simulated: Income Shares/Fixed Percentages of Income, "Post-Divorce Shares," Delaware-Melson, Equalized Standards of Living and Maintenance. The results of the simulations are then presented and discussed.

Equivalence Scales, Child Expenditure Estimates and Income-to-Needs Ratios

As was explained at the outset of this volume, child support guidelines are comprised of two components: estimates of the expenditures on children, and rules for apportioning the financial responsibility for the children between the two parents. For the simulations carried out, expenditures on children were estimated using the equivalence scale embodied in the established Statistics Canada Low Income Measures (LIMs). As has been mentioned above, this scale has been developed over a number of years at Statistics Canada and incorporates not only the best econometric evidence available, but also the findings obtained with other approaches to the estimation of child costs and the advice gained during extensive consultations with various Canadian social action organizations. The LIMs thus enjoy a certain support upon which a set of expenditure estimates can be based.**

---

*Simulations were also done for families with one and three children, and the results generally resemble those obtained in the two children case. Those results are available from the author. The simulations borrow from the methodology and presentation found in David Betson, Erik Evenhouse, Siobhan Reilly and Eugene Smolensky, "Trade-Offs Implicit in Child Support Guidelines," *Journal of Policy Analysis and Management*, Vol. 11, no. 1 (January 1992), pp. 1-20, where the US situation is studied.

**For detailed discussion of the LIMs and their development, see Michael Wolfson and John M. Evans, "Statistics Canada's Low Income Cut-Offs: Methodological Concerns and Possibilities," Statistics Canada Labour and Household Surveys Analysis Division Discussion Paper, 1989 and Michael Wolfson, John M. Evans and Brian Murphy, "Low Income Statistics: Methodological Issues and Recent Experience in Canada," cited in endnote 15.

The precise use of LIMs in estimating child expenditures has been explained above, but a brief recapitulation is appropriate. The LIMs incorporate the judgement that two adults require 1.4 times as much income as a single person to be as well off, two adults plus one child require 1.7 times as much income as a single individual, a four-person family 2.00 times as much and so on. It follows that the children's share of family income in, for example, our prototypical family of four can easily be calculated using this scale, and amounts to their .60 share out of the total needs of 2.00, or 30 percent.

Thus, in a family with an income of $50,000, expenditures on the children are associated with $15,000 of the total. (Note that the parents' shares are 1.00 plus .40 out of the 2.00 total, or .70, thus comprising the other $35,000.) This exercise is carried out at the various family income levels under consideration to generate the full range of expenditure estimates required.

The LIMs are also used to compute measures of family income adjusted for needs: Income-to-Needs Ratios (INRs) are obtained by dividing total family income by the LIM for each family. Values less than one therefore indicate that the family is in poverty, while values greater than one indicate proportionately higher standards of living.*

In summary, the Statistics Canada LIMs are used to generate estimates of children's expenditure requirements and to adjust total family for needs through INRs. The expenditure estimates are used in certain guidelines (e.g., Income Shares), while the INRs are used in the calculation of awards for the Standard of Living approaches and to compare the resulting economic well-being of the households involved in the pre- and post-divorce situation. The expenditure estimates are based on pre-tax income, while the adjusted incomes are with respect to the post-tax situation of the non-custodial parent *versus* the custodial household.**

---

*There is no official poverty line in Canada, but the Statistics Canada Low-Income Cut-Offs (LICOs) are often employed in a like manner, and the more recently derived LIMs can be thought of in a similar light. Specifically, the pre-tax 1992 LIMs peg the one-person low-income line at $12,148; the four person line at $24,300 (2.00 times the level for the single adult); with two adults and one child at $20,650 (1.7 the one-adult level).

**Statistics Canada has determined that the same "40/30" LIM scale applies in both pre- and post-tax situations.

THE GUIDELINES SIMULATED

The first guideline simulated is Income Shares. The calculations are very simple: the parents' gross (pre-tax) incomes are added together; the LIM equivalence scale is used to estimate the amount of gross income related to spending on the children at that level; these income requirements are split in proportion to the parents' gross incomes; and the non-custodial parent's share becomes the child support award. The use of the LIMs as the source of the expenditure estimates means that these are directly proportional to income; the Income Shares approach is therefore exactly equivalent to a Fixed Percentage of Income approach (following the discussion in the preceding chapter), with this percentage amounting to the 30 percent, which characterizes the children's share in a two-parent family.*

The second guideline is meant to be a very rough approximation of the current system of splitting actual expenditures on the children in the post-divorce situation in proportion to the two parents' incomes, or the well-known *Paras* formula. Post-divorce income requirements are estimated by applying the LIM equivalence scale (for one adult plus two children) to the custodial family's income, and the non-custodial parent's proportional share of these income needs is the child support award. This approach differs from the Income Shares guideline in the use of post-divorce spending estimates, rather than the "pre-divorce" estimates that characterize the standard guideline approach.

The procedure is, however, complicated by the fact that there is a feedback loop: estimated spending depends on custodial family income, including the award, while the award depends on the spending estimate. Therefore, an iterative procedure was adopted. The first round consisted of using the LIM equivalence scale to estimate the income requirements for the children based on the custodial parent's own income, splitting these financial requirements in proportion to the parents' gross incomes and making the non-custodial parent's share of this income the initial child support award. In the second round, the initial award is added to

---

*The Income Shares formula has also been implemented with a reserve, whereby parents with incomes below the LIM low-income line were not expected to make a payment. These results are available from the author upon request.

the custodial parent's own income, thereby increasing household income, the expenditure estimates and the second round award. This iterative process was continued until the change in award from one round to the next was less than one dollar.

Where the custodial parent's own income leaves the household below its pre-tax LIM — for this exercise, at earnings of $10,000 — the award is not reported, because it is difficult to predict awards under the current system in these circumstances. In the converse situation, where the non-custodial parent has an income below the LIM for an unattached individual, the award is simply declared to be zero, which is how the current system works.

This "Post-Divorce Shares" approach is, to repeat, meant to be only a very rough approximation of the current situation. Actual awards may look very different from those estimated, and the estimates could change significantly under another set of assumptions. For example, a change in the starting points, perhaps under the assumption of spousal support where the two parents' incomes were significantly different, could change the final awards substantially. Nevertheless, these simulations provide an interesting point of comparison.

The third guideline adopts the "Delaware-Melson" approach, which is in use in a few US jurisdictions, including its namesake, and which often comes up for consideration. This is an interesting hybrid approach, characterized by three principal aspects. First, parents with incomes below a certain minimum level are not expected to make any payment. Second, the minimum needs of the children are also established, and these are split in proportion to the parents' "surplus" incomes (i.e., beyond their own reserves). Finally, once the children's basic needs are met in this fashion, the non-custodial parent pays a fixed percentage of his or her income. In our case, the minimums are given by the LIMs, and the constant percentage is fixed at 30 percent, which corresponds to the Income Shares/Fixed Percentages guideline. The Delaware-Melson thus combines aspects of the income shares and flat percentage approaches, while fully integrating the concept of the "basic needs" (i.e., Standards of Living) of all parties involved into the formula.*

---

*Different minima could of course be adopted (e.g., provincial social assistance levels), and awards would shift accordingly. The general shape of the awards would, however, not change.

Table 5:

Child Support Simulations: Levels of Awards for Families with Two Children

Income - Custodial Parent	Guideline	Income - Non-Custodial Parent				
		$10,000	$20,000	$30,000	$40,000	$50,000
$10,000	Income Shares/Fixed %	3,000	6,000	9,000	12,000	15,000
	Post-Divorce Shares	n/a[a]	n/a[a]	n/a[a]	n/a[a]	n/a[a]
	Delaware-Melson	0	8,100	11,260	14,260	17,260
	Equal SOLs	1,530	7,100	12,930	19,780	26,940
	Maintenance SOL	5,940	13,540	22,770	30,920	40,120
$20,000	Income Shares/Fixed %	3,000	6,000	9,000	12,000	15,000
	Post-Divorce Shares	0	5,240	6,640	7,650	8,430
	Delaware-Melson	0	5,350	9,460	12,960	16,240
	Equal SOLs	-2,360	3,480	10,210	17,170	24,050
	Maintenance SOL	4,110	15,310	24,120	32,330	41,130
$30,000	Income Shares/Fixed %	3,000	6,000	9,000	12,000	15,000
	Post-Divorce Shares	0	5,920	7,780	9,230	10,400
	Delaware-Melson	0	4,230	8,350	11,980	15,380
	Equal SOLs	-5,970	840	7,580	14,290	21,010
	Maintenance SOL	4,440	14,860	24,760	33,030	42,670
$40,000	Income Shares/Fixed %	3,000	6,000	9,000	12,000	15,000
	Post-Divorce Shares	0	6,360	8,570	10,370	11,860
	Delaware-Melson	0	3,740	7,710	11,350	14,790
	Equal SOLs	-8,640	-1,920	4,610	11,140	17,430
	Maintenance SOL	2,800	13,380	23,440	32,730	42,440
$50,000	Income Shares/Fixed %	3,000	6,000	9,000	12,000	15,000
	Post-Divorce Shares	0	6,670	9,130	11,200	12,960
	Delaware-Melson	0	3,450	7,310	10,910	14,350
	Equal SOLs	-11,540	-4,990	1,330	7,430	13,940
	Maintenance SOL	1,840	12,290	23,090	32,440	42,290

NOTE: Calculations assume Ontario residency (with relevant taxes), that all income is earned and that there are minimal deductions. See the text for further details.

[a] Difficult to simulate using the established algorithm because a custodial family is not likely to have such a low level of income in the presence of social assistance. See the text for further discussion.

SOURCE: Calculations performed by the author.

The fourth guideline is the Equalized Standards of Living ("Cassetty") formula, where the two households' standards of living are equalized, as measured by post-tax INRs (which are, in turn based upon the post-tax LIMs). Finally, the fifth guideline follows the "Maintenance" principle, whereby the child's well-being is maintained at the "pre-divorce" level, as again measured by post-tax INRs.

RESULTS OF THE SIMULATIONS

Levels of Awards

Table 5 shows the awards generated by the five guidelines just described. There are obviously many numbers here, but these can be browsed by the reader, guided by a discussion of the most interesting and important aspects of the results. The first thing to notice is the clear illustration of the basic characteristics of the Income Shares/Fixed Percentages award: awards rise smoothly with the income of the non-custodial parent, but are constant across different income levels of the custodial parent; in short, awards are everywhere 30 percent of the non-custodial parent's income.

Next, the Post-Divorce Shares and Delaware-Melson guidelines have zero awards where non-custodial parents' incomes are lowest, reflecting the reserve, or set-aside, provisions in these guidelines. They then jump up sharply, as payments begin to kick in. Apart from this, there is no clear pattern across the first three awards in terms of any being higher or lower than the others. The first three guidelines might therefore be classed as generating broadly similar awards, albeit with substantial variation across particular cells.

This relative similarity is in distinct contrast to the two sets of awards based on Standards of Living. The Equalized Standards of Living formula is intuitively appealing to many people, as it is based on the principle of an equal sharing of the costs of the divorce across all family members. This approach generates some quite high awards, especially where the non-custodial parent has significantly higher income than the custodial parent, with the highest award amounting to almost $27,000 out of an income of $50,000.

The Equalized Standards of Living approach also generates some very low awards, however, and even some negative awards where there is a significant inequality in the opposite direction. Some might object to

Table 6:

Child Support Simulations: Pre- and Post-Divorce Standards of Living for Families with Two Children

Income - Custodial Parent	Guideline	Income - Non-Custodial Parent		
		$10,000 Cust/Non	$30,000 Cust/Non	$50,000 Cust/Non
$10,000	Pre-Divorce INR	1.05	1.65	2.19
	Income Shares/Fixed %	.91/.71	1.19/1.64	1.42/2.53
	Post-Divorce Shares	n/a[a]	n/a[a]	n/a[a]
	Delaware-Melson	.74/.93	1.30/1.48	1.49/2.40
	Equal SOLs	.83/.83	1.36/1.36	1.77/1.77
	Maintenance SOL	1.05/.42	1.65/.63	2.19/.84
$30,000	Pre-Divorce INR	1.65	2.31	2.87
	Income Shares/Fixed %	1.61/.71	1.79/1.64	1.98/2.53
	Post-Divorce Shares	1.53/.93	1.75/1.73	1.84/2.80
	Delaware-Melson	1.53/.93	1.77/1.69	1.99/2.51
	Equal SOLs	1.36/1.36	1.75/1.75	2.18/2.18
	Maintenance SOL	1.65/.57	2.31/.43	2.87/.61
$50,000	Pre-Divorce INR	2.19	2.87	3.45
	Income Shares/Fixed %	2.23/.71	2.44/1.64	2.63/2.53
	Post-Divorce Shares	2.13/.93	2.44/1.64	2.56/2.65
	Delaware-Melson	2.13/.93	2.38/1.77	2.61/2.57
	Equal SOLs	1.76/1.76	2.18/2.18	2.59/2.59
	Maintenance SOL	2.19/.81	2.87/.59	3.45/.65

NOTE: See notes, table 5.

the notion of negative awards, and would prefer to constrain awards to not flow from the custodial to the non-custodial parent in this way. However, once the basic philosophy of the Equalized Standards of Living approach is accepted, it is not clear why it should then be jettisoned whenever awards go in the opposite direction. On a practical matter, however, it might be difficult to sell a concept of *child* support awards with this characteristic.

The Maintenance principle of preserving the well-being of the children after the divorce is also intuitively appealing to many. The awards generated by this approach are, however, extremely high. For example, where the non-custodial parent has an income of $50,000, awards are everywhere greater than $40,000. More generally, in every cell but four, the award takes more than one-half of the non-custodial parent's income, and in the majority of all cases the payment represents more than 75 percent of the non-custodial parent's income. Part of the reason for these large transfers is that the custodial parent's tax rates are driven up by the large payments required to maintain the child's well-being at the pre-divorce level — thus at the margin, each dollar of payment goes a shorter distance towards the Maintenance target.

One final point is that the first four guidelines produce roughly similar awards where the incomes of the two parents are equal, while movements from these diagonal entries produce quite different awards. Thus, while each of the guidelines is characterized by some appealing underlying principles, these clearly take the awards in significantly different directions whenever the simplest cases are departed from.

Standards of Living

Table 6 shows the standards of living associated with the various guidelines in terms of Income-to-Needs Ratios (INRs). These have been described above, but the reader is reminded that INRs are defined as family income divided by the LIM low-income line for families of the given size; ratios below one thus indicate "poverty" status, while ratios greater than one represent increasing levels of economic well-being. "Pre-divorce" INRs are also shown — that is, the combined incomes divided by the appropriate LIM — to show the effect of divorce on the level of economic well-being. Results are presented for only three levels of income each side, so as to keep the display of results to a manageable scale.

Table 7:

Child Support Simulations: Non-Custodial Parent's Effective Tax Rates (Including Awards) for Families with Two Children

Income-Custodial Parent	Guideline	Income - Non-Custodial Parent				
		$10,000	$20,000	$30,000	$40,000	$50,000
	No-Award Tax Rate[a]	.09	.32	.36	.44	.41
$10,000	Income Shares/Fixed %	.31	.53	.54	.53	.58
	Post-Divorce Shares	n/a[b]	n/a[b]	n/a[b]	n/a[b]	n/a[b]
	Delaware-Melson	.09	.91	.54	.52	.57
	Equal SOLs	.19	.73	.74	.79	.80
	Maintenance SOL	.60	.82	.98	.85	.93
$20,000	Income Shares/Fixed %	.31	.53	.54	.53	.58
	Post-Divorce Shares	.09	.70	.42	.44	.46
	Delaware-Melson	.09	.70	.62	.57	.59
	Equal SOLs	.73	.74	.81	.80	.78
	Maintenance SOL	.42	1.17	.94	.85	.89
$30,000	Income Shares/Fixed %	.31	.53	.54	.53	.58
	Post-Divorce Shares	.09	.75	.46	.45	.48
	Delaware-Melson	.09	.62	.62	.58	.61
	Equal SOLs	.74	.81	.81	.79	.78
	Maintenance SOL	.45	1.10	1.04	.85	.96
$40,000	Income Shares/Fixed %	.31	.53	.54	.53	.58
	Post-Divorce Shares	.09	.78	.48	.46	.51
	Delaware-Melson	.09	.59	.61	.58	.61
	Equal SOLs	.81	.80	.79	.79	.78
	Maintenance SOL	.30	1.11	1.06	.95	.97
$50,000	Income Shares/Fixed %	.31	.53	.54	.53	.58
	Post-Divorce Shares	.09	.80	.50	.52	.52
	Delaware-Melson	.09	.57	.60	.58	.62
	Equal SOLs	.80	.79	.79	.79	.80
	Maintenance SOL	.22	1.08	1.13	.96	.98

[a] Rates actually fall off at the highest income levels due to the fact that the maximum deductions for unemployment insurance and CPP/QPP are already being met.
[b] Not calculable because the awards are not simulated at this income level of the custodial parent; see note, table 5.
SOURCE: Calculations performed by author.

For the first three awards, the household with the parent having the higher income winds up with the higher standard of living in every case. This affirms the importance of the parent's own income to the household's final level of economic well-being, even in the presence of child support. In fact, the custodial households generally have an advantage in this regard; for example the difference in the two households' INRs is greater in the bottom left cell of the table where the custodial family has the earnings advantage than in the top right cell where the advantage runs in the other direction. However, only non-custodial parents ever rise above their pre-divorce standard of living. Furthermore, in the actual population, individuals would tend to be clustered much more in the top right regions of the table than in the bottom left, leaving more of the non-custodial parents better off than their ex-spouses and children.

The Equalized Standards of Living results are interesting in that they show the inevitable losses resulting from the break-up of the family: such an equal sharing of the burden results in standards of living ranging from .75 to .82 of the pre-divorce situation. Finally, the Maintenance results show just how draconian the consequences of such an approach would be for non-custodial parents: they are left not only much worse off than the custodial parent and the children in terms of INRs but are actually in left poverty in every case.

Finally, we again see how the results are generally similar for the first three awards, and for the Equalized Standards of Living guideline as well when one looks at the diagonal entries where incomes are equal. It is only on the off-diagonals where there are significant differences in income for the two parents that the results diverge.

Implicit Tax Rates

Table 7 shows the implicit tax rates faced by the non-custodial parents, for whom rates are generally higher and where there is more likely to be the behavioural responses described in chapter 6. These are calculated as the proportion of income lost to taxes and other standard payroll deductions plus child support payments over the $10,000 of earned income up to the level indicated. These can be compared with the marginal tax rates in the absence of child support guidelines — that is, for a single individual — shown at the top of the table.*

---

*Actually, the calculations reflect the net change of all "tax and transfer" aspects of the tax system, including the loss in refundable tax credits as well as actual taxes paid out.

Table 8:

Child Support Simulations: Custodial Parent's Effective Tax Rates (Including the Effects on Awards) for Families with Two Children

Income - Custodial Parent	No-[a] Award Tax Rate	Guideline	Income - Non-Custodial Parent				
			$10,000	$20,000	$30,000	$40,000	$50,000
$10,000	.04	Income Shares/Fixed %	.07	.12	.18	.23	.32
		Post-Divorce Shares	n/a[b]	n/a[b]	n/a[b]	n/a[b]	n/a[b]
		Delaware-Melson	.04	.17	.23	.30	.40
		Equal SOLs	.42	.54	.55	.66	.68
		Maintenance SOL	.31	.43	.43	.42	.38
$20,000	.20	Income Shares/Fixed %	.25	.35	.44	.53	.55
		Post-Divorce Shares	n/a[b]	n/a[b]	n/a[b]	n/a[b]	n/a[b]
		Delaware-Melson	.20	.55	.60	.61	.59
		Equal SOLs	.55	.56	.67	.68	.66
		Maintenance SOL	.43	.46	.45	.41	.41
$30,000	.47	Income Shares/Fixed %	.55	.55	.55	.53	.51
		Post-Divorce Shares	.47	.52	.48	.45	.44
		Delaware-Melson	.47	.61	.60	.57	.55
		Equal SOLs	.56	.68	.68	.66	.66
		Maintenance SOL	.54	.53	.44	.44	.44
$40,000	.52	Income Shares/Fixed %	.50	.49	.49	.47	.46
		Post-Divorce Shares	.52	.46	.44	.42	.39
		Delaware-Melson	.52	.52	.52	.51	.49
		Equal SOLs	.67	.67	.65	.64	.65
		Maintenance SOL	.58	.54	.54	.52	.52
$50,000	.46	Income Shares/Fixed %	.44	.43	.42	.44	.45
		Post-Divorce Shares	.46	.41	.39	.38	.38
		Delaware-Melson	.46	.46	.44	.46	.48
		Equal SOLs	.65	.63	.63	.63	.65
		Maintenance SOL	.50	.50	.50	.50	.50

[a] See note previous table.

[b] Not calculable because awards where the custodial parent has earnings of $10,000 are not simulated; see note in Table 5.
SOURCE: Calculations performed by author.

Implicit tax rates with the guidelines are generally pretty high, especially beyond the very lowest income level, where there are generally low tax rates and some of the guidelines have set-asides. These rates might, therefore, cause some concern with respect to the behavioural responses discussed in chapter 6, including reduced labour supply, the hiding of income, nonpayment of awards and so on.

As for ranking the guidelines in terms of tax rates, those associated with the Income Shares/Fixed Percentages have the advantage of being the smoothest, with no particularly aberrant spikes — which is not surprising given the nature of the guideline. Note in contrast the roller-coaster rates at the lower income levels for the Post-Divorce Shares and Delaware-Melson awards, again reflecting their set-asides, after which awards rise precipitously. These rates would probably make the Delaware-Melson guideline unworkable in its present form, and at the very least it would require significant "smoothing" before implementation, which would in turn change it back into something resembling the Income Shares/Fixed Percentages guideline.

Not surprisingly, the implicit tax rates are highest for the two Standard of Living guidelines. For the Equalized Standards of Living formula, rates are generally 75 percent or higher; and higher still with the Maintenance approach, sometimes even rising above 100 percent, meaning that a non-custodial parent with a higher income would be left with less net income than another individual in a similar situation who had lower income. Such high implicit tax rates would surely make these guidelines unworkable in any practical sense.*

Table 8 shows the implicit tax rates for the custodial parent, with comparisons to be made between the non-award situation shown in the second column and the rates under each of the guidelines. Rates are not nearly as high as for non-custodial parents, for the obvious reason that they are not paying child support. In fact, although their implicit tax rates are usually higher with awards than without, due to the fact that the awards push them into higher tax categories, there are certain cases

---

*One must be especially careful with the notion of implicit taxes in the case of the Maintenance principle. Once the "pre-divorce" level was set, presumably the non-custodial parent would be able to keep any income after the transfer required to achieve that level was made. In this sense, while the implicit tax rates shown apply to comparisons across different individuals at the point of divorce, they overstate the true situation as it would unfold in a dynamic context. However, if the "pre-divorce" situation was updated, the rates shown would indeed apply everywhere.

where the full implicit tax rates are actually lower than in the non-award situation, because awards are higher where their earnings are greater.

SUMMARY

The empirical application of the guidelines may be summarized as follows:

- The simulations are based on a couple with two children considered across a range of incomes. The 1992 tax system is employed, with Ontario residency assumed.
- The children's income needs are estimated using the equivalence scale embodied in the Statistics Canada Low Income Measures (LIMs), which are also used to construct Income-to-Needs ratios (INRs) as a measure of economic well-being.
- Five guidelines are simulated: Income Shares/Fixed Percentages, Post-Divorce Shares, Delaware-Melson, Equalized Standards of Living (or "Cassetty") and Maintenance.
- In terms of the levels of awards, the Income Shares/Fixed Percentages, Post-Divorce Shares and Delaware-Melson guidelines could be grouped together, in that none produces awards generally higher or lower than the others; at the same time, there is significant variation across these guidelines for different combinations of custodial and non-custodial income.
- The Equalized Standards of Living guideline produces the greatest variation in awards, from large positive awards to substantial negative awards. The Maintenance formula, however, produces the highest awards of all, comprising over 75 percent of the non-custodial parent's income in the majority of cases, and over 90 percent at the highest income levels.
- For the first four guidelines, awards are very similar where the parents have similar incomes, suggesting a convergence of principles in this region. By contrast, awards vary significantly where incomes diverge.
- INRs are generally higher for the household with the parent having the higher income, thus affirming the importance of the parent's own income to the household's standard of living, even in the presence of child support.
- The INRs under the Equalized Standards of Living guideline

clearly show the loss in economic well-being associated with the break-up of the family into two separate households.

■ Conversely, the Maintenance guideline leaves the non-custodial parent to pay the full costs of the divorce *via* a precipitous decline in standard of living, while the custodial parent and children are left untouched. This obviously generates the greatest disparities in well-being in the post-divorce situation. In particular, the non-custodial parent is driven into poverty in every case.

■ Implicit tax rates are generally high for the non-custodial parent, but vary significantly from guideline to guideline. The Income Shares/Fixed Percentages guideline generates the smoothest taxes, whereas all other guidelines produce certain situations where the implicit tax rates are extremely high. Rates are especially high with the Equalized Standards of Living formula, and through the ceiling with the Maintenance approach.

CONCLUSION

There is a strong feeling in the country that something needs to be done about child support, and guidelines are at the top of the agenda. What should be done?

PUTTING GUIDELINES IN PERSPECTIVE

It is important to first consider that "the child support problem" may be as much — or more — about nonpayment as about the actual consistency and levels of awards, and the perceived need for higher awards might really be a displaced call for resolving the delinquency problem. If nonpayment is indeed the problem, policy should obviously be pointed in that direction; in any event, inordinately high awards should not be chosen due to any confusion among the level, consistency and collection aspects of the child support problem.

It is also important to remember that divorce necessarily results in declines in standards of living due to the loss of economies of scale associated with the break-up of the household. For example, the simulations presented above indicate that an equal sharing of the losses between the two households would result in a common decline in economic well-being of 20 to 25 percent in the case of families with two children. The divorce settlement is about how these losses are to be shared.

While the empirical results regarding the economic consequences of divorce presented at the beginning of this monograph suggest that the losses could perhaps be shared more equally in many circumstances, and advocates rightly assert that a new child support system might be one vehicle for achieving this, the fact that there are indeed losses needs to be accepted from the beginning. In particular, the simulations show that it is effectively impossible to maintain the children of the marriage at the pre-divorce standard of living — no matter how much we might wish to do this.

DIVORCE OUTCOMES AND THE GENDER EARNINGS GAP

The primary cause of the male-female gap in post-divorce incomes — and the associated disadvantages of children — is the gender earnings gap. It is unrealistic to suppose that child support guidelines are going to fill that gap, and therefore guidelines cannot be relied upon to eliminate the post-divorce divergence in the standards of living of men, women and their children.

This is because, during a marriage, there is income sharing between the parents as well as with the children, and child support guidelines are about the former, not the latter. This has direct implications for the children, however, since their well-being depends on the total amount of money available in the custodial household, and not just the amount of child support *per se*. Thus, in the presence of a gender earnings gap, the children's post-divorce well-being is going to be influenced by the income differences of the parents. Spousal support can play a role here, but to the degree the income gap between the parents remains, the child will tend to share in the standard of living of the custodial parent, who typically has the lower earnings. This means that if we really want to ensure the economic well-being of children at divorce, the gender earnings gap needs to be addressed.

In this regard, the good news is that the gender earnings gap is closing, and this trend should continue as women further increase their labour market participation and move up the occupation scale. The bad news, however, is that the progress is slow, and that women will probably never catch up to men without some dramatic change in the underlying socio-economic gender roles sustaining the gap.

Pay equity laws, affirmative action programs, scholarships for women to enter non-traditional occupations and other such policies can all help increase women's earnings, but their effects are — ultimately — limited. For example, pay equity programs can eliminate earnings differences between janitors and secretaries in a given enterprise (for better or for worse) but are unlikely to turn a secretary into a lawyer or equalize the pay of two lawyers, one of whom devotes considerably more time and energy to her family than does the other.

In short, there will remain a sizeable gender gap as long as women remain more oriented towards the family — for whatever reason — than men. For example, it is well documented that women bear a much larger share of the work in the home than do men, even when both have outside jobs, and that this division of time and effort has important implications for earnings and career growth. In fact, the continued growth of women's participation in the labour market is not just an indicator of how things have indeed changed in some respects, it is at the same time a smokescreen hiding what has remained the same — the different orientations towards family and career on the part of men and women.[20]

The "three-career family" is now the norm — the woman has primary responsibility in the home, plus a career, while the man is largely freed up from domestic tasks to concentrate more single-mindedly on his career. This leaves women at a fundamental disadvantage in their jobs, and until this imbalance is rectified the gender gap will remain and post-divorce outcomes will diverge.

This is not the place for a full-blown debate of the gender earnings gap. The point to be made here is that strong socio-economic forces underlie the gap, which will remain until there is change at this fundamental level. Post-divorce incomes will be equal only when it is men as often as women who stay home with the infant children; leave a meeting early to pick the kids up at daycare and prepare supper; turn down a promotion out of concern that it would be too demanding on his spouse and unfair to their children; and take the time off to stay at home with the kids when they are not feeling well. And similarly, earnings equality awaits the day that women choose a similar array of occupations as men; go back to work and leave a husband home to look after an infant child; and generally have similar attitudes regarding work to those of men.

It is this author's opinion that a more balanced existence on both sides would leave men, women and their children all better off — whether or not there was a divorce. It is also believed that this would require social change in terms of how we raise our children at a fundamental level, involving parenting, the schools and other institutions, the broader social environment, the media — in short, everything that affects who we are and what we become. One need only watch a few minutes of Saturay morning television — either the programs or the advertisements — to appreciate that we have a long way to go.

"Social engineering"? No, rather a true equality of opportunity. But this is beginning to go well beyond child support guidelines, to which we return.

The Case for A Fixed Percentages of Income Guideline

While guidelines based on a Standards of Living approach can be intuitively appealing in some respects, the attraction usually fades when it is realized how difficult it is to even conceive of fair solutions in any sort of dynamic context, while the transfers required would typically be so large as to make such an approach completely unworkable in any practical sense. They are, then, effectively out of the running — confirmed by the fact that such an approach has never been adopted in practice.

As for Income Shares guidelines, one colleague described the underlying principle of maintaining the custodial parent's support at the level it would be were the family still together, as "appealing, as long as you don't think about it too much." Furthermore, it, too, is fairly cumbersome to implement, due primarily to the requirement that information on both parents' incomes be available whenever awards are to be calculated or updated. In addition, any Income Shares approach can be fairly closely approximated — or even exactly replicated — by a much simpler Fixed Percentages guideline; thus any perception that such an Income Shares approach is any fairer than the simpler approach is largely an illusion.

This leaves the Fixed Percentages of Income approach, where awards depend on the non-custodial parent's income alone. Its advantages relative to other guidelines may be summarized as follows:

- Awards are easy to calculate, since they are simply fixed percentages of the non-custodial parent's income. This facilitates planning, since even in the pre-divorce situation awards could be easily determined by the couple themselves. This simplicity would similarly minimize associated legal proceedings, which is typically one of the principal motivations behind the adoption of guidelines.

■ Awards would be easy to collect. In particular, a Fixed Percentages guideline would work extremely well with the sort of deduction-at-source system of collection now in place in Ontario, and under consideration in certain other provinces. Child support payments would constitute nothing more than another deduction, perhaps becoming almost as standard and efficiently executed as UI and CPP/QPP payments.

■ Awards could be immediately and automatically updated — again, especially with a deduction-at-source system in place. In this way, the non-custodial parent would always be sharing his or her income with the child in the prescribed manner. This immediacy and simplicity may be compared with other guideline approaches, where updating requires the regular exchange of income information, and perhaps marginal tax rates, so that gross-ups can be performed. The simpler system can also be compared with the current child support regime, where it is necessary to go back to court to get a variation order whenever there is a "material change in circumstances."

■ The divorced parents would have the greatest economic independence possible, even as the non-custodial parent continued to share in the financial support of his or her child. Furthermore, the system adapts well to additional post-divorce changes in the family situation of the two ex-spouses.

■ The associated implicit marginal tax rates are the smoothest of all types of guideline, and therefore the unwanted behavioural responses (reduced labour supply, hiding income, nonpayment of awards and so on) are minimized.

■ The structure of awards can be easily amended, and can reflect the final balance of a wide range of considerations that might enter the choice of a guideline. This allows a great deal of flexibility when choosing the initial rates and amending these over time.

■ It represents a reasonable compromise across the other types of guideline in terms of the awards it generates. The simulations showed that the Fixed Percentages of Income awards were in the same general range as the comparative approaches, and rose smoothly with the non-custodial parent's income.

Some Details on the Structure and Functioning of a Fixed Percentages Guideline

This establishes the general advantages of a Fixed Percentages of Income approach. Beyond this, the author has less strong views on the precise specification of the percentages, but the following might constitute the sketch of a reasonable candidate.

The typical approach to the construction of a Fixed Percentages guideline should probably begin with the percentages associated with an Income Shares approach. Those derived from an application of the Income Shares method to expenditure estimates coming from the Statistics Canada Low Income Measures would be a sound starting point, and would generate percentages of 17.6, 30.0, 39.1, 46.2, and 51.7 for cases involving one through five children respectively. These percentages should be applied to gross (pre-tax) income, since this keeps the procedures simple, and has the desirable interaction with the tax system described in chapter 6.

Furthermore, it is this author's judgement that these percentages should be held constant across any changes in the family status of either parent. New family formation on the part of the custodial parent should not change the non-custodial parent's responsibility for his or her own child, while the non-custodial parent should not be able to remarry or procreate his or her way out of any pre-existing financial responsibility of this type.

On the other hand, these percentages reflect fair shares in the case where the non-custodial parent spends nothing directly on the child, and once there were any significant direct expenditures, the percentages should be amended accordingly.

The percentages could, in principle, vary with the age of the children, but this would require clear evidence with regard to how child costs vary by age and an assessment of how much this would complicate the determination and collection of awards. The percentages could similarly vary by income level, if this was thought to be important.

Needless to say, the system would work best with deductions at source, with payments then transferred through a central agency to the recipient. The agency would: have the most up-to-date information on the award and inform employers of existing awards as the employee started with the employer; keep track of any changes in the award due to, say, a change in the amount of direct expenditures paid by the parent, passing such amendments on to the employer so that the appropriate adjustment in payments could be made; help pursue any delinquent parents (or employers); and perhaps even provide some sort of payment insurance, at least in the short run, or even merely offer repayable loans.

Finally, there should be at least a minimum payment made by all non-custodial parents, no matter how low his or her income. It might be quite nominal, as little as, say, twenty-five dollars per month. There are two reasons for this. First, it would be good, in psychological terms, for both parent and child to know that the parent is making some contribution to the financial support of the child. Second, it would help with tracking individuals in the system.

Pros and Cons of a Fixed Percentages Guideline Relative to the Current System

Such a system would have a number of advantages over the current budget-based case-by-case system of determining awards. A Fixed Percentages Guideline would:

- mean the standardization of awards, thus eliminating the "roulette" nature of at least this aspect of divorce — in short, fairer awards;
- allow parents to know what the post-divorce outcome will be in advance, thus reducing uncertainty and facilitating better planning for all parties involved;
- allow for potentially easy — and even automatic — updating of awards, rather than the need to return to court for variations whenever there is a significant change in the situation;
- reduce conflict regarding child support during divorce proceedings, thus reducing the associated emotional duress as well as court costs; with the child support issue immediately resolved *via* a guideline, other aspects of the divorce might become more manageable as well;
- engender, perhaps, an enhanced sense of having fair treatment on the part of both parents, thus leaving them feeling better about the divorce experience generally and perhaps even leading to

greater cooperation in the post-divorce situation, including less resistance to paying the child support due.

There remain, however, various actual and potential disadvantages with a guideline approach:

- It does not reflect the particular circumstances of each case, and therefore might be either more fair or less fair overall than the current system.
- It may lead to the imposition of a set of awards that is generally too high or too low — that is, in addition to not allowing for the variation across cases just mentioned, it may actually lead to getting the general levels wrong.
- There is a possibility that the rigidity of guidelines could actually preclude better, more global agreements in certain cases — say, involving property transfers and so on. An extreme example is that the guidelines program implemented in England has actually set new awards without any respect for even *pre*-existing agreements of this sort.
- There is also the possibility that if awards were seen as unfair (too high or not flexible enough with respect to specific circumstances), there could be increased conflict, less post-divorce cooperation, greater resistance to making payments and so on. At the extreme, a bad guideline could discredit the idea so seriously that the whole idea might be written off the policy agenda.

A CAREFUL MIX: A GUIDELINE WITH FLEXIBILITY

One key, then, is that life is complicated, while guidelines are inherently simple; and while it is easy to think of guidelines as nice solutions to straightforward cases, the ultimate success of a particular guideline also rests on its ability to generate fair awards in a broad range of situations. All the same, no one expects guidelines to be universally applicable.

The question is, how broadly do we expect guidelines to apply? One reasonable compromise would be to have the guidelines as a starting point for all negotiations, with the idea that in the majority of cases the guideline would precisely determine the actual award but that in a substantial minority of cases the awards could shift somewhat from those specified by the guideline, including adjustments for the direct expenditures on the children by the non-custodial parent.

The obvious danger is that once the lid is off, all the problems of the current system could flood back. There quite clearly needs to be a reasonable balance between the force of the guidelines and flexibility, perhaps influenced by certain rules and directives to guide any award-bending that might be carried out.

Furthermore, any adjustments should conform to the general Fixed Percentages of Income framework, and adjustments should take the form of altering the percentage applied. For example, in working a property settlement into the deal, the award for two children might be reduced from 30 percent of gross income to 20 percent. All the other aspects of the guideline system would apply. In particular, awards would continue to be deducted at source, amounts payable would vary automatically with income and so on. In this manner, a system could have the advantages of the guideline approach, yet a reasonable amount of flexibility. Guidelines would be a source of achieving fair child support payments, not a strait-jacket.

An Alternative Solution: Contracts

Imagine, for a moment, an entirely different system, where divorce settlements, including child support, were prepared in advance of the marital disruption and put into effect as required. Explicit contracts of this type would have a number of advantages over the current system, which largely consists of attempting to clean up after the fact.

First, there would clearly be none of the ugly surprises that characterize the current system, and — as with guidelines — individuals could plan accordingly. Furthermore, even those who did not divorce would have the comfort of knowing their economic well-being was reasonably secure even in the event of a break-up.

Second, the settlement would be fair and efficient, because each major undertaking — marriage, having children, dropping out of the labour market etc. — would have been discussed, negotiated and agreed to by both parties in advance. For example, the couple might agree that if the marriage ended, one would pay the other 10 percent of his or her salary for a period of 15 years as compensation for the anticipated earnings losses associated with the latter's dropping out of the labour market to care for their child. Child support *per se* might add another 15 percent to the settlement. This contingent settlement would be fair for both parties; if not, it would not have been agreed to. Furthermore, the fact that these contracts would be worked out in advance — in a spirit of good will — would ensure a reasonableness and generosity of spirit often absent from divorce proceedings.

A third advantage of a contract system related to the second is that undertakings not mutually advantageous (*ex ante*) would not be entered into. For example, if no agreement could be reached regarding child and spousal support in the case of divorce, then the marriage would perhaps not occur, the couple would not have the child, there would be no absence from the labour market and so on. This is sad in a way, perhaps, but ultimately a good thing, in that if there is no agreement on the full consequences of the decisions taken, then the proposed undertaking is probably best left undone. Furthermore, individuals would then be free to find partners with whom agreements could in fact be reached, thus ensuring that life's major undertakings would be with partners with whom there was a true sharing of values, plans, responsibilities and so on.

In short, contracts could lead to better matching of individuals as couples — and perhaps fewer divorces as a result. In terms that some economists prefer, the marriage market would be made more efficient, due to the explicit nature of the decisions that are often assumed to be made implicitly anyway.

Fourth, agreements could be tailored to reflect the particular characteristics of each situation rather than some mathematical formula or some judge's impression of the individuals and their needs and responsibilities. Such a system could also allow for flexibility in the nature of the contract: some couples might prefer a once-and-for-all statement of broad principles which could be applied to a great range of particular eventualities, while others might prefer a more detailed agreement with regular updating.

Fifth, divorce settlements would cost very little to implement, since the agreements would simply be pulled off the shelf and applied as required. Of course there would be greater up-front costs involved with the contracting, but it is easy to imagine that these would be far less than the difficult, acrimonious and therefore costly negotiations involved in many divorces under the current system.

Finally, the settlements could include a broad range of items, including property settlements, custody arrangements in the case of children and so on. Thus each partner would be assured of an outcome which is acceptable overall — not just in terms of its financial elements.

ASSESSING A CONTRACTS SYSTEM

The contract idea is new, and the contracting problems should not be minimized. In particular, there might be a large number of contingencies to consider, and from time to time the agreement would have to be updated. Nevertheless, contracts of this general type are written all the time — insurance contracts for example — and standards would surely evolve very quickly. Thus the concept certainly seems technically possible. Furthermore, individuals consider the relevant issues anyway — what they want and expect and hope to get out of the union and even what might happen in the event of a divorce. Thus while the form of the contract would be new, the subject matter would certainly not be. Again, the deliberations would simply be more explicit than is currently the case.

One criticism might be that couples will simply not want to face the possibility that their marriages might fail, and will not want to address the situation in such an explicit fashion. This is, however, precisely why the exercise is so necessary. People *don't* want to think about divorce; they therefore often take decisions with no regard for the consequences should there be a break-up; and they — especially women — therefore then find themselves in a terrible plight if the marriage does in fact end. Contracts would protect individuals against this eventuality.

Some might suggest that the process of actually having to sort out such unpleasant business is hardly the way to start a relationship; that the associated updating of the contract would add extra stress to major undertakings such as having a baby; or that the process could even create conflict and bad will where before there was none. A response to this is that if the act of providing for a fair settlement in the unhappy event that things do not work out as planned *causes* a relationship to fail, perhaps it is better that the relationship ends at that point. In any event, such concerns would at most add a trade off element to be balanced against the advantages of such a system, and should not cause it to be dismissed out of hand.

Others might argue that women would be at a disadvantage in such a system, but the opposite seems more likely. For example, a woman with lower earnings from the beginning due to a career path tempered by a strong orientation toward the family she intends to have could demand an agreement that would compensate her for the non-market contributions she made. If a potential partner was unappreciative of these advantages or was otherwise unwilling to offer a fair deal, presumably there would be others who would better appreciate what the woman had to offer, and with whom she could strike a bargain. Of course "the marriage market" is not so efficient, cold and calculating as this suggests, but it is undeniably true that a great deal of sorting occurs, and contracts should result in matches where women's assets were more fully rewarded than is currently the case.

Thus, it seems likely that post-divorce incomes of men and women would be more equal with a contract system in place — more equal than under the current system; and more equal than all the fiddling with tax law, introduction of child support guidelines or spousal compensations might offer as well.

A contract system could even affect the nature of the marriage itself. For example, when faced with the long-term consequences of their decisions during the process of contract negotiations, men and women might move to a more equal sharing of family responsibilities. For example, a man might agree to pick up more family duties when faced with the spectre of a steep payment in the case of a divorce where the bulk of the family responsibilities are left to the wife.

Finally, in being better informed of the full range of potential costs and benefits of their decisions, individuals could be relied upon to be more responsible for their own actions. For example, the woman who dropped out of the labour market to care for her children would have a much better idea of what the full costs and benefits of this decision were; at the same time, the husband who agreed to the associated settlement to be invoked should the couple divorce would have his share in the consequences equally well defined. It would not be for the state to attempt to sort out all the elements which went into the decision, nor all of the consequences, since this would already have been done by the interested parties, and put into writing.

Here is an exercise. Think of the number of divorced people you know who never imagined things would turn out as they did — not only in terms of a divorce actually occurring, but also in terms of the resulting settlement. Think now of the couples you know who have recently started out in new relationships; most will baldly state that while they know the divorce statistics, they are sure that their own marriage will work, and that they are going to plan and live accordingly. Now consider that about one-half of those in the second group will at some point join the first — i.e., get divorced — and how the mutual protection of an agreement in advance might serve them well.

CONTRACTS, GUIDELINES AND MINIMUM GUARANTEES

How could contracts and guidelines work together? For the most part, they wouldn't necessarily have to, in that a well-developed contract system might make guidelines largely unnecessary. On the other hand, it could be argued that a certain default contract should exist, whereby those who chose to forego the contracting procedure would still be covered. A good default arrangement might also provide a very useful starting point — or even be adopted wholescale — in a great number of cases. With respect to child support, the default could be the Fixed Percentages guideline sketched out above.

The guideline default might also be useful if it was decided to impose certain constraints on contracts. For example, it might be determined that certain minimum payments had to be paid — especially where the custodial parent was at a low income level and likely to be dependent on socially provided benefits. In other words, while we might wish to allow for a "Murphy Brown" situation, where women were permitted to retain the full responsibility for the children to whom they gave birth (provided this was the mutual agreement), we might not wish to allow a non-custodial parent to walk away from supporting a child who would otherwise be on welfare. Finally, the guidelines could operate as the default where the couple was not in an established relationship and there was therefore no contract in place.

In short, it seems that a system that allowed for, and even encouraged, contracts, could co-exist with a child support guideline of the type proposed above. Most basically, the guideline would provide "the contract" for those who found they could do no better on their own; for those who simply did not want to deal with the whole contract idea; or for those who would otherwise violate a socially determined set of parameters regarding these contracts. On the other hand, those who wanted to take such decisions into their own hands and forge their own agreements would have that option. The state would provide a framework and intervene when necessary, but otherwise let couples live their own lives. The idea is a tad radical, but perhaps interesting?

CONCLUDING REMARKS

It sometimes seems difficult to be against child support guidelines. How can one side against a policy initiative that is at various times championed as a way to make divorce outcomes fairer for men and women, improve the economic situation of the children of divorced families and reduce the conflict and financial costs associated with divorce?

It is, however, this author's experience that reservations do in fact typically set in when an individual begins to understand more fully what guidelines are and what they do. For example, the Equal Standards of Living and Maintenance approaches are usually fairly quickly — if often sadly, dashing great hopes — abandoned as soon as it is seen how unworkable they would be in practice. In the search for a more viable approach, the Income Shares guideline, then, often seems to have an appealing foundation but only until it is thought about more carefully; disappointment typically follows when it is seen how the transfers it generates are in fact fairly moderate.

It is then usually realized how tough it is to find a guideline that is appealing in its underlying principles, fair in its application to a broad range of situations and relatively efficient to implement. In particular, throughout the process of becoming informed, the negative aspects of the rigidities that characterize awards determined by a guideline — as opposed to the great variety of situations that characterize divorced families — gradually sinks in, and discourages. There is also, typically, a growing appreciation that maybe the greater part of the child support problem is actually the nonpayment of given awards rather than the level of awards themselves. Are guidelines even the policy we really need?

And this is how one might in fact reasonably be against child support guidelines. It is reasonable to favour guidelines for what they can do in terms of the just-mentioned goals but it is also reasonable to reject the guideline option, perhaps turning instead to a reform of the existing system, including doing all that is possible to ensure that the payments due are in fact made.

It is hoped that this volume has helped in the process of informing the debate. It is no fun bursting bubbles, especially such well-intentioned ones as those associated with child support guidelines, but it is better to make informed policy choices than naive ones. After all, the policy goal should be to create a better system — if it is possible — and reject anything that is ultimately ill-founded or unworkable.

In the end, this author comes down on the side of adopting a child support guideline, but a guideline that is simple, flexible and, ideally, part of a broader system that relies in the first instance on individuals to work out their own contractual arrangements before any divorce is even on the horizon. Such a guideline should represent an improvement in terms of making divorce easier and fairer, with the resulting "rough justice" more "just" than "rough." It is at the same time accepted that such a guideline would also be limited in its likely achievements — for example, it is hardly going to lead to the elimination of child poverty among divorced families.

More wholesale change in divorce outcomes would require changes at a much more fundamental level, including great shifts in the basic gender roles that still exist. We should not expect the important, yet still moderate, intervention of child support guidelines to entirely change a situation that is more deeply rooted. Root problems require similarly deep solutions: there lies the real promise for the greatest change.

1. The points made here are discussed in greater detail in Ross Finnie, "Women, Men and the Economic Consequences of Divorce: Evidence from Canadian Longitudinal Data," *Canadian Review of Sociology and Anthropology*, Vol. 30, no. 2 (May 1993), pp. 205-41 and in Finnie, "An Analysis of the Economic Consequences of Divorce by Pre- and Post-Divorce Family Characteristics: Evidence from Canadian Longitudinal Data," *Cahier de recherche*, 92-02, revised (Quebec: GREPE, Département d'économique, Université Laval, 1994).

2. See Finnie "Women, Men" and "An Analysis of the Economic Consequences" for these adjustments.

3. See Finnie "Women, Men," and "An Analysis of the Economic Consequences" for more detailed discussions of the methodology and findings.

4. Statistics Canada, *Income Distributions by Size in Canada, 1992*, Catalogue 13-207 Annual, 1993.

5. For discussions of the evolution of child support law in Canada, see Mary Jane Mossman, "Family Law and Social Welfare in Canada," in Ivan Bernier and Andrée Lajoie (eds.), *Family Law and Social Welfare Legislation in Canada* (Toronto: University of Toronto Press, 1986) and E. Diane Pask, "Family Law and Policy in Canada: Economic Implications for Single Custodial Mothers and Their Children," in Joe Hudson and Burt Galaway (eds.), *Single Parent Families: Perspectives on Research and Policy* (Toronto: Thompson Educational Publishing, 1993), pp. 185-202.

6. *Paras* v. *Paras*, [1971] 1 O.R. 130(C.A.).

7. See Diane Galarneau, "Alimony and Child Support," *Perspectives on Labour and Income*, Vol. 4, no. 2 (Summer 1992), pp. 8-21 and Diane Galarneau, "Alimony and Child Support", *Canadian Social Trends* (Ottawa: Statistics Canada, Spring, 1993), pp. 8-11.

8. Federal Department of Justice, Canada, Evaluation of the Divorce Act, Phase II: Monitoring and Evaluation, Bureau of Review, May 1990.

9. Much of this chapter borrows from the more complete treatment

found in Ross Finnie and Daniel Stripinis, "The Economics of Child Support Guidelines," Cahier de recherche 93-02 (Quebec: GREPE, Département d'économique, Université Laval, 1993). See also Irwin Garfinkel, *Assuring Child Support: An Extension of Social Security* (New York: Basic Books, 1992) for an alternative treatment of child support guidelines in general.

10.   See Garfinkel, *Assuring Child Support*.

11.   Judith Cassetty, *Child Support and Public Policy: Securing Support From Absent Fathers* (Lexington, MA: O.C. Health and Company, 1978).

12.   Regarding the technical literature, see Martin Browning, "Children and Household Economic Behaviour," *Journal of Economic Literature*, Vol. 30, no. 3 (September 1992), pp. 1434-75 for an overview of the issues regarding the estimation of child costs. For the work recently done in Canada for the Justice Department as part of Federal/Provincial/Territorial guidelines project, see Martin Browning, "Measuring the Costs of Children in Canada: A Practical Guide," Technical Report prepared for theFederal/Provincial/Territorial Family Law Committee, TR1991-13a, January 1991; Martin Browning, "Expenditures on Children by Two-Parent Families in Canada," Technical Report prepared for the Federal/Provincial/Territorial Family Law Committee, TR1991-9a, May 1991; Joanne Fedyk, "Research Plan to Obtain a Reasonable Estimate of Expenditures on Children in Canada in the Context of the Child Support Guidelines Project," Technical Report prepared for the Federal/Provincial/Territorial Family Law Committee, TR1991-12a, January 1991; Joanne Fedyk, "Estimates of Family Spending on Children Using the Adult Good Model," Technical Report prepared for the Federal/Provincial/Territorial Family Law Committee, TR1991-10a, October 1991; Shelley Phipps, "How Much Does it Cost to Support a Child in Canada," Technical Report prepared for the Federal/Provincial/Territorial Family Law Committee, TR1991-14a, Spring 1991; Shelley Phipps, "Estimating Expenditures on Children in Canada," Technical Report prepared for the Federal/Provincial/Territorial Family Law Committee, TR1991-11a, May 1992). See also Finnie and Stripinis, "The Economics of Child Support Guidelines," for a more detailed accessible discussion of the issues as they pertain to

child support guidelines.

13. See Browning, "Children and Household Economic Behaviour," for a full discussion of the various concepts of child costs and how these correspond to the different estimating procedures that are implemented.

14. See Browning, "Children and Household Economic Behaviour," and David M. Betson, "Alternative Estimates of the Costs of Children from the 1980-86 Consumer Expenditure Survey," *Special Report*, no. 51 (Madison, WI: University of Wisconsin - Madison, 1990) for discussions of the full range of techniques.

15. See Martin Wolfson and John M. Evans, "Statistics Canada's Low Income Cut-Offs: Methodological Concerns and Possibilities," Statistics Canada Labour and Household Surveys Analysis Division Discussion Paper, 1989 and Martin Wolfson, John M. Evans and Brian Murphy, "Low Income Statistics: Methodological Issues and Recent Experience in Canada," Statistics Canada Labour and Household Surveys Analysis Division Discussion Paper, 1989 for work which finds a wide range of estimates across different methods for Canada, and Betson, "Alternative Estimates of the Costs of Children" and Thomas Espenshade, *Investing in Children: New Estimates of Parental Expenditures* (Washington, DC: The Urban Institute Press, 1984) for comparable US work. For the work done specifically for the Federal/Provincial/Territorial Committee, see: Browning, "Measuring the Costs of Children"; Browning, "Expenditures on Children"; Fedyk, "Research Plan to Obtain a Reasonable Estimate"; Fedyk, "Estimates of Family Spending"; Phipps, "How Much Does it Cost to Support a Child"; and Phipps, "Estimating Expenditures on Children."

16. Browning, "Measuring the Costs of Children," pp. 1, 70.

17. See Garfinkel, *Assuring Child Support,* for further discussion of these issues.

18. Finnie, "Women, Men."

19. See Finnie and Stripinis, "The Economics of Child Support Guidelines," for further discussion of some of the issues raised here.

20. See Katherine Marshall, "Employed Parents and the Division of Housework," *Perspectives on Labour and Income*, Vol. 5, no. 3 (Autumn 1993) regarding the different time uses of men and women in Canada, and Joni Hersch, "Male-Female Differences in Hourly Wages: The

Role of Human Capital, Working Conditions and Housework,"
Industrial Relations Review, Vol. 44, no. 4 (July 1991), pp. 746-59.

A P P E N D I X

The Divorce Act of 1985

The following are the relevant subsections of Section 15 of Bill C-47, the Divorce Act, regarding spousal and child support.

Objectives of order for support of spouse:
(7) An order made under this section that provides for the support of a spouse should
    (a) recognize any economic advantages or disadvantages to the spouses arising from the marriage or its breakdown;
    (b) apportion between the spouses any financial consequences arising from the care of any child of the marriage over and above the obligation apportioned between the spouses pursuant to subsection (8);
    (c) relieve any economic hardship of the spouses arising from the breakdown of the marriage; and
    (d) in so far as practicable, promote the economic self-sufficiency of each spouse within a reasonable period of time.

Objectives of order of support of child:
(8) An order made under this section that provides for the support of a child of the marriage should:
    (a) recognize that the spouses have a joint financial obligation to maintain the child; and
    (b) apportion that obligation between the spouses according to their relative abilities to contribute to the performance of the obligation.

RESPONSES

BY

DAVID M. BETSON

ELKE B. KLUGE

ELLEN B. ZWEIBEL

D A V I D M . B E T S O N

Fair Shares: Meeting the Financial Needs of

Children After Divorce

With the rising rate of divorce, individuals are becoming all too familiar with the problems surrounding child support. Not unlike taxes, child support stirs the emotions. It is rare to find a divorced parent who doesn't have a strongly held view on child support. In the US, non-custodial parents have formed interest groups to challenge what they believe to be the gross inequities in how child support awards are determined. They have taken their concerns to their legislatures and their grievances to the courts by challenging the constitutionality of the child support procedures. Their passion for their position is deep but often serves to cloud the real issues.

Ross Finnie should be commended on his excellent summary of the numerous issues surrounding child support guidelines. The discussion was balanced and especially dispassionate given its subject. His piece is clearly timely, since Canada is about to consider the adoption of child support guidelines. It will contribute to a reasoned debate on this important subject.

I have found this comment difficult to write since I would have written a monograph very similar to Finnie's. Most of the disagreements I have with him are minor, and are detailed below. I agree with him on the major issue: child support guidelines would be a prudent policy to adopt. I am not convinced, however, that his choice of the Fixed Percentages approach is the best. I hope to contribute to this discussion by offering some observations based upon developments of child support policy in the US, laced with theorizing about what constitutes a fair child support award.

WHAT'S HAPPENING SOUTH OF THE BORDER

During the late 1970s and early 1980s, researchers began to document a rising trend in child poverty in the US, which was mirroring the falling rate of poverty of the elderly population. In 1974, the Census documented that the trends in the poverty rates of these age groups crossed. Today, the poverty rate among children is more than double the poverty rate of the elderly.

Welfare policy was also undergoing a change. There was growing support for the idea that personal responsibility should be emphasized to combat the problems of poverty. Out-of-wedlock births and divorce were viewed as leading causes of child poverty. Child support was seen as one mechanism to enforce the personal responsibilities of parents for their own children, before the state provided aid.

Researchers responded by exploring the shortcomings of the child support system. Robins found that only 53 percent of children living with a single parent over the age of 18 years had an established child support award, and that of these, 26 percent never received a payment. As a result, only 35 percent of the children in single-parent families received any child support payment. Even then, the average payment was less than the average award.[1]

There was also a disturbing trend in the awards being made by the courts and payments received by custodial parents. Between 1978 and 1985, Robins documented that both the average award and the average payment dropped by roughly 25 percent in real terms. It became increasingly clear to analysts that initiatives had to be undertaken to address problems both in the establishment of child support awards and in their enforcement.

In 1988, President Ronald Reagan signed into law the Family Support Act. Title One of this legislation mandated states to adopt child support guidelines. The child support award directed by the application of these guidelines would be assumed to be the correct amount for the award unless the judge entered a written finding stating that the guideline amount would be inappropriate or unjust in the particular case.* The states were instructed to apply their guidelines uniformly throughout the state and in all cases appearing before the court. The primary purpose of this legislation was to address the perceived problem that, in similar divorce cases, judges were making a wide range of awards. The child support system was seen to be unfair since parents could manipulate their child support obligations by shopping for a judge who would be sympathetic to their position. To the extent that the non-custodial parent had more power to influence the child support award, the adequacy of the child support awards was being compromised.

By 1990, all states had adopted child support guidelines but there was little uniformity in their choices. Thirty-three states had adopted guidelines based upon the Income Shares standard, 17 had opted for the Fixed Percentage of Income standard, and three states had adopted guidelines based upon the Melson formula.** Even among states that followed the same basic approach in their guidelines, there was little agreement on the appropriate level of awards. Expressed as a percentage of the non-custodial parent's pre-tax income, the range of the guideline award was 11 percentage points in the Fixed Percentage of Income states and 15 percentage points for the Income Shares states.[2] Thus, while the Act may have reduced the amount of variation in the awards within the states, there still exists a great deal of variation across states.

Bassi and Barnow found the awards derived from state guidelines to be generally consistent with empirical estimates of the expenditures made on children in the US.[3] Yet, in a few cases, states required less support than would had been available for children in the average intact families. To the extent that this criterion measures the adequacy of support, then the question of whether guidelines awards sufficiently address the financial needs of the children remains.

The Family Support Act also legislated other initiatives in the child support area, including: state targets in the determination of paternity and hence child support awards in out-of-wedlock births; provisions that every two years modification orders be made in every child support case;

---

*This is referred to as "rebuttable presumption." From 1984 to 1988, states were required to have guidelines; however, these were only advisory to the courts.

**The District of Columbia, Guam and the Virgin Islands are included in the term "states."

and, in 1994, mandatory wage withholding for all child support cases. While the Act contained lofty goals for the child support system, many of these initiatives have not been implemented by the states. Hence much of the Family Support Act remains a promise of improvement of the child support system and is not yet a reality.

But Fair to Whom?

Unfortunately for many, divorce is becoming a common life event. By seeking divorce, a married couple admits to themselves that the unhappiness they find in their lives together is so great that they would be better off if they lived separately. Divorce marks the end of a stage of one's life and the beginning of another, one that holds out the promise of improvement. However, as Finnie points out in chapter 2, this new life is unlikely to mean a better economic situation. Furthermore, in the case of divorced families, it is the children and the custodial parent who are most likely to suffer an initial decline in their standard of living due to the combination of lower income and greater consumption needs.

Given these realities, what factors should be considered in determining an appropriate or fair level of child support? What may seem fair to one member of the family may seem very unfair to another. For example, non-custodial parents often argue that while they don't resent paying their fair share of what is actually spent on the children, they do resent paying for expenditures that improve the standard of living of their former spouse. However, as Finnie demonstrates, just as the standard of living of the children is inextricably tied to the economic resources of their parents prior to the divorce, so the economic fate of the children after divorce can't be separated from the fate of the custodial parent. This economic reality often serves as a pretext for the non-custodial parent to label almost all child support payments as unfair, thereby providing a reason not to pay.

Some would argue that, in the interests of fairness, children should not suffer any decline in their standard of living after their parents divorce. However, as the simulations show, the burden that the non-custodial parent would be asked to bear is quite substantial and in most cases would place him or her in poverty. Another argument suggests that the two households share in the economic burden in such a way that, after the divorce, their standards of living are equal. This position implies that if one party suffers a decline, both must. In the US, it is difficult to find many supporters of this highly egalitarian standard. To understand why, one need only look at child support in the same terms as we do taxes and transfers.

For Americans, it is inconceivable to even contemplate taxing individuals and transferring the money to others in order to make both parties equally well off. Winners should win in the economy, not through redistribution. In a similar vein, taxpayers often feel the *burden* of taxation much more than the perceived *benefits* that supposedly arise from taxation.

Child support is like the tax system in that non-custodial parents do not like the idea of having their income taken from them and not having control over how it can be spent. In some regards, child support payments can be more onerous than taxes. Taxes can quickly change when your income or spending changes; child support payments, by contrast, don't automatically drop when you lose your job. Equally important is the fact that the benefits of the child support payments are diminished in the eyes of the non-custodial parent by the knowledge that the payments are making the custodial parent better off.

Support for taxes is generally easier to obtain if the tax receipts can be shown to be directly related to a given expenditure. Perhaps this explains why the majority of states in the US have adopted an Income Shares standard for child support, which establishes as a reference point not the standard of living of the custodial family but a particular level of spending on the children. By setting the explicit goal of achieving the same level of spending on the children that would have been obtained had the couple not divorced, the Income Shares standard strikes an interesting compromise between the interests of the non-custodial parent and those of the custodial parent and the children. Targeting the pre-divorce level of spending on the children encourages the impression that the children's standard of living is to be maintained. As Finnie shows in his monograph, this clearly is a false impression. Yet, making spending on children the core principle of the standard helps to reinforce the non-custodial parent's impression that his or her payments are being used for expenditures on the children. Through a formula by which both spouses are instructed to share in these expenditures, the standard promotes the impression of fairness to both parties in the divorce.

A Closer Look at the Income Shares Standard

A common complaint from non-custodial parents is that custodial parents aren't contributing their fair share to the raising of the children and in some cases aren't even spending all of the child support payments on the children. Is this possible? Unfortunately, the answer is yes.

To demonstrate this claim, let us assume that the equivalence scales implicit in Canada's Low-Income Measures correctly portray how parents spend on their children both in intact and single-parent families. Thus for two children, an intact couple is assumed to spend 30 percent of their total expenditures on their children. In a single-parent family, the parent is assumed to spend 41.2 percent of her or his total expenditures on the two children.

Let us consider a case where the custodial parent has an income of $20,000 and the non-custodial parent has $40,000. Under the Income Shares approach, the basic obligation of both parents to their children is determined by what they would have spent on them prior to the divorce. This would be equal to 30 percent of their combined income of $60,000 or $18,000. The non-custodial fair share of this basic obligation would be equal to the proportion of the couple's combined income earned by the non-custodial parent. In this example, the non-custodial parent's obligation would be 67 percent of the $18,000 or $12,000. The custodial parent's share would be the remainder, or $6,000.

But what will be the spending on the children if the award of $12,000 is actually paid? The custodial family's income is now $32,000. According to the Canadian estimates of child expenditures in single-parent families, 41.2 percent of this income will be spent on the children. This implies that $13,184 will be spent on the children, an amount far short of the $18,000 envisioned in the standard. Critical non-custodial parents would point out that the custodial parent is only contributing $1,184 to the financial needs of the children or roughly only 20 percent of their fair share.* They are not holding up their end of the bargain.

While this example demonstrates the concerns of the non-custodial parents, it depends upon the assumed consumption behaviour of the

---

*If the non-custodial parent's income is $50,000 then the basic obligation would equal $21,000, of which the non-custodial parent's fair share would be $15,000. However, after receiving the child support payment of $15,000, only $14,420 (41.2 percent of $35,000) would be spent on the children.

custodial parent. In Finnie's world, the child support payment is assumed to be spent on the members within the household in the same proportion as the custodial parent's income was spent prior to the child support award.* However, it is not unreasonable to believe that a higher proportion of the child support payment will be spent on the children than the proportion spent from the custodial parent's income. In this example, if the custodial parent spends 81.3 cents of every dollar of child support on the child and not the 41.2 cents assumed in the example, then the full amount stipulated in the child support award ($18,000) would be spent on the children.

Clearly the validity of the objections raised by non-custodial parents rests upon the knowledge of how child support payments augment spending on children in single-parent families. Unfortunately this is something we don't know much about. But the non-custodial parent's concerns about the actual level of spending on children may suggest that the appropriate point of reference is indeed the pre-divorce level of spending. By voicing their concern, are not non-custodial parents saying that their view of a fair award is grounded in the level of spending on children after the divorce?

CAN JUDGES ITERATE?

Finnie provides another set of simulations of awards based upon the proportional sharing of the post-divorce expenditures on the children. These simulated awards were meant to serve as a rough approximation of the current procedures for awards under what is known as the *Paras* formula. As Finnie notes, the calculation of this award is not as straightforward as the Income Shares. This standard's award is meant to reflect the proportional sharing of the post-divorce spending on the children; however, this spending will, in turn, depend upon the size of the award. If such an approach does indeed reflect current Canadian practice, then Canadian judges must be solving a lot of potentially nonlinear equations to arrive at their awards.

Finnie suggests using the following iterative procedure. The first step would be to calculate the amount of spending on the children using only the custodial parent's income and then compute an award based

---

*In other words, the marginal propensity to spend on children is assumed to be equal to the average propensity and to be unaffected by the income source.

upon the proportional sharing of this level of spending. The procedure would then be repeated — except this time, the amount of spending would be based upon the custodial parent's income plus the award as computed in the previous stage. This procedure would be repeated until the difference in computed awards in any two consecutive iterations was no greater than a dollar.

It has been my experience that the legal profession has difficulty enough using look-up tables, let alone this extensive iterative procedure. I doubt whether the reported simulations really replicate even a rough approximation of the current awards. While the spirit of the post-divorce spending standard may correspond to the approach taken in current awards, I wouldn't be surprised if the judges stopped at the first stage. In other words, the current system would be better approximated by examining what the spending would be on the children taking only the custodial parent's income into account and then performing a proportional sharing of that amount.

The difference between this calculation and the Finnie calculation is quite significant. Let us again consider the example where the custodial parent has income of $20,000, the non-custodial parent has $40,000. Using the LIM equivalence scales, we would estimate that 41.2 percent of the custodial parent's income would be spent on the two children, or $8,240. The non-custodial parent's share of this amount would be $5,493, a substantial difference from the $7,573 resulting from Finnie's method of calculation.*

Finnie's calculation of the Post-Divorce Shares standard imposes an additional constraint — namely, that the custodial parent must earn at least a poverty-line income and that the payment of the award must never place the non-custodial parent in poverty. While these provisions may indeed be a part of Canada's current system of awards, they tend to lead to some confusion when we compare this approach with other standards presented in table 5. The inclusion of this provision has a strange and perhaps undesirable effect on the pattern of awards. Consider the column in table 5, which depicts the awards for a non-custodial parent

---

*The amount described here as Finnie's calculation doesn't match the figure presented in his table 5 because I don't take into account the tax implications of child support payments or his "low-income" safety provisions — under which the incomes of custodial parent and non-custodial parent never drop enough to put either parent below the poverty line. These differences still don't wholly account for the significant gap between the two awards. Finnie computes an award of $7,650 for this example.

with an income of $40,000. As the custodial parent's income rises from $10,000 to $50,000 in $10,000 increments, the simulated Post-Divorce Shares award would rise as follows: $9,930; $7,650; $9,230; $10,370; to $11,200. I would think such a U shape pattern of awards would be troubling, especially to non-custodial parents. Consider the potential frustration of a non-custodial parent whose spouse was earning $10,000 and who turned down a job paying $20,000. If the custodial parent were to accept the job, the child-support award would fall by more than $2,000 but this would be more than offset by the additional $10,000 of income coming into the custodial parent's household. Financially, both the non-custodial parent and the children would be better off if the custodial parent took the job.

I found the use of the poverty line as a minimum income in the calculation of the award to be an interesting provision. In the US, many states instruct the judge to deem that the custodial parent has an income even if he or she doesn't report any. In most cases, such deemed income is the amount that would be earned from a minimum wage job. Finnie's use of poverty-line income in calculating awards seems to amount to an assumption that the custodial parent has access to public-assistance payments that would place he or she at the poverty line and that it is reasonable to include these benefits in the calculation. In the US, public-assistance benefits aren't included in the calculation of awards. The focus in the US has been what is available to be spent on the children from private sources only.

Equally troubling in Finnie's method is the sharp increase in awards when the non-custodial parent's income rises above the poverty line. The award jumps to $7,650 from zero when the non-custodial parent's income doubles from $10,000 to $20,000, crossing the poverty line. In the US, many states using the Income Shares standard have adopted self-support reserves, such as the one proposed by Finnie, to protect the non-custodial parent. However, to avoid the high "tax rates," as in the Finnie proposal, the states have gradually phased in the full amount of the non-custodial parent's fair share of child support over a wider range of income. The non-custodial parent would not be required to pay any child support if he or she were below the poverty line. But as income rises above the poverty line, he or she would be expected to pay an increasing percentage of the child support award. For example, at income of 125 percent of the poverty-line amount, the payer would contribute 25 percent of the obligation. At 150 percent, the figure would rise to 50 percent. At twice the poverty-line income, the full contribution would be made.

COST OF CHILDREN

Estimates of parents' expenditures on their children are critical elements of the standards Finnie considers. Since he assumes that child expenditures are a constant proportion of a family's income, the Income Share standard is transformed into a fixed percentage of the non-custodial parent's income.* While the assumption of constant percentages provides some justification for the Fixed Percentage standard, is it correct?

Based on my own research and the literature I have reviewed, I have come to the conclusion that child expenditures do represent a constant proportion of a family's total *current expenditures*.[4] However, there is a distinction to be drawn between a family's total expenditures and its pre-tax income. The difference between these two concepts is the amount of taxes paid and the amount of savings set aside by the family. At low levels of income, the difference may not be great; however, as the family's resources rise, the difference becomes proportionately greater due to the progressive nature of taxes and a rising average propensity to save. Hence my reading of the evidence indicates that expenditures on children are a *falling* proportion of a family's pre-tax income. For example, consider a high-income family whose pre-divorce tax payments and savings totaled 40 percent of their income. The expenditures on the children would be 30 percent of the family's total expenditures, which, in turn, represent 60 percent of their pre-tax income. Computing child expenditures on the basis of expenditures rather than income would lead to a lower award. An Income Shares award would be 40 percent lower than the figure obtained under Finnie's calculation.

---

*Let s equal the constant percentage of income devoted to children. The basic obligation in the Income Shares approach would equal $s(Ic + Inc)$ where Ic is the custodial parent's income and Inc is the non-custodial parent's income. The award would then be equal to

$$\text{Award} = \frac{Inc}{Ic + Inc}\, s\,(Ic + Inc) = s\, Inc,$$

which is the fixed percentage of the non-custodial parent's income.

Selecting a fixed percentage standard based upon some average level of spending would lead to awards at lower incomes that are less than what is actually being spent on the children. At higher than average incomes, parents would be required to pay more in child support than the amount dictated by the levels of spending on their children.* While some may be pleased with this result, the inappropriate use of the estimates of spending patterns undercuts any rationale one might provide for the guideline.

The empirical research on parents' spending on their children reflects the common sense finding that as a child grows older, it costs more to raise the child.** The consequence of such a finding is that any system of awards that doesn't take into account the age of the children will provide awards that are too high when the child is young and too low when the child is older. Thus, if the divorce occurs when all the children are young, it would be prudent of the custodial parent to save some of the payments for use when the children are older. But what is troubling is cases where the children are already older when the divorce occurs. The awards appropriate for the average-age child are too low for older children. Several states in the US have adopted age-specific guidelines; however, this further complicates an already complicated procedure.

Finnie uses a single set of estimates of the percentage of income devoted to children in families. While the percentages implicit in Canada's LIMs may be appropriate for use in Canada, it is important to recognize there is little agreement on these percentages. For example, based upon my own research, I estimate that an intact family with one child would spend 25 percent of total household expenditures on the child. This compares to the 17.6 percent implicit in Canada's LIMs. The difference becomes smaller for two children, where I estimate that 35 percent of total expenditures are devoted to the children, compared to the 30 percent under the LIMs. The consequence of these differences is that award schedules can vary significantly according to assumptions about the costs of children and differing concepts of fairness.

---

*To provide for a partial remedy, the child support calculation could be converted to a net income basis. However, this opens the way for a wide range of manipulations.

**The costs of the children are somewhat U-shaped, with the costs initially falling as the child reaches school age. When the child enters his or her teens, the costs then rise.

FAIR MODIFICATIONS

Establishing a fair award at the time of divorce is difficult enough; trying to decide what is still fair at a much later point in time compounds the difficulty. As Finnie notes, the logic of the award standards dissipates over time, as income and family situations change. For example, how meaningful is it to talk about how the remarriage of the non-custodial parent should affect an Income Shares award when the point of reference for this standard is the pre-divorce situation of the original family? All the same, the way in which modifications are made is as important as the original setting of the award in promoting the efficiency and fairness of the child support system.

Proponents of frequent and regular modifications stress that such procedures would promote fairness. When the non-custodial parent's income rises, the children should receive higher benefits, just as they would if the parent still lived with them. Conversely, when the non-custodial parent's income falls, the children should be expected to share in the loss.

However, these benefits should be measured against the potential costs of frequent modifications. If child support obligations were automatically updated whenever the non-custodial parent's income changed, then the level of financial uncertainty faced by the custodial parent could rise substantially. He or she could never count on a regular child support payment. In a real sense, we would have increased the risks attached to divorce beyond the level associated with the current situation, where the only uncertainty arises from not knowing what the initial award will be.

If modifications were never made, then the marginal tax rates discussed by Finnie would all be zero. The impact of the child support system would be restricted purely to income effects, and this is likely to encourage rather than discourage greater work effort on the part of the non-custodial parent. Child support systems that provide for frequent or automatic modifications, such as envisioned by Finnie in the Fixed Percentage standard, would create marginal tax rates or substitution effects tending to discourage the parent's initiative to augment his or her income. As Finnie demonstrates, the magnitude of the implicit tax rates in many of these standards can be substantial in the case of non-custodial parents but almost nonexistent or sometimes even negative for custodial parents. The question of the fairness of this structure of tax rates, and not just its efficiency costs, should be considered.

For these reasons, I am convinced that modifications of awards should be done quite infrequently if at all. However, if awards remain fixed in nominal terms, then the adequacy of the awards diminishes over time, thereby compromising the welfare of the children. To address this real concern, I would propose that awards be adjusted yearly to reflect changes in the cost of living.

I am in agreement with Finnie's position that modifications due to changes in family situation should not be made. Despite the additional financial responsibilities remarriage carries, I don't believe remarriage by either spouse should be grounds for a modification of a child support order. The original responsibilities haven't diminished just because the parent has taken on new ones. I do believe in the principle of "first in line, first in right."

However, if orders are to be modified based upon changes in family situations, then such modifications should apply to both parents. Recently, in Indiana, the Supreme Court amended the child support procedures to allow either parent to seek a modification in his or her award if the parent has taken on the financial responsibility of an additional child. Thus, if a non-custodial parent remarries and has another child, then he or she can seek to reduce child support payments. In the same way, if the custodial parent has another child, then he or she can seek an upward modification of the original order, to reflect the additional financial responsibility. What is good for the gander should also be good for the goose.

CONCLUSIONS

Finnie concludes by stating his best case for the Fixed Percentage standard. His reasons for favoring this approach are based primarily upon the simplicity of calculation and administration. Personally, I do not find these justifications convincing enough to warrant the adoption of a fixed percentage formula for child support without a careful consideration of other standards.[5]

Finnie correctly notes that perhaps the most important goal in child support policy is not setting the award but collecting it. But I would suggest that "fair" awards are easier to collect than "unfair" awards. The real reason why we should worry about the fairness of the child support system, especially from the non-custodial parent's perspective, is that we are concerned about the potential collectability of the awards. What good is an award if it is never paid?

It is hard for me to believe that an award based upon a fixed percentage of the non-custodial parent's income would ever be considered fair by a majority of parents. What parents or any litigants seek from the courts is a consideration of the facts of their case. They don't seek "cookie cutter" justice. The virtue of standards such as the Income Shares or Post-Divorce Shares approach is that they both provide a concrete rationale for the determination of an award. The Fixed Percentage approach lacks any underlying rationale unless one tries to rest it on the untenable assumption that children expenditures are a constant proportion of one's income. Basically, I find this approach arbitrary and it is difficult for me to believe that any arbitrary formula could ever be viewed as fair.

Finnie notes that the perception that other approaches such as the Income Shares standard are fairer than the Fixed Percentage approach is an illusion. While I agree that this observation is largely correct, I would add that sometimes illusions are important. US economists have noted that the "pay-as-you-go" financing structure of our social security system, combined with collection of social security taxes from employers and employees, only serves to give workers the impression that they had paid for their retirement benefits. But the illusion serves the public by providing apparent reasons for supporting the program. In the case of child support, as long as the divorced couples view the process as fair, that is all that counts.

The potential advantages of a fixed percentage formula in collection are overstated. If every non-custodial parent with the same number of children faced the same percentage rate then there would be clear advantage to the approach. But to the extent that judges order deviations from the standard on a case-by-case basis, this advantage quickly evaporates. With regard to the automatic modifications that are possible under this standard, I doubt the wisdom of modifying awards, as I explained above. Moreover, the practicality of at-source deductions of payments seems to hinge upon the assumption that the non-custodial parent is paid a wage or salary by his or her employer. In fact, implementation of a fixed percentage award for self-employed individuals such as farmers would become an accounting nightmare.

The point of these remarks is to say that I don't find the case for the

Fixed Percentage standard all that strong. I think that all the alternatives have their advantages and disadvantages, and these should be debated.

Do I think the use of guidelines is preferable to current practice? Yes, I do, and for the same reasons as Finnie suggests. But that is not important. The real challenge in the debate is to determine what constitutes a fair and adequate child support award. Child support is becoming too crucial a source of financial support for children not to be publicly discussed and debated. Child support payments should not be left to the whims of judges. Fairness to all parties, parents and children, can and should be improved. Ross Finnie's work should play an important part in this debate.

1. Phillip Robins, "Why Are Child Support Awards Amounts Declining?", *IRP Discussion Paper,* no. 885-89 (Madison: University of Wisconsin-Madison, 1989).

2. See Laurie Bassi and Burt Barnow, "Expenditures on Children and Child Support Guidelines," *Journal of Policy Analysis and Management,* Vol. 12, no. 3 (Summer 1993).

3. Bassi and Barnow, "Expenditures on Children."

4. See David Betson, "Alternative Estimates of the Cost of Children," from the 1980 to 1986 Consumer Expenditure Survey, final report to the Department of Health and Human Services, Assistant Secretary of Planning and Evaluation, 1990.

5. David Betson, Erik Evenhouse, Siobhan Reilly and Eugene Smolensky, "Tradeoffs Implicit in Child Support Guidelines," *Journal of Policy Analysis and Management,* Vol. 11, no. 1 (Winter 1992).

E L K E   B .   K L U G E

CHILD SUPPORT GUIDELINES: A QUICK GLANCE

FROM A PRACTITIONER'S PERSPECTIVE

I have practised Family Law for over a dozen years and welcome the introduction of child support guidelines. They will deprive me and other family law practitioners of many hours of work spent (and billed) on clients' files but will leave the consumers of our legal services with greater financial resources to look after their children and re-establish their lives after marriage breakdown.

Guidelines, whether presumptive or merely advisory, will not be a cure-all, of course. Doing away with arbitrariness is to be welcomed; but being unable to use discretion poses its own risks. However, not unlike the limited discretion given to judges dealing with property divisions or equalizations — where a judge can find that the statutory provisions turn out to be "unconscionable" or "inequitable" in any given case — the child support legislation need not tie the hands of judges. Moreover, it could provide to separating spouses and their children a predictable and inexpensive means of determining the amount a custodial parent will receive by way of child support and, conversely, the obligation of the other parent to pay such support.

In my experience, and I believe that most of my colleagues would agree with me on this point, a legal system that is perceived as fair works better for all concerned. There are far fewer enforcement problems or attempts to avoid payment of support when the awards are perceived as fair. Awards that are viewed as arbitrary will inevitably leave at least one party feeling wronged by the process and trying to defeat its result.

Most parents who separate do not institute court proceedings to resolve their disputes. They either make casual arrangements or enter into formal separation agreements. While a divorce cannot be granted without a court proceeding, the vast majority of divorce judgments either contain no child support provisions or incorporate, by consent of both parents, provisions to which they have agreed orally, in writing or in Minutes of Settlement.

Of those separating couples who do institute court proceedings to resolve issues arising from their separation, very few proceed to trial. Most settle their disputes at some point before a trial commences. Why? Aside from the emotional trauma, it is simply too expensive and takes too long (often years) to have a dispute resolved by a trial judge.

Most child support awards determined by judges or other court officials such as Masters are interim child support orders granted after a party has brought a motion to the court. These interim orders are usually in effect until either a final order is made (at a trial — which, again, is rare) or another means is found to resolve the issue. What often happens is that the amount of child support set in the interim order becomes the yardstick against which proposals for a permanent and final resolution are measured. If the interim child support order is high, the recipient will not be inclined to settle for a lower amount — parents who had to go to court to resolve the matter tend not to be inclined to be conciliatory at this stage. If the support award is low, the payer will not be inclined to agree to pay more. In either event, the longer the high or low amount is paid, the more the children's custodial or primary parent is likely to adjust his or her spending patterns to adapt to the amount awarded. Most people, in my experience, do not feel comfortable incurring increasingly greater debt in order to arrive at the amount that should really be spent on the children. On the other hand, parents who receive high awards are unlikely to put the extra money away for a rainy day. It certainly would not be in that parent's best legal interest to do so since it would prove that the amount initially awarded was unreasonably high.

Given the importance of the interim child support award, we should have a closer look at how these interim orders come about. They are usually made on the basis of hastily prepared materials, after brief argument by two opposing counsel, by a harried judge who may well have another 20 motions on his or her list that morning and who may not have had a chance to read any of the materials prepared by the lawyers. The lawyers, of course, obtained their information at a time when their clients are likely most angry, hurt, confused and uncertain about what is to happen within the next month or so, never mind the next few years.

Perhaps the preceding paragraph presents too bleak a picture. There are, of course, times when caring, concerned and knowledgeable judges weigh carefully the evidence presented to them by well-prepared counsel who have taken the necessary time (expensive as it may be for their clients) to prepare a detailed financial picture of the family prior to the breakdown, careful budgets for the children and cogent oral arguments. Unfortunately, this scenario is not the norm. If it were, there would not be so much difference between child support awards in cases where the financial facts are relatively similar. In other words, the system would work better and guidelines would not be required.

As to the enforcement of support orders, my experience has been that steady progress has been made since I first started to practise in 1980. The Ontario Support Deduction scheme, implemented relatively recently, appears to be working well most of the time and reciprocal enforcement provisions between various provinces and states and countries are becoming increasingly effective. In the window of a Vermont post office, I recently noticed a poster with half a dozen or so pictures. On closer examination, I realized that this was a poster with photographs of parents who had failed to pay child support. An interesting approach, I thought, but in my view far less effective than a scheme which, as a result of its inherent or at least perceived fairness and predictability, would have the result of far fewer failures to pay child support.

While the implications of the *Thibaudeau* decision of the Federal Court of Appeal are not yet entirely clear and the ruling is unlikely to be the last word on the matter, I would, in any event, welcome amendments to the Income Tax Act (Canada) to allow flexibility in the structuring of child support from a tax perspective. If we ignore, for the sake of this discussion, the *Thibaudeau* case, the Income Tax Act obliges the recipient of child support to include the amounts paid in income and permits the payer to deduct the amount paid. Often, especially when there is wide disparity in the respective incomes of the payer and the recipient, it is beneficial for the payer to receive the tax deduction (at his or her higher marginal tax rate) and to have the recipient include the amount as income (at his or her lower marginal tax rate) — the payer can afford to pay more because his or her "real, after tax" payments are lower. Occasionally, however, it is the lower income-earning parent who pays child support to the higher income-earning parent or, as a result of receiving support, the recipient moves into a higher tax bracket than the payer. In such cases, it would be beneficial if provisions under the Income Tax Act allowed parents to agree (or if a judge could order) that the payer not receive a deduction for support, and conversely, that the recipient need not include the amount of child support in his or her income. There is considerable flexibility respecting income tax treatment when properties are transferred between spouses on marriage breakdown. Likewise, parties can agree (or judges can order) that third-party payments and support payments made and received before a written separation agreement is concluded or an order is made be treated as tax deductible to the payer and included in the income of the recipient. Surely, similar flexibility and tax planning could be provided for in child support matters generally.

If one of the principal reasons for the current tax treatment is to enable more money to be freed for child support, it would appear only equitable to allow parents to opt out of the deduction/inclusion system in cases where the current tax treatment would lead to a reduction in money available for spending on the children. One option (in recognition of the fact that many couples do not consult lawyers) might be to allow no tax deduction for child support (and require no inclusion) unless the parents specifically opt for the deduction/inclusion method.

While it has been suggested that the Income Tax Act be revised simply to allow no deduction of child support for the payer and, conversely, require no tax to be paid by the recipient (which is the case in the US and in many other countries), such a change in the Income Tax Act, if it were retroactive, would have the undesirable effect of engendering a monumental rush of variation applications on the part of payers who would want to reduce payments on the grounds that the "real, after tax" dollars received under the new scheme would be much higher than the "real, after tax" dollars paid under the old one. The lawyers would likely be the only winners in this scenario. Interestingly, the first three phone calls I received after the *Thibaudeau* decision was announced were from payer parents. Each asked me, first, whether the decision curtailed the right to deduct the support paid. When I answered no, the next question from all three callers was whether they were now entitled to reduce the child support they were paying.

Finally, I have read Professor Finnie's paper and other materials respecting the various guidelines under consideration. It appears to me that the Fixed Percentages of Income of the paying parent would be the easiest guideline to apply at all stages where an award must be determined, especially at the interim support stage. While a reluctant payer may try to hide income, that situation is not all that unusual even now and can be remedied by income attribution. Similarly, if basing child support on a fixed percentage of the payer's income would produce an inequitable (or "unconscionable" — a higher test) result, either because it would impose a hardship on the payer or would be inadequate to meet the needs of the child in the recipient's care, judicial discretion may alleviate concerns in this regard. Most awards would not deviate from the results achieved from applying the fixed percentages of income. As a consequence, parents would then know ahead of time or at any stage how much one must pay and the other would receive. Most people, when told "that's how it is," will accept the inevitability of it; since there is not much that can be done about it, they will adjust to the reality. The clients will not have spent a fortune on legal fees, judges will have more time to deal with other matters and, in the long run, we will all benefit from the consequences — except, perhaps the lawyers, who are probably not the people whom our government's social policy is there to protect.

ELLEN B. ZWEIBEL

WHY CHILD SUPPORT GUIDELINES ARE ON THE

FAMILY LAW REFORM AGENDA

After divorce or separation, custodial mothers and their dependent children have an appallingly high rate and depth of poverty; while the custodial mother and children experience a decline in standard of living, the non-custodial father's standard of living often improves, or at least stays the same.

Alienation, long-term financial insecurity and a profound sense of unfairness are the legacy of a system where custodial mothers and children experience the bulk of the economic impact of family break-up, all the while observing a non-custodial father living in more comfortable circumstances. These circumstances prompted the Federal/Provincial/ Territorial Family Law Committee (Family Law Committee) to consider replacing the current case-by-case, evidence-based determination of child support awards with a guideline formula approach.

Defining the main objectives of child support guidelines is crucial. These objectives shape the research questions asked, the criteria applied in measuring outcomes and the response to deficiencies identified by the research. They also shape the tradeoffs considered acceptable and the specific features incorporated in the guideline adopted.

The principal goals of child support guidelines are to improve upon the adequacy and equity of current child support awards. These are the

Family Law Committee's *first* stated policy objectives.[1] Representatives from a wide range of community and advocacy organizations, family lawyers and researchers specializing in family and support issues confirmed these principal goals at several national and regional research consultations and workshops.[2]

Ross Finnie inappropriately downplays these objectives. Instead he asserts that the principal goal of child support guidelines is to "reduce arbitrary variations" to achieve "uniform justice."* Uniformity in and of itself is of limited value: *consistently low* child support awards are still low. Child support guidelines must do much more than duplicate the *status quo* in a standardized fashion.

As of yet, in the child support guideline debate, I am neither a proponent nor a detractor. Listening to the diverse voices of the community representatives, advocacy groups and other Canadian and US researchers, I have been cautiously evaluating the potential of guidelines and considering the impact of many substantive and technical features. In this response, I will provide supplemental and contrasting views to those of Finnie on just a few of the many guideline design and evaluation issues.

THE NEED TO BROADEN THE CHILD SUPPORT REFORM AGENDA

Child support guidelines apportion private family resources. Although the link between low child support payments and the depressed economic circumstances of women and children is clear, this type of private family law reform will have little positive impact for a significant number of divorced and separated families. Many families who were able to sustain a basic or moderate standard of living with both parents' combined incomes will no longer be able to do so in separate households.

Early in the guideline consultation process, community and advocacy organizations began calling for an expanded agenda to include a public maintenance advance system and stronger collection mechanisms. In a public maintenance advance system, the government advances a basic support amount whenever private support is inadequate, unavailable or

---

*Finnie lists post-divorce economic planning as a second goal and increasing average amounts becomes only "a third, oft-cited goal." Improving equity between custodial and non-custodial households doesn't make his list.

difficult to enforce. The state support amount is treated as an advance on the private family obligation and the state takes over the responsibility of enforcing the private award.[3] As a strictly private measure, child support guidelines were viewed as working best if they are part of this type of broader, integrated public support strategy.

This view parallels the approach of the University of Wisconsin, Institute for Research on Poverty which, in 1977, began work on developing a Child Support Assurance System (CSAS).[4] This is an integrated public and private solution which holds non-custodial parents to a formula-based child support obligation, ensures collection and guarantees a minimum, non-income-tested assured benefit for custodial mothers. A non-income-tested benefit was preferred over a targeted welfare model because it more successfully cushions all children from the substantial decline in their economic situation, is less likely to discourage custodial mothers' workforce participation and allows recipients to avoid the stigmatization of an income-segregated benefit.[5]

To date, only the guideline formula and enforcement components of the Wisconsin CSAS have been adopted in the United States. However, as guideline limitations become more apparent, the full CSAS approach is re-emerging on the US political agenda. There are now Congressional Bills to establish a national child support assurance system and demonstration projects.[6]

The three-pronged private/public approach could more directly address the economic vulnerability of custodial parents and children. As a representative of the Ontario Immigrant and Visible Minority Women's Organization explained:

> The danger of seeing the problem in fragments, of not looking at the whole picture, is that you risk making assumptions that ripple into other laws so that laws play off each other, leaving women falling through the gaps.[7]

In broadening the agenda for child support policy reform, more gaps are closed.

THE CRITERIA FOR MEASURING ADEQUACY AND EQUITY

The Family Law Committee has been collecting information on current awards and is expected to recommend a guideline approach by the summer of 1994. Whether the guideline improves upon existing awards can be evaluated on the basis of two criteria.

Adequacy

Child support guideline awards should reduce the number of poor and financially insecure custodial households whenever there are enough resources to share between the two households. Generally, families with incomes below Statistics Canada's Low Income Cut-off Lines (LICOs) are considered relatively poor. Although financial insecurity is a more subjective concept, families whose incomes are less than 30 percent above the LICO can be considered financially vulnerable — that is, without sufficient resources to deal with economic pressures or emergencies.

Small increases over current awards are illusory and will not justify replacing the current system. Guideline awards are generally determined when the family initially breaks up, before either parent has remarried and gone on to have other children. Under guidelines, child support awards are then decreased, typically, for the first family when the father remarries and starts a second family. Considering the higher and quicker remarriage rate for men, small initial increases under guidelines will quickly disappear. Similarly, downward adjustments from joint or shared custody arrangements will also cancel out nominal increases.

Even if the recommended guideline appears on paper to increase support awards for families in the low and middle-low income groups ($30,000 combined income), overall, they are still unlikely to translate into better standards of living for the custodial households. This is true for several reasons. First, the award will often impoverish the non-custodial father, leading to routine deviations from the guideline. Second, collection will be difficult and unlikely. Third, given the income levels and resources of the custodial mother, she will likely need to rely on some form of social assistance. Although provincial social assistance systems vary in their treatment of child support, benefits are, in general, either reduced dollar for dollar or are subject to a small ($50-$100) exemption, which the custodial mother can keep.

Equity

Guidelines are not expected to achieve absolute parity between the two households. However, the economic impact of the family break-up should be more evenly distributed.

Where families have the resources to maintain both households at a reasonable standard of living, a guideline is inappropriate if it leads to a situation in which the non-custodial father's standard of living duplicates or rises above the family's pre-separation standard of living while that of the custodial mother and children hovers uncomfortably close to the poverty level or is disproportionately low. As a corollary to this, guidelines should be able to respond to unexpected declines in the custodial mother's income. For example, suppose the custodial mother's income decreases because her employer cuts down her employment hours or she is laid off. To avoid gross inequities, the guideline should respond by increasing the resources for the children under these circumstances.

DOUBLE STANDARDS: IGNORING CUSTODIAL MOTHER'S NON-MONETARY COSTS, RECOGNIZING NON-CUSTODIAL FATHER'S ACCESS AND JOINT CUSTODY COSTS

Finnie claims that the non-monetary costs borne by the custodial mother are in effect cancelled out by the psychological benefits of living with the children full time. From a practical perspective, he suggests that the relevant calculations are impossible. His notion that cooking dinner becomes "play" if the child is present is suspiciously reminiscent of the Mary Poppins' approach to chores: "*In every job that's to be done there is an element of fun, you find the fun and snap, the job's a game.*"[8] His idealized vision of the custodial parent's life ignores all the research documenting the greater tension, urgency and fragility in the work-family balance experienced by single custodial parents.[9]

On the other hand, several sections later, he proposes adopting guidelines that reduce the support amounts owed by non-custodial fathers to reflect access and joint custody costs. This he suggests is "only an accounting exercise" with "no complicated theory to consider." There is no suggestion that these costs are cancelled out by the non-custodial father's increased pleasure from the child's company. Let us now unpack the severe policy ramifications of this double standard.

What Are Non-monetarized Costs?

"Non-monetarized costs" is a general term often used to refer to non-market production. The term is, in part, a misnomer. These extra-costs are "non-monetary" not because they couldn't be given a dollar value but because they are generally left out of the traditional national accounts framework.[10] The importance and value of non-market production is becoming more widely recognized. In an effort to "extend measures of production," Statistics Canada has launched a series of studies to estimate the dollar value of labour input to household production in Canada.[11]

In the context of the child support debate, non-monetarized costs collectively refer to three kinds of extra costs associated with child rearing: increased responsibility and time spent on household and child rearing or nurturing tasks; increased direct and indirect costs; and employment opportunity costs.

1. *Increased responsibility and time spent on household and child rearing or nurturing tasks*. The division of labour with respect to parenting, generally disproportionately assumed by the mother when parents live together,[12] is often exaggerated when parents live apart. Everything from supervising homework, driving to activities and assisting with socialization skills are routinely handled on a daily basis by the custodial mother.*

Studies on the relative amounts of time spent with the residential and non-residential parent confirm that the custodial mother absorbs the majority of nurturing tasks.**

---

*Empirical evidence supports this general observation. A study by a large business in the northeastern US reported that female single parents spent an average of 18.89 hours per week caring for children, for a total work week (paid labour, home chores and child-related activities) of 75.31 hours. In contrast, male single parents without custody spent an average of 8.5 hours per week on child-related care, for a total work week of 65.16 hours. Karen Czapanskiy, "Giving Credit Where Credit is Due: The Role of the Noneconomic Contribution of the Physical Custodian in Establishing Child Support," in *Critical Issues Critical Choices: Special Topics in Child Support Guidelines Development* (Washington: Women's Legal Defense Fund, 1987), p. 144, citing Diane S. Burden, "Single Parents and the Work Setting: The Impact of Multiple Job and Homelife Responsibilities," *Family Relations*, Vol. 35 (1986).

**Diane S. Burden, "Single Parents and the Work Setting: The Impact of Multiple Job and Homelife Responsibilities," *Family Relations*, Vol. 35 (1986), pp. 146-147, citing studies by Frank Furstenberg, Judith Wallerstein and Deborah Lupenitz, all of which found a low level of continuing contact between the non-custodial father and children.

2. *Increased direct and indirect costs.* A range of services previously provided by the other adult must be purchased for the first time. In the two-adult household, one adult can babysit while the other takes care of domestic tasks, attends school meetings or enjoys leisure time. Assistance with certain household tasks such as home or car repairs must now be purchased.[13] Some expenses such as work-related child care may be incurred for the first time or be increased.

The need to be near schools, shopping, play areas and public transportation or to maintain stability by remaining in the old neighbourhood can dictate a choice of more expensive housing.* Greater time pressures on single parents result in costly substitutions of convenience products and purchased services. There is also less time for achieving economies through comparison shopping.[14]

3. *Employment opportunity costs directly related to the children's presence in the household.*** Child-rearing responsibilities put constraints on availability for overtime, shift work, job-related travel, job choice and location. The double burden of work and homemaking has a negative effect on most women's workforce earnings.[15]

Custodial mothers have even less flexibility than mothers in a two-adult household. Custodial parents report many child care-related changes in their employment patterns, including arriving at work late or

---

*A Manitoba study focusing on post-divorce home ownership reports that lone-female parents pay significantly more of their gross income toward rent and home ownership costs (principal, interest and taxes). Eighteen percent of lone-female parents paid more than 30 percent of their income on these costs as compared to 14.5 percent of all other persons in the study. Freda M. Steele, *Executive Summary: Economic Consequences of Divorce on Families Owning a Marital Home* (Winnipeg: CMHC, 1990).

**This discussion ignores the cumulative effect of past and present child-rearing responsibilities on women's future labour market participation and employment earnings. Spousal support is sometimes used to address this issue.

leaving early, missing work, reduced availability for travel, reduced workload, quitting a job and being fired.* In the words of two mothers interviewed for a case study by the Canadian Advisory Council on the Status of Women (CACSW):

> I need a flexible job. [My son] has an eye appointment every six weeks because he got glasses when he was [one year] and they're monitoring him closely; his day care closes at 5:30 and children are always getting colds and stuff. So I need to be able to take time off. The problem is that flexible jobs are not as well paid.
>
> I changed jobs because I could not do a 6 a.m. shift and my career is stonewalled because I cannot do a graduate degree because I have no time or money.[16]

These are the "non-monetarized costs" that increase dramatically for custodial mothers and also increase the economic disparity between the custodial mother and non-custodial father's household.

"Non-monetarized costs" have an impact on guideline-based support awards in another way: the economic estimates of child-rearing costs incorporated into guidelines leave them out. The economic models used to calculate expenditures on children[17] all use Statistics Canada Family Expenditure Data Base (FAMEX). This is a consumer spending survey of child-rearing costs in two-adult households. It does not include non-monetarized costs of providing services to the children or earnings foregone because of child rearing. The underestimated total costs of raising children in two-adult families then become the amount apportioned

---

*Donna S. Lero and Karen L. Johnson, *110 Canadian Statistics on Work and Family* (Ottawa: Canadian Advisory Council on the Status of Women, 1994), pp. 29-30. In a US study, these types of pressures were reported by 90 percent of sole-custody mothers and 73 percent of sole-custody fathers. Karen Czapanskiy, "Giving Credit Where Credit is Due: The Role of the Noneconomic Contribution of the Physical Custodian in Establishing Child Support," in *Critical Issues, Critical Choices: Special Topics in Child Support Guidelines Development* (Washington, DC: Womens' Defense Fund, 1987), pp. 144-45, summarizes a study by Geoffrey Greif. In her summary, she compares the experience of sole-custody fathers and mothers as follows: arriving late or leaving early (35 percent men, 32 percent women), missing work (34 percent men, 32 percent women), reduced work-related travel (32 percent men, 9 percent women), reduced workload (19 percent men, 9 percent women), quitting a job (6 percent men, 12 percent women), being fired (4 percent men, 7 percent women).

between the parents in the child support guideline. Finnie's proposal to base child expenditures on the equivalence scales embodied in Statistics Canada Low Income Measures (LIM) does not avoid this under-estimation problem since the LIM equivalency scale is also based on FAMEX.

Thus, "non-monetarized" costs may be left out twice: first, in the estimates of the child-rearing costs incorporated in the guideline; second, by not giving any recognition to the increase in these costs for custodial mothers.

It is possible for a guideline formula to give some recognition to these costs. For example, the CACSW recommends incorporating a higher self-support reserve for the custodial mother to reflect her heavier load of the routine parenting responsibilities, the double load of work and parenting, the indirect and hidden costs and her lost employment opportunity costs.*

Adjusting Support Payments in Recognition of Visitation and Co-parenting Costs

In making downward adjustments in support awards for time spent with the non-custodial parent, one must be careful not to compound the effect of not having credited the custodial mother with any of her extra time and costs. Some US state guidelines allow a downward adjustment in support payments when the child spends more than the "typical" amount of time with the non-custodial parent. Thirty percent of overnights per year is often used to define the point where an adjustment is appropriate. This would be roughly 110 days a year or in more graphic terms, two overnights per week plus six vacation days.[18]

Finnie objects to ignoring the non-custodial parent's expenses at points below any "arbitrary cut-off point." This would "not only be unfair, but might also make it difficult for many non-custodial parents to provide for the child in the manner in which they should be able."

---

*Canadian Advisory Council on the Status of Women, *Evaluating Child Support Policy* (Ottawa: CACSW, 1992), p. 33. US commentators suggest several others, including: computing a monetary value for the work and treating it as income to the non-custodial parent; not imputing income to the parent who foregoes income-generating work to care for children; not reducing child support as the custodial parent's income rises; and increasing child support when the non-custodial parent fails to comply with regular visitation schedules. Karen Czapanskiy, "Foreword," in *Essentials of Child Support Guidelines Development: Economic Issues and Policy Considerations* (Washington, DC: Women's Legal Defence Fund, 1986), p. 20.

Instead, he suggests that we start with the recommended payment where there is sole custody with no visitation or joint custody costs and then "fine tune," i.e., downwardly adjust, for different visitation and joint custody arrangements.

Under this proposal, the non-custodial father gets a double benefit. He doesn't have to compensate the custodial mother for her labour or her increased costs. But he gets recognition for any time he spends with the child.* Surely if time spent with the non-custodial father is viewed as creating some limited savings for the custodial mother, then just as clearly the custodial mother has even greater overall costs when the non-custodial father fails to exercise "typical" visitation. Joint and shared custody, residence and extended visitation arrangements increase the overall costs of raising children. In general, custodial mothers start with insufficient employment earnings and receive insufficient child support. They often just cannot afford adjustments for custody and visitation variations. It is presumed that lengthy periods of visitation or shared residence and custody arrangements will decrease some of the primary custodial mother's expenses. However most costs are fixed.

Joint or shared custody is challenging, and many parents who start off with this ideal find that they cannot realize their good intentions. Over time, their original co-parenting plan looks more like the traditional primary custody and visitation arrangement. To avoid serious hardship to the custodial parent, the guideline formula must be capable of quickly adjusting to the real visitation pattern.[19]

To the extent that a guideline uses a custody or visitation adjustment, five principles should be observed:

1. The variation should never impoverish the custodial household or make the mother financially insecure. Many custodial households cannot absorb a decrease in support.

2. The decrease in support should not exceed the custodial mother's actual savings from non-fixed costs such as food and entertainment.

3. The variations should allow a reduction only for the additional time spent over a defined normative threshold.

4. There must be a quick, cheap and effective review mechanism

---

*Underlying this model is the stereotype that women naturally and appropriately put their families first, sacrificing their own financial security in order to fulfil their role as nurturers. For fathers, the opposite stereotype operates as he is compensated for having accepted any responsibility.

available to the custodial mother to have the full support payment re-instated for non-compliance with the custody or visitation arrangement.

5. There must be a mechanism for increasing support when non-custodial fathers do not comply with the defined normative threshold.

Although I do not share Finnie's particular concerns about using a threshold cutoff, other guideline commentators have noted a different set of problems and have offered equitable solutions. Several US states use an "apportionment and offset" adjustment, which dramatically decreases child support as soon as the number of agreed-to overnight visits exceeds the defined threshold. Child support is then apportioned completely on a time basis and the non-custodian receives a full credit for any and all time spent with the child. For example,[20] suppose the state guideline called for a $446 payment where each parent earned $2,000 gross per month and when the non-custodial parent spent the "typical" 30 percent of time with the children. If that parent increased his time with the children to 40 percent (about 3 days per month) the "apportionment and offset" adjustment would reduce support to approximately $89. The extent of this effect will of course vary with the income spread of the parents. However, it always produces a considerable decrease.

A more equitable method is a "percentage reduction" adjustment. Additional time over the 30 percent also results in a credit. But the credit reduction is based only on the additional time spent above the threshold. In the example above, the reduction in support would be the difference between 30 and 40 percent or a more manageable 10 percent of the total support payment.

CHILD SUPPORT GUIDELINES AND THE CANADIAN INCOME TAX TREATMENT OF CHILD SUPPORT

In the US and Australia, jurisdictions that pioneered child support guidelines development, payments have no income tax consequences for either the custodial or non-custodial parent. The custodial mother knows that she can spend the full amount of the support payment she receives.

In Canada, current income tax policy allows payers to deduct the full child support payments from their taxable income and requires recipients to include the full child support payments in their taxable income. The custodial mother cannot spend the full child support payment; she needs to consider how much she will pay in income tax first. The main rationale for the deduction/inclusion provisions is that they are expected to produce higher support payments. Since taxable income is shifted from the non-custodial father (who is presumed to be in a relatively high marginal tax bracket) to the custodial mother (who is presumed to be in a relatively low marginal tax bracket), there is an overall tax savings that is supposed to be available to increase resources for child support. To make this theory work, the custodial mother's child support payment must be "grossed up" to at least cover her increased tax liability. Otherwise the system would merely make the custodial mother fully liable for the non-custodial father's taxes on his child support obligation.

The appropriateness of this deduction/inclusion scheme has come increasingly under attack by policy and advocacy organizations. The National Association of Women and the Law (NAWL) and the Canadian Advisory Council on the Status of Women (CACSW)[21] each have resolutions calling for the repeal of the Income Tax Act's deduction/inclusion provisions.[22] The Society for Adequate Parental Support of Children (SCRAPS) has been organizing rallies and circulating petitions.[23] On March 22, 1994 Beryl Gaffney MP for Nepean introduced a private member's motion calling for the repeal of the inclusion portion of the current policy. Then, on May 2, 1994, in *Thibaudeau v. the Queen*,[24] the Federal Court of Appeal ruled that the inclusion portion of the current policy violates section 15 of the Charter of Rights and Freedoms and is therefore unconstitutional. An appeal to the Supreme Court is likely.

The deduction/inclusion income tax system complicates the fair implementation of child support guidelines. As the Family Law Committee itself noted, although tax consequences should be an element of every child support determination, there is evidence to suggest that these calculations may not always be made and there is no guidance on how the benefits of the deduction should be shared between the parties.[25]

The recent *Thibaudeau* decision highlighted yet another problem that has been documented in academic writing: the tax policy behind the deduction/inclusion provisions assumes that the non-custodial father's tax savings will always be greater than the tax liability of the custodial mother. In fact, two different case studies[26] showed that the reverse was true in a significant portion (29 percent[27] and 39 percent[28]) of the families studied: the non-custodial father's tax saving was less than the custodial mother's increased tax liability. The deduction/inclusion benefit theory does not work for these cases and family law is faced with an impossible conundrum. The father cannot afford to gross up the award but, because of the tax system, the mother will receive considerably less support than she needs.

These tax problems and others[29], carry over into the implementation of guidelines. The Family Law Committee's *Research Report*[30] tentatively dealt with the income tax issue by incorporating a separate gross-up calculation as part of every child support guideline considered. This is a good beginning, but it will not deal well with the cases where the father's savings are less than the mother's increased liability. A full gross-up may undermine the guideline's underlying principle and may impoverish fathers in certain income groups.

Finnie suggests that any Income Share or Fixed Percentage guideline could be based on pre-tax incomes, with no separate tax adjustment. He states that this maintains the underlying principle of the Income Shares approach because the total dollars spent on the children is the same. In the Appendix, he illustrates this with an example of a family with two children where the total family income of $50,000 is earned by the non-custodial father.* Single income-earning families are a decreasing portion of two-parent households** and after divorce and separation custodial mothers by necessity are in the paid workforce. But more importantly, this example avoids facing the extent to which the Canadian income tax system undermines another fundamental principle of the Income Shares method: apportionment of the total child rearing costs based on relative income levels.

For example, let us assume the same total family income of $50,000, but this time have it earned $30,000 by the non-custodial father and $20,000 by the custodial mother. The total amount to be spent on the

---

*In the example, the non-custodial father is left with $17,500 net disposable income, (after paying both child support and his income taxes). Finnie views this as appropriate because this is what the father's net disposable income (net of children's expenses and income tax) would have been if the family had not separated. It should be noted however, that when the family lived together and spent $15,000 on the children, the remaining $17,500 after tax income supported two adults. After separation, because of the child support tax deduction, the father has the full $17,500 to spend on himself and the mother has only $15,000 to support a three-person household.

**Dual earners represent the majority of husband-wife families with children. In 1988, both parents were employed in 58 percent of two-parent families with children under age 13. Donna S. Lero and Karen L. Johnson, *110 Canadian Statistics* (Ottawa: Canadian Advisory Council on the Status of Women, 1994), p. 12.

children is still $15,000. The father will contribute $9,000 (60 percent) in a child support payment and the mother will contribute the remaining $6,000 (40 percent) from her own income.

The Income Tax Act deduction/inclusion provisions will then have the following effects. The deduction will reduce his after-tax cost of support to $6,259.* The inclusion will increase her tax liability and hence her contribution by $2,861. Of the original total $15,000 in child-rearing costs, he now pays approximately 42 percent ($6,259/$15,000) while she absorbs approximately 58 percent ($8,861/$15,000). This is almost a complete reversal of the original 60/40 apportionment intended under the Income Shares Method. Notice also that in this example the assumption that his tax savings will be greater than her increased tax liability did not hold: instead her tax increase was greater than his tax savings. As a result, the total they spend on the children ($6,259 + $8,861) is now $15,120, slightly greater than the original $15,000. The increase is, of course, the increase in taxes created by the deduction/inclusion provisions.

The current income tax deduction/inclusion provisions are a significant hurdle for the implementation of child support guidelines.

TRADEOFFS

Finnie greatly contributes to the child support guideline debate by emphasizing that guideline development is an art not a science, that there are significant tradeoffs to be identified and evaluated and by offering his ideas on many difficult issues. I am not convinced that the particular version of the Fixed Percentage of Income approach he favours is either simple or fair. It cannot really be simply routinely deducted like a payroll tax since the employer would have to have information on the father's custody and visitation arrangements to adjust the percentage. It is not particularly fair to use a simple percentage in cases where the children have extraordinary expenses, or to expect the custodial mother to shoulder the full burden of work-related child care expenses. As well, a

---

*Both the non-custodial father's tax savings and the custodial mother's increased tax liability were calculated by comparing the difference in their tax liabilities with and without the application of the child support deduction/inclusion provisions. Tax rates, credits and deductions were based on the 1992 Income Tax Act, an average provincial tax rate of .546 of federal tax was used and refundable child tax credits and GST tax credits were included.

Fixed Percentage Guideline will never adjust the support amount during periods when the custodial mother's income involuntarily decreases because her employer cuts down her employment hours or she is laid off.

During the next year the debate will intensify as the Family Law Committee moves closer to its legislative goals. This book will contribute to that debate and to the follow-up research necessary to monitor the actual effects of child support guidelines in the Canadian context.

1. *Child Support: Public Discussion Paper* (Ottawa: Queen's Printer for Canada, 1991), p. 7.

2. Research Consultation on the Feasibility of Child Support Schedules, (Vancouver, March 29-30 1990); Ontario Women's Directorate, (Toronto, November 6, 1991); National Association of Women in the Law (West Coast Branch) and Society for Children's Rights to Adequate Parental Support, (SCRAPS) Joint Consultation (December 1991); Critical Review of Child Support Guidelines Workshop, Canadian Advisory Council on the Status of Women (Ottawa, May 1992).

3. For a general discussion of public maintenance advance systems, see Irwin Garfinkel & Patrick Wong, "Child Support and Public Policy," in Organization for Economic Cooperation and Development, *Lone-Parent Families: The Economic Challenge* (Paris: OECD, 1990) 101, pp. 113-15 and Karen Bridge, *An International Survey of Private and Public Law Maintenance of Single-Parent Families* (Ottawa: Dept. of Supply and Services, 1985), pp. 17-21. Jurisdictions that have developed PMA systems include Sweden, France, Germany, Austria, Switzerland and Norway.

4. Irving Garfinkel, *Assuring Child Support* (New York: Russel Sage Foundation, 1992), p. 42. See also, Irving Garfinkel, Sara S. McLanahan and Philip K. Robins (eds.), *Child Support Assurance: Design Issues, Expected Impacts, and Political Barriers as Seen From Wisconsin* (Washington, DC: The Urban Institute Press, 1992).

5. Non-income-tested programs were also viewed as having less administrative costs per recipient. Finally, if eligibility were not restricted to poor persons, it is likely there would be greater political support for higher benefit levels. Garfinkel, *et. al.*, *Child Support Assurance*, p. 163.

6. National Child Support Assurance System Bill, H.R. 4051 (1994); Child Support Assurance Act of 1992, S. 2343; Downey/Hyde Child Support Enforcement and Assurance Proposal, Subcommitte on Human Resources, Committee on Ways and Means, US House of Representatives, September 1992.

7. Canadian Advisory Council on the Status of Women, *Evaluating Child*

Support Policy (CACSW: Ottawa, 1992), p. 3.

8. At which point Mary and the Banks children magically and musically play at tidying up the messy nursery. *Mary Poppins,* Walt Disney Productions, 1964.

9. D.S. Lero and L.M. Brockman, "Single-Parent Families in Canada: A Closer Look," in B. Galaway and J. Hudson (eds.), *Single-Parent Families in Canada: Perspectives on Canadian Research and Policy* (Toronto: Thompson Educational Publishing 1993), p. 107.

10. For a summary of the issue with references to earlier research, see Morley Gunderson and Leon Muszynski, *Women and Labour Market Poverty* (CACSW: Ottawa, 1990), pp. 24-27.

11. William Chandler, *The Value of Household Work in Canada*, 1992, National Income and Expenditure Accounts, 4th quarter 1993, Statistics Canada, catalogue no. 13-001. See also, Chris Jackson, *The Value of Household Work in Canada*, 1986, National Income and Expenditure Accounts, Technical Series Number 19 (Statistics Canada: Ottawa, July 1992).

12. Donna S. Lero and Karen L. Johnson, *110 Canadian Statistics on Work and Family* (Ottawa: Canadian Advisory Council on the Status of Women: 1994), pp. 8, 21 and 22; Gunderson and Muszynski, *Women and Labour Market Poverty*, p. 25.

13. Carol S. Bruch, "Problems Inherent in Designing Child Support Guidelines," in *Essentials of Child Support Guidelines Development: Economic Issues and Policy Considerations*, Proceedings of the Women's Legal Defense Fund's National Conference on the Development of Child Support Guidelines (Washington: WLDF, 1986), p. 43. See also Marilyn Ray Smith and Jon Laramore, "Massachusetts' Child Support Guidelines: A Model for Development," in *Essentials of Child Support Guidelines*, p. 274, citing Carol S. Bruch, "Developing Standards for Child Support Payments: A Critique of Current Practice," *U.C. Davis Law Review,* Vol. 16 (1982), p. 49.

14. Bruch, "Problems Inherent in Designing Child Support Guidelines," p. 43.

15. Lero and Johnson, *110 Canadian Statistics*, pp. 5, 27 and 29. See also Dianne Pask and M.L. (Marnie) McCall (eds.), *How Much and Why* (Calgary: Canadian Institute for Law and the Family, 1989), pp. 58-59.

16. CACSW, *Evaluating Child Support Policy*, p. 19.

17. *The Financial Implications of Child Support Guidelines: Research Report* (Ottawa: Queen's Printer for Canada, 1992) and Robin A. Douthitt and Joanne Fedyk, *The Cost of Raising Children in Canada* (Toronto and Vancouver: Butterworths, 1990).

18. For a comprehensive discussion of the issues related to guidelines and visitation and co-parenting costs, see Marianne Takas, "Improving Child Support Guidelines: Can Simple Formulas Address Complex Families?", *Family Law Quarterly,* Vol. 26 (Fall 1992), p. 171.

19. Takas, *Improving Child Support Guidelines.*

20. Example taken from Takas, *Improving Child Support Guidelines.*

21. See CACSW, Recommendation B5.5, *Tax Deductibility of Alimony/Maintenance Payment* (June 1977); National Association of Women and the Law Resolution Number 25 (February 24, 1991). See also National Symposium on Women, *Law and Administration of Justice: Recommendations from the Symposium,* June 11, 1991, (Department of Justice, 1992), pp. 49-50.

22. *ITA* ss. 56(1)(b), (c) and (c.1) and 60(b), (c) and (c.1).

23. SCRAPS and SCOPE (Support and Custody Orders for Priority Enforcement) organized a rally on Parliament Hill on June 27, 1992, calling for the repeal of the deduction/inclusion provisions. See Anna Asimakopulos, "Mothers protest tax on child support," *The [Ottawa] Citizen,* June 28, 1992, p. A12.

24. Federal Court of Appeal file A -1248-92.

25. *The Financial Implications of Child Support Guidelines*, pp. 91-92

26. Ellen Zweibel and Richard Shillington, *Child Support Policy: Income Tax Treatment and Child Support Guidelines* (Toronto: The Policy Research Centre on Children, Youth and Families, 1993); Affidavit of Nathalie Martel, filed by Justice Department in *Thibaudeau,* using 709 cases from the Department of Justice: "Child Support Award Database."

27. Affidavit of Nathalie Martel.

28. Zweibel and Shillington, *Child Support Policy.*

29. The gross-up calculation is sensitive to changes in the custodial mother's income and her marital status, suggesting the need for frequent adjustments under any guideline.

30. *The Financial Implications of Child Support Guidelines.*

Rebuttal

by

Ross Finnie

———

Rebuttal

Reply to Betson

Professor David Betson's remarks offer some interesting and useful discussions on a range of topics not dealt with in my text, elaborations and different perspectives on some issues I do address and ultimately a different preferred guideline from the one I propose. I enjoyed his comments and respect our differences.

I particularly enjoyed Betson's detailed treatment of issues of fairness, and how he does not shrink from meeting some of the thornier issues head on. For example, he notes how an Income Shares approach can actually result in the non-custodial parent paying considerably *more* than his or her assigned share if actual expenditures on the child drop from the pre-divorce level — as they often do. This is part of the reality of child support, and should be accepted and dealt with. However, I would hasten to add that spending on the children drops to the degree the custodial family's income drops, and thus our sense of fairness probably needs to go beyond simple comparisons of post-divorce spending shares — as Betson would probably agree.

Betson's discussion also deals particulary well with the problems associated with updating awards, again with a focus on issues of fairness, plus a treatment of the more practical matters such as the associated implicit tax rates. Betson is clearly looking for a real-world guideline, and I applaud him in his attempts to balance what we might ideally want in a guideline with what we can have in a practical sense.

In the end, Betson prefers an Income Shares guideline with no updating except for standard adjustments for the cost of living. While he recognizes that a Fixed Percentages of Income guideline could generate similar awards, he believes that individuals would perceive an Income Shares approach to be the fairer guideline, and would therefore feel better about the process and ultimately be more likely to cooperate. It is a different set of trade offs from those I choose — but as I state in the opening paragraph of my monograph, "That's the child support debate."

REPLY TO KLUGE

With Elke Kluge — a practising lawyer rather than an academic — we again find issues of fairness front and centre. And again, as with Betson, Kluge believes it is crucial that the system for determining child support be perceived as fair, largely because she believes this will minimize attempts to avoid payments. In particular, Kluge offers a very useful description of the present system for determining child support and how it is very often difficult to reach a settlement that strikes both sides as fair — and in many cases only after sizeable outlays of time, energy and money relating to legal proceedings.

Hence Kluge comes down in support of guidelines in general, and the Fixed Percentages of Income guideline I have proposed finds her favour. Interestingly, this practitioner, who sees so many different cases and who represents both custodial and non-custodial parents, emphasizes the need for flexibility. In other words, she sees using the formula as a base, which would in fact precisely determine the great majority of awards, but around which there could be deviations according to the particular circumstances of the situation.

REPLY TO ZWEIBEL

When I suggested Professor Ellen Zweibel as a commentator for this volume, it was with the idea that she would provide an alternative point of view. The results have not been disappointing in this regard.

Zweibel's comments are interesting and represent a very useful contribution to the child support debate. However, I disagree with her analysis on six major points which I address in order of increasing importance.

Adequacy and Equity

Zweibel asserts that "[t]he principal goals of child support guidelines are to improve upon the adequacy and equity of current child support awards," and then suggests that I "inappropriately downplay these objectives."

However, on the very first page of the Introduction it is spelled out that "getting child support right is central to ensuring economic justice between the divorced parents and vital to the economic well-being of the children involved." Furthermore, two of the volume's central concerns — perhaps *the* central concerns — are determining the level of awards generated under different guideline options and evaluating the resulting levels of well-being of the two households involved.

However, I do, in fact, enumerate other guidelines issues — that is, issues other than the level of awards and related equity issues — and thus the complete list is perhaps longer than Zweibel might prefer. This compilation is, however, not meant to reflect my own opinion but rather to comprise a more complete inventory of the issues found in the guidelines literature.

Broadening the Agenda

We are generally in agreement that child support should be one item on a broader agenda. For example, we both feel that collection is important. I offered a concrete suggestion in this regard — automatic payroll deductions — which Zweibel suggests might be difficult to implement. On the other hand, she offers no alternative proposal, so one is left to wonder what she has in mind, especially since the guidelines she seems to prefer are much more complicated, and would therefore be even more difficult to operate than those I propose.

As for an expanded Child Support Assurance System (CSAS), while such a program should be applauded to the degree it transfers money to needy and deserving families with children while preserving work incentives to the extent possible, a couple of thorny questions regarding fairness and the efficiency of government spending need to be addressed.

In particular, the lack of an income test (Zweibel proposes none) means that to some degree such a program will transfer income to families who are otherwise deemed to have adequate incomes — that is, when the custodial parent has a comfortable income on his or her own. As a result, some might suggest that such funds would be better spent on poor families generally rather than only on those who happen to have a delinquent father.

The idea of effectively offering a short-run line of credit to non-custodial parents, while at the same time helping to collect from non-custodial parents, is more clear-cut. It would help custodial families get through temporarily difficult situations without a massive commitment of public funds and without introducing the equity and efficiency problems a full-blown CSAS might engender.

A Preferred Guideline

Zweibel offers a number of suggestions for the construction of a child support guideline. For example, she calls for a substantial increase in award levels generally; expresses particular concern for custodial families with incomes up to 30 percent above the poverty line; advises not letting the father's standard of living rise above the pre-divorce level; cautions about driving fathers into poverty; advocates making payments rise when the custodial parent experiences a fall in earnings due to circumstances beyond her control; and so on.

However, various specific suggestions do not a guideline make. One of the central themes of the book is that each approach has its advantages and disadvantages, and the "art-plus-science" aspect of determining awards is to construct a guideline that strikes the preferred balance. Zweibel seems to have certain suggestions that imply a Standards of Living approach, others that are consistent with an Income Shares approach; taken together, these imply a sort of Delaware-Melson guideline. This is all very fine, except that in not coming out to clearly identify her preferred guideline she leaves us with nothing concrete, and no advice as to how to deal with all the problems described in the main text regarding the approaches she advocates.

Non-monetarized Costs

Zweibel was clearly amused by the suggestion that meal preparation could be considered anything but work for which the custodial parent should be compensated. Let's again move beyond this specific example to look at the general principles involved: there are certain non-monetary costs and benefits attached to having custody — let's call them the extra burden of parenting *versus* the advantages of being able actually to live with one's own children. The custodial parent gets one along with the other. Zweibel does not consider the advantages of having custody, only the costs, which she enumerates. (Or, from the other perspective, she does not wish to consider the disadvantages of *not* having custody.) Thus I find her treatment unbalanced and unfair.

As for the categorization of costs, I am certainly in agreement that any costs that could be taken into consideration, depending on the precise additional monetary (or monetarizable) costs associated with raising children in a single-parent family should indeed be taken into account under any formula where payments depend on the custodial household's actual spending on children or post-divorce standard of living. On the other hand, such considerations would not enter into a formula based on the Income Shares approach, precisely because this method is based on relative incomes rather than on the actual post-divorce standard of living.

Zweibel is also correct in stating that some costs, such as certain opportunity costs related to labour market activity, are not easily estimated, and one might wish to adjust a given formula accordingly. However, the extra monetary expenditures associated with the absence of one parent are indeed reflected in the LIMs, which represent my preferred equivalence scale. In other words, single-parent families *are* included in the FAMEX; there *have* been estimates of the different costs of single-parent *versus* two-parent families; and the LIMs reflect these cost estimates through the assessment that the costs of a first child in a single-parent family are equal to those of a second adult rather than an extra child *per se*.

The Double Standard of Counting and Not Counting Time — Adjustments for Visitations

I propose starting awards at a level that is fair in the cases where there is no visitation — and hence where no costs are borne directly by the non-custodial parent — and then adjusting awards to reflect any direct spending associated with visitation. Such adjustments would not be dollar-for-dollar but would rather reflect the increased overall costs from the joint parenting and a fair division of those higher costs.

Zweibel suggests that, "[u]nder this proposal, the non-custodial father gets a double benefit. He doesn't have to compensate the custodial mother for her labour or her increased costs. But he gets recognition for any time he spends with the child." That certainly does seem unfair. But let's return to the principles at hand to understand my point.

The principles underlying my proposed adjustments are simple. Parents should share the financial costs of raising their children; it is too difficult to try to fit the non-monetary costs and benefits associated with custody into a formula; and direct spending on the child should be taken into consideration. Furthermore, the principles should apply symmetrically; we should not, that is, treat the custodial and non-custodial parents differently, as Zweibel proposes. There is, then, no "double advantage" for men; indeed, there is no advantage at all.

Furthermore, the specific manner in which Zweibel proposes to take the direct spending of the non-custodial parent into account is, to my mind, seriously flawed. First, she wants no adjustment up to the point where the children spend 30 percent of their time with the "non-custodial" parent. This, of course, raises all the equity issues presented in the text. For example, in the case of two non-custodial parents with similar basic award obligations, the parent who spends no time with his children would pay the same amount as one who has his children almost a third of the time. How can the award be fair in both situations? It is impossible, and this approach should be abandoned.

Zweibel then suggests that a basic standard of time should be established, and if the children spend *less* time than this with the non-custodial parent, payments should be *increased*. This begins to look like a smooth type of adjustment, such as the one I have proposed, but one which has "full payment" applying when the children spend fully 30 percent of their time with the non-custodial parent. Is this fair? Why not instead make a *full* payment correspond to *no* direct spending — as it logically should — and adjust from there?

But it is not, in fact, especially clear exactly what Zweibel advocates, because elsewhere in her text she talks about an adjustment that *begins* at the 30 percent mark. One option she reviews is to have awards drop precipitously at the 30 percent point — from a monthly payment of $446 when the children spend 30 percent of their time with the non-custodial parent to $89 when the time rises to 40 percent (in the example she gives). To my mind, such a "brick wall" adjustment seems both unfair, for reasons which have been mentioned already, and dangerous in terms of the importance it imparts to calculating the time spent with each parent and the incentives regarding the time to be spent in the two households in the critical range where awards vary so much. This is not an attractive option.

Zweibel's preference is to have a much more moderate adjustment, whereby a change in the percent of time the children spend with the non-custodial parent from 30 to 40 percent would lead to a "more manageable" adjustment of 10 percent in the total support payment. Now think more closely of what this means: the children spend 40 percent of their time with the father, yet his award is still at 90 percent of what it would be were they to spend no time at all in his care. Is this fair?

Finally, Zweibel suggests that one of the reasons the adjustments should be so small is due to the fixed nature of many of the costs of having custody. But this can work both ways. What of the father who needs enough housing for his children's visits even though they spend only a proportion of their time in his care? What about the other costs associated with establishing a second household? The fixed nature of such costs would suggest the need to perhaps make even *greater* adjustments in child support payments and probably at *lower* visitation levels.

In summary, I stand by the smooth adjustments I outlined in the main text to reflect the direct spending on the children associated with visitation, on the grounds of both efficiency and fairness.

Income Tax Treatment — Correcting the Calculations and the Story

Zweibel has been one of the most vocal proponents for changes in the income tax treatment of child support awards, and her research is in fact heavily referenced in the recent *Thibaudeau* case. Her opinions on this matter are thus to be taken very seriously.

Here is the scenario as it appears in text. The father earns $50,000, the mother zero, there are two children, and thus under an Income Shares approach the award is set at $15,000 (30 percent of gross income). Under the proposed guideline, and current tax system, the full $15,000 is transferred to the woman. If we suppose that her marginal tax rate is zero at her low level of income, she gets to keep the full $15,000.

Now let us consider the situation under the reversed tax treatment which would likely result were the *Thibaudeau* decision to hold, i.e., when the taxes are paid by the payer and not by the recipient. The

Income Shares approach would generate an award of $7,500, the appropriate amount in terms of *net* income. (A gross income requirement of $15,000 translates into $7,500 of actual spending on the children, which the father pays in its entirety. Readers are advised to review the appendix of chapter 6 if they are unclear on this critical point.) No tax is due, but the net award is obviously only one-half the level of the award that would hold under the current tax treatment and the guideline based on gross income. Why is this?

By basing the award on gross income and handing this amount over to the woman, my proposed guideline passes the full benefit of the current tax system to her. In this case, under the current system the deduction saves the father taxes at the rate of 50 percent on the dollar; the mother pays no taxes on this full amount (because of her low income), and thus the net amount of the award is doubled. In short, the money the father would have paid in taxes is instead transferred to the woman; and to the degree to which her marginal tax rate is lower than his, her net award is higher. By contrast, the proposed tax changes would leave the woman with considerably less net income, as the advantages of the tax shifting available under the current system would no longer exist.

Let us now consider the award under Zweibel's alternative scenario of incomes of $30,00 and $20,000. She is correct in arriving at an award of $9,000 in gross terms. Assuming Zweibel's tax treatment, the woman is left with a tax bill of $2,861 and a net award of $6,139. Zweibel then states that "[o]f the original total of $15,000 in child-rearing costs, he now pays approximately 42 percent ($6,259/$15,000) while she absorbs approximately 58 percent ($8,861/$15,000). This is almost a complete reversal of the original 60/40 apportionment intended under the Income Shares method."

Zweibel's fundamental error is to not differentiate between *gross income requirements* and *net spending on the children*. It has already been explained that the $15,000 gross income requirement translates into $7,500 net, which represents the actual spending on the children. Thus her calculations are wrong. If we continue to assume that spending on the children is kept at the $7,500 pre-divorce level, then his net payment is actually a full *83 percent* of the spending on the children ($6,259 of $7,500) — well beyond the 60 percent specified by the Income Shares approach, and obviously double the amount arrived at in Zweibel's erroneous calculation.

Why do things work this way? Because, once again, the proposed guideline is based on gross income and passes the full advantage of the current tax system over to the woman.

Now, let us compare the award in this alternative scenario to what it would be in a "post-*Thibaudeau*" tax world. The $15,000 gross income requirements of the children would translate into an actual spending estimate of $7,500, and the man's share would be 60 percent of this, amounting to $4,500. Although this is a net amount, free of taxes, the woman again receives a *larger* net transfer under the current tax system and an Income Shares approach based on gross income than under the sort of tax reversal that may result from the *Thibaudeau* case.

There is no magic here. Again, the current system passes the tax liability from the payer to the recipient and, given the typical relative income patterns between the two, the total tax burden to the (ex)couple is reduced. The proposed guideline based on gross income passes this benefit onto the recipient, thus typically resulting in higher net awards. If upheld, the tax reversal suggested by *Thibaudeau* would throw this advantage away, and reduce awards commensurately.

Now, it must be admitted that where the recipient is in a higher income tax category than the payer, there is no such advantage and the current tax system works against the couple. We might argue as to how many cases there are of this type. Zweibel refers to the findings of her "case study" (this is the wrong term — what she actually has is a sample, and an unrepresentative one at that) and other work by the Department of Finance to note that there are in fact both winners and losers under the present regime. Of course; but the more representative Finance figures suggest an overall benefit to divorced couples of around $330 million per year, which would be lost should the tax treatment be reversed. Furthermore, the biggest winners under the current regime are the poorest women and their children.

Finally, a guideline based on gross income would be much easier to implement — as with, say, a system of automatic deductions at source — and would maintain the incentives to actually make payments which hold under the current tax system.

Ross Finnie was an Assistant Professor in the Department of Economics at Université Laval from 1989 to 1994. His core research interests are the gender earnings gap and the economics of divorce. For the past two years, he has been acting in a consulting role to the Department of Justice regarding child support guidelines.

David M. Betson is the Director of the Hesburgh Program in Public Service and an Associate Professor of Economics at the University of Notre Dame. Prior to that, he was a Research Associate at the Institute for Poverty at the University of Wisconsin at Madison and a Research Economist in the Department of Health, Education and Welfare. He has advised numerous states on the design of their child support guidelines.

Elke B. Kluge has practised family law with the Ottawa law firm Soloway, Wright, Victor for the past eight years and, prior to that time, in Victoria, BC. She has taught family law at the Ontario Bar Admission Course and at the University of Victoria. For a number of years, Kluge was also a separated and then divorced custodial parent.

Ellen B. Zweibel is Professor of Law at the University of Ottawa, Faculty of Law, Common Law Section. She has an L.L.M. in income taxation and teaches in the areas of income tax, tax policy and family and property law. She has written and consulted widely on the taxation of child support and the development of child support guidelines.

Jean-Michel Cousineau, *La Pauvreté et l'État: Pour un nouveau partage des compétences en matière de sécurité sociale*

OTHER PUBLICATIONS OF INTEREST:
Elisabeth B. Reynolds (ed.), *Income Security: Changing Needs, Changing Means*

RECENT IRPP PUBLICATIONS
Education:
Edwin G. West, *Ending the Squeeze on Universities*
Peter Coleman, *Learning About Schools: What Parents Need to Know and How They Can Find Out*
Bruce Wilkinson, *Educational Choice: Necessary But Not Sufficient*
City-Regions:
William Coffey, *The Evolution of Canada's Metropolitan Economies*
Andrew Sancton, *Governing Canada's City-Regions: Adapting Form to Function*
Governance:
F. Leslie Seidle (ed.), *Rethinking Government: Reform or Reinvention?*
F. Leslie Seidle (ed.), *Equity and Community: The Charter, Interest Advocacy and Representation*
Public Finance:
Paul A.R. Hobson and France St-Hilaire, *Toward Sustainable Federalism: Reforming Federal-Provincial Fiscal Arrangements*

These and other IRPP publications are available from:
Renouf Publishing
1294 Algoma Road
Ottawa, Ontario
K1B 3W8
Tel.: (613) 741-4333
Fax.: (613) 741-5439